PMP® Certification
A Beginner's Guide

About the Author

George G. Angel, a certified Project Management Professional (PMP), is founder and owner of Eagle Business Services, LLC, a project management education and consulting company since 1994. He has successfully managed projects for over 30 years at IBM and was an innovative global education program manager for ten years.

As a leader in project management education, George has extensive experience in business, project and program management education, course development, teaching, and consulting. He provides high-quality training and consulting services to a broad range of clients, including universities, state and federal government, international corporations, and private companies of all industries and sizes. He also delivers classes using a multitude of methods, including virtual classroom, online, and face-to-face to thousands of students from over 60 different countries.

George achieved IBM's Executive PM Certification in 2001 and served on their PM Profession Review Board for over six years. He has also been a professional speaker at Project Management Institute (PMI) conferences, symposiums, and teaches PM classes and workshops at Colorado State University (CSU) since 2000.

When not writing, teaching, or consulting, George can be found hiking, biking, skiing, scuba diving, or relaxing on the beach with his wife, two daughters, and their husbands. You can contact him through the www.eagle-business.com website or send an e-mail to george.angel@q.com.

About the Technical Editor

Ricardo (Ric) Rothschild is a Certified PMP and IBM Certified Executive Project Manager with global and enterprise-wide project management experience. He is a 24-year veteran of project management and is currently an IBM Service Executive managing a large global strategic outsourcing contract for an international bank. He has managed projects with budgets in excess of US$20M, from server/workstation migrations to complete technical transformations for IBM's outsourcing clients.

Ric also teaches project management classes at Colorado State University (CSU) and serves on the IBM Project Management Review Board. In addition, he is an international instructor and Delivery Program Manager education lead for IBM Americas (U.S., Latin America, and Canada).

He has worked and taught classes from England to Singapore, Canada to Argentina. Ric is fluent in English, Spanish, and Portuguese, with a working knowledge of German.

He lives in Colorado with his wife and two children, where they enjoy the outdoors and various professional and youth sports. Ric has volunteered hundreds of hours coaching and leading youth sporting programs. You can contact him via e-mail at ric.rothschild@comcast.net.

PMP® Certification
A Beginner's Guide

George G. Angel, PMP

New York Chicago San Francisco
Lisbon London Madrid Mexico City
Milan New Delhi San Juan
Seoul Singapore Sydney Toronto

Cataloging-in-Publication Data is on file with the Library of Congress

McGraw-Hill books are available at special quantity discounts to use as premiums and sales promotions, or for use in corporate training programs. To contact a representative, please e-mail us at bulksales@mcgraw-hill.com.

PMP® Certification: A Beginner's Guide

1234567890 DOC DOC 019

ISBN   978-0-07-163370-3
MHID   0-07-163370-7

Sponsoring Editor   Megg Morin
Editorial Supervisor   Janet Walden
Project Manager   Vipra Fauzdar, Glyph International
Acquisitions Coordinator   Meghan Riley
Technical Editor   Ricardo (Ric) Rothschild
Copy Editor   Bart Reed
Proofreader   Claire Splan
Indexer   Claire Splan
Production Supervisor   Jean Bodeaux
Composition   Glyph International
Illustration   Glyph International
Graphic Artists   Becky Drager and Beth Bilka
Art Director, Cover   Jeff Weeks
Cover Designer   Jeff Weeks

To my wife Pam and my girls, Dawn and Candy, for your love and editorial and moral support, with thanks and best wishes. You are the wind beneath my wings. I could not have completed this book without you.

Contents at a Glance

Contents

Part II The Nine Knowledge Areas

Acknowledgments

This book, like any other, is the end product of a lot of hard work by many people. I'd like to thank some of the people who were involved with the creation of this book.

First, a big thanks goes out to Megg Morin, acquisitions editor at McGraw-Hill. Megg stepped back and let me run with this project yet was there to provide great suggestions and guidance. She did a wonderful job to ensure things ran smoothly. Also thanks to Ricardo (Ric) Rothschild, my friend, co-instructor (wing man), and the technical editor for this book.

Many thanks go out to my students at Colorado State University (CSU) for their interest in project management and the great questions and input they provided through the years to give me the ideas for this book. Special thanks goes to Chris Bonar and his wife Susy. Along with Megg, they planted the seed that grew into this book and turned into a dream opportunity for me. Also a big thanks to my fellow instructors (Lee Varra-Nelson, Terry Skaggs, Jeff VanBuskirk, and Ric Rothschild) at Colorado State University who provided input and reviews to help make this book a useful resource for our project management classes. Thanks also to Shane Cadwell and Matt Pellant at the Budweiser Events Center (BEC). They provided great case study examples for the real-world view of project management. Additional thanks go out to the production and editorial folks at McGraw-Hill, including Meghan Riley, editorial supervisor Janet Walden, copy editor Bart Reed, and proofreader and indexer Claire Splan. My thanks to Beth Bilka and Becky Drager for their help with illustrations, and to Vipra Fauzdar of Glyph International.

The last big thanks go to my wife Pam, for letting me follow my dreams, for being my navigator, my editor, and my best friend who keeps me on the right track in our adventures toward a wonderful life together, and for putting up with me all these years.

Introduction

This book's focus is on bridging the gap between being a project manager (PM) and being a globally recognized Project Management Professional (PMP). It takes you through the everyday challenges of managing projects and provides tips on how to prepare for and pass the PMI exam.

The differentiators in this book are the straightforward approach to project management details, the proven examples, and the collection of checklists and references that serve as a guide for even the most experienced project managers.

This book takes you through the fundamentals of project management using real-world examples of what works and what doesn't work in this dynamic profession. It also demonstrates how sound PM principles can improve the efficiency and effectiveness of you and your project team by providing sample documents and a real project case study that build on the topics discussed throughout the book.

Project management is recognized as one of the fastest-growing professions in many of today's industries—software and hardware product development, government, military, construction, and information services (just to name a few). It is rapidly becoming a required skill for career advancement and improved project and program management success.

This book helps PMs better understand the importance of balancing project constraints (barriers) and providing timely and accurate project status communications to all key stakeholders.

It is also important to note that this book is just a starting point in this large and growing profession. I hope it whets your appetite for more on the topic of project management.

Assumptions

This book assumes the readers have varying degrees of knowledge and experience—from little (or no) formal PM experience to more advanced experience. Because of this range of experience, this book is designed to be a primer and to confirm the further steps needed to be a more successful project manager.

Organization

Because this book is designed to meet the needs of a wide range of project managers—it is broken into two major sections. The first section, which consists of Chapters 1–3, discusses the value and benefits of PM certification and serves as an introduction to Project Management Institute (PMI) PM credentials and the PMI exams. The first section "bridges the gap" between being a PM and becoming a certified PMP.

The second section contains Chapters 4–12, which detail the nine knowledge areas, and Chapter 13, which explains how to effectively bring a project to successful closure.

If you are not familiar with PM credentials or are not sure you want to pursue PMI certification right away, you definitely want to start this book from the beginning. If you have a few years of project experience and already know about PMI and the benefits of their credentials, you may want to jump right into the knowledge areas, starting at Chapter 4.

Now here's a brief summary of the book's organization and contents.

Part I: Essentials of Project Management and PMP Certification

This part of the book looks at project management from a real-world perspective and then offers insight into the benefits of project management (PM) credentials.

Part I has three chapters:

- **Chapter 1:** Bridging the Gap Between PM and PMP
- **Chapter 2:** The Emerging World of Project Management
- **Chapter 3:** Project Management Process Groups

Part II: The Nine Knowledge Areas

Part II contains ten chapters, starting with Chapters 4–12 covering PMI's nine knowledge areas, and ending with Chapter 13, which discusses how to successfully close a project. Here's a list of the knowledge area chapters:

- **Chapter 4:** Project Integration Management

- **Chapter 5:** Project Scope Management

- **Chapter 6:** Project Time Management

- **Chapter 7:** Project Cost Management

- **Chapter 8:** Project Quality Management

- **Chapter 9:** Project Human Resource Management

- **Chapter 10:** Project Communications Management

- **Chapter 11:** Project Risk Management

- **Chapter 12:** Project Procurement Management

Chapter 13, "Closing the Project: Are We There Yet?", explains the importance of properly closing the project and offers a check list for effectively bringing the project to successful completion.

Tips, Notes, Try This, and Ask the Expert Elements

This book also includes Tips, Notes, Try This, and Ask the Expert series elements. These elements are intended to share a specific experience, address a common problem, or highlight key information that will help you understand the topic better and provide helpful information toward your PMI exam application, preparation, and successful completion of these highly sought-after credentials.

Project Management Institute (PMI), Inc.

This book ties directly to the fourth edition of the *PMBOK Guide*[*] and can be read in tandem with it chapter for chapter, or you can jump into any of the chapters to focus on specific areas of interest.

This book not only will help you improve your project knowledge, but also will help explain the *PMBOK* by offering real-world project examples and tips to increase your success on your projects and assist in preparing you for the PMI exam.

[*]Project Management Institute *A Guide to the Project Management Body of Knowledge (PMBOK® Guide) - Fourth Edition*, Project Management Institute, Inc., 2004. Copyright and all rights reserved. Material from this publication has been reproduced with the permission of PMI.

Part I

Essentials of Project Management and PMP Certification

Chapter 1

Bridging the Gap Between PM and PMP

Key Skills & Concepts

- A brief history of project management

- Reasons for getting certified

- Benefits of certification/credentials

- PMI and the *PMBOK®* Guide

- PMI credentials

- PMI exams

- PMI exam objectives

- How to apply and prepare for a PMI exam

- The various learning styles

- Study tips and what to expect on exam day

- Maintaining PMI credentials

There is a huge difference between being a project manager (PM) and managing projects as a globally recognized credentialed Project Management Professional (PMP). The difference can often be seen in the reduced number of failed projects. As project managers develop the skills needed to effectively manage projects and then go on to get certified, their success rate typically increases, as does their salary. In fact, according to Payscale .com, median salaries for PMPs are up to 30 percent higher than those for non-PMPs. Depending on the city you work in and the number of years of experience you have, salary increases range from 6 to 30 percent. PMPs in the United States enjoy salaries from $56,000 to over $115,000.

To quantify the increase in project success rates, The Standish Group studied more than 40,000 projects over a ten-year period and reported that project failures declined to 15 percent of all projects—a vast improvement over the 31-percent failure rate reported in 1994. The reason, they say: "People have become much more savvy in project management.

When we first started the research, project management was a sort of black art."[1] In a later article, Standish Chairman Jim Johnson goes on to say that mangers have a better understanding of the dynamics of a project. Johnson cited three reasons for the improvement in software quality: "better project management, iterative development and the emerging Web infrastructure."[2]

To get a better understanding of these changes, let's talk first about project management in general. It is in practically everything we do—creating a new technology, designing an office building or a new home, managing a major event (such as the Olympics), and running a fundraiser for a church or school. Project management principles can also be used in our personal lives—remodeling a basement or kitchen, designing a landscape, and planning a wedding or a family vacation. A large number of these projects are done with little or no formal training. Because projects by definition are unique in nature, we tend to manage them in various ways to different degrees of success. Most of the time when the project reaches the end, everyone is fairly happy with the results.

Looking throughout history, we see project management goes back thousands of years (some say to the beginning of time). Look at the pyramids of Egypt (some are dated back to 2550 B.C.), the Roman aqueducts (Appia was believed to be the first one built, in 312 B.C.), and the Great Wall of China (built between 221 B.C. and 206 B.C.). Many of these engineering marvels are still standing today (with some renovation).

How do you suppose these marvels were designed and built? Project management. Project management existed in one form or another early on, and our ancestors somehow mastered it without scope statements, communications plans, or task schedules.

Even though many early project managers were successful, their processes were independent (ad hoc), inconsistent, and mostly not replicable. Thus the need for structure—documented, proven, and repeatable processes; tools and techniques; methods and project management discipline.

Even some "successful" projects were anything but a success by today's standards (that is, on time and on budget). As a more recent example, take the Sydney Opera House—one of the most recognizable images of the modern world. It was designed by Jørn Utzon of Denmark in 1957 and deemed, at the time, a spectacular failure. Even though it is now revered as an icon of Sydney, it was originally labeled a "white elephant" and "acoustic nightmare." When construction started on the Sydney Opera House in 1959, it was estimated to cost AU$7 million and take five years to build. It was finally completed in 1973 (9 years behind schedule) at a cost of over AU$100 million (AU$93 million over budget.) Even though this project failed to meet the traditional project management success metrics, it is considered a huge success.[3]

Introduction to Project Management Institute (PMI)

A lot of us have been managing projects longer than we care to admit, and for the most part we have been doing pretty well, mainly going on instincts and "gut feelings." However, the growing need to modernize has caused the world of project management to really take off. The 1950s marked the beginning of the modern era of project management as we know it today.

This new era ushered in the need for a framework of globally recognized standard processes, tools, and methods. A small group of project management professionals recognized this need and in 1969 founded a nonprofit organization called the Project Management Institute (PMI). PMI began documenting a proposed set of project management standards they called a "white paper" (an authoritative guide) in 1987. Their intent was to standardize project management information and practices. The white paper later became the original *A Guide to the Project Management Body of Knowledge (PMBOK® Guide),* published for the first time in 1996. This guide became recognized as a worldwide standard and provided common processes, principles, knowledge areas, tools and techniques, and a global project management discipline. PMI saw the need to take this new discipline into the twenty-first century and make it official by creating an examination for project managers to validate their ability to understand the new standards. To do this, PMI launched the Project Management Professional (PMP) certification exam in 1994. Since that time, the PMP credential has skyrocketed in popularity.

To demonstrate the emerging demand for certified PMPs, you need only look at the job postings for project managers. Only a few years ago, advertisements for project manager jobs stated, "PMP certification a plus." Now they read, "PMP certification required." This is true for public and private sector companies as well as government agencies who are requiring their PMs get certified.

To meet this increased demand, PMs are getting serious about acquiring those important initials after their names. The number of PMPs has grown exponentially since 1998, when there were only 11,000 PMPs worldwide. In June 2009, the number of PMPs exceeded 350,000—and this number continues to grow by over 4,000 per month.

For those who don't have the three years of PM experience leading project teams that are needed to go after the PMP certification, there is the Certified Associate Project Manager (CAPM) credential available from PMI.

NOTE
There were over 8,000 CAPM credential holders worldwide at the end of May 2009—and the numbers are continuing to grow.

Why Get Certified? What's in It for Me?

Anything worthwhile, such as getting certified, requires commitment. A lot of people wonder, "Why should I subject myself and my family to the extra time it takes to prepare for the PMI exam, especially in today's demanding work environment?" Most of us are already working long hours, on several different projects at the same time, and with less time for family and friends.

With the current economic times, there are fewer jobs available and many qualified workers who are more than willing to put in the extra time to get certified, making them eligible to compete for top project management positions.

Sounds pretty competitive—so why put yourself through the extra work? The biggest reason I believe starts with the feeling you get when you walk out of the test center with a "Congratulations, you passed" letter in your hand, knowing you reached a goal that millions of project managers are thinking about pursuing. A chill runs down your spine, and the smile on your face can be spotted a mile away. You want to tell the world, "I have arrived. I passed the PMI exam!"

Then come the real benefits. You will be able to "talk the talk" (know a common language to be able to communicate with project managers on a global basis) and "walk the walk" by being able to apply standard proven processes on global projects.

Your family and friends will be proud of you because they know the time and energy you put into studying for the PMI exam. Your boss and coworkers will admire your commitment and achievement. Some companies even reward employees that rise to the level of certification with recognition bonuses, salary increases, and/or promotions for their dedication.

Benefits of Achieving Certification/Credentials

The benefits go far beyond the initial congratulations. Once you are certified, you have a newfound sense of awareness and understanding, knowing there is a worldwide recognized standard that provides a roadmap to guide you toward improved project results.

You can be content in knowing there are thousands of project managers across the globe facing the same challenges you are—and in some cases stumbling over similar barriers and "potholes." Your job is made a little easier with the realization that you are not alone on your project.

Here's a summary list of the benefits of certification:

- Demonstrated commitment and proof of professional achievement
- Increased customer and team credibility
- Increased marketability

- Potential for higher compensation
- A better understanding of how to manage resources
- Improved communications skills

NOTE
If you are already familiar with PMI's credentials or if you are not planning to pursue certification just yet, that's okay. Please feel free to jump to Chapter 2. You can always come back to Chapter 1 as a reference when you are ready for more information regarding exam eligibility, PMI credentials, or exam information.

The PMI Family of Credentials

PMI offers a comprehensive certification program for project managers with different levels of experience. The program supports a career framework in the project management profession. PMI's credentials and professional development can help business professionals start, build, or advance their careers in project management, program management, and scheduling and risk management.

Five Levels of PMI Credentials

PMI credentials establish your dedication and proficiency in project management. To attain one of PMI's credentials, you must satisfy defined education and professional experience requirements. To better understand PMI credentials and the requirements needed to obtain certification, review the following definitions and then refer to Table 1-1 (later in this chapter) for the necessary requirements, project roles, and details.

Certified Associate in Project Management (CAPM)

The CAPM credential is geared toward people who contribute to a project team but who are not leading or directing the team (see the PMP credential, explained next, for those who are leading and directing project teams). The CAPM credential recognizes a person's ability to demonstrate their capabilities by:

- Having a fundamental knowledge of the *PMBOK Guide*
- Understanding the standard *PMBOK* processes and terminology
- Demonstrating knowledge of basic project management practices
- Being responsible for individual project tasks in their area of expertise (e.g., finance, marketing, legal, customer care, market research, fulfillment, processing).
- Contributing to the project team as a subject matter expert (SME)

Project Management Professional (PMP)

The PMP credential is for people who are leading and directing a project team. PMPs are

- Responsible for all aspects of the project through its entire life cycle

- Capable of leading and directing cross-functional teams in delivering project results

- Able to demonstrate sufficient knowledge and experience to apply a methodology to projects within the constraints of schedule, budget, and resources

- Responsible for managing risk, communications, stakeholder expectations, and effectively performing their duties in a professional manner

Program Management Professional (PgMP)

PMI's Program Management Professional credential is specifically developed to acknowledge the qualification of the professional who leads the coordinated management of multiple projects toward a strategic goal and ensures the ultimate success of the overall program.

A sample of the PgMP's capabilities are

- Responsible for achieving an organizational objective by overseeing a program that consists of multiple projects

- Defines and initiates projects and assigns project managers to manage cost, schedule, and performance

- Maintains alignment of program scope with strategic business objectives

- Effectively monitors and responds to the needs of the PMs in their program

PMI Risk Management Professional (PMI-RMP)

The PMI Risk Management Professional credential recognizes knowledge, skills, and experience in the area of project risk management. A Risk Management Professional provides expertise in the specialized area of assessing and identifying project risks, along with plans to mitigate threats and capitalize on opportunities.

RMPs are typically:

- Responsible for identifying project risks, assigning owners and reviewing mitigation plans

- In direct support of project managers and the project team as a contributing member

- Able to document a minimum of three years of project risk management experience

PMI Scheduling Professional (PMI-SP)

The Scheduling Professional credential recognizes the specialized skills needed for developing and maintaining the project schedule.

Scheduling Professionals are

● Responsible for creating and maintaining the project schedule

● In direct support of the project manager and project team as a contributing member in managing the overall schedule

● Able to document a minimum of three years of project scheduling experience

PMI Credentials

To begin the process of becoming certified in one of the PMI credentials, you first need to determine your level of experience and eligibility. Table 1-1 should help with this process.

	CAPM	PMI-SP	PMI-RMP	PMP	PgMP
Full name	Certified Associate in Project Management	PMI Scheduling Professional	PMI Risk Management Professional	Project Management Professional	Program Management Professional
Project role	Contributes to project team	Develops and maintains project schedule	Assesses and identifies risks, mitigates threats, and capitalizes on opportunities	Leads and directs project teams	Achieves the organizational objectives through defining and overseeing projects and resources
Eligibility requirements	High school diploma or global equivalent **AND** 1,500 hours experience **OR** 23 hours PM education	High school diploma or global equivalent 5,000 hours project scheduling experience 40 hours project scheduling education **OR** Bachelor's degree or global equivalent 3,500 hours project scheduling experience 30 hours project scheduling education	High school diploma or global equivalent 4,500 hours project risk management experience 40 hours project risk management education **OR** Bachelor's degree or global equivalent 3,500 hours project risk management experience 30 hours project risk management education	High school diploma or global equivalent 5 years project management experience 35 hours project management education **OR** Bachelor's degree or global equivalent 3 years project management experience 35 hours project management education	High school diploma or global equivalent 4 years project management experience 7 years program management experience **OR** Bachelor's degree/global equivalent 4 years project management experience 4 years program management experience

Table 1-1 PMI Credentials

	CAPM	PMI-SP	PMI-RMP	PMP	PgMP
Steps to obtaining credential	Application process + multiple-choice exam	Application process + multiple-choice exam	Application process + multiple-choice exam	Application process + multiple-choice exam	Three evaluations: application panel review + multiple-choice exam + multi-rater assessment
Exam information	3 hours; 150 questions	3.5 hours; 170 questions	3.5 hours; 170 questions	4 hours; 200 questions	4 hours; 170 questions
Fees for PMI members	US$225	US$520	US$520	US$405	US$1,500
Credential maintenance cycles and requirements	5 years; must retake the exam in the fifth year to recertify	3 years; 30 Professional Development Units (PDUs) in project scheduling	3 years; 30 PDUs in project risk management	3 years; 60 PDUs	3 years; 60 PDUs

Table 1-1   PMI Credentials

NOTE
To be eligible for the PMP credential, a candidate must meet the education and professional experience listed in Table 1-1, and all the project management experience must have been accrued within the last eight consecutive years prior to application submission.[4]

For additional details and the latest information, go to the PMI.org website (click "Get Certified" to see the guidelines).

Reasons People Pursue PMP Certification

PMP is the premier certification credential for project managers. When a random audience was asked why they were pursuing this credential, the majority of the responses were for career advancement (50 percent) and the next highest reason was a recommendation from an employer (21 percent). You can see all the responses in Figure 1-1.[5]

Ask the Expert

Q: **Which credential is right for me?**

A: It depends. The best way to determine the answer to this question is to look at your experience, your level of education, your current and future job role, and your aspirations. Each credential is designed to stand alone (no one credential serves as a prerequisite for another). However, you can pursue multiple credentials. Each credential complements the others.

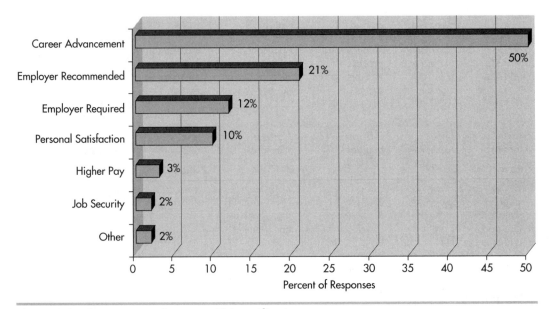

Figure 1-1 Reasons people pursue PM certification

Examples of Credential Eligibility

To put this credential eligibility in perspective, let's look at three people with different levels of experience to see which credential is right for each of them:

- Joey has a minimum of 1,500 hours experience working on project teams but has not led a project himself. He has a high school diploma and over 23 hours of project management education. Joey has a good foundational understanding of the *PMBOK* process groups, knowledge areas, and concepts.
  Joey should go for the CAPM-level credential (he is eligible with either 1,500 hours of experience or the 23 hours of PM education). The CAPM focuses on the *PMBOK*. With only 150 multiple choice questions (compared to 200 in the PMP exam), it measures one's ability to understand the PM fundamentals according to the *PMBOK Guide.*

- Suzy has over three years (36 non-overlapping months) of project management experience leading and directing project teams over the past eight years. When she adds up her hours managing projects she has more than 4,500 hours and Suzy has a bachelor's degree. She also has over 35 hours of formal project management education. Suzy has demonstrated her ability to "think on her feet" in real live project situations and has a good grasp of project management principles, methods, and processes, according to the *PMBOK Guide.*

Suzy should go for the PMP-level credential. She understands that the PMP exam focuses on the ability to apply sound judgment to project situations.

- Suzy's sister Mary currently has a high school diploma (no college degree). She does have a minimum of 7,500 hours of project management experience leading and directing project teams over a five year (60 non-overlapping months) period in the last eight years. Mary also has over 35 hours of formal project management education, so she is also eligible to sit for the PMP exam.

Demystifying PMI Exams

Most people (myself included, before I took the test) are confused and intimidated by PMI exams. This is normal and expected because few people want or like to take tests, especially with the cost, the time to prepare, and the level of commitment to pursue this three-to-four-hour event (note that the PMP exam was eight hours prior to April 1998). So, the good news is the exam is now only three to four hours, depending on the type of exam you take. Plus, the majority of the exams are computer-based testing (CBT), which means "touch screen" for less paper processing and quicker scoring (and to align with the electronic generation). That's right, you get the results in minutes after you complete the exam right on the screen.

There is also a growing number of PMI Registered Education Providers (REPs). These are recognized companies, universities, and organizations that offer project management courses and certificate programs designed to help you prepare to successfully pass the exam.

In order to further demystify the exams, let's start with a quick review of the five types of examinations PMI currently offers. The PMI exam types align with the credentials mentioned earlier, so only a brief summary of the types is provided here. To begin, the two most common PMI exams are

- PMP (Project Management Professional)
- CAPM (Certified Associate Project Manager)

The newer PMI exams are

- PgPM (Program Management Professional)
- PM-SP (PM Scheduling Professional)
- PM-RMP (PM Risk Management Professional)

What's more, you have two ways to take PMI exams:

- Computer-based testing (CBT)
- Paper-based testing (PBT)

NOTE

There are strict requirements to qualify to take the paper-based test. To be eligible, the candidate must live at least 186.5 miles (300 km) from a PMI test site. Also, there is a reexamination fee should you need to retake the test. (See the PMI.org website for the latest fee amounts.) You are allowed to retake the exam up to three times during your 12-month approved period. The reexamination fee must be paid prior to each sitting for the exam.

Differences Between the Exams

Because the PMP certification exam was introduced first, it has the highest number of credentialed PMs. It is by far the most sought-after exam of all the credentials. Because of its popularity, we will focus mostly on the details of the PMP exam.

According to PMI, the PMP exam is designed to determine your ability to demonstrate proficiency in each of the five process groups (also known as "domains"): Initiating, Planning, Executing, Monitoring and Controlling, and Closing.

The PMP exam is composed of 200 multiple-choice questions. Of the 200 questions, 25 are considered "pretest" questions. Pretest questions do not affect the score and are used in examinations as an effective and legitimate way to test the validity of future examination questions. All questions are randomly placed throughout the examination. Each question on the exam is developed and independently validated by global work groups (credential holders) and assigned a complexity rating.

Each exam is unique in that the system selects a random group of questions for each participant and the number of correct answers needed to pass the exam depends on the complexity of the questions selected. For example, if many of the questions in your exam are higher in complexity, then you can pass with a slightly lower number of correct answers—say, 69 percent as opposed to 70 percent. (These percentages are examples only and are subject to change without notice.)

The allotted time to complete the PMP computer-based examination is four hours. The CAPM, on the other hand, has 150 multiple-choice questions, with three hours allotted to complete the test. These time limits are tightly controlled at the test center and, in general, most people feel they have more than enough time to complete the exams. You can sign in and out to take short breaks, eat a snack, and so on—however, the clock is still ticking.

Candidates for the CAPM credential must be able to document their contribution to projects as subject matter experts (SMEs) and team members. They may also serve as

How to Save Money on the Cost of the Exam

The PMP exam costs US$555 in 2009 for the first sitting (for CBT). However, if you are a member of the PMI organization, you receive a big discount on the exam. The discount is approximately US$150 (and subject to change).

Membership also offers savings on chapter meetings, books, events, and so on. Therefore, it is recommended that you join the PMI chapter nearest you for at least one year (the year you plan to take the exam). Some employers will even pay for a year of membership dues because the savings (discount) on the exam fee alone is offset by the cost of a year of PMI membership dues.

The annual cost of membership in PMI averages around US$130, depending on the chapter, and you can join additional special interest groups (SIGs), such as IT (Information Technology), IS (Information Systems), and SD (Software Development). Each SIG runs around US$20 to US$30 per year.

project sponsors, facilitators, liaisons, or coordinators on the projects they participated on, but are not responsible for leading or directing the project team (which is the role of the project manager).

Exam Blueprint

The PMP examination is developed based on the PMP examination blueprint contained in the Project Management Professional Examination Specification. The exam blueprint details the percentage of questions contained in each project management process group. Table 1-2 shows the percentage of questions in each process group/domain included on the exam.

Process Group/Domain	Percentage of Questions	Number of Questions
Initiating	11%	22
Planning	23%	46
Executing	27%	54
Monitoring and Controlling	21%	42
Closing	9%	18
Professional and Social Responsibility	9%	18
	100%	200

Table 1-2   Exam Blueprint

NOTE

The percentages and the number of questions shown in Table 1-2 are subject to change. For the latest PMP exam or CAPM exam blueprint percentages, go to the PMI.org website.[4]

PMI Exam Objectives (Skills Tested)

The PM must be able to make sound decisions and apply good judgment in order to move the project forward to achieve schedule and budget deadlines. As a PM, you must be able to address various real-world situations and work through them quickly to solve the many different problems faced by you and the project team.

The applicant's skills tested (such as communications, risk management, cost and time management, team building, and so on) vary depending on the type of exam taken. For example, the PMP exam focuses on the PM's ability to apply their knowledge, tools, techniques, and methods to effectively manage projects, whereas the CAPM exam focuses on the fundamental processes and more academic view of project management (straight from the *PMBOK Guide*).

NOTE

Because this book is focused on project management, as opposed to program management we will focus primarily on the PMP and CAPM exams.

PMP Exam Objectives

The PMP Role Delineation Study conducted by PMI states that candidates for the PMP credential must

- Perform their duties under general supervision and be responsible for all aspects of the project for the life of the project

- Lead and direct cross-functional teams to deliver projects within the constraints of schedule, budget, and scope

- Demonstrate sufficient knowledge and experience to appropriately apply a methodology to projects that have reasonably well-defined project requirements and deliverables

Overall, the PMP exam is designed to determine your ability to demonstrate proficiency in leading and directing project teams in each of the five process groups listed next.

1. **Initiating the Project Process Group:**
   - Conduct project-selection methods
   - Define project scope
   - Document risks, assumptions, and constraints
   - Identify and perform stakeholder analysis
   - Develop project charter
   - Obtain project charter approval

2. **Planning the Project Process Group:**
   - Define and record requirements, constraints, and assumptions
   - Develop the project management plan
   - Identify the project team and define roles and responsibilities
   - Create the Work Breakdown Structure (WBS)
   - Define activities, estimate resources, and determine the budget
   - Develop the schedule and change management plan
   - Plan communications, quality, and procurement
   - Identify risks and define risk strategies
   - Conduct project kick-off meeting

3. **Executing the Project Process Group:**
   - Execute activities defined in the project plan
   - Ensure common understanding and set expectations
   - Implement the procurement of project resources
   - Manage resource allocation
   - Implement quality management plan
   - Implement approved changes
   - Implement approved actions and workarounds
   - Improve team performance

4. **Monitoring and Controlling the Project Process Group:**
   - Measure project performance
   - Verify and manage changes to the project

- Ensure project deliverables conform to quality standards
- Monitor all risks and initiate a response strategy

5. Closing the Project Process Group:

- Obtain final acceptance for the project
- Obtain financial, legal, and administrative closure
- Release project resources
- Identify, document, and communicate lessons learned
- Archive and retain project records
- Measure customer satisfaction

NOTE

Notice how the verbs vary among the process groups, especially between the Initiation and Planning process groups (i.e., *define, identify, develop*) and the Execution process group (i.e., *execute, ensure, implement,* and *manage*). This is to further emphasize the change in the fourth edition of *PMBOK* to be more action-oriented, using a "verb noun" format (Plan Risk) versus a "noun-verb" format (Risk Planning). This seems like a small change; however, it makes a big difference when it comes time to create the WBS or the schedule for your project.

Even though the professional and social responsibilities are not covered in the *PMBOK Guide*, there are a number of questions (approximately 18) on the PMP and slightly fewer on the CAPM exam. These questions relate to the ethical application of project management and are broken into four value categories in the Code of Ethics and Professional Conduct guidelines area. The value categories are

- Responsibilities
- Respect
- Fairness
- Honesty

The focus areas for professional and social responsibilities are as follows:

- Ensure individual integrity
- Contribute to the project management knowledge base
- Enhance professional competence
- Promote interaction among stakeholders

CAPM Exam Objectives

Overall the CAPM exam focuses on the PM's ability to work in a project team and understand the domains/process groups, nine knowledge areas, and 42 processes, according to the *PMBOK*. As previously mentioned, the CAPM is based more on the academic view of project management according to the *PMBOK* as opposed to the applied practitioner view as tested in the PMP exam.

The CAPM exam questions tend to be straightforward compared to the more situational (what would you do if) questions you will find in the PMP exam.

Expected Results (First-Time Pass Rate)

The first-time pass rate is tightly controlled by PMI and changes occasionally and without notice; however, history indicates that the target is about 70 percent, compared to only 50 percent in 1998. This means seven out of ten people taking the PMP exam for the first time, on average, are smiling when they leave the test center. Unfortunately, three on average are not smiling and will have to try again later.

PMI raised the bar significantly in the 2005 PMP exam when the percentage of correct answers needed to pass increased to over 80 percent. This drove the first-time pass rate of people taking the exam down to less than 60 percent. Fortunately, PMI revisited those results quickly and adjusted the test scoring back to around 70 percent to pass. PMI tends to be shy about publishing this information, and it rarely has been shown on the website since 2004.

How to Apply for a PMI Exam

Once you have selected the credential that is right for you, you submit an online application form to sit for the exam. Directions for the application, current pricing, and additional details are also available on the PMI website. Again, you have two ways to take a PMI exam: computer based and paper based (you must be physically located further than 186.5 miles from a contracted PMI test facility to qualify for paper-based testing).

Once your application has been reviewed, you will receive approval or denial within a matter of 5–10 business days. Once approved, you have up to one year to schedule and sit for the exam.

TIP

Start the registration process as early as possible and schedule a planned date to take the exam. This will make it real and help drive you to complete the process.

Ask the Expert

Q: Is the exam as hard as everyone says? And how much study time does it take?

A: It depends on your level of experience, your commitment to learn the language from PMI's perspective, and the amount of time you plan to prepare for the exam.

NOTE

The PMP exam can be tricky, with a high number (over 90 percent) of situational questions that require you to select the "best" answer from the PM's perspective and PMI's point of view. It is not a test of information from the *PMBOK*, as with the CAPM exam; you have to be able to determine which answer is best.

The exam is difficult and ever changing. The biggest changes occurred in 1998 when PMI went to the computer-based exam, and again in September 2004 when PMI raised the bar on the requirements to pass the PMP exam (such as possessing project management experience actually leading and directing project teams). This change was made right after PMI launched the CAPM exam (for people that participate as a project team member). The most recent changes in these exams occurred July 2009 when PMI aligned to the latest *PMBOK*.

TIP

Many people feel they over-studied for the exam and it was not as hard as they thought it would be. I suggest you allow two to four months to prepare for the exam, depending on how well you take tests and your level of project management experience.

PMP Exam Application Checklist

It is best to apply for the exam online through the PMI.org website (select Career Development | Certification & Credentials | Obtain a Credential and then click the Apply for a Credential button).

The following application checklist is a summary of the top three steps you need to take to apply for a PMI exam:

1. Complete the online application form, providing all the key information. Be sure to provide your name exactly as it appears on your government-issued identification card. You also need to fill out the experience verification section according to the credential exam you are applying for, and provide documentation of the 35 hours (minimum) of education you've obtained.

TIP

Save a tree! You do not have to provide all the supporting documentation of your project experience unless you are audited. The backup documents are not sent to PMI unless requested.

The time it takes to complete the application depends on the amount of detail and research necessary for credential eligibility (for example, you will need contact information and details from previous projects).

2. Affirm that you have read and understand the policies and procedures outlined in the credential handbook which is available on the PMI.org website.

3. Submit your payment according to the Credential Payment Process (you will not be able to schedule your exam until full payment is received).

PMI will review your application and provide an approval code. You will then need to contact a Prometric test center near you and call to schedule an exam date.

NOTE

Prometric is an independent group that provides comprehensive testing and assessment services to companies and organizations such as PMI across the globe. They offer an extensive, professional, and secure testing network from which tests are delivered in over 7,500 locations across 160 countries.

Manage the Exam Preparation Like a Project

A good project manager is organized, gains satisfaction from checking off tasks, and can manage the exam as if it were a project (because it is). You can use the following steps as your project plan:

1. Review the courses and credentials available.

2. Review the requirements and eligibility.

3. Determine which exam is right for you and apply for it (see the "Timeline of the PMP Credential Process" section).

4. Build a project plan to guide you toward achieving your goals (and stick with it).

5. Set a realistic target date with key checkpoints to ensure you are on track.

6. Schedule the exam date and mark it on your calendar. (Now it is real!)

7. Allow some "down" time during the training and preparation process.

8. Tell your boss, coworkers, and family that you are going into training.

9. Monitor your progress and continue managing the process as a project.

10. Remember to stay focused on the exam using the tools and resources available (study materials and your support group) to make successfully passing the exam happen.

11. Once you pass the exam, celebrate!

Timeline of the PMP Credential Process

As with other credentials, there is a timeline or flow for the PMP credential that must be followed to apply for a PMI exam. Remember that the time it takes to apply for the PMP credential will vary depending on how organized you are with your project information, contacts, and so on, needed to complete the submission form. Also remember you will only need to provide the detailed supporting documentation if you are audited, so please don't plan to send mounds of paper to PMI.

The following bullets are from the "About PMP Credential" section of the PMP Credential Handbook at www.pmi.org. The handbook can be downloaded and used as a reference when the time comes to begin your application process.

- The application submission window is open 90 days from the receipt of the application.
- The applicant completeness review (by PMI) takes five business days (when submitted online).
- The applicant payment process must be completed and confirmed before you can schedule your exam with Prometric.
- The audit process (if the application is selected by PMI for audit) takes five business days.
- Examination eligibility period is one year from the date of application approval.
- The certification cycle is three years from the date the exam is passed, then you need to recertify.

NOTE

To recertify once you attain a PMI credential, you must participate in the Continuing Certification Requirements (CCR) program to maintain active certification status. Additional details are provided in the "Maintaining Your PMI Credential" section later in this chapter.

Start Training

It is never too early to start training—and by this I mean *physical* training. I actually set up an exercise bike in the bedroom with a rack on the handle bars to rest my study material on for easy reading. Then set up a schedule (I chose three nights per week, one hour per night) to start with and then gradually increased the duration and frequency as I got closer to the test date. After coming home from the office, I would spend at least 40 to 60 minutes going over exam preparation material while working out on an exercise bike. This allowed me to be in good shape both physically and mentally for the exam.

What to Expect on the PMP Exam

You should expect lots of situational-type questions. Remember the PMP exam tests your ability to apply project management knowledge to a given situation.

Here are some examples:

1. The project sponsor has indicated he will be making a lot of changes to the scope of the project during the Initiation and Planning phases. What is the *best* approach the project manager should take to manage the expected changes?

   A Meet with the sponsor and tell him the changes will add cost to the project.

   B Send a note to the sponsor's boss to figure out a way to assign him to another project.

   C Include the sponsor early in the project to understand his needs and expectations. Work with him to ensure he is aware of and is in agreement with the change process.

   D Just say no to changes—they are distracting to the project team.

Answer: C.

2. During a project team meeting a software engineer indicates a need to provide a larger (newer technology) system to meet the long-term needs of the customer. The engineer admits this change will delay the project, but it needs to be done. As the project manager, you remind the team for the need to focus on the approved plan. This is an example of what?

   A Time management process

   B Cost management process

   C Scope management

   D Work Breakdown Structure

Answer: C. Although it could be argued that this is a time/schedule management impact or even a cost management issue, it really goes back to the original scope of the project. Managing scope effectively keeps other constraints (time and cost) under control.

Moving the Exam Date (Change Happens)

Once you are approved, you can contact Prometric to schedule your exam date within the 12-month approved PMI window to take the exam. Changing the exam date is *not* recommended. However, there may be certain circumstances that force you to move your exam date. Some reasons that would be accepted by PMI for moving the examination date include medical emergency, military deployment, and death or serious illness in the immediate family.

Rescheduling requires that you contact the test center directly no later than two business days prior to your scheduled exam date. You must provide your PMI identification number, group ID number, the location and type of exam you are scheduled to take, and the reason for rescheduling.

Balancing Competing Demands

With the advent of portable, easy access to the Internet/intranet, it is far too easy to work extra hours even when you are on vacation. Many bosses have come to expect, or even demand, a higher level of accessibility to their employees. To be competitive, we feel the need to "stay connected," so we keep pushing ourselves because we are afraid of falling out of favor with the boss, losing our job, or not getting that promotion we deserve. With the current economic times, there are fewer jobs available and scores of qualified workers who are more than willing to put in the extra time on the job and to get certified to increase their marketability.

When it comes to studying for the exam, you will find it far too easy to get distracted and lose focus. You will need to balance a variety of competing demands for your time, especially if you have a family with kids. Between your job, your family, and your friends, how will you ever find the time it takes to prepare for the exam? The answer is focus, commitment, and a support structure. If you can maintain focus and use your support group to help you meet your commitment to yourself, the satisfaction and rewards of passing the exam are immeasurable.

Tools to Use to Prepare for the Exam

Many books are available to help you learn about project management, to build your knowledge, and to help prepare you for the PMI exam. The tools available to help you study for the exam (such as flash cards, sample exam question workbooks, and downloads) are plentiful, thus it may be difficult to determine which ones are right for you. The only way to choose is to first look at your own learning style. You need to determine what makes you feel most comfortable and what style works best for you. Here are some examples:

- Dawn is a fast study and is usually not intimidated by tests (well, maybe a little). She is very organized and learns best by seeing the words and goes as far as rewriting her class notes in neat, color-coded script. She likes descriptive scenes, diagrams, and posters, always reads directions, and seeks out pictures to help visualize and understand the message. Dawn is using a "visual" learning style. Dawn used the *PMBOK*, a popular PMP exam-preparation workbook, flashcards, and her own color-coded notes.

- George tends to sound out the words and uses a phonetic approach to learning. He is eager to talk. He tends to get distracted by sounds and noises (such as the television) and prefers verbal instructions rather than reading directions. George is using an "auditory" learning style. He studied for the PMP exam using recorded tapes he created with key study material. He listened to the tapes often while on the way to work, walking the dog, mowing the lawn—all to help "burn in" the material.

The information in Table 1-3 is an extract paraphrased from Colin Rose's 1987 book *Accelerated Learning*. This table helps you determine your learning style; read the word in the left column and then answer the questions in the successive three columns to see how you respond in each situation.

When you...	Visual	Auditory	Kinesthetic & Tactile
Spell	Do you try to see the word?	Do you sound out the word or use a phonetic approach?	Do you write the word down to find if it feels right?
Concentrate	Do you become distracted by clutter or movement?	Do you become distracted by sounds or noises?	Do you become distracted by activity around you?
Meet someone again	Do you forget names but remember faces or remember where you met?	Do you forget faces but remember names or remember what you talked about?	Do you remember best what you did together?
Contact people on business	Do you prefer direct, face-to-face personal meetings?	Do you prefer the telephone?	Do you talk with others while walking or participating in an activity?
Read	Do you like descriptive scenes or pause to imagine the actions?	Do you enjoy dialog or hearing the characters talk?	Do you prefer action stories or are not a keen reader?
Do something new at work	Do you like to see demonstrations, diagrams, slides, or posters?	Do you prefer verbal instructions or talking about the subject with someone else?	Do you prefer to jump right in and try new things?
Put something together	Do you look at directions and pictures?	(not applicable)	Do you ignore directions and figure it out as you go along?

Table 1-3 Learning Styles

Study Tips

Depending on your learning style you will need to decide what study tips work best for you. Many people find it helpful to obtain or record key materials, definitions, formulas, inputs, tools and techniques, and outputs for the various processes and then play back the tapes during their training/study periods. Sample exams, flash cards (some can be downloaded to your personal digital device), CDs, and more are available.

I chose to record key topics, and I replayed the recording while walking the dog, working in the yard, and so on. I covered one knowledge area per week over a planned study (training) period of 12 weeks. At the end of each week, I got up early on Saturday morning and took all the sample exam questions I could get my hands on for practice. At key intervals, I would take the entire practice exam from my handy PMP exam preparation study guide to get used to a 3-to-4-hour sit for the exam. I did this three times, until I felt comfortable in that test-taking mode.

A good friend of mine only used sample exam questions from various sources and would spend hours taking and retaking the sample "exams" until he felt good about his answers. He passed the PMP on the first try.

Countless online and face-to-face exam-preparation classes and workshops are available to help you prepare for the PMI exam. These usually cost anywhere from US$350 to US$1,200, depending on the provider, the duration of the class, the location, and the provider's success rate.

NOTE
Check with your local PMI chapter or other education providers in your area for available classes or study groups.

The Key Is to Stay Focused and Committed

Focus is the key; if you get distracted easily like many of us do, you will need to work harder at staying focused on exam preparation. It is far too easy to put it off, even for a night, then two, and before you realize it, weeks or even months have passed.

There is a saying (quoted by an IBM system programmer in the book *The One Minute Manager* by Kenneth H. Blanchard, Ph.D. and Spencer Johnson, M.D.), that goes like this: "How do you get a year behind on a project?" Answer: "One day at a time."

This is where the commitment comes in to play. You will need the training discipline we mentioned earlier and the support of your family, friends, and coworkers to make this happen. Allow for some down time to relax and get re-energized during the training cycle, but you will need to stay focused.

TIP

How to stay focused? Answer: Make it real; go into training mode and ask your support group (friends, family, boss, and co-workers) to allow you the study time you need. You may have to remind them of your commitment and the date (put it on your calendar in bold print).

Exam Day Has Come

You must arrive to the testing center 30 minutes ahead of your scheduled start time. You must bring an original government-issued ID that has both a photo and a signature that matches your name exactly. The identification must include English characters (or a translation). It can be a valid driver's license, military ID, or passport. You must sign in and provide your unique PMI-approved identification code (you may be asked to provide your confirmation number from Prometric as well).

You will be provided with scratch paper, pencils, and a calculator. Items not allowed in the test area include cell phones, pagers, food, drinks, books, notes, jackets, sweaters, and personal belongings. Also, visitors and children are not allowed in the testing facility.

Once you sign in, are seated at your computer, and begin the exam, it is best to do a quick brain dump of all the formulas you remember onto a page of scratch paper while they are fresh in your mind. This serves as a quick reference later on when you get to those questions in the exam.

The computer-based examination is preceded by a tutorial and followed by a survey, both of which are optional and can take up to 15 minutes each to complete. The time used to complete the tutorial and survey is not included in the four hours allotted for the PMP exam or the three hours allotted for the CAPM exam. I suggest you take the tutorial to get settled in and to better understand the computer-based exam process.

Use the "Mark for Review" Option on the Exam

If you are not sure of the correct answer for any question, you can mark it for "review" with the touch of the computer screen. At the end of the exam, you can select the option to review all marked questions. This will take you back through all the questions you marked for later review.

NOTE

You can also select the "Review All Questions" option, which I do *not* recommend because the system takes you back to the beginning of the exam. Valuable time is taken going back over all the questions.

Once you are comfortable with your answers, press End (complete). The system will then ask if you are sure you want to end the exam. At this point you might think, "What do they know that I don't?" The tendency is to second-guess yourself. Instead, just press Yes, and after a short time (which seems like several minutes) you will be presented with a screen that either states "Congratulations, you passed" or reads sorry you did not pass the exam, in which case you need to try again later. Again, you can retake the test up to three times within the 12-month window from your approved date.

When you receive the "Congratulations, you passed" message and printout from the test facilitator, then go celebrate! You deserve it for all your hard work.

Maintaining Your PMI Credential (CCRs/PDUs)

Once you become certified, you will want to maintain your credentials. This is necessary to demonstrate your continued participation in the PM profession. The program for maintaining your credentials is called Continuing Certification Requirements (CCR). Your certification/CCR cycle begins the day you pass the exam and ends on the same date three years later for all credential holders.

To meet the CCR requirements, you need to participate in professional development activities in which you earn professional development units (PDUs). PDUs are used to quantify approved professional activities. Typically, you earn one PDU for one hour spent in a planned, structured professional development activity.

Each credential requires a certain number of PDUs per three-year credential cycle. Refer to the PMI.org website under the CCR for the latest information because these numbers are subject to change. The 2009 credential requirements are detailed in Table 1-4.[4]

Credential	Number of PDUs Needed in the Three-Year Cycle
PMP (Project Management Professional)	60 PDUs.
PgMP (Program Management Professional)	60 PDUs.
PMI-SP (PM Schedule Professional)	30 PDUs in the specialized area of project scheduling.
PMI-RMP (PM Risk Management Professional)	30 PDUs in the specialized area of project risk management.
CAPM (Certified Associate Project Manager)	No PDUs. Retaking the CAPM exam is required in the last year of your five-year cycle to recertify.

Table 1-4 PDU Requirements by Credential

There are currently ten different types (or categories) of PDUs and various ways to obtain them. The most common is formal academic education (Category 1), offered through continued education programs with PMI registered education providers (REPs). These are companies, training facilities, or other academic providers that register with, and are recognized by, PMI to meet their educational requirements for classes offered outside of PMI. Other ways to obtain PDUs include professional activities and self-directed learning (Category 2).

NOTE

For Category 1 PDUs, one hour of classroom contact usually equals one PDU.

Ask the Expert

Q: What is the best way to maintain my credential?

A: The best way is to follow these steps:

1. Start early by establishing a strategy for attaining your PDUs before your cycle begins. For example, set reminder dates on your calendar for any planned PMI events or education. Don't wait until year three of your cycle to start applying for PDUs.

2. Maintain a personal folder of all your PDU claim documents. The claim documents should be printed from the online registration process at the PMI.org website. This information will be valuable if your reporting form is randomly selected for audit.

3. Report activities soon after completion while dates and topics are fresh on your mind. This makes it easier to complete the Activity Reporting Form.

4. Take advantage of the opportunity to transfer PDUs from one cycle to the next. You can transfer up to 20 PDUs earned in the last year of your current cycle if you exceed the 60 total needed for the three-year cycle.
   For example, say you earn 20 PDUs the first year of your credential cycle, 30 PDUs the second year, and 30 PDUs in the third year. You have a total of 80 PDUs in your three-year cycle (you only need 60). In this scenario, you can carry over 20 PDUs from year three to your next recertification/CCR cycle. This is a great way to get a head start on the next cycle.

5. Make sure you have the registered program number for all REP classes you complete, which is required on the Activity Reporting Form.

Easy PDUs

You can even claim PDUs for reading project management material, magazines, and trade journals, collaborating with fellow PMs, and participating in free webinars and podcasts, which are often offered as demos and teasers for many PM education providers. You are limited to five such PDUs per year (subject to change without notice).

NOTE

If you do not maintain an active certification status by meeting the CCR program requirements, your credential will expire and you will no longer be allowed to refer to yourself as a credential holder unless you retake the exam and pass.

Your participation in continuing education activities indicates to your peers, employers, and clients that you are committed to ongoing professional development. Staying current on standard practices and policies as well as keeping up with the latest processes and methods are all helpful in managing your projects in a professional, effective manner.

References

1. "Standish: Project Success Rates Improved Over 10 Years," from Application Development Product Coverage. January 15, 2004 (http://www.softwaremag.com/L.cfm?doc=newsletter/2004-01-15/Standish).

2. "Standish Group Report: There's Less Development Chaos Today," by David Rubinstein. March 1, 2007.

3. *ArchitectureWeek,* April 23, 2003 and Ibid.

4. PMP Credential Handbook (www.pmi.org).

5. *PMI Today,* a supplement to *PM Network* magazine, November 2008.

Chapter 2

The Emerging World of Project Management

Key Skills & Concepts

- Definition of a project

- Difference between projects, programs, and operations

- Definition of project management

- How the world of project management is emerging

- Different views of project management

- Role of the project manager

- Importance of communications

- Organizational structures

- How to measure success on a project

- The "Ready, fire, aim" dilemma

- The AIM strategy

- Why projects fail and what you can do about it

The best way to describe how the world of project management is emerging is to start by defining what a project really is. What does project management really mean and what is the role of the project manger?

In this chapter and throughout this book, we will look at project management from two different perspectives. These views are different in nature, based on the extent of formal training and experience you may have. Yet, when the views are combined, they provide synergy and benefits to you as a project manager.

Here are the two project management perspectives:

- **The real-world view**   Managing projects using common-sense instincts
- **The Project Management Institute (PMI) view**   Managing projects using globally accepted standards

Before we go into the different views of project management, let's look at the definition of a project, program, and operation and review project management in general.

What Is a Project?

Even though project management has been around a long time, there still tends to be a fair amount of confusion, even among experienced project managers, concerning the definition of a project. People often use the term "project" to describe everything from designing software or building a new hybrid (fuel-efficient) car, to building a new house, planning a major event, installing new computer equipment, finding a way to fix a problem, or setting up an ice cream stand.

So, what is the correct definition of "project"? I suggest we first look to the experts in the PM profession. According to PMI, a project is "a temporary endeavor undertaken to create a unique product, service or result."[1] The temporary nature of projects indicates a definite beginning and end. Projects are put in place to create a unique product, service, or result. Most everyone has a pretty good idea about what products and services are, but what about "results"? This was added to the 2004 version of the *PMBOK,* and it means that the results of the project may far outlive the project itself—for example, Mount Rushmore was a massive sculpture project completed in 1941 now has over 2 million visitors a year; reduced pollution from hybrid cars will benefit the planet far beyond the design project; and increased savings due to automated systems—these are all results from projects.

To be a little more specific, let's look at some of the characteristics of typical projects. All projects should have the following characteristics:

- They are temporary in nature—that is, they have a definite start and a definite end (if a project is long term and never ends, it is likely a program or an ongoing operation).

- As mentioned, projects create a unique product, service, or result (even if the project has been done before, there is something unique about it, such as the location, team members, materials, and so on).

- They have (or should have) clearly defined goals and objectives (if it is open ended or changes over time, it is likely a program or an ongoing operation).

- The end of the project is reached when its approved objectives have been achieved.

What Is a Program?

Programs are different from projects in that they usually are a collection (or group) of projects, they tend to be longer in duration, and have no defined end date. An example would be NASA's space shuttle *program* (officially called Space Transportation System [STS]), which consists of multiple projects and the ongoing maintenance/operation of several aircraft, such as the Columbia, Challenger, Discovery, Atlantis, and Enterprise.

Program management is a way for us to bundle (or group) similar projects and support operations into a logical manner. Grouping projects into a program makes them easier to assign and manage. A project management education program, a government welfare program, a specific software application program—they all tend to be ongoing and usually include many projects and subprojects.

What Is an Operation?

Usually an operation is the activity of operating something (such as a machine or a business). On a larger scale, a company may have multinational operations. In the world of project management, the key words to look for to help distinguish operations from projects or programs are *enhancement* (for example, improving existing software application code or adding a process to enhance [or improve] the operation of computer installations), *daily activities,* or *ongoing.*

Operations are usually repeatable activities performed to establish a product (for example, an assembly line operation to manufacture cars).

A good way to clarify the differences between projects, programs, and operations is to think about the characteristics of each, as detailed in the preceding definitions, and then look at the examples presented in Table 2-1.

Event/Activity	Project	Program	Ongoing Operation
Design software	X		
Testing software	X (if new)		X (if repetitive)
Maintain the software once promoted to production			X
Manage a group of software application products		X	
Design a hybrid car	X		
Set up an assembly line to build hybrid cars	X		
Assemble/build hybrid cars			X
Plan a major event (like a wedding)	X		
Develop a new PM class on risk management	X		
Manage a new class as part of a series of PM courses		X	

Table 2-1 Examples of Projects, Programs, and Operations

Ask the Expert

Q: What happens when a person is called a project manager yet is responsible for various aspects of a program and even daily operations (systems availability, staffing, and so on)?

A: There are times when the staff is limited and the person in charge of leading the project is expected to be all things (one-stop shopping) across the entire program. When the PM is handling daily operational issues and problems or a long-term program (multiple projects or subprojects), then the specific project tends to get neglected. The end result, at best, is controlled chaos, and the most likely result is uncontrolled chaos. When a person is subjected to this cross-section of responsibilities, they can rarely focus on the specific project and often fail at the project management level. If you find yourself in this situation, the solution in my opinion is to work with the sponsor(s) to verify the priorities of the project (or program) and reason with them to allow you to have the staff needed or time required to focus on the project at hand.

TIP

There is no hard-and-fast rule on what is called a "project." Therefore, don't correct your boss or project sponsor when they tell you to go manage a "project" that may not be one by definition. Simply smile and take comfort in knowing the difference for yourself, and do your best to help train the rest of the world a little along the way.

What Is Project Management?

Now that you know what a project is and have seen some examples of projects, programs, and operations, let's talk about project management. What is project management, and what does the PM need to do to perform this dynamic role?

In practice, project management is all about being able to look across the entire project—from the requirements (what the customer wants) to what is being accomplished (what needs to be done to meet the customer requirements). In Chapter 8, you will see this referred to as *meeting specifications* and *fitness for use*—for example, does the product, service, or result do what we said it will do (provide the functions and features as specified) and work the way we designed it to work in order to meet the approved requirements of the project (fitness of use)?

Project management may involve staffing the project team (who will do the work) and planning, estimating, and managing the schedule (when each phase of the project will be completed) as well as the cost of the project. Note that hiring or assigning the team members may be managed by the Human Resources (HR) department (or the Contracts and Procurement department in some companies), and the PM may not get to pick the team members to work on the project. They may be preassigned or provided by a functional manager as part of a "pool" of resources.

According to PMI, project management is the application of knowledge, skills, tools, techniques, and practices to project activities to meet project requirements. This is accomplished through the appropriate application and integration of the 42 logically grouped project management processes in the *PMBOK*. (Note: The key word is *application*.)

TIP

The PMP exam focuses on the PM's ability to *apply* knowledge and skills to solve various problems, to be able to think on their feet (that is, to be able to manage in many different situations).

The Project Management Institute (PMI) View

PMI's view of project management is to have a globally recognized discipline with a standard accepted framework to assist in the pursuit of improved project success. PMI's vision is to provide a network of highly skilled professionals to share experiences and knowledge and to help promote the project management profession.

Strong PM skills are not easy to acquire and in many cases need to be developed over time by working on real projects; this is one field that can't be totally learned from books. PM skills must be developed and practiced to ensure success. That is why PMI calls us "practitioners" and requires on-going recertification every three years.

PMI recognizes that project and program managers face many variables and challenges and at the end of the day it all comes down to being able to apply sound project management judgment, leadership, and organizational skills to balance the competing project demands. This constant balancing act, if done well, can help you reach a higher level of success on your projects. PMI's goal is to provide the broader perspective and assist the PM community to strive for continuous improvement.

As a project manager, you should constantly watch for and manage the various aspects of a project: time (schedule), cost (budget), and scope. At the end of a project, according to PMI, its success is measured by product quality, timeliness, budget compliance, and the degree of customer satisfaction.

The Real-World View—Managing Projects Using Instincts

Many of us apply project management skills in our daily jobs and in everyday activities using sheer gut instincts (often referred to as managing by the "seat of our pants"). Many project managers are put into projects with little or no formal training and must trust their instincts.

A large number of project managers perform well using nothing but common sense. Others perform poorly and don't even know it. They tend to make the same mistakes over and over, developing bad habits that may never be realized or corrected.

The good news is that common sense goes a long way, and chances are you have been managing projects with good to reasonable success much longer than you might realize. Think about putting on those puppet shows as a kid, working on school projects (there's that word again, *projects*), and planning a surprise birthday, anniversary, or wedding party for a friend or family member—*all* of these are examples of projects.

Common sense and gut instincts are at the core of being a good, solid project manager. However, having good instincts is great up to the point where you have to lead others and present the project status to the stakeholders (that is, anyone affected by the project). For that you need more than common sense—you need a common language.

Once you learn the language of project management, the standard processes, and the tools, then the "ah-ha" moments come (when you see the link between what you do instinctively and what these components are called in the professional world of project management).

As a project manager, you need to see the bigger picture (across the entire project, as previously mentioned) and be able to identify risks; to communicate effectively; to address the various needs, concerns, and expectations of the stakeholders; and most importantly to balance the competing project demands and constraints (limitations or barriers.)

Competing Project Constraints

Regardless of which project management book you read (and there are many), you will hear about the need for the PM to balance competing demands and constraints. This used to be called the "triple constraints," and was shown as a triangle with Time, Cost, and Scope on respective sides of the triangle.

To put this in perspective, a friend of mine when faced with the challenge of balancing project demands often says, "Good, fast, or cheap—pick any two," meaning that if you want something good and fast, it will likely cost more; if you want it good and cheap, it may take more time. Any change to the triple constraints throws the triangle out of balance.

Because of the dynamics of managing projects in today's complex world, we need a broader view beyond just the three primary constraints. Most authors agree on Time (often shown as "Schedule") and Cost (often shown as "Budget"), but the third key component varies between "Scope," "Quality," "Resources," and "Risk." PMI recognizes that multiple components must be managed (balanced) and therefore has pulled away from using the term "triple constraints" in favor of calling these "competing constraints."

The basic concept is still the same in that the project manager and team must balance the key components to keep them in line with the project sponsor's requirements. If time (the schedule) is compressed (for example, the customer needs the solution sooner), then the other components of the constraints shift, thus increasing cost or decreasing quality and potentially affecting the scope of the project. If scope changes, then time and cost are surely effected. The key is to clearly understand the driver (or main component) of the project constraints. For example, the primary driver on the Olympics project is time—making sure the torch is lit at a specific time on a specific date, even if the paint is not dry on the bleachers.

Project stakeholders have different priorities and sometimes changing demands, which makes the balancing act extremely difficult. This is why I often refer to project managers as "jugglers." We constantly have to keep the plates spinning and all the balls in the air (so to speak) at the same time.

Finally, I believe there is another side to these constraints that is rarely mentioned— and that is keeping the team happy. If the PM is focused on the team as the number-one asset to the project, the rest of the pieces tend to fall into place. If the team is happy, working well together, and focused on the requirements, the project has a much higher chance for success.

What Is a Portfolio? What Is Portfolio Management?

In the world of project management, a *portfolio* refers to a collection of similar projects or programs and other work that is grouped together at a company level. The auto industry is a prime example. A large company such as Toyota has a portfolio of various brands, models, and styles—they design and manufacture the Camry, Corolla, Rav4, Highlander, Prius, and more, with cars, trucks, and SUVs.

Portfolio management refers to the centralized management of one or more portfolios, which includes identifying, prioritizing, authorizing, managing, and controlling projects and programs as well as the governance of the collective work to achieve specific strategic objectives.

Table 2-2 provides an overview of project, program, and portfolio management. It compares how projects, programs, and portfolios differ in key areas such as how they are planned, managed, and measured, and how scope is defined.

Introduction to the Project Management Office (PMO)

Project management offices (PMOs) are emerging mostly in larger companies to set up a common approach to providing standards across many projects. When projects are managed inconsistently, the overhead cost of setting up, running, and reporting using different types of reports, tools, and procedures can be prohibitive.

	Projects	**Programs**	**Portfolios**
Scope	Projects have defined objectives. Scope is progressively elaborated upon (that is, it builds) throughout the project life cycle.	Programs have a larger scope and provide more significant benefits.	Portfolios have a business scope that changes with the strategic goals of the organization.
Change	Project managers expect change and implement processes to keep change managed and controlled.	The program manager must expect change from both inside and outside the program and be prepared to manage it.	Portfolio managers continually monitor changes in the broad environment.
Planning	Project managers progressively integrate high-level information into detailed plans throughout the project life cycle.	Program managers develop the overall program plan and create high-level plans to guide detailed planning at the component level.	Portfolio managers create and maintain necessary processes and communication relative to the aggregate portfolio.
Management	Project managers manage the project team to meet the project objectives.	Program managers manage the program staff and the project managers; they provide vision and overall leadership.	Portfolio managers may manage or coordinate portfolio management staff.
Success	Success is measured by product and project quality, timeliness, budget compliance, and the degree of customer satisfaction.	Success is measured by the degree to which the program satisfies the needs and benefits for which it was undertaken.	Success is measured in terms of aggregate performance of the portfolio components.
Monitoring	Project managers monitor and control the work of producing the products, services, or results that the project was undertaken to produce.	Program managers monitor the progress of program components to ensure the overall goals, schedule, budget, and benefits of the program will be met.	Portfolio managers monitor aggregate performance and value indicators.

Table 2-2 Comparative Overview of Project, Program, and Portfolio Management

PMOs also provide "governance" (controlled direction) to projects and programs. The word *governance* originates from the Greek verb *kubernáo*, which means *to steer* and was used for the first time in a metaphorical sense by Plato. It then passed to Latin *(gubernare)* and then on to many other languages. The term *governance* as used in the industry—especially in the information technology (IT) sector—describes the processes that need to exist for a successful project.[2]

Governance works best when standards are selected and enforced across projects and programs within a portfolio or organization.

Ask the Expert

Q: Are there standard templates and real-world examples of scope statements and other project documents to help me manage my project in a more consistent manner?

A: Yes. I recommend an Internet search on "PM Templates" for a wealth of project management freeware and great examples used in real-world projects like the one from Dr. Gary Evans at http://cvr-it.com/PM_Templates/. You can also talk to fellow project managers inside and outside your team/organization for examples as well.

NOTE

The message here is to use the tools available (never reinvent the wheel if you don't have to) to manage projects in a shared learning environment (working together to learn from one another and gain synergy). Most project managers are happy to offer templates they have designed or used on successful projects to share their knowledge and experience.

Being Audit Ready

When it comes to projects, in the corporate world we often say, "It is not a question of *if* your project will be audited, but *when* it will be audited." Therefore, it is important to stay organized and maintain the documents of the project by keeping them current and accurate.

The best way to be "audit ready" is to have a project control book (PCB), preferably in an electronic database, team room, Microsoft SharePoint, or other form of a central repository to ensure easy access by the project stakeholders. The PCB should also be included in the overall Project Management Information System (PMIS). The PMIS is where you should keep all your project plans and output documents (status reports, risk and communication plans, schedule updates, approved changes, and so on).

With a PMIS comes the responsibility to keep it current, which means version control (making sure you have the latest version of all project documents). Being "audit ready" means being able to demonstrate you are effectively managing all aspects of the project. It is a great feeling to walk out of a project audit with no negative findings and no action items because you were able to show that your project is well organized, current with all documents, and that you are in control of the project.

The Role of the Project Manager

The project manager is the "glue" that holds the project together. The PM is responsible and accountable for the project and must take charge as the project leader.

To be a good leader, the PM must be a good communicator, be organized, play well with others (that is, be team oriented), and be a team builder/motivator. The PM must be willing (and able) to take calculated risks, be an advocate for the team, be able to solve problems, and understand stakeholders' needs and expectations. As the person responsible for project success, the PM is in charge of all aspects of the project, including but not limited to the following:

- Developing the project management plan and updating it as needed to ensure currency, accuracy, and applicability

- Keeping the project on track (budget, schedule, scope, and deliverables)

- Managing risk and providing timely and accurate reports on project status/metrics

- Managing stakeholder needs and expectations

Ideally, the PM should be assigned to the project early in the project life cycle to assist in developing the project charter, planning documents, and establishing the project team (depending on the type of organizational structure, the team may already be assigned or may be assigned by the functional manager based on location, skills, and availability).

The role of the PM is distinct and should be focused on the project. If, for example, this person is a functional (line) manager in addition to being assigned the PM role, there will likely be conflicting demands on their time and requirements.

Being a good project manager requires a specific set of competencies (skills). According to PMI, there are three dimensions (layers) of project management competency:

- **Knowledge**   This refers to what the PM knows about project management.

- **Performance**   This refers to what the project manager is able to do or accomplish while applying their project management knowledge.

- **Personal**   This refers to how the project manager behaves when performing within the project or related activity. Personal competency encompasses attitudes, core personality characteristics, and leadership—the ability to guide the project team while achieving project objectives and balancing the project constraints.[3]

Even though the role of the PM varies based on the size, type, and complexity of the project, the fundamental skills required are universal (the primary PM skills and disciplines can be plugged into practically any industry). This is not to say "one size fits all," because projects by definition are unique. However, project management as a skill is extremely versatile and can be used in a broad spectrum of applications.

Finally, a good project manager must be a strong leader to effectively control the project. Being a leader means taking control of the project.

TIP

The true measure of success for you as a project manager is when team members say they want to work with you on future projects. The only way you gain this kind of trust and dedication is by being an advocate for the team, being able to admit when you have made a mistake, and by being honest and respectful. This will go a long way toward establishing your credibility and integrity.

I recommend the following action steps for taking control of either a new or existing project:

1. *Get (and stay) informed.* Be a sponge and absorb as much about the project as possible by reviewing project requirements, the project management plan, output documents, the contract, work orders, change requests, and the status reports of the project. This means listening more than talking. One of my previous managers has a saying that goes like this: "My daddy always said I have two ears and one mouth, so I should listen twice as much as I talk."

2. *Document key issues and concerns.* Review actions and options with key individuals first to understand as much as possible about pervasive (chronic) issues, staff issues, customer contacts, organizational structure, environmental factors, and organizational assets (standard tools, templates, forms, and so on) as appropriate and available.

3. *Meet with the customer to begin establishing a relationship* in order to understand their concerns as well as what they like and don't like when it comes to the project, the team, and the deliverables.

4. *Bring these steps together by holding a project kickoff meeting* using all the information collected to establish yourself as the leader of the project. This is where steps 1–3 pay off, because you need to demonstrate your awareness of the project, the stakeholders, project objectives, customer expectations (hot buttons), and overall status. You need to provide clear direction (a plan) and reiterate the roles, responsibilities, and assignments using proven project management tools, techniques, and processes to show your competency as the project manager.

Ask the Expert

Q: Once you are assigned as a project manager, what is the best way to take control of a project?

A: The best way to take control of a project is to establish yourself as the leader (not by being bold or dictatorial, but by showing interest, knowledge, and professionalism). When you (as the project manger) take responsibility and accountability for the project, you show the team you are in control. Being in control also means you need to support your team in their effort to deliver the approved scope of the project. Being firm but fair helps lead to positive results.

Importance of Clear Communications—Learn the Language

Being able to speak and understand the language of project management is essential to the combined success of the project stakeholders, and the project itself.

On average project managers spend about 90 percent of their time communicating. Communications occur in many different ways: formal, informal, written, verbal, and nonverbal (through body language).

The types of communications are varied and should be tailored to meet the needs of the project. Some common forms of communications on most projects include the project management plan document, various process documents (for example, the Work Breakdown Structure [WBS]), communications plan, various written reports, status meeting minutes, emails, phone messages, and general discussions with project stakeholders. The project manager is either communicating or planning communications during the majority of their time on a given project. Multiply this several times over if the PM is managing multiple projects or programs at the same time. This becomes quite a juggling act for the project manager.

The primary purpose of project communication is to ensure every one associated with the project is rowing in the same direction (on the same page), and making sure everyone on the project understands the deliverables, roles, responsibilities, schedule, and expected results.

The best way to keep everyone focused is through clear two-way communications. To communicate effectively you need to learn the language of project management. Using this book, you will learn how to keep the team focused on the project. Given the importance of communication management, you can bet it is a key PMI knowledge area (to be discussed in more detail in Chapter 10 of this book).

Three Takeaway Points from This Chapter

Understanding the importance of applying clear communications, common processes, tools, techniques, and practices in a consistent manner is essential for quality delivery and measured results on your projects. Many of my students, associates, and clients often ask for the "magic bullet" to successful project management—that is, what are the key focus items that will help me manage my project more effectively?

In my opinion, there are three primary points that will assist you in achieving your goals to effectively manage your projects:

- **Stay focused on the end goals and objectives**   It is very easy in the real world to get distracted by the many requests from sponsors, potential risks identified by the team, changes in scope, and the natural tendency to want to add value (do more) to the project. Change management as a process can help you and the team stay focused on the approved scope and goals of the project.

- **Use the tools available**   It is important to use standard tools and templates from the *PMBOK,* from your project management office (if available), from other projects in your group or company, and from the Internet. Also, you can acquire shareware tools at no cost (or low cost) to help you track and manage the cost, schedule, and scope of your project.

- **Work as a team**   Remember the number-one asset on a project is the team. As a project manager, you cannot do it all. The best way to ensure the team is working together is through clear communications and rewards/recognition when things are done right.

NOTE
There is a saying in the PM world that goes like this: "If you have more than one person on a project, you have a team, and if you have a team, you have conflict." Therefore, be aware of the ongoing need to keep the team informed, engaged, and focused. As a PM, you must provide clear direction to the team for success.

Roles of the Stakeholders (Who Are They and Why Do We Care?)

I have mentioned the term *stakeholders* several times in this chapter and want to take a minute to define who they are and their importance to the project.

- **Who are project stakeholders?**
  Answer: Anyone or any organization that is positively or negatively affected by the project.

● **Why should we care who the project stakeholders are?**
Answer: The project cannot exist without stakeholders; they are the sponsors (provide the budget), the customer, the end users (or customers) of the product produced by the project, and the project team (including the PM) responsible for bringing the project to a successful close to meet the needs of the other stakeholders. The stakeholders are so important to the project, PMI added Identify Stakeholders as a new process in the Initiating process group. It is extremely difficult to meet stakeholder needs if we don't know who they are.

Try This   Who Are the Project Stakeholders?

Say you are the overall project manager working on a major event (such as a concert). It is your job as PM to identify all the stakeholders (including whom to call boss) on the project.

Take a few minutes and write a list of who you think the stakeholders are for an events center and then compare your list to the following:

● Corporate sales representative.

● Marketing representative.

● Contract manager.

● Finance (Pricer).

● Business office manager.

● Event manager.

● Ticket sales (box office).

● Operations manager and team.

● Changeover project manager and team (setting up the venue for concert seating).

● Hundreds of part-time employees, including security, ushers, lighting, sound, dressing room setup (to meet artist requirements), food, merchandising, audio/video (AV) technicians, post-event cleanup, parking, traffic control, and, of course, the people attending the event.

● The artist and performing band, riggers, wardrobe, makeup artist, and managing agent.

● The boss. This is the person to whom you report and are accountable to on the project. The person you call "boss" varies depending on where you are in the pecking order (chain of command). At the end of the day, the project manager is the "boss" of the project, and of course the sponsor (the person or persons paying for the project) is the "boss" of the project manager. Remember everyone has a boss (usually several).

Project Framework

The project management framework provides a basis for understanding project management. The framework sets the stage for the overall structure of the project. It lays the foundation for the type of organization, the types of products, services, and deliverables, and the results to be achieved from the project. Key to understanding the project framework is the project life cycle.

The Project Life Cycle

The life cycle of a project can differ in type and terms used. Software development is a good example, where you have concept, development, test, implementation, and closing phases (remember, projects should have a beginning and an end). Because of the high potential for change, the project and associated PM plan are iterative in nature, meaning they go through what PMI calls "progressive elaboration" throughout the project's life cycle. Progressive elaboration involves continuously looking for ways to improve on the work and results of the project. As the project evolves, you learn more, you have more information (more "knowns" and less risk), and with information comes knowledge. This increase in knowledge allows the project team to manage a higher level of detail as the project evolves.

No matter how large, small, simple, or complex the project, in general all projects have a basic structure:

- Initiating the project (getting it started)
- Organizing and preparing the project through planning (planning the work)
- Carrying out the work of the project (working the approved plan) and monitoring/controlling results
- Closing the project

In summary, a project life cycle is a collection of sequential (but sometimes overlapping) project phases.

Project Phases

Project management is all about organizing the work of the project in manageable logical chunks (groups or categories of work). With the many dependencies that exist on a project to get from one phase to the next, it is almost like managing many subprojects or subsets of the project. Take the case of setting up an ice rink for a hockey game or any other show on ice event. Clearly the event will not occur unless the ice is properly frozen, and even if the ice rink is ready for play, unless marketing, advertising, and the box office do their jobs, no tickets will be sold or delivered. These are often considered project phases especially when setting them up for the first time. Once these steps become repeated, documented, and approved, the steps may ultimately become ongoing operations.

Also consider a project that is coming to a close. Even though you are in the final phase of the original project, the closing phase becomes, and should be managed like, a project. Closing a project (as you will see in Chapter 13) takes on a project life cycle and should be managed accordingly.

Organizational Structures

There are many different organizational structures as well as multiple methods of managing projects. However, it is best to focus on the basic structures (especially if you are planning to take the PMI exam.)

Basic Organizational Structures According to PMI

Organizational structure is an enterprise environmental factor that can affect the availability of resources and influence how projects are managed. Organizational structure refers to the way a company or group is formed or aligned. The basic structures (according to PMI) are as follows:

- **Functional**   This is usually hierarchical (line managers) or by skill (plumbers, event planners, programmers, security administration, and so on). With this type of organizational structure, the power tends to be retained by the functional manager, not the project manager.

- **Matrix (Weak, Balanced, and Strong)**   This is usually a pool of people aligned similarly to the functional structure; however, they are used across multiple projects and organizations and have much more flexibility in cross-coverage between projects. Weak, Balanced, and Strong relate to the level of power or authority the PM has in the matrix organizational structure.

TIP

Don't get these confused with the term *tight matrix,* which means to have the project team co-located (working) in the same room or building.

- **Projectized (aligned and managed by project)**   This structure provides the project manager with the highest level of authority of all the structure types because the team usually reports directly to the project manager. However, there are disadvantages. For example, when a project ends, the PM and team will have to find a new home (project); otherwise, they close with the project.

NOTE

Remember organizational structures are part of the enterprise environment factors (EEFs) that need to be considered on your project. These EEFs can affect a number of areas of your project, such as how you obtain resources (people and equipment), how you execute your project, how payments are made, and so on. Some companies may have a combination of these structures or spin-offs they use to manage their business and projects. Because of the importance of EEFs, more information is provided in Chapter 3 of this book.

Organizing the Project (Using Different Breakdown Structures)

Several tools are available to assist the PM in organizing a project. The most common are the Work Breakdown Structure (WBS), the Risk Breakdown Structure (RBS), Resource Breakdown Structure (also RBS) and the Organizational Breakdown Structure (OBS).

The WBS is extremely beneficial to helping identify the work of the project and to break the work into manageable chunks (groups or categories.) The WBS provides a way to systematically carve out (identify) what needs be done to meet the deliverables of the project. The WBS also provides a way to capture key categories of work and put them into logical groups (work packages) that can be assigned to different work groups or departments. The WBS is "deliverables oriented," meaning the WBS should be developed around the deliverables of the project.

TIP

A deliverable is a product of work completed on a project. Deliverables are sometimes described as inputs or outputs. One person's output is the next person's input, until the project is complete. An example of a deliverable is a training manual, or survey results that are needed as an input to the type of classes that need to be developed to meet a particular program curriculum.

It is important to note that PMI is really big on the WBS—it is mentioned many times in the *PMBOK Guide.* When you take a PMI exam, you will likely see many questions concerning the WBS. As a mater of fact, creating the WBS is a process in the Project Scope Management knowledge area, and we discuss this in more detail in Chapter 5 of this book.

The OBS typically shows the organization's departments, units, or teams aligned to the project activities or work packages they are responsible for delivering. The OBS shows "who" is doing the work of the project.

The Risk Breakdown Structure (RBS) shows how the risk should be managed. The RBS should show the risk events that have been identified, the analysis of impact and probability, and the risk event owner should the risk occur. Risk response strategy and how to manage risk on the project is covered in detail in Chapter 11 of this book.

The Resource Breakdown Structure (RBS) breaks the work down by type of resource, such as programmers, plumbers, electricians, testers, trainers, and so on.

Now that you are up to speed on the primary breakdown structures (BSs) and their use, let's look at how project success is achieved.

Success Is in the Eyes of the Customer

The customer is always right, right? It is important to know that in the real world, the customer is not always right; however, the customer is always the customer, right? So we have to be sensitive to the customer's needs and expectations.

According to PMI, customer satisfaction is a measure of success on a project. It is important to keep the customer in the loop and involved in many aspects of the project planning, tracking, and areas of risk, communications, and so on.

Customer needs and expectations can be a dichotomy. Needs are usually fairly precise and measurable, whereas expectations vary early and often, depending on "selective amnesia." For example, the customer often remembers the extra features you presented in the sales pitch but they may conveniently forget those features were not purchased based on affordability. Yet, they are still expecting the extras. The customer may change focus on what they want at the end of the project for various reasons (this is especially true when requirements or scope are unclear going into the project). These and a host of other reasons can cause "scope creep" or even "scope leap" (that is, when project requirements change significantly from the start of the project to the end).

In general, the measure of success on any project should be quality delivery (on time and on budget) based on customer-approved scope and deliverables.

NOTE
PMI states that in general all conflicts on the project should be resolved in favor of the customer. Therefore, make sure you are in close communication with the project sponsor (customer) to help ensure you meet their needs and expectations (which at the end of the project is the true measure of success). In the real world, however, this could be viewed as a "Yes-Man" approach and could be costly. So, what is the answer? The answer is to be very aware of the customer needs and expectations, and add value to the project without giving away the store (extras at no additional cost).

Try This ## What Does the Customer Want?

Suppose you are the project manager on a kitchen remodeling project. You hire a plumber (subcontractor) to do the plumbing and sink installation. You obtain the bid from the plumber, and when you roll this into your overall bid with the other work, the total estimate is three months to complete the project at a cost of $30,000. You present the bid to the customer,

(continued)

they agree, sign a contract, and the work begins. You are two months into the project and the plumber tells you (the PM) that the special fixtures (brushed nickel sink and faucet) are back-ordered and will delay the project by six weeks. As a competent PM, you discover that the fixtures are available at a higher cost from an alternate supplier in another state. The purchase of the fixtures from the alternate supplier will cost an additional $3,000.

Now that you have the analysis (expected impact) you take it to the customer and they have a decision to make. Here are the key questions that need to be answered from the customer:

1. How important are the special fixtures? Are they willing to allow the project to be delayed? If time is not important and they really want the brushed nickel fixtures, they may decide to accept the delay.

2. If time or cost is important (say the customer has a special event planned at their home and the delay will spoil the plans), are they are willing to go with alternative standard fixture selections, saving the extra time and cost. Or are the special fixtures so important that they are willing to pay extra for the additional cost and shipping?

As the PM you need to learn from this lesson and establish a strategy to prevent this from happening in the future. The best strategy for the PM is to frequently check project status with the team to minimize the risks of this type of problem occurring again. You must be prepared and have action (back-up) plans to help mitigate the risks should they occur. In summary, the strategy as a PM should be to plan well to help ensure there are no (or minimal) surprises!

Adding Value to the Project

There are ways to add value to a project without giving away the store. How is this possible, you ask, especially given that value is often very difficult to measure? You can add value by consistently showing integrity in how you manage the project. Provide on-time and accurate status reports even if the story is not good—being behind schedule or over budget are real situations, and you do not want to hide, ignore, or delay bad news in your status reports.

Always present the impact to the project in clear terms. More importantly, present a plan of action or alternative options so the sponsor can make an informed decision on where the project needs to go next. Try to anticipate the questions: If you were the customer, what would you want to know about a risk event and the possible impact? Is it a threat or possible opportunity? Is it going to cost more or delay the project in any way?

Try This Building a Corral for Rodeo Animals

Suppose you are the PM on a project to build a corral. As your team is digging the post holes, they encounter an unforeseen event—they hit solid rock. The equipment is damaged, and the impact to the project is a two-week delay and a $1,000 repair to the equipment.

Because you are an experienced PM, you know the first step is to assess the situation. You gather the team together and discuss the situation. One of the team members mentions she has probed the ground around the rock and found that the soil is more favorable if the fence line were to be moved ten feet in from the original boundary. This would allow the team to continue building the corral around the remaining property. If you remain on the original fence line, you will need to bring in special equipment at great expense, and you not only have a delay, but also a big impact to the cost of the project.

What do you do?

Your answer should be to balance the competing demands: time, cost, and scope. It is best to determine the priorities from the customer to determine what is more important. Once the priority is clear and you realize that time is of the essence, it appears that moving the fence line in ten feet is the best approach. It will save time and money. You present this as the recommended option to the customer in the form of a change request. Once this is approved (signed) by the customer, you direct the team to move the fence line and proceed with the project.

It is important to remember to report the status (finding) to your sponsor and other stakeholders honestly in a professional and timely manner. Provide a best estimate of impact to the project. You always want to provide the all-important recommended action plan as to how to best solve the problem and to keep it from happening again in the future. This is how you add value and gain the much needed trust and confidence from the customer, other key stakeholders, and sponsors.

Case Study Introduction

Now that we have walked through a couple real-world examples, I would like to introduce a case study that we will use throughout this book to help apply the concepts discussed along the way.

Many of my students frequently ask for real-world examples in a case study format that tie into the discussions in class concerning scope management, risk management, and so on. Others have asked if there is a book with a real case study that builds over the course of the book and ties into the project management knowledge areas and process groups in the *PMBOK*. So, by popular demand and in an effort to meet their request, here goes....

I have chosen this case study based on real-world examples that have occurred at a major events center in northern Colorado. I think you will find these events informative, interesting, beneficial, and entertaining. The objective is to learn from the experiences of this case study and to apply this experience to your own projects. The best way to learn about project management successes is to see the events in action—and if we can discuss events that are of an interesting nature, we may be able to have some fun along the way as well.

With permission from the Budweiser Events Center (BEC), I will showcase some of their event projects in this case study. The center, located in a development called The Ranch, is owned by Larimer County and managed by Global Spectrum, a public assembly facility management company with more than 80 facilities throughout the United States and Canada.

We will start from the contract phase of the project, when an agent, manager, or promoter contacts the events center to host an event such as a concert, rodeo, ice skating show, or hockey game. This case study will build from start to finish and tie into the PMI process groups and knowledge areas. You will witness (in text) the setup for concerts and managing the change over to rodeos and then to ice hockey.

Through various interviews with the events center director, operations manager, and changeover project managers, you will see how The Ranch makes these events happen on time and on budget almost all the time.

We will start with Phase I of The Ranch facilities project, which includes six buildings and roughly 150 acres of site work. First, let's look at some of the challenges of the project in designing facilities containing buildings adaptable to the hundreds of events hosted each year. Then we will cover specific project management processes and methods used to help tie everything to project management.

The biggest challenge is clearly "flexibility"—the ability to meet the needs of a multitude of events, especially considering the dangers presented by rodeo animals, flying pucks at hockey games, and sometimes demanding concert artists.

The next challenge is the logistics of transforming the center for a variety of events. The venue must be adaptable with a reasonably short changeover time and be able to handle a wide range of lighting, sound, and video requirements, as well as scoreboards and so on. On event day, the concerns are security, crowd control, merchandise sales, and food and beverage services.

Now that I have introduced the case study and set the stage (so to speak) on the many variables and challenges, let's move on to the different approaches used for these and other projects and some of the dilemmas that can occur.

Many different approaches can be used to manage projects. As mentioned previously we tend to manage using our personal experiences, and instincts. These methods work in some cases, but in many cases they don't. We fall into certain habits (some of them bad), and as everyone knows, habits are often hard to break. The most common habit is often referred to as the "Ready, fire, aim" dilemma.

The "Ready, Fire, Aim" Dilemma

Too often we get ahead of ourselves on projects. We live in a world in which most people are used to, and expect, instant gratification. We want an all-in-one, state-of-the-art gadget that is a phone, camera, personal planner that plays music and can shine our shoes, all at the same time. The end result is distractions—and lots of them. This can lead to a "jump the gun" mentality, where we frequently start doing the work without having a clear scope and then wonder why we continue to miss the target.

This tendency comes to light in the book *The Toyota Way Fieldbook*, by Dr. Jeffrey Liker, who cautions against the tendency in most Western companies to short-change the problem-solving process:

> "One of the signs of a 'Ready, fire, aim' culture is the tendency to 'jump' immediately from the 'problem' to the 'solution.' In many cases the problem may be mentioned casually and much time is spent proposing various 'solutions' before the 'problem' has been clearly defined. At this stage in the process it is likely that a symptom has been observed rather than the true problem."[4]

The Toyota problem-solving approach is implemented in four steps:

1. Develop a thorough understanding of the situation and define the problem.

2. Complete a thorough root cause analysis.

3. Consider alternative solutions while building consensus.

4. Use Plan-Do-Check-Act (PDCA)—the Shewhart-Deming cycle:

   - **Plan**   Develop an action plan.

   - **Do**   Implement solutions rapidly.

   - **Check**   Verify result.

   - **Act**   Make necessary adjustments to the solutions and action plan and determine future steps.

   - Finally, reflect and learn from the process.[5]

The "Ready, fire, aim" dilemma was painfully realized when a PM began working on a nine-month project without clearly defined requirements. There was no project charter to authorize the project. Because this was a new and exciting software application product and had never been done before, the PM decided the requirements and features were to be "open-ended" code. The work needed to start immediately, and the customer was excited about the potential of this new product. At every meeting the customer brought many great ideas to the team for additional features they wanted added to the code. Because of the added features, the PM kept adding more and more people to the project. As you can imagine, at the end of nine months they had some good code, but a very unclear product that tried to do everything—from paying bills online to automatically balancing your checkbook. However, they couldn't get it to work reliably. They needed more time. Unfortunately, the customer ran out of patience, time, and money and decided to take the development work back in-house. "Thanks for the hard work," they said, "We will take it from here." The customer and service provider were not happy with the results and the project was deemed a failure.

In looking at our "Ready, fire, aim" dilemma, let's go back to the first word: *Ready*. If everything is done properly, we are ready to begin when we have a project charter, we know what the project deliverables are, and we can begin the planning cycle (the "aim" part).

Many projects begin without anyone knowing who the real customer is or what the requirements are, and yet we continue to jump right into that "new opportunity." We gather a team of people and schedule the kickoff meeting (PMI is big on kickoff meetings). We may not even have all the details of the project yet, but we *fire* it off. We introduce the project (or what we think the project should be), we set target dates (based on when the sponsor wants the project completed—usually a date out of thin air), and we start building the project, only to find we are building the wrong solution, in the wrong place, with down-level specifications. Oh my!

Project management is all about communication, and yet we rarely ask questions or make sure we understand what the sponsor wants or expects from the project manager and team.

In this discussion, the word *fire* ahead of the word *aim* alludes to us pulling the trigger of a gun before we actually aim it. You will never hit the target if you don't aim. This comes from years of being pushed to deliver results without knowing exactly what the customer wants. The customer always knows what they want, right? This is like a kid watching commercials on TV at Christmastime and his wish list changes and grows with every series of commercials.

To close on the "Ready, fire, aim" dilemma, let's talk about aim. We always seem to be in such a hurry to do the work even if the scope is not clear, that we don't take the time to plan (aim). And then we wonder why we continue to miss the target.

Ask the Expert

Q: What is the solution to the "Ready fire, aim" dilemma?

A: The solution is what I call the "AIM strategy." Many of my clients agree that sponsors are quick to throw a project at them without any thought for the time it takes to complete the project, the planning needed, or even how much it will cost. Many sponsors just want a problem to go away fast or to be first to market with a new product or service. The AIM strategy breaks the solution down into a manageable flow and allows the PM and team to systematically analyze the problem, implement a solution, and effectively manage the project.

You would think a concept as basic as planning (aiming) before executing the project (firing) would be something we would do instinctively, and yet we do it so rarely that it causes a high percentage of failed projects—we keep making the same mistake over and over again!

I often wonder why we don't take the time to aim (that is, plan our projects). The only excuse I can come up with is that we are so distracted we fool ourselves into thinking that we don't need to take aim before we fire (or we don't think at all and simply react to the pressure). The cost to industry and to ourselves in lost time and energy is enormous.

So, what are the lessons learned? If we properly prepare (get ready with adequate planning) and take the time to aim before we fire off a project (that is, ensure the proper processes, procedures, and expectations are in place), many headaches can be avoided.

How do you know if you have the right order? What is the proper sequence of planning a project to avoid stepping in front of the proverbial bullet? For an answer, let's look at the AIM strategy.

AIM Strategy

To better understand the AIM strategy, let's look at why we need a strategy in the first place. A strategy requires planning. Looking at the *PMBOK Guide,* you will see that the majority of processes (20 of 42) are planning processes. This should be your first clue to take a deep breath and think about what it takes to manage a project. We need to prepare not only the project itself, but how we are going to manage it.

Far too often when projects are priced, we rarely consider the cost of project management, the time it takes to build the team, and how to manage the flow of information. Rarely do we take time to actually build communication and risk plans, document and verify the scope of the project, look at the process groups to see where we are in the life cycle of the project, or determine which processes are needed and appropriate to help us effectively mange the project. Instead, we just jump right into "fire"!

The AIM strategy is all about staying focused on the task at hand and understanding what the goals are before pulling the trigger to start the project. This requires planning and coordination, and this is where we need to look at the whole project, to ensure we have a solid PM strategy.

What Does AIM Stand for?

First, *analyze* the situation and get involved with the key stakeholders, develop the plan as a team, and obtain formal acceptance (approval) for the project plan.

Second, *implement* the approved plan.

And last but not least, *manage* the whole project and nothing but the project. If you stray, which is far too easy to do with the many distractions mentioned earlier, your project is likely to fall into the category of a failed or troubled project.

Why Projects Fail and What You Can Do About It?

First, let's review what constitutes a failed or troubled project. The definition varies based on the size, type, and complexity of the project. According to The Standish Group, which specializes in independent research and analysis of IT project performance, project results can be divided into three categories:

- **Projects that succeed**   The project is completed on time and on budget, with all features and functions as initially specified.

- **Projects that are challenged**   The project is completed and operational but over budget, over the time estimate, and offers fewer features and functions than originally specified.

- **Projects that are impaired**   The project is canceled at some point during the development cycle.

Reports from The Standish Group and other sources show that approximately 30 percent of projects succeed, over 50 percent are challenged in some way, and less than 20 percent fail, which is an improvement from several years ago when over 30 percent of projects failed for one reason or another.

Business requirements change so quickly these days that, unless the project manager is fully aware of the issues at a business level, even a project that delivers the planned scope within time and cost may be deemed unsuccessful because its deliverables are no longer relevant to the business.[6]

Statistics from the Gartner Group state that 30 percent of IT projects never come to a fruitful conclusion. On average, 51 percent exceed budget by 189 percent while only delivering 74 percent of the originally stated functionality.[7]

Factors that drive poor performance range from lack of disciplined project management to lack of communication between the IT organization and the business unit directors. It is essential that the project managers have a solid understanding of the enterprise's business objectives so they can continually measure the project in terms of delivering these business objectives.

Here are several factors that drive failed projects:

- Project sponsors are often not committed to the project objective. They have a lack of understanding of the project and are not involved in the project strategy and direction. They may have their own agenda, pet projects, or pet peeves concerning other projects.

- Some projects do not meet the strategic vision of the company, or the direction has changed. When business needs are not clearly defined, the result is a project that does not add value to the bottom line or enhance business processes.

- Projects are started for the wrong reasons. Some are initiated purely to implement new technology without regard for whether the technology is right for the business needs.

- Staffing is often a reason for failure. For example, not enough dedicated staff (project managers and project team members) is allocated to projects. Project team members may lack experience and do not have the required qualifications.

- Incomplete project scope. There's no clear definition of the project's benefits and how they will be delivered.

- The project plan is nonexistent, out of date, incomplete, or poorly constructed. Not enough time and effort are spent on project planning.

- Project value management is not put into practice to evaluate the baseline cost agreed upon during baseline transfer against actual costs spent at any given time.

- Insufficient funds and incorrect budgeting are a major reason for projects not delivering their goals and objectives within the quality framework required.

- Formal project management methodologies and best practices aligned to the company's specific needs aren't used to assist project performance.

- Projects don't go through a normal signoff using a proper postmortem (Lessons Learned) process to build a reference model for future use.

Here are some things you can do to help keep your projects from failing:

- Use proven project management disciplines.

- Ensure clear two-way communication.

- Work with the stakeholders to focus on the end results (including end users).

- Manage change, risk, scope, time, and cost diligently.

- Review and report status frequently and honestly.

- Be an advocate (cheerleader) for the project team (catch them doing something right).

- Use project management standards (tools and resources available) for planning, executing, and controlling the project.

- Verify the overall health of the project by asking yourself and the team the following questions:

  - Were deliverables produced on time, within the approved scope, and within the approved budget?

  - Did the project satisfy the business requirements of the stakeholders (for example, was the problem solved or solution accomplished)?

  - Has the project met the business value goals (that is, cost savings, increased market share, or streamlined processes needed to improve quality)?

  - Most importantly, do the business owners (sponsors) believe the project was successful? Did you deliver a quality product and meet stakeholder expectations?

Projects Fail for Many Reasons

Keep in mind that projects may be deemed a failure for reasons outside of your control as a project manager. Even when everything is executed properly, there may be changes in direction, strategy, funding, or limited availability of key skilled staff members to effectively complete the project. As a project manager, you need to keep these influencing factors in mind and realize there are times when projects are considered failures through no fault of your own. It is difficult not to take this personally. Still, you must perform a Lessons Learned session, document the issues as well as what worked and what didn't work (including input from the customer), and then move on. We discuss this in more detail in Chapter 13.

At the end of the day, the success or failure of a project depends entirely on measured results and perception—a project may be on time and on budget, but may not meet the customer's expectations.

Pop Quiz

By now you should have a better understanding of what constitutes failed projects; things you can to do to help prevent projects from failing; what a project is; what project management is; the three takeaway points; the AIM strategy, and what a program is. To test yourself on these important topics, take the following simple pop quiz:

1. What is a project?

2. What is a program?

3. What are the three takeaway points from this chapter?

4. What does AIM stand for?

5. Name three reasons why projects fail.

Take a few minutes and write down your answers. Then refer back to the appropriate sections in this chapter for confirmation or check out the answers that follow.

Answers:

1. A project is a temporary endeavor to create a unique product, service, or result. It has a definite start and end, is usually short term in duration, and has clearly defined goals and objectives.

2. A program is a collection of projects, usually has no end date, and tends to be longer term in duration.

3. The three takeaway points are

- Stay focused on the end goal and objectives of the project.
- Use the tools available to help effectively manage the project.
- Work as a team (remember, the number-one asset on the project is the team).

4. AIM stands for

- *Analyze* the situation and get involved with the key stakeholders, develop the plan as a team, and obtain formal acceptance for the project plan.
- *Implement* the approved plan.
- *Manage* the whole project and nothing but the project.

5. Here's a sample summary list of reasons of why projects fail:

- Lack of project management discipline

- Lack of user (key stakeholder) involvement

- Lack of project sponsors committed to or involved in the project strategy and direction

- Projects not meeting the strategic vision or business needs of the company

- Projects started for the wrong reasons

- Lack of properly trained or skilled people to work the project

- Lack of cultural skills and ability to manage in a multicultural environment

References

1. *A Guide to the Project Management Body of Knowledge (PMBOK® Guide), Fourth Edition,* (PMI–Project Management Institute Global Standard: Newtown Square, PA), 2008, page 5.

2. Wikipedia, http://en.wikipedia.org/wiki/Governance.

3. *A Guide to the Project Management Body of Knowledge (PMBOK® Guide), Fourth Edition,* (PMI–Project Management Institute Global Standard: Newtown Square, PA), 2008, page 13.

4. Liker, Jeffrey K. and David Meier, *The Toyota Way Fieldbook: A Practical Guide for Implementing Toyota's 4Ps* (McGraw-Hill: New York), 2004, page 325.

5. Liker, Jeffrey K. and David Meier, *The Toyota Way Fieldbook. A Practical Guide for Implementing Toyota's 4Ps* (McGraw-Hill: New York), 2004, page 313.

6. TechForum, "The Top 10 Reasons Why Projects Fail," issued by AST Group (Johannesburg), July 12, 2001.

7. Ibid.

Chapter 3

Project Management Process Groups

Key Skills & Concepts

- Importance of the five PMI process groups

- Initiating a project

- Introduction to the nine *PMBOK* knowledge areas

- Inputs, tools and techniques, and outputs

- Application of project knowledge

- Mapping processes to knowledge areas and process groups

- Closing process group

- Code of ethics and professional conduct

This chapter further defines, identifies, and describes PMI's five process groups as well as briefly introduces the nine knowledge areas and their associated processes required for most projects. This chapter also details PMI's Code of Ethics and Professional Conduct, why this is important for project managers and project teams, and what to expect in this section on the PMP exam.

What Are Process Groups?

Process groups serve as independent domains (or groups) of processes that are tied to a particular phase of a project. They are often iterative in nature, meaning they build on one another. Each process group has associated project management processes that are linked by respective inputs and outputs; for example, the output of one process often becomes the input to the next process.

PMI recognizes and endorses five basic process groups (sometimes referred to as *domains*). "These five process groups have clear dependencies and are typically performed in the same sequence on each project. They are independent of application areas or industry focus."[1]

A process group can also be performed independently, for example, planning a project that doesn't get funded or closing a project at the end of its life cycle where closing the project is a project in itself.

The five process groups are briefly described as follows:

- **Initiating process group**   Defines and authorizes the start of a project or a phase
- **Planning process group**   Establishes the scope of the project, refines the objectives, and defines the course of action required to attain the objectives of the project
- **Executing process group**   Integrates people and other resources to complete the work of the project
- **Monitoring and Controlling process group**   Includes those processes required to track, review, and regulate the progress and performance of the project and identify areas where changes or corrective action needs to be taken to meet project objectives
- **Closing process group**   Includes those processes performed to finalize all activities across all process groups to formally close the project or phase

TIP

If you are planning to take the PMP exam, it is important to note that the questions on this exam align with the five process groups and not the knowledge areas (as in the past.) The reason for this, in my opinion, is that it is more important to know when a process should occur relative to the five process groups rather than which knowledge area it happens to fall into.

Process groups provide a logical sequence of events rather than simply grouping processes into their area of knowledge. For example, Identify Stakeholders is one of the Project Communications Management knowledge area processes. However, it is extremely important to initiate this process early in the project management life cycle, which is why it is grouped in the Initiating process group. This can be a bit confusing because all the PMI-recognized processes are associated with their respective knowledge areas *and* the processes are grouped in one of the five process groups (see "Mapping Processes to Knowledge Areas and Process Groups" later in this chapter for more details.)

Ask the Expert

Q: Do most project managers use process groups to manage real-world projects?

A: Project managers frequently make use of these process groups and knowledge areas instinctively and may not even realize they are doing so. Even experienced project managers without formal training use these process groups and often could not tell you what the process groups are called.

(continued)

For example, this was evident when my daughter started planning her wedding. Even though she has no formal PM training (although I like to think there was some learning by osmosis from living with me for so many years), she instinctively sat down and wrote out her idea of the perfect wedding, thus initiating the project (in project management terms we call this "developing the project charter," which is the first process in the Initiating process group). Her documented view of the wedding set up the criteria/requirements to be met for this project to be successful. These requirements were the input to the project charter and to the scope statement.

Next, my daughter and her fiancé put together a list of participants, who they wanted as attendants, who they wanted to preside over the ceremony, and their invitation list. In doing so, they identified the stakeholders, which is the second process under the Initiating process group. Not even realizing it, my daughter had just completed the first process group of any project (initiating).

Next, she approached my wife and me to negotiate the size of the wedding and preliminary budget. Her estimated number of attendees came to 200. Based on her expectations and research, she was able to provide a best-guess estimate of the cost. This is known as a rough order of magnitude (ROM) cost estimate, which is one of the processes in the Project Cost Management knowledge area under the Planning process group.

Once my wife and I reviewed the estimate and were convinced my daughter and her future husband were serious about keeping the budget reasonable without us having to take out a second mortgage on our home, we all agreed. This became our formally accepted project charter (even though we didn't call it that). With the charter and the budget estimate in hand, we officially "authorized" the project to begin. We emphasized that the check she received represented an agreement, and if they overspent the budget, the extra cost would be out of their pocket. If they spent less than the budgeted amount, she and her new husband could apply any leftover dollars to their honeymoon (which is exactly what they were able to do).

Establishing a budget and issuing the check for the total wedding up front turned out to be a great idea because it kept my wife and me from being involved in every little detail and from having to negotiate for each item along the way. This approach also kept my daughter from feeling guilty about the cost of a particular item (such as the wedding dress or the cake) because she had the decision to make and the budget to manage. Talk about a lesson learned (a key project management principle)! I highly recommend this approach for all parents of a bride because it really instills a sense of ownership in the wedding project and forces the bride and groom to manage their budget well or suffer the consequences.

I must admit the credit for this great idea goes to one of my PM students at Colorado State University (CSU) who was going through planning her own wedding during the time she was taking a project management fundamentals class. We actually used her wedding as a team project during this eight-week class. It was great to see even the older men in the class take such an active role in helping plan her wedding, using all the project management processes and knowledge areas as we discussed them in class. The bride was able to use the work of the team to make her wedding project a complete success, and the class had fun as a team working the project.

The process flow diagram shown in Figure 3-1 provides an overall summary of the basic flow and interactions among process groups and specific stakeholders. Also note that the Monitoring and Controlling process group overlaps the other process groups.

Initiating Process Group

As you might imagine, the Initiating process group should be the first in the series of process group activities and consists of those processes performed to define a new project or a new phase of an existing project. This process group is focused on obtaining authorization to start the project or phase.

The Initiating process group includes only two processes:

- Develop project charter.
- Identify stakeholders.

Develop the Project Charter

The project manager should be assigned as early in the project life cycle as possible, either during or shortly after the project charter is written because this is when things can go well if the PM is represented or can go wrong if a PM is not assigned.

Note that some projects are only authorized or funded (budgeted) for one phase, such as a "feasibility study" or concept phase, to determine whether the project is appropriate and will provide the correct solution to meet the business need or solve the problem that needs to be resolved by the project.

You have probably seen a project charter in one form or another—and may not have realized it. The charter can come in many different flavors/forms. It can be formal (such as a contract), informal (such as a phone call from your boss or customer), or in writing (such as an e-mail or memo). If at all possible, it is best if you can get it in writing even if only in an e-mail. Some additional examples are provided in the following list (additional details can be found in Chapter 4):

- **Informal**   A work order or service order/request to upgrade a computer system, thus changing the scope of the project
- **Informal**   An e-mail from your boss telling you to get a team together and fix a design problem on a software application
- **Formal**   A written contract for any product, service, or result (an example of a result would be a project to consolidate work to decrease production costs by 10 percent)
- **Formal**   A statement of work (SOW), service agreement (SA), project change request (PCR), service request (SR), or request for service (RFS) to modify or change a project

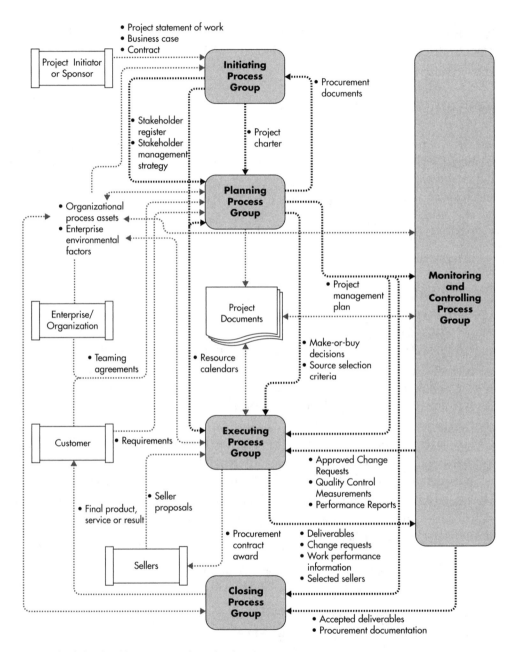

Figure 3-1 Project Management process interactions. (Project Management Institute *A Guide to the Project Management Body of Knowledge [PMBOK® Guide]–Fourth Edition*, Project Management Institute, Inc., 2004. Copyright and all rights reserved. Material from this publication has been reproduced with the permission of PMI.)

Identify Stakeholders

The Identify Stakeholders process is the first in the Project Communications Management knowledge area and is extremely important within the Initiating process group.

As mentioned in Chapter 2, stakeholders can be anyone who is positively or negatively impacted by the project. It is the project manager's responsibility to identify the stakeholders of the project. Additional details on this process are provided in Chapter 10 of this book.

Manageable Phases

It is common (or should be) to divide projects into separate manageable phases. Identifying stakeholders and knowing their expectations for the different phases of the project makes the phases more manageable. Repeating the initiating processes at the start of each phase helps keep the project team focused on the key deliverables for each project phase. This doesn't mean creating or obtaining a new project charter at the beginning of each phase but means ensuring you have authorization to proceed to the next phase of the project.

TIP

Setting and verifying key measurements and jointly determining project success criteria with key stakeholders will help ensure project success. The success criteria—once documented, approved, and communicated—provide key indicators of the health and progress of the project and will help you manage the primary project constraints more effectively. An example of a success criteria is having an events center facility fully set up, tested, and ready to host a concert prior to curtain up time.

It is also important to involve the customers and other key stakeholders identified in the Initiating process group as it generally improves the probability of shared ownership, deliverable acceptance, and customer/stakeholder satisfaction.

Planning Process Group

This group consists of processes performed to establish the total scope of the project, to define and refine objectives, and to develop the course of action required to attain the approved objectives. The planning processes make up almost half (20 of 42) of the *PMBOK* processes and help the project manager develop the project management plan and documents that will be used to carry out the project. As you would imagine, the processes grouped into the Planning process group occur early in the project life cycle when there are many unknowns. The risk for failure is increased if the planning processes are not performed, are unclear, or not communicated properly.

Figure 3-2 helps clarify the interaction of the different planning processes included in the Planning process group. The reference number shown at the top of each process box maps to its chapter and section of the *PMBOK*.

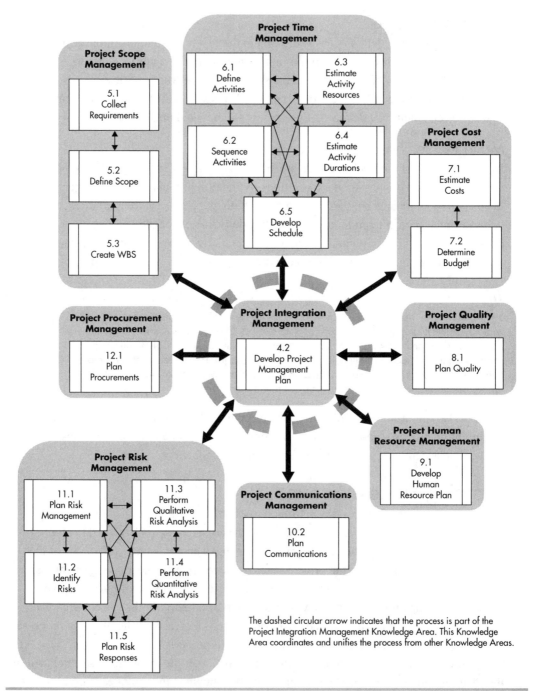

Figure 3-2 Planning process group. (Project Management Institute *A Guide to the Project Management Body of Knowledge [PMBOK® Guide]–Fourth Edition*, Project Management Institute, Inc., 2004. Copyright and all rights reserved. Material from this publication has been reproduced with the permission of PMI.)

Ask the Expert

Q: **Does the project manager really need a project management plan if the project has been done before?**

A: Yes, the PM should have a documented and approved project plan to serve as a guide to how the project is to be managed, to help ensure the accountability and audit readiness of the project, and to help ensure success. The plan can later be refined into an operations guide for repeat projects. In either case, you need a documented plan to guide the work of the project.

    For example, let's say you are working on the event changeover project for a large convention center and the requirements for the next event are to set up a rodeo. Because this project has been done before, you begin the process by setting up the usual corrals, gates for bull and bronco riders, and so on. Then you hear over lunch that this is a 4-H Special Olympics rodeo, and the main events are goat roping and mutton busting—there will be no bulls and broncos. You've just lost several hours if not days of setup time and money because you didn't fully understand the requirements.

Poor planning and lack of project management discipline are two common reasons for project failure. Therefore, it is essential to develop a solid project plan and to work the plan (don't just let it collect dust in a desk drawer or in your briefcase).

The iterative multidimensional nature of project management creates an atmosphere for repeated input and feedback loops for further consideration and analysis. Remember, everyone likes to make informed decisions, and the more information you can provide, the better the chances of hitting the target.

TIP

Success is not possible unless you plan first and then verify, verify, verify the scope and deliverables of the project.

The Planning process group is all about revisiting one or more of the planning processes and possibly some of the initiating processes in a progressive fashion to ensure the requirements are clear and communicated properly and the work of the project is in line with the scope and deliverables to be provided by the project. This iterative progression detailing of the project management plan is often called "rolling wave planning," which means you keep coming back and checking for the ripple effect—in other words, when you identify a risk or make a change to the project, you are likely to affect something else and will need to update scope, budget, or schedule along the way.

Executing Process Group

This is where the real work begins, and as you would expect, the largest portion of the project budget is usually spent during the executing processes. This is where the majority of the team is engaged and performing the work of the project. This group consists of eight processes that are performed to complete the work defined in the project management plan (refer to Table 3-1, later in this chapter).

The goal of the project manager in the Executing process group is to coordinate the people and other resources as well as integrate and perform the activities of the project to meet the requirements by satisfying the approved specifications (see Figure 3-3).

Monitoring and Controlling Process Group

This process group is the "eye in the sky," so to speak, making sure the project is going according to the project plan as well as reviewing and tracking the overall attainment and performance of the project per the approved scope and deliverables.

This step is where many projects fail—the PM either is too distracted with the daily work, or is in too much of a hurry to effectively monitor the overall progress of the project. In many cases, the PM simply does not have enough resources (people) to effectively measure progress, or is just not familiar with the tools and techniques to effectively monitor and control the project. In any event, things slip when the PM takes their eyes off of this process group.

There are ten processes in the *PMBOK* Monitoring and Controlling process group. Some of the key processes include determining how you and the team will track progress, deciding what tools and techniques you will use to measure the progress, and how you will report that progress (type of reports, frequency, and so on) to the key stakeholders of the project (see Figure 3-4).

Closing Process Group

The Closing process group is all about bringing the project (or phase) to an orderly and hopefully successful completion. The Closing process group contains two processes that are performed to finalize all activities across all project process groups:

- Close project or phase.
- Close procurements.

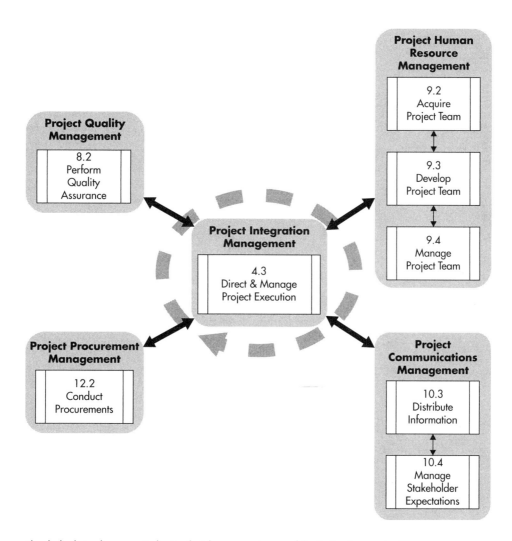

The dashed circular arrow indicates that the process is part of the Project Integration Management Knowledge Area. This Knowledge Area coordinates and unifies the process from other Knowledge Areas.

Figure 3-3 Executing process group. (Project Management Institute *A Guide to the Project Management Body of Knowledge [PMBOK® Guide]–Fourth Edition*, Project Management Institute, Inc., 2004. Copyright and all rights reserved. Material from this publication has been reproduced with the permission of PMI.)

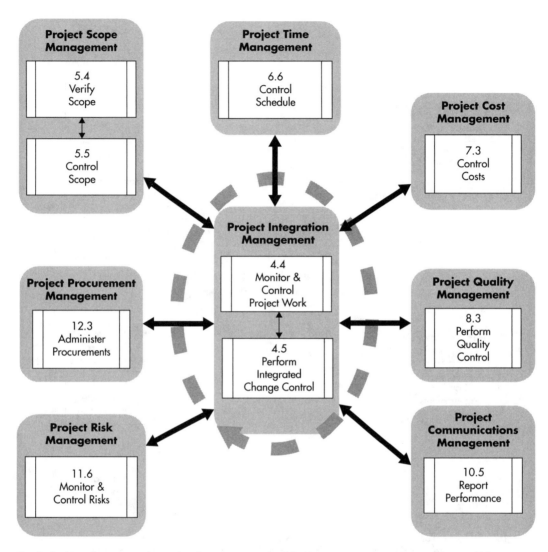

The dashed circular arrow indicates that the process is part of the Project Integration Management Knowledge Area. This Knowledge Area coordinates and unifies the process from other Knowledge Areas.

Figure 3-4 Monitoring and Controlling process group. (Project Management Institute *A Guide to the Project Management Body of Knowledge [PMBOK® Guide]–Fourth Edition*, Project Management Institute, Inc., 2004. Copyright and all rights reserved. Material from this publication has been reproduced with the permission of PMI.)

The steps involved with the Closing process group are essential for the formal completion of the project or phase or to meet contractual obligations. Once the processes are completed, a number of signoffs (formal acceptance) should occur. For example:

- Conduct post-project or phase-end review.

- Document open issues relating to changes or the tailoring of project or processes.

- Document lessons learned from the team and customer. (You should use this step all along the way, not just at the end of the project. It works best if done at the end of each phase of the project to help identify issues and to track corrective action as appropriate.)

- Apply all appropriate updates to organizational process assets.

- Archive all relevant project documents in the Project Management Information System (PMIS) as appropriate.

- Close out all outstanding procurements (purchase orders, accounts payable, accounts receivable, supplier agreements, equipment rentals or leases, software licenses, and so on).

- Obtain acceptance from the customer or sponsors.

Ask the Expert

Q: What happens when the project manager receives an invoice for subcontractor (vendor or supplier) services three months after the project is officially closed?

A: If the invoice is for legitimate services provided for approved work from an approved supplier, then the invoice must be paid.

The key questions that need to be reviewed and addressed are: How was this invoice overlooked? What steps should have been taken to ensure it was accounted for as part of the Closing process group? The main thing is to do what you can to ensure this doesn't happen on other projects in the future.

TIP

Missing or late invoices are far too common. The best approach is to set up a project closeout check list using the project management plan documents, information system, and all the startup phase deliverables to help ensure a clean closeout of the project.

Introduction to PMI Knowledge Areas

Knowledge areas are fields of specialization, such as project integration management, scope management, time management, cost management, quality management, human resource management, communications management, risk management, and procurement management. Knowledge areas apply to all projects or phases to some degree and can, in some cases, be used to organize project startup. This section provides only a brief introduction to knowledge areas; more details are provided in Chapters 4 through 12.

Each of the nine knowledge areas contains project management processes and crosses over some or all of the five process groups. For example, the Project Integration Management knowledge area contains the following six processes and the associated process group for each is shown in parentheses:

- Develop project charter (Initiating process group).

- Develop project management plan (Planning process group).

- Direct and manage project execution (Executing process group).

- Monitor and control project work (Monitoring and Controlling process group).

- Perform integrated change control (Monitoring and Controlling process group).

- Close project or phase (Closing process group).

Keep in mind that true knowledge comes from the project manager's and the project stakeholders' experience, decision-making skills, capabilities, and willingness to take pride, ownership, and accountability in the project. The true measure of success on any project is when the team respects the project manager and is willing to work on future projects with the PM.

With that in mind, the *PMBOK* should be used as a guide that offers globally recognized processes, terms, and methods. However, at the end of the day, the PM is responsible for the application of knowledge, skills, tools, and techniques for project activities to meet project requirements.

In the remainder of this section, we briefly introduce the nine knowledge areas according to PMI, starting with Project Integration Management, as well as a brief introduction to process inputs, tools and techniques, and outputs.

Project Integration Management

This knowledge area includes the processes and activities needed to identify, define, combine, unify, and coordinate the various processes and project management activities within the project management process groups. Project integration is the capstone (that is, it brings the project together) and is crucial to project completion and provides the key components of project management. Another key ingredient to success is managing stakeholder expectations and meeting the approved requirements and objectives of the project in accordance with the approved charter.

Here's a list of the Project Integration Management processes and associated process groups in parentheses (as a reminder the numbers for each process map to the chapters and sections in the *PMBOK*):

- 4.1: Develop project charter (Initiating process group).
- 4.2: Develop project management plan (Planning process group).
- 4.3: Direct and manage project execution (Executing process group).
- 4.4: Monitor and control project work (Monitoring and Controlling process group).
- 4.5: Perform integrated change control (Monitoring and Controlling process group).
- 4.6: Close project or phase (Closing process group).

Project Scope Management

This knowledge area includes the processes required to ensure that all the work required (and only the work required) to complete the project successfully is identified. Managing project scope is primarily concerned with defining and controlling what is and is not included in the project.

Here's a list of the Project Scope Management processes:

- 5.1: Collect requirements (Planning process group).
- 5.2: Define scope (Planning process group).
- 5.3: Create WBS (Planning process group).
- 5.4: Verify scope (Monitoring and Controlling process group).
- 5.5: Control scope (Monitoring and Controlling process group).

Project Time Management

This knowledge area includes the processes required to manage timely completion of the project.

Here's a list of the Project Time Management processes:

- 6.1: Define activities (Planning process group).
- 6.2: Sequence activities (Planning process group).

- 6.3: Estimate activity resources (Planning process group).
- 6.4: Estimate activity durations (Planning process group).
- 6.5: Develop schedule (Planning process group).
- 6.6: Control schedule (Monitoring and Controlling process group).

Project Cost Management

This knowledge area includes the processes involved in estimating, budgeting, and controlling costs so the project can be completed within the approved budget.

Here's a list of the Project Cost Management processes:

- 7.1: Estimate costs (Planning process group).
- 7.2: Determine budget (Planning process group).
- 7.3: Control costs (Monitoring and Controlling process group).

Project Quality Management

This knowledge area includes the processes and activities of the performing organization that determines quality policies, objectives, and responsibilities so the project will satisfy the needs for which it was undertaken.

Here's a list of the Project Quality Management processes:

- 8.1: Plan quality (Planning process group).
- 8.2: Perform quality assurance (Executing process group).
- 8.3: Perform quality control (Monitoring and Controlling process group).

Project Human Resource Management

This knowledge area includes the processes that organize, manage, and lead the project team. The project team is composed of people with assigned roles and responsibilities for completing the project.

Here's a list of the Project Human Resource Management processes:

- 9.1: Develop human resource plan (Planning process group).
- 9.2: Acquire project team (Executing process group).
- 9.3: Develop project team (Executing process group).
- 9.4: Manage project team (Executing process group).

Project Communications Management

This knowledge area includes the processes required to ensure the timely and appropriate generation, collection, distribution, storage, retrieval, and ultimate disposition of project information. It is important to note that project managers spend the majority of their time communicating.

Here's a list of the Project Communications Management processes:

- 10.1: Identify stakeholders (Initiating process group).
- 10.2: Plan communications (Planning process group).
- 10.3: Distribute information (Executing process group).
- 10.4: Manage stakeholder expectations (Monitoring and Controlling process group).
- 10.5: Report performance (Monitoring and Controlling process group).

It is important to note that the communications management processes are interrelated and overlap with processes in the other knowledge areas. Good clear communications are essential to the overall success of the project.

Project Risk Management

This knowledge area includes the processes of conducting risk management planning, identification, analysis, response planning, monitoring, and control on a project. The objectives of risk management seek to increase the probability and impact of positive events, and decrease the probability and impact of negative events in the project.

Here's a list of the Project Risk Management processes:

- 11.1: Plan risk management (Planning process group).
- 11.2: Identify risks (Planning process group).
- 11.3: Perform qualitative risk analysis (Planning process group).
- 11.4: Perform quantitative risk analysis (Planning process group).
- 11.5: Plan risk responses (Planning process group).
- 11.6: Monitor and control risks (Monitoring and Controlling process group).

Project Procurement Management

This knowledge area includes the contract management and change control processes required to develop and administer contracts and purchase orders issued by the authorized project team members. It also includes administering contracts issued by an outside organization (the buyer) acquiring the project from the performing organization (the seller) and administering contractual obligations placed on the project team by the contract.

Here's a list of the Project Procurement processes:

- 12.1: Plan procurements (Planning process group).

- 12.2: Conduct procurements (Executing process group).

- 12.3: Administer procurements (Monitoring and Controlling process group).

- 12.4: Close procurements (Closing process group).

Inputs, Tools and Techniques, and Outputs

Every process has inputs, tools and techniques, and outputs. These components provide links (or common threads) from one process to the next. Many of the processes have the same inputs. For example, enterprise environment factors and organizational process assets are the inputs to almost all the knowledge area processes and should be considered even if not specifically identified in each process.

TIP

Any time you see a particular topic mentioned frequently in this book or the *PMBOK*, you should take note, because this means the topic is viewed as highly important by PMI and you can bet it will likely be on the PMI exam. This is especially true with process inputs, tools and techniques, and outputs (watch for the ones repeated often between processes and focus on them if you plan to take a PMI exam).

Enterprise environmental factors refer to both internal and external environment factors that surround or influence a project's success. An enterprise is nothing more than an organization (including corporations, small and large businesses, nonprofit institutions, and government bodies). In practice, the term *enterprise* is used more often to describe larger organizations than smaller ones.

Environmental factors may come from any or all of the enterprises involved in the project. These factors may enhance or constrain the project management options and may have a positive or negative influence on the outcome. The various environmental factors are to be considered as inputs to most planning processes and include, but are not limited to, the following:

- Organizational culture, structure, and processes

- Government or industry standards (regulatory agency regulations, codes of conduct, product standards, quality standards, and workmanship standards)

- Infrastructure (existing facilities and capital equipment)

- Existing human resources (skills, disciplines, and knowledge)

Ask the Expert

Q: Can you provide an example of how enterprise environment factors may affect a real project?

A: Yes. A Fortune 50 company initiated a service agreement (contract) to have a project team come into their offices to conduct a physical (wall-to-wall) inventory of their computers. The cost estimates were developed based on a certain set of assumptions. As the project plan was developed and verified, the customer informed the project manager that their organization's culture and structure (enterprise environmental factor) is "management by consensus." This meant that they have a committee of managers that sets certain policies. In this case, the company policy required all the people conducting the inventory to first go through four hours of training on sensitivity in the workplace (for example, how to be respectful of the employees' time when conducting the data-collection process). Also, the entire inventory team had to provide very detailed background information and sign nondisclosure statements because some of the buildings where they would be conducting inventories were highly confidential research and development centers. As you can imagine, with all the additional requirements and constraints, the cost and the time to conduct the inventory more than doubled.

The moral to this story is that you need to fully understand the environmental factors prior to the final agreement for the time, cost, and scope of the project.

- Personnel administration (staffing and retention guidelines, performance reviews, training, overtime policies, and time tracking)
- Company work authorization systems
- Marketplace conditions, stakeholder risk tolerances, political climate
- Organization's established communication channels

Further, an input is something that needs to be considered as part of the influencing factors to complete a process. Inputs to a particular process are often the outputs from the previous process. In some cases there tends to be a logical sequence, and in other cases the processes may be totally independent.

Tools and techniques are the methods in which the information (input) is applied to get the process to the intended output. For example, you may use "expert judgment" as a tool or technique to help ensure you have the right skilled resources to review the input and provide expert recommendations on how the input information or conditions may affect the output.

Finally an output of any process is the finished product or result of the process—for example, the project charter is the output of the Develop Project Charter process.

Project Processes

"A *process* is a set of interrelated actions and activities performed to achieve a prespecified product, service, or result. Each process is characterized by its inputs, the tools and techniques that can be applied, and the resulting outputs."[2] In simple terms, a process serves as a guide (*what* needs to be done) as opposed to a procedure (*how* to do the work by using a series of steps to accomplish an end).

Processes tend to overlap and interact in a variety of ways. Some processes run in series, where one process can build on the next. However, many processes are repeated within the different process groups or phases of the project. The good news is the project manager and project stakeholders get to decide which processes are appropriate for their specific project.

In order for a project to be successful, the project team must

- Select the appropriate processes required to meet the project objectives.
- Use a defined approach to meet the requirements of the project.
- Balance competing demands of scope, time, cost, quality, resources, and risk to produce the specified product, service, or result the project is intended to address.

Now that you have a better understanding of project processes, the next step is to group them into process groups (domains or categories).

The project management team is responsible for selecting the appropriate processes to meet and comply with the requirements of a project.

Each process and its inputs, tools and techniques, and outputs should serve as a high-level guide for the project management team. The project management team should "tailor" each process to the individual needs of the project. Project management processes tie directly into the five process groups. All processes interact throughout the project via their inputs and outputs. According to PMI, successful project management includes actively managing these interactions to successfully meet project requirements.

Global Standards

Global standards are crucial to the project management profession because they ensure that a basic project management framework is applied consistently worldwide. The American National Standards Institute (ANSI) has recognized PMI as a standards development organization.

With the increased focus on project management across the globe, it has become more and more important to operate in a common, consistent manner wherever possible.

PMI provides generally recognized "good practices" for processes, applications, skills, tools, and techniques to enhance the chances of success over a wide range of projects. This, however, does not mean the knowledge should always be applied uniformly across all projects.

PMI offers a standard vocabulary for discussing, writing, and applying project management concepts. Having a globally recognized standard in terms, methods, and processes is an essential element of a professional discipline such as project management.

Several recommended standards can be found in the *PMBOK* and in some of the inputs of many of the processes. Earlier we discussed enterprise environmental factors and how they must be considered as inputs to most all processes (especially the planning processes). Another key input that needs to be considered as an input to most all processes is organizational process assets. This is where standard processes reside. The organization's processes and procedures for conducting work include the following standards:

- Organizational standard processes such as company polices (safety and health, ethics, project management policy, standard project audits, and quality policies)

- Standard guidelines, work instructions, proposal evaluation criteria, and performance measurement criteria

- Standard templates (Risk Breakdown Structure, Work Breakdown Structure, project schedule network diagrams, and contract templates)

- Communication requirements and guidelines

- Change control procedures and approvers (including how project documents will be modified)

- Risk control procedures (including risk categories, probability definition, and impact analysis)

Mapping Processes to Knowledge Areas and Process Groups

A Guide to the Project Management Body of Knowledge (PMBOK Guide) is a collection of processes and knowledge areas generally accepted as best practices within the project management discipline. It is also an internationally recognized standard (IEEE Standard 1490-2003) that provides the fundamentals of project management, regardless of the type of project being managed—construction, hardware/product development, software development, engineering, aviation, automotive, and so on.

Table 3-1 maps the 42 *PMBOK* processes to both the nine knowledge areas (in the first column) and the five process groups (across the top of the table).

NOTE

Each process is identified by its *PMBOK* chapter and section number. For example, 4.1 is the Develop Project Charter process, which is discussed in Chapter 4 of the *PMBOK* and is the first process in the Project Integration Management knowledge area.

The Importance of Planning

To see the importance of planning a project, simply look at the number of planning processes in the *PMBOK*. As previously mentioned, the majority (20 of 42) of the processes are planning processes.

In the real world, projects are far too often managed with little, if any, planning. We are lucky if we get three hours (much less three days or three weeks) of actual planning before we begin the work of a project. This, in my opinion, is due to current culture (especially in the United States) where we have grown to expect instant gratification. Between watching the problems of the universe being solved in a 30-minute television show and the wonders of modern technology (phones that play music; take pictures; receive up-to-the-minute sports scores, traffic, and weather forecasts; and use global navigation systems), it is no wonder we have little or no patience. We are multiplexing our way into loss of sleep, frustration, accidents, and potentially death. Empirical proof shows that our cultural changes and distractions (in the interest of improved productivity) are hazardous to our health. The following is from an article titled, "Drivers on Cell Phones Kill Thousands, Snarl Traffic," by Robert Roy Britt, posted at LiveScience.com:

> "Cell phone distraction causes 2,600 deaths and 330,000 injuries in the United States every year, according to the journal's publisher, the Human Factors and Ergonomics Society.
>
> The reason is now obvious:
>
> Drivers talking on cell phones were 18 percent slower to react to brake lights, the new study found. In a minor bright note, they also kept a 12 percent greater following distance. But they also took 17 percent longer to regain the speed they lost when they braked. That frustrates everyone.
>
> 'Once drivers on cell phones hit the brakes, it takes them longer to get back into the normal flow of traffic," [David] Strayer said. "The net result is they are impeding the overall flow of traffic.'"[3]

Knowledge Areas	Project Management Process Groups				
	Initiating	Planning	Executing	Monitoring and Controlling	Closing
Project Integration Management	4.1: Develop Project Charter	4.2: Develop Project Management Plan	4.3: Direct and Manage Project Execution	4.4: Monitor and Control Project Work 4.5: Perform Integrated Change Control	4.6: Close Project or Phase
Project Scope Management		5.1: Collect Requirements 5.2: Define Scope 5.3: Create WBS		5.4: Verify Scope 5.5: Control Scope	
Project Time Management		6.1: Define Activities 6.2: Sequence Activities 6.3: Estimate Activity Resources 6.4: Estimate Activity Durations 6.5: Develop Schedule		6.6: Control Schedule	
Project Cost Management		7.1: Estimate Costs 7.2: Determine Budget		7.3: Control Costs	
Project Quality Management		8.1: Plan Quality	8.2: Perform Quality Assurance	8.3: Perform Quality Control	
Project Human Resource Management		9.1: Develop Human Resource Plan	9.2: Acquire Project Team 9.3: Develop Project Team 9.4: Manage Project Team		

Table 3-1 Mapping Processes to Knowledge Areas and Process Groups

(continued)

Knowledge Areas	Project Management Process Groups				
	Initiating	Planning	Executing	Monitoring and Controlling	Closing
Project Communications Management	10.1: Identify Stakeholders	10.2: Plan Communications	10.3: Distribute Information	10.4: Manage Stakeholder Expectations 10.5: Report Performance	
Project Risk Management		11.1: Plan Risk Management 11.2: Identify Risks 11.3: Perform Qualitative Risk Analysis 11.4: Perform Quantitative Risk Analysis 11.5: Plan Risk Responses		11.6: Monitor and Control Risks	
Project Procurement Management		12.1: Plan Procurements	12.2: Conduct Procurements	12.3: Administer Procurements	12.4: Close Procurements

Table 1-1 Mapping Processes to Knowledge Areas and Process Groups

Ask the Expert

Q: How long, on average, should one spend planning on a 12-month project?

A: It all depends on the uniqueness of the project (has it been performed before, or is it a unique first time project), the experience of the team and project manager, and the level of commitment from the sponsors and other stakeholders). Also, is there a clearly defined scope and an approved project charter?

The answer also will vary depending on the country in which the project is being performed. For example, in Asia planning is a way of life, and project teams often will spend several months on this phase. One of my students from Korea stated that in his country planning would take approximately eight to nine months on a 12-month project. Granted, the planning process is viewed differently in different countries. In the U.S., we usually want to dive right in and begin the project prior to having a clear scope, a charter, or, in many cases, approved funding.

So what is the right amount of planning? On average, I would suggest 100 hours for every 1,000 hours of work on the project. The key thing to remember is the real answer to the amount of planning needed depends entirely on the variables previously mentioned and the experience of the PM and the project team. We must first aim at the target before we fire (start the project) to ensure our chances at hitting the target.

The same is true with project activities—the project team and manager are constantly being distracted. Because over 90 percent of the PM's time is spent communicating, the unscheduled interruptions of phone calls, new concerns and issues, and project changes are like a juggling act. With the urgent demands from the project stakeholders and almost immediate response expected from everyone, it is no wonder we don't take the time to plan properly how to manage a project.

PMI Code of Ethics and Professional Conduct

PMI formed the Ethics, Standards and Accreditation Group in 1981. This group has evolved through the years. However, the topic of ethics, standards, and accreditation is so dynamic and has gone through so many changes that it is published as a separate document rather than as part of the *PMBOK*.

In 1997, the PMI Board determined the need for a member code of ethics, which was approved in October 1998 as the Project Management Institute Code of Ethics and Professional Conduct. It is only briefly mentioned in the fourth edition of the *PMBOK* (released in December 2008.)

TIP
You should not be fooled by the Project Management Institute Code of Ethics and Professional Conduct's minimal appearance in the *PMBOK*. There are several questions (approximately 16–20) on the PMP exam concerning this area, which is viewed as essential by PMI and the business world to ensure the high standards and integrity of project managers around the world.

PMI's Code of Ethics and Professional Conduct is specific about the basic obligation of responsibility, respect, fairness, and honesty. It requires PM practitioners to demonstrate a commitment to ethical and professional conduct, including complying with laws, regulations, and organizational and professional policies. Acceptance of the code is required for PMP certification by PMI.[4]

The Code of Ethics and Professional Conduct has been renamed at least three times through the years and has expanded to include a new structure and two key areas called "Mandatory Standards/Requirements" and "Aspirational Codes." With all the changes to this section and only a small amount of coverage in the *PMBOK,* it is best to view the latest details on the PMI.org website. The document can be downloaded from http://www.pmi.org/PDF/AP_PMICodeofEthics.pdf.

To better understand the reason for the code of ethics and its purpose, let's look at PMI's Vision and Applicability statement.

Vision and Applicability Statement

As practitioners of project management, we are committed to doing what is right and honorable. We set high standards for ourselves and we aspire to meet these standards in all aspects of our lives: at work, at home, and in service to our profession.

The PMI Code of Ethics and Professional Conduct describes the expectations we have of ourselves and our fellow practitioners in the global project management community. It articulates the ideals to which we aspire as well as the behaviors that are mandatory in our professional and volunteer roles.

The purpose of this code is to instill confidence in the project management profession and to help an individual become a better practitioner. We do this by establishing a profession-wide understanding of appropriate behavior. We believe that the credibility and reputation of the project management profession is shaped by the collective conduct of individual practitioners.[5]

Persons to Whom the Code Applies

The Code of Ethics and Professional Conduct applies to all PMI members and individuals who are not members of PMI but meet one or more of the following criteria:

- Nonmembers who hold a PMI certification
- Nonmembers who apply to commence a PMI certification process
- Nonmembers who serve PMI in a volunteer capacity

Structure of the Code

The Code of Ethics and Professional Conduct is divided into sections that contain standards of conduct that are aligned with the four values identified as most important to the project management community.

Each section of the Code of Ethics and Professional Conduct includes both aspirational standards and mandatory standards.

Aspirational Standards   The aspirational standards describe the conduct we strive to uphold as PM practitioners. Although adherence to the aspirational standards is not easily measured, conducting ourselves in accordance with these standards is an expectation that we have of ourselves as professionals and it should not be viewed as optional.

NOTE

The conduct covered under the aspirational standards and the conduct covered under the mandatory standards are not mutually exclusive; that is, one specific act or omission could violate both aspirational and mandatory standards. Also, both aspirational and mandatory codes are further divided into values of Responsibility, Respect, Fairness, and Honesty.

Here are examples of respect under the aspirational standards:

- As practitioners in the global project management community, we inform ourselves about the norms and customs of others and avoid engaging in behaviors they might consider disrespectful.

- We listen to others' points of view, seeking to understand them, and we approach directly those persons with whom we have a conflict or disagreement.

Mandatory Standards/Requirements   The mandatory standards establish firm requirements and in some cases limit or prohibit practitioner behavior. Practitioners who do not conduct themselves in accordance with these standards will be subject to disciplinary procedures before PMI's Ethics Review Committee.

As practitioners in the global project management community, we require the following of ourselves and our fellow practitioners:

- **Regulations and Legal Requirements**

    - We inform ourselves and uphold the policies, rules, regulations, and laws that govern our work, professional, and volunteer activities.

    - We report unethical or illegal conduct to appropriate management and, if necessary, to those affected by the conduct.

- **Examples of Respect Under the Mandatory Standards**   As practitioners in the global project management community, we require the following of ourselves and our fellow practitioners:

    - Negotiate in good faith.

    - Do not exercise the power of our expertise or position to influence the decisions or actions of others in order to benefit personally at their expense.

    - Respect the property rights of others.

Ask the Expert

Q: I have a trusting relationship with my team and project sponsor and don't feel I should enforce rigid change control on my project. Why should I take extra time for "bookkeeping" when it is not needed?

A: Clearly you have to manage the sponsor and team in a trusting and effective manner; however, there are times when a simple "do me a favor" request from the sponsor, a team member, or other stakeholder is a request to look the other way or to perform "extras" on the project without proper change management. These "favors" often pose a conflict of interest and should *not* be performed because there will likely be consequences. As a project management professional, you should be prepared for these requests and respond in a straightforward professional manner.

The term in the world of project management for providing extras (that is, giving away something that is not in the scope of the project) is "gold plating." Gold plating is often viewed as a bad thing although many people feel it is a good thing and they want to provide the extras to show commitment to the project. However, there is a big difference between gold plating and providing added value on your project. If you understand the difference, you can always provide high-quality "value-added" management to the project without giving away things that are not in the scope agreement.

Value-added service can come in the way of streamlining a process (making it more effective or efficient) and offering suggestions to the stakeholders to save time or money. Showing integrity and operating in an honest manner is what the PMI Code of Ethics and Professional Conduct is all about.

What to Expect on the Exam

To give you an idea of what to expect on the PMP exam when it comes to the PMI Code of Ethics and Professional Conduct section, here are a couple sample questions:

1. A project you are managing is at the end of the Closing phase and during the Lessons Learned meeting the customer informs you of a number of activities and deliverables that have not been completed. What do you do first?

 A Tell the customer you will check on the incomplete deliverables and get back to them within a few days, even though you know these deliverables are not in the project scope.

 B Review the project deliverables in question during the meeting to understand the status and the customer's expectations to ensure you reach formal acceptance for all approved deliverables.

 C Ask the customer for their schedule and compare it to your own schedule.

 D Tell the project team to work overtime to complete the deliverables.

Answer: B. Openly reviewing and discussing the project activities and deliverables with all the stakeholders (including the customer) shows respect and helps ensure you are clear on the expectations, the status, and what it will take to obtain formal acceptance from the customer prior to closing the project. (Note: Both PMI and I are big on "formal acceptance." Getting signoff in writing or even in the form of an e-mail helps you stay audit ready on your project.)

2. You have just been assigned as the project manager for a new global project and have been told by one of the four sponsors to work only with him (Bob) because the other three sponsors live in different countries with different time zones. Bob asks you to conduct a project kickoff meeting (face-to-face for local team members and via conference call for international team and sponsors) and tells you *not* to invite the other sponsors because "they are too busy." What should you do?

 A Work only with Bob because this will make communications much easier.

 B Insist on inviting the other sponsors.

 C Notify the other sponsors that Bob doesn't want them invited to the meeting.

 D Talk to Bob to better understand the reasons for not inviting the other sponsors and strongly encourage him (politely insist) to allow you to include the other sponsors.

What Else Is Missing from the *PMBOK*?

Remember, the *PMBOK* is only a guide. It cannot possibly cover all the aspects and variations documented in the many text books, journals, and articles across the globe. Therefore, don't expect to use only the *PMBOK* when preparing for the PMP exam. You will need a good cross-section of knowledge, experience, and problem-solving capability and be able to apply all your skills to real-world situations to pass the PMP exam. If this tip makes you nervous and you are thinking you might not have enough PM experience to pass the PMP exam, you should consider taking the CAPM exam, which is based mostly on the *PMBOK Guide.*

Answer: D. It is important to ensure all sponsors of the projects have the opportunity to participate in the kickoff meeting so they can provide their input, expectations, and support. The sponsors are making an investment in their share of the project and have specific expectations for the end results. Thus, they need to be included in the kickoff meeting.

References

1. *A Guide to the Project Management Body of Knowledge (PMBOK® Guide), Fourth Edition,* (PMI–Project Management Institute Global Standard: Newtown Square, PA) 2008, page 41.

2. *A Guide to the Project Management Body of Knowledge (PMBOK® Guide), Fourth Edition,* (PMI–Project Management Institute Global Standard: Newtown Square, PA) 2008, page 37.

3. http://www.livescience.com/technology/050201_cell_danger.html.

4. PMI Code of Ethics and Professional Conduct, http://www.pmi.org/PDF/AP_PMICodeofEthics.pdf.

5. Ibid.

Part II

The Nine Knowledge Areas

Chapter 4

Project Integration Management

Key Skills & Concepts

- Overall integration management
- Project selection process (how projects are born)
- The project charter and who owns it
- Jumpstarting a project
- Project management plan (planning the work)
- Execution of the project (working the plan)
- How to know whether the project is on track
- Importance of the closing phase of the project

Think of Project Integration Management as the project manager flying over the project on a daily basis 1,000 feet in the air to see how everything is going. Are all the boats rowing in the right direction? Are the barriers (levies, dikes, and dams) all holding properly, or is there a flood coming that could break down the barriers and ruin the project?

As the project manager, it is up to you to be the pilot in command, the eye in the sky, the one who keeps the project moving forward as planned. It is up to you to provide clear direction and support to all the stakeholders while keeping everyone focused on the end results (project objectives). The Project Integration Management knowledge area also involves reporting the progress and overall status of the project accurately and in a timely manner to ensure adjustments can be made if needed.

Integration management is also about the team. Is the project team fully staffed, do they have the right skills, are they at the right place at the right time? Do they have all the information, tools, and support they need to manage their portion of the project? Are the team members clear on the goals and objectives of the project? Are they playing well together? Are they productive? These are only a few of the questions you need to ask yourself and address to effectively manage project integration across the entire project.

The PM must effectively manage the interdependencies between groups and individuals to ensure a smooth flight while traveling through the project life cycle and different knowledge areas. Integration management not only entails making choices about resource allocation, but is also about making tradeoffs among competing objectives and alternatives to solve problems and address concerns/issues before they become problems.

If the PM is too close to the details of the project, they will not be able to see the bigger picture beyond the project itself. The PM needs to think strategically (from beginning to end) and look at the whole project, not just the pieces and parts. This is where Project Integration Management is essential and if done properly will help ensure success on your project.

Project Integration Management According to PMI

Project Integration Management (which was introduced in the 2000 version of the *PMBOK)* is the first knowledge area in the *PMBOK* (Chapter 4) and probably the most important in that it crosses all five process groups. It sets the overall framework of how the project will be managed.

PMI states that Project Integration Management includes the processes and activities needed to identify, define, combine, unify, and coordinate the various processes and activities with the project management process groups.

In the context of project management, integration management includes a variety of characteristics, such as being able to articulate project deliverables (what are the products of the project?) and taking integrative actions to make sure all the work products and packages (activities) fit together properly. This also includes successfully managing stakeholder expectations and meeting all approved project requirements (which is easier said than done).

Ask the Expert

Q: Is it easier to manage integration of the project without including the team?

A: Many PMs feel they can conduct integration management faster on their own without the involvement of and questions from the team. This may work for a little while early in the project life cycle; however, without the team's input or involvement, the PM misses a wealth of knowledge, experience, and, most important, "buy-in" (acceptance) from the team. Even though the PM must be the "pilot in command" of the project, integration management revolves around the team and works best if the team is involved.

TIP
Integration management is a "team sport," and the project manager cannot do it all. Therefore, it is of the utmost importance to include the team in the integration management process activities.

Overview of Project Integration Management Processes

The Project Integration Management knowledge area, according to Chapter 4 of the *PMBOK*, includes the following six processes:

- **4.1: Develop project charter (Initiating process group)** The process of developing a document that formally authorizes a project or a phase of a project to begin and documenting the initial requirements needed to satisfy stakeholder needs and expectations.

- **4.2: Develop project management plan (Planning process group)** The process of documenting the actions necessary to define, prepare, integrate, and coordinate all subsidiary project plans.

- **4.3: Direct and manage project execution (Executing process group)** The process of performing the work defined in the project management plan to achieve the project's objectives.

- **4.4: Monitor and control project work (Monitoring and Controlling process group)** The process of tracking, reviewing, and regulating the project's progress to meet the performance objectives defined in the project management plan.

- **4.5: Perform integrated change control (Monitoring and Controlling process group)** The process of reviewing all change requests, approving changes (as appropriate), and managing changes to the deliverables, organizational process assets, project documents, and the overall project management plan.

- **4.6: Close project or phase (Closing process group)** The process of finalizing all activities across all the project management process groups to formally complete the project or phase.

NOTE

Project phases can actually be projects or subprojects unto themselves. For example, closing the project involves the same process groups and knowledge areas that should be used for managing the whole project. The same can be true with any of the project phases. I have seen many cases where the project plan and schedule were aligned with and grouped by the project phases or process groups, in essence breaking the project down into more manageable subprojects.

Project Integration Management is complex, and often the time and cost to perform this knowledge area are overlooked during estimating processes. We usually do a pretty good job of estimating the cost of the work necessary to complete the finished product or solve the problem the project is created to address; however, we tend to underestimate the cost to manage the time and effort it takes to oversee and integrate the overall project.

Integration management includes setting up meetings, building the team, setting up a tracking mechanism, collecting information, addressing issues, and reporting project status. A project manager needs to be assigned early in the project life cycle to focus on the project for these reasons. Far too often the existing operations manager or program manager is expected to oversee the project because they will inherit the product or result of the project. And, of course, they are expected to manage the project in their spare time and at no extra charge. A host of activities are involved with integration management, and these activities are rarely considered as part of the project. Because the work of the project will benefit the ongoing operations, it is often assumed the project work will be done by the daily operations manager and operations support team without cost or schedule impact. This is a great idea if it works; however, it rarely works.

For example, suppose a business need is identified to reduce the cost of call center operations by 10 percent for the Get It There (GIT) Trucking Company. A project manager is brought in to identify a solution. The PM and solutions team agree that an automated VRU (voice response unit) would expedite call handling with fewer handoffs and thus reduced time and cost. The estimated time to complete the project is two months. The project proposal is reviewed and approved for immediate implementation. However, instead of assigning a PM to initiate and manage the project, the GIT Trucking Co. executives feel they can save additional cost by having the call center's operations manager oversee the project in addition to his full-time operations job because he will own the solution once it is installed. Do you think this will work? No, because the operations manager already has a day job (and coincidentally has very little project management experience). Therefore, both roles will be done poorly. Between lack of PM experience and the distractions of the day-to-day operations, the operations manager will be too distracted to perform well in either function.

The Selection Process: How Projects Are Born

Projects are usually born (initiated) for one of two primary reasons:

- Business needs or opportunity (increase revenue, decrease cost, and so on)
- Problem that needs to be solved (for example, equipment failure causing lost productivity or a construction project to stimulate the economy)

Think about it: All the projects you have ever worked on probably fall into one of the two categories mentioned.

Business needs can manifest themselves as a perceived problem or a reason to change the way a company is doing business (or change the products they sell). Because business needs may often be perceived and are not a direct result of a real problem, I use both the primary reasons just mentioned as drivers in the project selection process.

For example, take an IT (Information Technology) project to consolidate the number of servers. The justification for this project is to reduce cost and to increase reliability of the servers. The need to reduce cost is a business need (to be more competitive), and the need to increase reliability not only reduces outage and service problems but also saves money and improves customer satisfaction. All great benefits that can justify the project (a project is born).

Usually the company's executive committee, together with its subcommittees, identifies the need for projects and approves project funding (budgetary) commitments. This committee or delegate is responsible for establishing the strategic direction and plans for ensuring that projects are consistent with the organization's overall strategy. It is also responsible for ensuring approved policies or practices are followed.

Define the Business Need/Opportunity or Requirement

The best way to get a project approved is to identify the opportunity, benefit, or business need for the project. If the benefits (results of the project) outweigh the cost and time to create the product or service, then the project proposal should be an easy sell. If the project is to satisfy a safety or regulatory compliance requirement, it may be mandated.

TIP

Most companies or organizations have project review boards or PMOs that serve as a governing body to determine which projects are worthy to be funded and chartered/approved.

The project statement, justification, or proposal should explain, in clear business terms, how the project will address specific needs or opportunities. Why should the company spend time and money on this project? Here are some examples of how to help satisfy business needs, opportunities, or a regulatory requirement:

- Streamline/improve quality, reliability, or effectiveness of a product or the efficiency of a service, procedure, or operation.

- Meet mandated or regulatory compliance requirements of an internal or external authority (Sarbanes-Oxley, OCC, OSHA, FDA, ISO, ITIL, and so on).

- Reduce operating or overhead costs or increase revenue.

- Gain market share or provide a strategic business advantage.

- Improve the skills of the team to enhance their ability to perform more effectively (through education, on-the-job training, or mentoring).

Here are some additional details that can (or should) be provided in the discussion of the business need/opportunity to help provide a better understanding of the project:

- How the need/opportunity was recognized and who benefits.

- A best estimate of the size or impact of the need/opportunity in specific terms.

- Results or contributing factors, such as increased workload, reduction in staff, budget or time constraints, increased risk, and the need to introduce new technology.

- Alternatives, risk analysis, advantages, and disadvantages.

- The potential cost of the project if approved and the potential cost if no action is taken (for example, a continued failure rate of 15 percent if no action is taken). You should be as specific as possible with failure or improvement rates.

Remember, the information you provide in the project proposal will help the project sponsors make informed decisions and will help promote support for the project. The business need or opportunity can be better justified if it is based on sound information and facts. Unfortunately there are many variables and you may not always have the answers.

Famous Words in Project Management: "It Depends"

A fellow PM instructor (and friend of mine) frequently says, "The two magic words in project management are 'It depends.'" This is true because every project tends to be unique in one way or another. No matter how many times a project is performed, many variables make each time different, and the way the project is managed depends entirely on these variables.

Project managers have to be able to solve problems, handle different situations, and be able to think on their feet to come up with the best answer based on the information available at that time. If it were easy, anyone could do it, right?

Project Methodology and Sample Checklist

In the PM classes I teach at businesses and universities, two questions are frequently asked by my students:

- What is a project methodology?
- Are sample checklists and templates available for the different aspects of a project?

I'll answer the second question first: Yes, hundreds of sample checklists and templates are available from the Internet and from fellow project managers. Project managers are usually more than willing to share their tools and techniques, such as checklists, sample documents, and so on. To get an idea of what is available, simply perform an Internet search for "PM Templates." Some are available at a fee, of course, but many are free "shareware." One such website (discovered by a student in my class) is a website showing a fantastic list of templates. They are explained clearly, organized well, and cover a host of topics on project management. The website is owned by Dr. Gary Evans, PMP, and the URL is http://www.cvr-it.com/PM_Templates/. The templates from CVR/IT Consulting LLC are free for personal use, or for governmental and nonprofit agencies. However, there is a nominal licensing fee for commercial use, which is well worth the cost.

Now let's tackle the first question: What is a project methodology?

Per Wikipedia, *methodology* is defined as follows:

1. The analysis of the principles of methods, rules, and postulates employed by a discipline.
2. The systematic study of methods that are, can be, or have been applied within a discipline.
3. A particular procedure or set of procedures.

Methodology includes the following concepts as they relate to a particular discipline or field of inquiry:

1. A collection of theories, concepts, or ideas
2. A comparative study of different approaches
3. A critique of the individual methods[1]

Methodology refers to more than a simple set of methods; it refers to the rationale and the assumptions that underlie a particular study or approach relative to the method.

Many companies are realizing the importance of a standard approach, or methodology, to help ensure consistency and a greater degree of success across the projects and programs they manage. To do this in an organized manner, more companies are creating project management offices (PMOs). As part of its charter, the PMO is responsible for ensuring and maintaining a documented project management (PM) methodology for use across all projects. This methodology is designed to meet the needs of all segments of the organization. It serves as a guide to the organization concerning the projects it selects, to project teams as they plan the work and report the status of their projects, and to management as it supplies the required oversight.

Often the chosen PM methodology is designed around the *PMBOK,* and in other cases companies develop their own PM methodology. Either way, it is important to remember the *PMBOK* is only a guide (not a methodology). A PM methodology should work equally well on large and small projects. Standard templates are typically part of the methodology, and hundreds of great templates are available on the Internet or within your company's PM methodology (if one exists). If your company doesn't have an approved standard PM methodology, now is a good time to create one. Your boss will see the benefits and shower you with bonuses, keys to the VIP washroom, and executive parking... or at least a pat on the back.

The best way to set up a clearly defined project methodology is to use a set of tried and true checklists. One constant with project managers around the world is that we love checkmarks, and checkmarks work best on a checklist. To this end, I have included several bulleted and numbered checklists in this chapter for your use and enjoyment.

A standard project management methodology is extremely beneficial and the goals are quite simple. Per CVR/IT Consulting LLC, the following goals or objectives should apply when defining a PM methodology:

- Provide a common point of reference and a common vocabulary for talking and writing about the practice of project management.

- Increase awareness and use of good project management practice by those charged with the responsibilities defined in the methodology.

- Define the roles of the executive committee, sponsor, project manager, stakeholders, and other team members and obtain consensus within the organization about critical success factors (CSF).

- Create the basis for a collaborative environment where everyone engaged in technical project work understands what is required of them and why those requirements are key factors for improving project results.[2]

Project Integration Management Processes: Charter to Close

To better understand Project Integration Management, we need to look at the individual processes. The details of the six processes in the Project Integration Management knowledge area are defined and explained throughout the remainder of this chapter.

1. Develop Project Charter Process

What is a project charter? In simple terms it is the authorization for a project or phase of a project to begin. It also authorizes the project manager to be assigned and allows the PM to begin assigning resources (people and equipment) to the project. In other words, it is the green light for the project to officially begin.

When Does a Project Officially Become a Project?

In reality, many projects are born long before they receive the official charter. PMI views the project charter as the first official authorization and recognition of a project or phase of a project. There are many ways for a project or phase to begin, and many organizations don't even use or recognize the term *project charter.*

TIP

The term project charter is not commonly used in many government agencies and public and private sector companies. It is more often referred to as one of the following: work order, service request, statement of work (SOW), request for service (RFS), contract, work initiative, work action, grant, or any of a number of other different names (especially on government contracts).

The Develop Project Charter process is the first in the series of 42 processes in the *PMBOK* and occurs during the Initiating process group. It is the process of developing a document that formally authorizes the project. It is also the process for documenting the initial requirements that satisfy the stakeholders' needs and expectations; defining the product, service, or result of the project; and outlining acceptance criteria.

Here's a list of some of the key activities that should occur during this process:

- Identify project sponsor(s).
- Identify and document project deliverables (what is expected from the project).
- Identify and document project constraints (limitations).
- Determine project success criteria.

- Document project assumptions.

- Develop and analyze cost-benefits.

Where Does a Project Charter Come From?

The project charter can come in many forms and in different names. It may be formal, such as a contract or letter of agreement (LOA), or informal, such as a call or e-mail from your boss or the customer telling you to proceed with the project or phase. It is best if the charter is in writing to minimize confusion and to meet audit requirements.

To clarify the term *project phase,* let's use as an example a specific project to estimate the cost of designing a new fuel-efficient car. The approval may be to conduct a preliminary review or feasibility study (concept phase analysis) to determine whether there is sufficient business justification to proceed. The prudent approach to any project is to first determine whether it is doable or can be cost-justified before the company commits to the project in its entirety.

In today's economy, many companies are not able to afford long-term investments and need to realize benefits and ROI (return on investment) sooner than later, thus the need to take projects in smaller steps using fewer investment dollars.

Sample Components of a Project Charter Template

As mentioned, many great templates and forms are available that provide a good starting place for documents such as the project charter. Here is a summary list of the key components of a sample project charter template:

1.0: General project information

- 1.1: Project name

- 1.2: Sponsors (who is funding or will be the primary benefactor of the project)

- 1.3: Document history (for tracking changes and version control)

2.0: Identify stakeholders and contacts (project manager, team lead, etc.)

3.0: Project description

- 3.1: Project purpose, business need, opportunity, or justification (problem to be solved)

- 3.2: Project objectives (measurable outcomes, such as reduce cost, increase performance, increase sales, etc.)

- 3.3: Deliverables or major milestones (products of the project, such as working software code, training manual, completed call center, user test document, etc.)

- 3.4: What the project is intended to do and not do
- 3.5: Risks or constraints (barriers/limitations)

4.0: Financial or resource information

- 4.1: Budget assumptions
- 4.2: Reporting strategy (frequency and format)
- 4.3: Type of estimate
- 4.4: Funding source(s)

5.0: Acceptance criteria

- 5.1: Approvers
- 5.2: Change control process

6.0: Final signoff (formal acceptance signatures) of the charter[3]

NOTE
When filling out a template, remember that all projects are unique in some way, so the template might not fit the project exactly. Therefore, consider all the inputs, tools and techniques, and outputs of the processes to ensure you haven't missed anything.

Case Study: Sample Project Charter Alternative

In our case study, the Budweiser Events Center (BEC) uses their contract with the client (artist, performer, promoting agent, or organization) as their project charter. The contract also serves as important input to the scope of the project.

In the case of BEC, contracts usually have a "rider" (technical data sheet) that specifies the artist's (organization's) requirements, which vary based on the nature of the event. Here are a few of the key components:

- Compensation and how payment is made/received
- Event date and ticket "on-sale" date
- Advertisement and merchandise sales
- Contract cancellation and liability insurance
- Permits needed and special security/staffing
- Advancing requirements such as the following:

- Production setup requirements (power, rentals, spotlights, and so on)
- Dressing rooms needed and special requirements such as food and beverage
- Stage configuration, sound and audio/video (AV) special effects, and other lighting
- "Backline" band equipment or gear not being provided by the band/performer

These requirements are then documented in an "event data sheet" that serves as the formal communications document for the event. The next step is then to begin the setup process for that particular event. This is referred to as "building conversion" or "changeover," and the process involves the following steps:

1. Transferring the physical setup requirements from the previous event to the next scheduled event.
2. Scheduling the labor for the event (ticket sellers, merchandise sellers, ushers, ticket takers, security, parking, law enforcement, fire marshal, medical, conversion labor, cleaners, operations staff, fire panel monitor, house audio/visual, electricians, stagehand labor, runners, and supervising staff).

Who Owns the Project Charter?

Because the project charter is the official authorization document of the project, it should be initiated by the primary champion or executive owner (sponsor). Because most high-level managers are not usually document creators, it is up to the project manager to draft the charter, review it with the sponsor, and obtain formal acceptance or approval of the document. This can even be in e-mail format, as long as it is in writing.

Ask the Expert

Q: Who owns the project charter?

A: The project sponsor responsible for the financial resources of the project owns the project charter. The sponsor is usually the person who promotes or supports the benefits of the project to higher levels of management. In the real-world, however, the project manager (or project leader) usually documents the details of the charter and obtains approval for the project to begin.

Definition of a Project Sponsor

According to Dr. Gary Evans (CVR/IT Consulting LLC):

> "The Sponsor is the individual [or individuals], generally an executive, who is responsible for the strategic direction and financial support of a project. A Sponsor should have the authority to define project goals, secure resources, and resolve organizational and priority conflicts."

> "It has been shown, but may not be generally recognized, that lack of project sponsorship can be a major contributor to project failure. Conversely, an appropriately placed and fully engaged Sponsor can bring a difficult project to successful conclusion. Assumptions that a formal Sponsor is not needed (or for political reasons can be avoided) are misplaced. Steering committees are no substitute. A powerful but uninvolved Sponsor is no help. Even big-budget and highly visible projects require a formal Sponsor."

Here's a sample list of sponsor responsibilities (from Dr. Gary Evans):

- Champion the project from initiation to completion.
- Participate in the development and selling of the project business case.
- Present the overall vision and business objectives for the project.
- Assist in determining and approving the final funding and project direction.
- Serve as executive liaison to key stakeholders (for example, senior management, department directors, and support managers).
- Support the project team.

For best results, it is also important for the project manager to be assigned early in the initiation phase so the charter can be reviewed and/or developed by the person responsible for the execution of the project.

The project sponsor needs to provide the direction, executive sponsorship, and expectations that need to be met to consider the project a success. These components must be considered as key inputs to the project.

Develop Project Charter Inputs, Tools and Techniques, and Outputs

As a reminder, every process has inputs, tools and techniques, and outputs. An input often comes from the output of the previous process, so there is a logical progression in many cases.

Process Inputs   As mentioned previously inputs are items that need to be considered for the process to be administered. Further, *input* is a term denoting either an entrance or changes inserted into a system or process. The quality of the input can be crucial to the value of the output of the process, which brings us to the famous saying "garbage in, garbage out" (GIGO). There are several inputs to the Develop Project Charter process, as listed here:

- Project statement of work (SOW)
- Business case
- Contract
- Enterprise environmental factors
- Organizational process assets

Tools and Techniques   Tools and techniques are used to analyze the inputs received for a particular process. Subject matter experts (SMEs), focus groups, and specialists are often used as consultants; they can be considered to be the tool or technique used to assess the inputs for a process. These experts apply their knowledge and experience to help determine the best approach to accomplish specific outputs of the process. In the Develop Project Charter process, there is only one tool and technique—and it is simply expert judgment. Note that the SMEs may have (and certainly can use) a variety of tools and techniques to help them develop the project charter.)

Outputs   The outputs of a process are the documents or results being developed as part of the process. For example, the single output of the Develop Project Charter process is the project charter.

When the project charter (or alternative authorization document) is received, the project manager needs to dive right in and jumpstart the project.

How to Jumpstart a Project

Projects usually come at you with little warning. You get a tap on the shoulder from your boss (usually via e-mail or a phone call) with the all-too-familiar line, "Have I got an opportunity for you." And as always, the project is high priority and needs to begin immediately. So what do you do?

Ask the Expert

Q: How do I "hit the ground running" to jumpstart a project?

A: I suggest you use a standard checklist and templates from previous similar projects or you can use the sample checklist I provide in this section. The key is to have a checklist ready before you receive "the call."

Once a checklist is chosen, the next step is to select the templates that can be used. Templates can be your friend or your enemy. They are great for getting your thoughts flowing and to apply synergy based on other people's experiences. However, if the templates you select are used as "fill-in-the-blanks" forms, you and your team could waste countless hours doing work collecting information or answering questions that really don't apply to your project. A template is just a shell until you fit it into your project. I have seen many project managers and project teams lose focus and creativity on their project when using templates if they simply fill in the blanks with little thought of how it fits their project.

The best way to collect and organize the templates is to put them in a binder or electronic folder—often referred to as a project control book (PCB.) The PCB provides a great way to organize documents or templates so you can dive right in when starting a new project or updating an existing project.

To help you begin, I've provided a sample PM jumpstart checklist. Although your actual checklist will likely be different from this one, the good news about project management is that the fundamentals tend to apply to most all projects. With that in mind, here is the sample checklist:

1. Review project objectives from the project-selection process. What is the problem to be solved? What is the business need or opportunity to be addressed?

2. Identify/verify the project sponsor (or sponsors) who need to be satisfied that the project does what is expected of it. The PM's job is to identify the sponsors and other stakeholders on the project (in other words, know your audience).

3. Obtain the project charter and other inputs (contract, work order, service request, and so on) to review what is authorized (in scope) in the project.

4. Acquire the project team and other resources needed to perform the work. In some cases, a letter of commitment from management for key resources (especially "mission-critical" or highly skilled people) is recommended to ensure their availability.

5. Assess and maintain staff technical proficiency and provide training where needed.

6. Gather the team to begin introductions and conduct skill and capability reviews.

7. Review constraints (financial, resource, time, and so on) to help establish the scope.

8. Document and review the scope statement with key stakeholders and obtain scope verification from the project sponsor(s).

9. Create a Resource Assignment Matrix (RAM) and Organizational Breakdown Structure (OBS) and review these with the team.* (This should include backup resources.)

10. Schedule a kickoff meeting to officially announce the project, get everyone on the same page, set the ground rules, show the project structure "chain of command," and so on.

11. Develop the project management plan including tools and techniques needed to manage the project.*

12. Develop the Work Breakdown Structure (WBS).*

13. Begin development of the project schedule (time management).*

14. Begin cost estimating (cost management) with input from the stakeholders.*

15. Conduct risk management assessment and assign owners to the high-priority risks.*

16. Develop the project communications plan, including format and frequency. Review this with the stakeholders for approval and determination of how issues will be tracked and managed.

17. Once the project is underway, begin the *PMBOK* execution and controlling processes.

18. Review the project status on a regular basis and report the status to key stakeholders weekly (or as needed, based on the size, type, and complexity of the project).

19. Set up a Project Management Information System (PMIS). This is often called an electronic "team room" or "central database repository." Its purpose is to allow the project manager and team to store the project plan and output documents for easy access and audit readiness.

* With team involvement—Keep in mind the team development "forming stage" may have certain constraints, such as personality conflicts, lack of skilled resources for the assignment, lack of commitment, and lack of trust from a team member or from a manager. Therefore, it is important to allow time for the team to get to know one another on a new project.

Bruce Wayne Tuckman is an American psychologist who has carried out research on the theory of group dynamics. In 1965, he published one of his theories called "Tuckman's Stages," where he states that "Groups initially concern themselves with orientation accomplished primarily through testing. Such testing serves to identify the boundaries of both interpersonal and task behaviors. Coincident with testing in the interpersonal realm is the establishment of dependency relationships with leaders, other group members, or pre-existing standards. It may be said that orientation, testing and dependence constitute the group process of *forming*."[4]

The best approach to help form a project team is to make time for the team members to get to know one another and for you to get to know the team members—they are your number-one asset on the project.

Once the project initiation (startup) has begun and the preliminary team is formed, it is time to lock in (verify) the project deliverables.

What Are the Project Deliverables?

A project deliverable is the product of work done on a project, such as a blueprint of a building, a test script for software testing, or a specific training manual. Deliverables are sometimes described as inputs or outputs. One person's outputs are the next person's inputs. A deliverable can be a "product" of the project. It should be a unique and verifiable product, service, or result that must be produced to complete a process, phase, or the project itself.

Project deliverables include both the outputs that comprise the product or service of the project as well as ancillary results, such as project reports and other documents. Deliverables can be described at a summary level or in great detail, depending on the needs of the project.

TIP

As important as it is to clearly identify project deliverables, it is equally important to identify and document what is excluded from the project as well. Project exclusions should be precise to leave very little room for confusion or challenges of what is and is not included in the project scope. An example of project exclusion is, "The training manual will only be provided in English." Or, "Special sound effects and laser light show equipment for the concert must be provided by the artist, not the events center."

The only way to be completely clear on the project deliverables is to collect and verify the requirements of the project with the sponsor(s). The requirements usually dictate the deliverables.

Try This Who Provides the Requirements?

A famous rock star's booking agent contacts the events center manager to book the BEC (Budweiser Events Center) for a concert. The requirements for the stage placement, seating, and special effects (for example, pyrotechnics/fireworks) pose a safety hazard. The booking agent is contacted and he is insistent on the requirements as stated. What do you do?

Answer: Even though the customer (booking agent) provides the requirements, if these requirements pose a hazard or are in conflict with a city or fire ordinance, they will need to be changed. Otherwise, the event cannot go on as requested.

The requirements must be clear, documented, approved, and pose no conflicts in the safe delivery of the project. Once the requirements are approved, the project manager should schedule a kickoff meeting and begin developing the project management plan. Note that there can be more than one kickoff meeting; however, there should be at least one fairly early in the project life cycle to get everyone up to speed quickly and to formally announce the project scope, the deliverables, the team, sponsors, and so on.

The Kickoff Meeting

The kickoff meeting helps set the stage (framework) for the project and demonstrates the team's importance in the planning and execution process. So who should attend? A sample list is shown below:

- Project sponsor(s)
- Project manager
- Project leads (coordinators)
- Project team members and support personnel
- Key subject matter experts (SMEs)
- Others as appropriate:
    - Administrator or scribe (to take minutes of the meeting)
    - Financial representative (person tracking budget and expenses)
    - Customer, end-user management, or lead representatives

What topics are covered in the kickoff meeting? It depends (you knew that was coming, right?) on the size, type, and complexity of the project. If the project is an extension of an existing project, this step should be pretty easy. If, however, it is a totally new project with a totally new team and new technology, this can be labor intensive. At the end of the meeting, the attendees should leave with a clear understanding of the following:

- Project organization, key stakeholders, and team members assigned. Where the plan and output documents, meeting minutes, and assignments will be posted and stored (preferably in an electronic team room). How to access and update the product documents.

- The project charter, including goals and objectives of the project.

- The scope of the project and how the scope will be managed (for example, through formal change control).

- Success factors (measured deliverables and results expected).

- General schedule, budget, and preliminary next steps (action items).

- Benefits or business results expected upon completion of the project.

- Known issues, constraints, or risks that need to be considered going into the project.

- Key assumptions and milestones, if identified.

- Activities planned for the next several days/weeks.[5]

With the kickoff meeting complete, you are now ready to develop the more detailed overall project management plan with input from the team (remember this should be a team sport).

2. Develop Project Management Plan Process

The Develop Project Management Plan process involves documenting the actions necessary to define, prepare, integrate, and coordinate all the other work plans of the project. It defines how the project will be executed, monitored and controlled, and then closed.

The project management plan, once developed, serves as a guide to how the project will be managed. This guide should be used as a working document. It should be used for various purposes and is the first step in demonstrating that the PM is effectively managing the project based on an approved methodology and formal plan.

At the end of the day (or the end of an audit), the true measure of control over a project is whether the PM has a plan and is working (managing) the plan.

The primary owner of the project management plan is the project manager. The project manager has total responsibility and accountability for the overall project and its successful completion. To succeed, the project manager must work closely with the sponsor, the team, and other key stakeholders to ensure adequate plans are put in place for all aspects of the project, including (but not limited to) resources, funding, risk management, communications, schedule, and change control.

In some cases on real-world projects, the project manager may not be assigned to the project until the planning or even execution phase (after the project has started), in which case there may be a handoff or orientation meeting to bring the PM up to date on the agreements made during the initiation phase. In these cases, the project manager must thoroughly review all the materials previously collected or created as well as ensure they are reasonable in scope and delivery capabilities and are approved. Once approved, and all project history and current status have been reviewed, the PM must then finalize the project management plan development.

Try This Plan the Work

In Chapter 2, I mentioned the "Ready, fire, aim" dilemma. This is the stage where you can avoid this dilemma. Planning the work of the project will help ensure a smooth project. There are far too many variables—thus the importance of planning.

Consider the following: Your boss comes to you on Monday and says, "You are the new project manager of a software development project to create a tracking system for downloads from the EZtrackmusic.com website and you need to deliver the project plan to the sponsor on Friday." What is the first step to get you started?

This is a great time to begin the first step of the AIM strategy:

1. *Analyze* the situation, including what needs to be done, target dates, limitations, and possible roadblocks and barriers.

2. Lock in a preliminary plan first at the team level. A good approach is to use a checklist (such as the "Sample Checklist for PM Management Plan Development" shown next.)

3. Then take the plan forward for review and validation by the key sponsors/stakeholders.

Once approved, you now have a plan to work from for your new project.

Sample Checklist for PM Management Plan Development

The following sample checklist can be used to assist in the Develop Project Management Plan process (note that many of these steps are also included in the project jumpstart check list):

1. Develop a detailed project management plan with the assistance of the project team.

2. Create a Work Breakdown Structure (WBS), Organizational Breakdown Structure (OBS), and Risk Breakdown Structure (RBS) with assistance from the project team.

3. Develop or assist in the development of a scope statement, project schedule, and communications plan.

4. Create a preliminary risk management plan (including owners and contingency plans) and cost benefit analysis (as appropriate).

5. Create a procurement plan. This plan will vary depending on organizational structure (for example, a centralized procurement department versus a decentralized procurement department, where the PM has more involvement and control).

6. Develop the project budget, assumptions, exclusions, and the tracking and reporting plan. Note that it is important to identify and document the type of estimate used (for example, order of magnitude or definitive).

7. Obtain management commitment, a document of understanding (DOU), statement of work (SOW), or contractor (vendor/supplier) agreement for key resources to clearly state the work they are expected to perform.

8. Assign resources to the project and assign work packages from the WBS to specific team members (resource plan or resource assignment matrix [RAM]).

9. Approve project quality management processes and procedures, measurements and tracking format, and reporting frequency.

10. Develop a baseline and obtain approval (baselining the plan means to establish a starting point or a point of reference for comparing against for changes).

Once these items are complete, as the PM you must provide clear direction and ongoing management of the project management plan. It is all about planning the work and working the plan. The plan also serves as a guide to how you are planning to manage the different aspects of the project.

Case Study: Example of a Project Management Plan

In the case of the BEC (Budweiser Events Center), their project management plan is the "Event Data Sheet," which is created by the Event Manager using a standard process and template that clearly defines how the project is to be managed down to the following items:

- The schedule (including event date, setup date, sound check, and doors open times)
- Contacts (including promoter, tour manager, production contacts, operations manager, media/PR manager, box office, finance/HR, concessions, and catering)
- Box office information (including attendance/seating and ticket handling)
- Staff (number of supervisors, number of staff needed for each category—sound/lights, runners, receptionists, cleaning, video, pyro shooter, and so on)
- First responders (local law enforcement, emergency medical, fire department)

- Security (including parking lot, entrances, loading dock, and dressing rooms)
- Parking lot management
- Concessions/catering
- Setup (stadium seating, stage, tables, dressing rooms, and so on)
- Show production (trucks, buses, food/beverage, stagehand labor, and so on)
- Miscellaneous

The standard format and flow of the Event Data Sheet offers consistency in how events will be managed regardless of the type of event. From the customer's point of view, the measure of success will be whether the project is completed on time, within budget, and at an acceptable level of quality.

Develop Project Management Plan Inputs, Tools and Techniques, and Outputs

According to the *PMBOK*, inputs to the Develop Project Management Plan process are as follows:

- Project charter
- Outputs from the previous planning processes
- Contract
- Enterprise environmental factors
- Organizational process assets

The tool and technique for this process is expert judgment, and the output is the actual project management plan.

Don't be fooled by the single tool and technique and output for this process, because the project management plan is essential to the success of the project and is a compilation of all the key components of the project. The project management plan can be a fairly large document with many volumes or it can be small in size, depending on the complexity of the project. The PM plan should be used to guide the execution of the project. It will be the first place someone (such as a new team member or an auditor) goes to understand the project and how it is to be managed. The copies/files should be date stamped and clearly marked with a version number so there is no confusion over which is the latest version to be used for reference by the PM and the team.

TIP

The project management plan should be used early and often throughout the project life cycle. It should be a "working document" and readily available in a centrally located file cabinet or an electronic team room (such as a Wiki or SharePoint location). It is extremely important to keep the document up to date and accurate without multiple versions. The rule of thumb is to keep the current and previous two (v-2) versions for reference.

3. Direct and Manage Project Execution Process

This is where the actual work execution begins. The bulk of the project budget is spent during this phase of the project. As project manager, you need to exercise your leadership skills and put them into action. Be proactively involved, constantly looking for ways to keep the team focused on the deliverables of the project. Provide clear direction. Be available to the team and ensure they have the tools necessary to do their job. Ensure schedules are being met, and work the details of the project plan to anticipate breakdown or risks, such as missed handoffs. For example, you should be aware of dependencies where someone needs to provide information or work products to allow the project "assembly line" to continue operating.

The project manager, along with the team, directs the performance of the planned project activities as well as manages the various technical, operational, and organizational interfaces that exist within the project to achieve project objectives.

Project Execution Activities Checklist

During the project execution phase, it is helpful for the project manager and project team to perform their work in an organized fashion. As always, a good way to begin is with a checklist of key activities.

TIP

Notice that the action words (verbs) change during the execution phase (*perform, maintain, manage,* and *review*) when compared to the earlier initiation phase (*develop, create,* and *assign*). In most cases, the verbs will change during each phase of the project life cycle.

The following list includes some key activities that should be considered when executing the work of your project (note that the order of activities may change depending on the needs of your project):

1. Perform activities to accomplish project requirements and deliverables.

2. Create project deliverables per approved requirements.

3. Implement the planned methods, processes, and standards.

4. Maintain the project management plan and output documents from other processes.

5. Manage risks and make sure an owner is assigned to each of the highest-priority risks.

6. Work with risk owners to ensure mitigation plans and response action plans/procedures are in place and being monitored as well as managed should the risks occur.

7. Maintain staff levels and technical proficiency, providing training and mentoring where needed (including sellers, vendors, and suppliers, as appropriate).

8. Manage productivity and the schedule to ensure the work is being done on time.

9. Manage communication with all stakeholders, including timely and accurate reporting.

10. Manage day-to-day activities and provide clear direction to team members.

11. Review project status, comparing budgeted costs to actual costs and the value of the work performed (Earned Value analysis) on a regular basis (weekly is recommended).

12. Manage the scope, budget, and schedule and update them based on approved changes.

13. Make recommendations and adjustments as needed to improve the project.

14. Manage quality results to ensure compliance.

15. Manage the change process and participate in the Change Control Board (CCB) to approve product/project changes.

16. Document lessons learned and implement approved process improvements.

Direct and Manage Project Execution Inputs, Tools and Techniques, and Outputs

The inputs, tools and techniques, and outputs for the Direct and Manage Project Execution process are detailed in Table 4-1.

Inputs	Tools and Techniques	Outputs
Project management plan	Expert judgment	Deliverables
Approved change requests	Project Management Information System (PMIS)	Work performance information
Enterprise environmental factors		Change requests
Organizational process assets		Project management plan updates
		Project document updates

Table 4-1   Direct and Manage Project Execution Inputs, Tools and Techniques, and Outputs

Clearly defined processes and a firm understanding of inputs, tools and techniques, and outputs are great; however, in the real world of project management, something invariably gets in the way—time or cost constraints, resource turnover, skills or experience limitations, misguided (or distracted) project sponsors with unrealistic expectations, risk events, and so on. Therefore, managing projects in the real world is sometimes easier said than done.

Try This Sky's the Limit: Pet Projects Are Out of Scope

You are a seasoned project manager for an international project, and the primary sponsor (director) is a good person who knows a lot about the project. However, he has his own "pet" sub-project that is not funded and is outside the scope of the project you are managing. The director has asked you to write a proposal to get funding for his pet project and he wants it completed ASAP. You are fully committed right now for your in-scope deliverables and you politely explain to him that his request is outside the scope of your project. The director gets very upset and says you are *not* a team player. How do you handle the situation?

A. Write up the proposal to prove you are a team player and to get him off your back.

B. Hold your ground (be firm) in your position and remind him that his request is not part of the funded project and you will not have time to work on his pet project.

C. Negotiate with the director and tell him you will write the proposal; however, you need more time on the original project from him in return.

D. Tell the director that his plan to get additional funding is a good idea and you will be happy to assist in the proposal when time allows; however, his request needs to go through the approved change control process to assess the impact to the funded project.

Answer: D is the best answer in this case. However, this is easier said than done, because the director can impact your career and your future by telling others you are not a "team player" or even firing you. Unfortunately, this sort of thing happens occasionally when one plays by the rules.

If all project sponsors were easy to work with and stuck to the approved scope statement, anyone could be a project manager. At the end of the day, you have to stand firm on managing scope and feel that you are doing the right thing—which sometimes means updating your resume and being prepared for a change.

4. Monitor and Control Project Work Process

The Monitor and Control Project Work process involves tracking, reviewing, and regulating the progress of project activities necessary to meet performance objectives defined in the project management plan. This process needs to be implemented early during plan execution to ensure the project is on track. Many tools and procedures are available to assist the project manager and team with this process.

The PM must constantly keep an eye on the project, team performance, change requests, the issues and concerns that surface, and the risk events that occur to ensure the project is under control. The following is a simple list of some of the things the PM needs to watch for during the Monitor and Control Project Work process:

- Monitoring and controlling the quality of the deliverables of the project

- Comparing the actual project performance against the approved project management plan

- Assessing performance to determine if corrective or preventive actions are needed

- Monitoring risks and identifying, analyzing, and tracking new ones

- Maintaining timely and accurate status reports and updates to the information system (including up-to-date documents, version control, and audit readiness)

- Providing accurate forecasts to update the current cost and schedule

- Monitoring the implementation of approved changes as they occur

As for the inputs, tools and techniques, and outputs of this process, there are only a few differences from the previous process, and they are listed here:

- **Inputs**   Project management plan and performance reports, such as current status, accomplishments, scheduled activities (any overdue or coming-due activities?), open issues that may impact the project, and, of course, forecasts (are you on track?).

- **Tools and Techniques**   Expert judgment is used to interpret the information provided by the Monitoring and Controlling processes, and the PM (in collaboration with the team) determines any actions required to ensure the project performance matches expectations.

- **Outputs**   The outputs for this process focus on change requests and updates to the project management plan and other documents, as needed.

Try This Keeping Your Eyes Wide Open: Accurate Progress Reporting

A project team lead (Joey) has reported for the last three weeks that he is 85 percent complete on a "test script" work package he has been working on for the application test group. It appears there is either no progress on this activity or Joey has failed to accurately update his report. However, when asked about it, he replies with a definite "Yes, progress is being made and I am on schedule," which should mean about 98 percent completion. The test group lead (Mary) says she has not seen any progress on the test script and that this activity is on the critical path of the project and will affect the end date if not provided. What do you do?

A. Request that Joey show you the test script and hand-carry it with Joey to the test group to verify it is usable for the upcoming test sequence.

B. Ask Joey to update the status report to accurately reflect the 98 percent completion.

C. Work out the details with Joey one-on-one and then schedule a checkpoint meeting with all appropriate team members to verify the current status of the script and its readiness for handoff to ensure there are no surprises.

D. Let it go because Joey knows people in high places and you don't want to rock the boat.

Answer: C. It is best to work out the details with Joey first and then get with the appropriate team members (especially for activities on the critical path) to help ensure proper progress of activities, accurate reporting, and a smooth handoff of dependencies to meet the project schedule.

One of the key outputs mentioned during the Monitor and Control Project Work process is "change requests." Change requests may include the following:

- Taking corrective action to resolve a problem.
- Taking preventative action to avoid a problem.
- Repairing a defect in a project component. (The action taken may be to repair or replace the component.)

5. Perform Integrated Change Control Process

The Perform Integrated Change Control process involves reviewing all change requests as well as approving and managing changes to the project deliverables, organizational process assets, scope, project documents, and the project management plan. The change process (like the risk management process) should be conducted early and often through the project life cycle.

Process Activities

This process includes, but is not limited to, the following change management activities:

- Ensuring a change management system is in place to review, analyze, and approve change requests in a timely manner (including a request form, log, and work order).

- Identifying the people authorized to request and approve project changes.

- Ensuring only approved changes are implemented.

- Managing and enforcing the change control process.

- Coordinating changes across the entire project. (for example, a proposed schedule change will often affect cost, risk, quality, and staffing.)

- Documenting and communicating the complete impact of change requests.

- Updating appropriate documents, deliverables, and activities based on approved changes.

Importance of Change Control (Be Stubborn on Change)

I love to use the quote "Change is inevitable, except from a vending machine" (unknown source) when teaching my PM classes—it is always good for a laugh (except in some countries where it is lost in translation). One of my students even gave me a placard with this quote on it, which I prominently display for all to see (in my home office).

Change happens, and as a project manager you can't "just say no." Instead, you must be willing to accept change because it is real—and sometimes it can even benefit the project, resolve regulatory requirements, or enhance the finished product (as long as the change is approved by the appropriate stakeholders/sponsors). Change control is best managed when you have a clearly defined process and an identified Change Control Board (CCB) with authorized decision makers to review and vote on requested changes.

This process focuses on first having an approved change process. The process involves the collection of change requests, logging and reviewing all change requests, analyzing the potential impact to the project, obtaining proper acceptance (or deferral/rejection) of the change, and last, making sure you document and communicate changes. Remember, change tends to have a ripple effect to the project deliverables, organizational process assets, project documents, and the project management plan itself.

Typically, there are two different types of changes:

- Changes that impact the project's constraints (and may increase cost, time, or scope).

- Daily operational changes, such as shift coverage, material adjustments, and so on, that may not impact the overall project's cost, schedule, or scope.

TIP

All changes should go through a change control system—especially anything that potentially impacts the project's scope, cost, or schedule. All changes must be reviewed and approved prior to implementation. In the real world, many project managers have a certain amount of authority in making daily change decisions without going through the full-blown change process. This can be risky, though—depending on the size, type, and complexity of the project; the criticality of the project; as well as the trust and confidence in the project team.

Change Control System

The best way to manage change is to establish a change control system (an electronic tool or database is recommended) to more easily document change requests, log and track the change requests, and document the response action to the requests. This system doesn't have to be elaborate or expensive; it can be simple and should include at least these three components:

- A request form (keep it simple—a one-page request form in the project team room)

- Tracking log with response (can be an ordinary spreadsheet)

- Work order (requirements, direction, response strategy, guidance, and back-out plan)

Response actions in the tracking log are typically one of the following:

- Accept

- Reject

- Defer (postpone)

TIP

The most important action for all changes is to document and communicate the response. The response action/status should go first to the requestor, then to the team so that everyone is crystal clear on the request and the response.

Also, in the change management process it is good to have categories or priorities of changes with an approved response time. Here's an example:

Urgency:

- **1 = Emergency change**   For example, one-to-four-hour fix required if something is broken and impacts a high number of users. This could be a system outage, down network, out-of-service train, and so on.

- **2= Normal change**   For example, three-to-five-day response time, with accepted solution or workaround (temporary fix).

It is also important to track the results of a change to determine whether or not it was successful. If it failed, how will the results be tracked and reported? (Usually, results are recorded in a standard template and reported weekly or at least monthly with action plans and future planned change activity.)

The only way to effectively manage change is to have a regularly scheduled change control meeting (usually weekly; the meeting can be cancelled if no change requests are submitted for the change review period). You should identify key representatives (authorized decision makers and SMEs) in the meeting to vote on the change requests and to identify potential risks or conflicts if changes are approved for implementation.

TIP

A single change may not pose a serious risk to the project; however, when coupled with or installed out of sequence with other changes, it could fail or cause other things to fail. Also, when unauthorized changes are forced into the system, they can catch you by surprise. If they are installed without going through the proper review and approval channels, this is a recipe for failure.

Try This Having a Crystal Ball: Fix It Before It Breaks

You are the PM on a software application development project and the IT manager (Bob) comes to you with a request for the installation of a new software product he just read about in a trade journal. Bob is so impressed with this product—the "Fix It Before It Breaks" (FIBIB) Wizard—that he wants it installed on 500 laptops before the end of next week.

The normal change process takes at least two weeks, but Bob, who has been a good friend and customer, is asking you to expedite the change because it will make him a hero with his end users (customers). What do you do? Take a few minutes to formulate your response and then look at the following answer.

(continued)

Answer: Politely sit down and say, "To ensure I get the request accurate, let's fill out the request form together. It will just take a few minutes, and it will give me the specifics to ensure we get this right. We will also need to discuss the level of urgency because the change will need to go through the emergency change process."

After reviewing the priority with Bob and questioning him on management approval, Bob decided not to submit the request. This was a good thing because it turned out he did not have approval from his manager to request the change and the software product requested was "beta" (still being tested and not yet available to the general public).

The moral of the story is

- Follow the change process, and

- Ask questions to fully understand the importance, level of sponsorship from management, and level of priority of all changes.

Perform Integrated Change Control Inputs, Tools and Techniques, and Outputs

The key inputs to this process are the project management plan and, of course, change requests. The tools and techniques are the people (expert judgment) and the change control meetings. Outputs are the status of the change request as well as updates to the project management plan and updates to other project documents.

Ask the Expert

Q: Who is responsible for turning out the lights and closing the door on a project?

A: The janitor, right? Well, that would be the PM. And, like a warranty period on a new product, a project should have a set time period for closing down, even after the lights are turned out and you think the doors are closed and locked. This period of time allows for any residual charges or delayed billings (invoices) that can come in after the project is complete. Time is needed to compile and report final performance and accomplishments to ensure assets and people have been officially transferred (to pay final utility bills, vendor services, and such).

The best way to effectively turn out the lights on a project and make sure you don't miss anything is to use a project "closeout" check list. A good input to this check list is the "startup" check list you used when you initiated the project (assuming you have one). Closing a project is like opening it in reverse—but the closing phase should be more complete because you will have identified things along the way that have been added or were missed during the startup phase.

6. Close Project or Phase Process

Closing down a project is as important as the startup/initiation phase. The closing phase should be handled as a project in itself and oftentimes is difficult because the team members are aware the project is going away and they want to focus on their next project. Most project teams start abandoning the ship toward the end of the project because no one wants to be the last person out the door. This attitude makes it more difficult to manage a project during the closing phase.

You'll have numerous important considerations to make during the closing phase of a project, and the following list represents only a sampling of those things. The actual list you use depends on the specifics of your project.

1. Determine the targeted project close date and develop a right-to-left plan schedule (back into the schedule by working from the must-finish-on "close" date).

2. Close out all open action items and develop action plans for any product deficiencies, open issues, and follow-up activities needed to satisfy the approved deliverables.

3. Create a project closure document and review it with the customer and team.

4. Conduct a final customer acceptance meeting and take meeting minutes (distribute and retain a copy of the minutes).

5. Obtain customer and management formal acceptance of the completed project (in writing, if possible) and retain the acceptance document for audit purposes.

6. Find homes (new assignments) for the project team members and project assets.

7. Conduct a Lessons Learned assessment meeting (include the customer). Note that you should be collecting lessons learned throughout the project, not just at closure.

8. Close out any financial accounts or accounting charge codes.

9. Assist as needed with any post-project delivery activities.

10. Assist purchasing and contract administrators in contract closeout.

11. Archive all project documents (ensure record retention complies with company and outside audit or regulatory agency requirements).

12. Celebrate success with the key stakeholders and project team.

A big dilemma during the closing phase is that there may be a mountain of documentation (paperwork) to go through, much of it old and outdated. So how do you handle this dilemma?

The answer is, get the team together for a casual dress day, get a large shredder and file boxes, and then carefully go through and organize the documents files and such (you don't want to throw away important papers and you don't want to keep old documents that have been replaced or updated with newer versions). This is where electronic storage media comes in handy because it is small and easy to store.

Try This Pass the Shredder: Closing the Project Is So Therapeutic

Doug is one of your lead project coordinators on a ten-month project. There were a number of problems on this project, and the team was pushed hard to complete on time and on budget—which they did. After the celebration lunch, you go back to your office feeling pretty good about the successful completion—and there is Doug shredding all the project documents. You stop him and ask, "What are you doing?" Doug smiles and replies that he is closing down the project by shredding the project documents, and that it feels very therapeutic. What do you do?

Take a minute to formulate your response and then look at the following answer.

Answer: You stop him immediately, collect all the documents from Doug, determine which were shredded, and try to recapture them from softcopy (or other sources) to ensure all key documents are retained for audit purposes. You inform Doug that the latest project documents must be stored in a safe place to ensure you meet record retention and other business control and audit requirements.

In my experience, closing the project is one phase that is often neglected. You should plan for closing the project at the beginning of the project. That is what project integration is all about—looking across the entire project (charter to close) and planning adequate time and resources for the all-important closing phase.

The biggest factor that may negatively impact the closing process is when the project was not clearly defined in the first place or may have experienced significant or uncontrolled changes. In many cases, the project was not truly a project to begin with (for example, on-going operations or programs). If your project seems to be never ending, you might want to go back to the basic definition of a project (definite end date) and see if it still meets the criteria.

The closing phase of projects is generally where the gap between noncertified PMs and certified PMPs is the widest. Our natural instincts tend to be to wrap up the project as it ends. Often we forget about the length of the runway needed to gracefully shut down the systems, close the financial accounting, conduct Lessons Learned meetings, make arrangements for record retention storage, and most importantly, obtain the "formal acceptance" (signoff from the sponsor or customer) of the closing phase of the project. Chapter 13 provides more details on effective project closure.

References

1. Wikipedia, http://en.wikipedia.org/wiki/Methodology

2. CVR/IT Consulting LLC, http://www.cvr-it.com/PM_Templates/

3. Project Charter Lite template from CVR/IT Consulting LLC

4. Bruce Tuckman's model on team development, http://www.infed.org/thinkers/tuckman.htm

5. Project Management Best Practices. Project Start-Up: The Project Kick-off Meeting, http://oa.mo.gov/itsd/cio/projectmgmt/PDF/Chapter4V3-1.pdf

Chapter 5

Project Scope Management

Key Skills & Concepts

- The importance of scope statements

- Taking meeting minutes to improve communications

- How to manage scope on your project

- Who owns and should provide project requirements

- The importance of clearly defined documented requirements

- The five scope management processes

- Scope creep and scope leap

- Creating a Work Breakdown Structure (WBS)

- Project completion criteria

As the project manager on a large project many years ago, I was conducting a kickoff meeting and presenting the scope statement to the team when the project executive (PE) sponsor spoke up and said, "Hold on! Scope is a mouthwash, and we don't talk about it to the customer!" He went on to say, "Whatever the customer wants, as long as they are willing to pay for it, they will get it." Knowing the importance of scope management, I cringed and had the feeling of being on a ship that was rolling on very high waves with no sign of land in sight.

My response to the PE was a bit abrupt when I stated, "Scope is not a mouthwash, and, yes, we do need to talk about it." The PE said, "If the customer is willing to pay, we will do whatever they ask." Because I didn't want to make a scene in front of the team, I chose to ease up and approach him later (one on one). When I spoke to him about the importance of scope management, he wouldn't budge. It was his customer and his project after all, and he had the final word. He was the boss, and the boss may not always be right, but the boss is always the boss, right?

The PE's decision made it painfully clear the scope of the project was going to be wide open. The next step was to take a deep breath and look at the potential impact to the project, the team, and the customer. For a brief moment, my gut was saying, "Update your résumé and move on!" However, project managers are not quitters. As a team we pulled together and performed an impact analysis based on the number of requests already received from the customer. Based on these results, I made the decision to seek out and obtain a temporary change management tool (database) and called a meeting to implement a control process to track the change requests.

In the change meeting, we introduced a very simple (three-step) change process to the PE, the customer, and the team. Everyone agreed the process was needed, and weekly meetings to review and approve changes would be implemented to help manage the process. We captured the minutes of the meeting, which included a list of attendees, details of the process, and formal approval to implement the change process. The minutes were communicated, distributed, and posted in an electronic team room folder, and the approved process was implemented immediately.

At first the change process was a little difficult for everyone to get used to, but all agreed that it was the right thing to do. Before long it became a habit.

As expected, the changes did flow, and at the end of the first three months of the project, we had 40 pages of requests in the tracking log. I called another meeting and raised the red flag as to the impact on the team, the delays caused by the high number of changes, and the additional cost in terms of person hours to keep track of all the change requests. The PE acknowledged the need for additional resources and brought in a full-time change control agent to manage the requests. That helped; however, the PM and project team were distracted with all the changes that continued to come in, and soon the project schedule slipped and costs soared.

At the end of six months the customer's chief financial officer (CFO) raised a big red flag to the chief executive officer (CEO) on the additional cost, which turned out to be 30-percent higher (several million dollars) than the original approved budget. The CEO called for an independent (external) audit. The project team was interviewed extensively by the auditors, and the change process and minutes of meetings were reviewed as well. The biggest saving grace was the fact that we had a documented and approved change control process that was being managed and enforced. Because of this finding, the auditors ruled in favor of the project team. As a result of the finding, the customer CEO made significant changes and set tighter controls over who could request and approve changes. The number of changes went down by over 60 percent, allowing the project support teams to focus on the planned activities of the project, and most everyone (except the managers creating all the changes) lived happily ever after.

We not only realized the importance of change and scope management, but also the importance of keeping meeting minutes. The minutes from the meeting introducing the change process saved the day!

TIP

To help ensure proper focus on and response to important documents such as minutes to meetings, I highly recommend using the following closing statement for meeting minutes and other important communications:

"If any information is misstated or omitted in this document, please reply with corrections or suggestions within seven business days. No response implies acceptance of this document as written."

Definition of Scope Management

Scope management involves the processes of defining and documenting all the work (and only the work) required to successfully complete the project. Scope is the essence of the project—it defines what the project is all about, the deliverables to be provided, and the foundation on which the team builds. Once the scope is defined for your project, it should be documented in a *project scope statement,* which is a narrative description of the objectives and purpose for the project as well as the specific business need or problem to be solved. The document should clearly state key contacts, key milestones (major events), the project target completion date, and so on. The next step is managing what is included and not included (exclusions) in the project scope statement. The last and most intensive part of scope management is the act of constantly checking to ensure all the work is being completed and managed effectively to ensure the integrity of the approved scope of the project.

What Are Project Deliverables?

Deliverables are tangible products (usually stated at a high level, such as milestones) that the project will produce. They describe what the customer or project sponsor will get at key intervals and when the project is complete. They also state exclusions, or what will not be included in the project. [1]

Table 5-1 provides some examples of project deliverables.

Ask the Expert

Q: What is the best way to manage scope on a project?

A: Once scope is verified, the best way to manage scope is through an agreed-upon, documented, communicated, and enforced change control process.

NOTE

Regular change control meetings (I recommend weekly) are essential to allow the PM and team to stay focused on scope, risk, and other key aspects of the project.

Includes:	Design of a new service.
	Specifications for a new automation.
	A feasibility study for a product or project.
	A customer-level procedures manual.
	A user's guide or training manual.
	A new voice response system for a call center.
	Installation of standard lighting and sound equipment for the concert event.
Excludes:	Implementation of the new service.
	Implementation of the feasibility study recommendations.
	The user's guide will not be available in other languages (English only).
	Training material will not be provided in printed form (electronic form only).
	Maintenance or on-going support of the new system.
	No "backline" equipment for the concert will be provided without advance reservations.

Table 5-1   Examples of Project Deliverables

Project Completion Criteria

Project completion criteria may be listed by project phase, by functional department, or as a milestone. The criteria should describe what will be created in terms of deliverables and their characteristics. It should also describe what will constitute a successful phase completion.

The scope statement should contain clearly expressed criteria for success, describing quantitatively what must be accomplished at the completion of the project. A good rule of thumb is to have four to seven (maybe more on a large project) concisely documented criteria presented in a "priority" list or table showing the expected results of the project.

Case Study: Sample Completion Criteria

Let's take a look at our case study for the Budweiser Events Center (BEC) and examine a concert to determine project completion criteria. We first look at the scope of the project and list out the items that, if done properly, will constitute a successful project.

The BEC-assigned event manager uses an Event Data Sheet (EDS) to document the details of the contract. Once completed, the EDS serves as the project plan. In this case the Event Data Sheet serves the same purpose of the project scope statement and outlines all the major support group activities that apply to the event. The EDS also outlines all

Priority	Criteria	Measure of Success	Owner
1	Conduct a safe and secure event.	No injuries and no incidents on premises or in parking lots.	Event Manager & Director of Operations
2	Meet or exceed financials.	Hit targeted box office and sponsorship sales and stay within approved budgets.	Director of Marketing
3	Provide excellent service as host to concert promoter and guests.	Client receives 8 or higher (on a 1–10 scale) on guest response surveys.	All staff
4	Meet or exceed facility and equipment objectives.	No performance interruptions due to equipment or facility failure, and quality sound and lighting effects.	Operations Manager
5	Meet or exceed concession and merchandise sales.	Concession and merchandise sales to meet per-capita targets.	Concession and Merchandise Manager

Table 5-2   Sample of BEC Project Completion Criteria

the work that must be done, when it should be done, and by whom (subproject owners are assigned to ensure accountability). As you can see in this case, a single document can serve many purposes.

The best way to document completion criteria is to look at the work to be done and then pick the top deliverables as measures of success. Review these with the customer and project sponsor and once approved they become your approved completion criteria. Table 5-2 provides sample project completion criteria for BEC.

Project Scope Management Processes

Five processes are included in the Project Scope Management knowledge area:

- **5.1: Collect requirements (Planning process group)**   The process of defining and documenting stakeholder needs to meet project objectives

- **5.2: Define scope (Planning process group)**   The process of developing a detailed description of the project and product of the project

- **5.3: Create WBS (Planning process group)**   Involves subdividing the project into smaller, more manageable components

- **5.4: Verify scope (Monitoring and Controlling process group)**   The process of formalizing acceptance of the complete project deliverables

- **5.5: Control scope (Monitoring and Controlling process group)**   Involves monitoring project status and product scope as well as managing changes to the approved scope baseline

These processes and the processes in other knowledge areas interact with each other and are interdependent.

It is also important to recognize the difference between project scope and product scope:

- Project scope is the work that needs to be accomplished to deliver a product, service, or result with approved specified features and functions.

- Product scope is the feature or function identified, designed, and approved for the product that the project is to produce.

TIP

The processes used to manage project scope vary based on the size, type, and complexity of the project and by the applications, tools, and techniques needed to produce the product, service, or result of the project.

1. Collect Requirements Process

This process is one of two new processes added to the fourth edition of the *PMBOK* in December 2008. In my opinion, this is one of the most important processes due to the impact on the project if not done properly.

One of the biggest reasons for project failure is incomplete or inaccurate requirements. The Collect Requirements process is one of 20 processes grouped with the Planning process group in the *PMBOK*. This means it should be performed during the planning phase.

Gathering requirements can be an art form in itself. Because of this and the importance of requirements to the success of the project, I will spend a fair amount of time on this process. Gathering and agreeing on requirements is fundamental; however, this does not necessarily imply that all requirements need to be fixed before any architecture and design are done, but it is important for the project team to understand what needs to be built.

The best place to start with the Collect Requirements process is to first look at the goals of the project. These goals represent planned outputs or results of what should be accomplished as a result of the project.

Collecting requirements should involve review and analysis of information and business/ organizational needs. What is it the company or group needs done, and what do they expect

Ask the Expert

Q: What is the best way to collect requirements?

A: The best way to collect meaningful requirements is through interviews. The trick is to get with the right people to interview. If you talk to the wrong people, you may get skewed, bogus, or varied information and expectations, which will waste time and money. Also, interviews help to establish relationships and show that you are willing to listen and learn and that you care about the people involved in the project.

How do you know you are interviewing the right people to gather requirements?

First, make sure you talking to the key sponsors, end users, or other stakeholders who have a vested interest in the project results. Next, make sure the people you interview are knowledgeable about the project and expected results. Once you have the input from key sponsors/stakeholders, you need to document, communicate, and most importantly validate the requirements.

Remember, there are many techniques for conducting interviews. One technique may work well on a given day with a specific person and may not work for someone else in another circumstance.

at the end of the project? The answer to these questions should be the cornerstone of the scope of the project. Requirements should match the scope, and the scope must map back to the project charter. (See a trend here?). By now you should be getting a better feel for how one process links to the next and more fully understand the importance and interdependency of the inputs and outputs of each process.

Interview Techniques for Gathering Requirements

Good interview techniques for gathering requirements are "all in the approach," and because projects and project managers are unique, the approach taken to collect requirements varies. To demonstrate this, I offer three distinctly different approaches and you can pick which works best for you:

- **Open approach**   This is where the PM and team have a high degree of trust and open communications, and the PM frequently allows time for checking and rechecking requirements to ensure they are clear and aligned with the deliverables of the project.

- **By the book**   This is where the PM may be a bit rigid in the way they collect requirements. They stick to the rule book (so to speak) and are somewhat resistant to change once the requirements are collected.

- **The "one-sided" interview** In this case, the interviewer maintains eye contact and will ask only a few open-ended questions. This is an unusual but effective technique and it does take some practice (unless you are the silent type already). This technique is rare and not recommended but, since I have seen it used a few times I wanted to make you aware of its existence.

Too often time is of the essence and we don't seem to do a good job interviewing people to learn about the details and expectations prior to initiating the project. It seems our interview tactic is more like this:

- **The impatient interviewer** The attitude of the impatient interviewer is, "Who has time for interviews anyway? We know what this project is about and what to deliver, so why waste the time interviewing stakeholders? Let's move forward; we can adjust later if we have to."

When we don't take the time to properly interview the people most knowledgeable about the project is when the PM and team get into trouble. It is best to take an open-minded approach and to learn about the project details for the best results.

TIP
Interview techniques tend to vary depending on the situation, how well you know the people involved, the location, and cultural considerations. For example, in Australia it is said that people don't care how much you know until they know how much you care, meaning Australians are wary of authority and of those who consider themselves "better" than others. According to the authors of *Kiss, Bow, or Shake Hands,* in conducting an interview, you should "be modest in interactions, and downplay your knowledge and expertise. Let your accomplishments speak for themselves."[2]

Another good alternative to collecting requirements is to form focus groups or facilitated workshops to obtain valuable opinions and input (more details on these methods will be covered later in this chapter).

Who Owns and Provides Requirements?
The project sponsor who is providing the funding and/or authorization to begin the project owns the requirements. This person is responsible for providing the requirements and expectations for the project. In some companies, the project sponsor is also called the "champion" or "requestor." No matter what name they go by, that person should clearly state what they want as the product, service, or result (for example, a 10-percent increase in revenue, an 8-percent reduction in cost, or 12-percent improved call center response time.)

Requirements Should Map to the Project Goals and Objectives

The business or organization's goals and objectives will dictate which requirements are important. Also, requirements are best divided into project requirements and product/or service requirements. The primary purpose for collecting requirements is to allow the project team to focus on what the project will deliver. The deliverables and the product, service, or result of the project must map back to the customer's business or organization's needs and expectations.

Business objectives can be described in two different ways:

- **Hard objectives**   Relate to the time, cost, and operational objectives (scope) of the product or process. Here are some examples:

  - Reduce event staffing expenses by 15 percent.

  - Reduce utility cost by 10 percent.

  - Reduce maintenance/operational expenses by $25,000 per year.

- **Soft Objectives**   Relate more to how the objectives are achieved, and may include attitude, behavior, expectations, and communications. Here are some examples:

  - Improve customer service by developing a unique way for all staff to address guests when they arrive.

  - Improve the timeliness and accuracy of the building changeover process through improved communications and active participation by the team.

  - Improve intercompany communication by discussing event requirements one month in advance with all departments.

Try This Dealing with Unusual Demands: The Customer Wants What?

The year is 1994 and a well-known musician has booked a date for a concert at a popular events center. His agent has provided a "rider" requirement in the contract to have five bowls of plain blue M&Ms available in the dressing room one hour prior to stage time. (This was before blue M&Ms were even available.) What do you do?

- **A.** Contact Mars Candy Company for a special order (although there's likely not enough time for this).

- **B.** Get out the spray paint. (But then how do you paint the little *m*'s back on?)

C. Tell the promoter blue M&Ms are not available.

D. Contact the promoter to see if an alternative color is acceptable.

Answer: D. You contact the promoter to verify the requirement, and she says she was just joking and any color will do. (By the way, blue M&Ms were introduced in 1995.)

There are many types of requirements, and most tie back to the needs of the business, opportunities to be capitalized on, problems to be solved, or help focus on improved quality. Most requirements are straightforward and easy to understand; however, two of the requirement types are worth more discussion: functional and nonfunctional requirements.

Functional vs. Nonfunctional Requirements

Identifying requirements can be like trying to nail Jell-O to a tree—it gets a little wiggly and the consistency tends to change with the weather. Let's look at functional and nonfunctional requirements.

Functional Requirements   Functional requirements are used to describe the capability of a product. They often describe characteristics that the product must have if it is to provide useful functionality for its operator (what the product will do). Functional requirements are typically stated in general, nonspecific terms. Here are some examples:

- The system will produce an updated easy-to-read report.
- The conference will educate suppliers on the product development process.
- The new data-retrieval unit will deliver data faster than the old one.
- The vacation will be at the seashore to provide warmth and relaxation.
- The new dog house will accommodate a full grown St. Bernard.

Nonfunctional (Technical) Requirements   Nonfunctional requirements tend to revolve around areas such as service levels, performance, safety, security, regulatory compliance, and supportability. Often nonfunctional requirements are referred to as "technical requirements" or "performance requirements" that focus on the properties or features the product of the project must have. They describe what the product needs to do so that it meets the functional requirements. Here are some examples:

- **Usability requirements (based on the intended user):**
  A newly trained call center service representative will be able to use the problem ticket tracking system, with nominal errors or assistance.
  The audio/visual equipment directions in the classroom will be easy to follow.

- **Performance requirements (how fast, big, accurate, safe, reliable, and so on):**
  The new dog house must be four feet high and have a 24-inch-wide door.
  The garment must be 100-percent waterproof during one hour of exposure to three inches of rainfall per hour.

Collect Requirements Inputs, Tools and Techniques, and Outputs

We'll now cover the inputs, tools and techniques, and outputs for the Collect Requirements process, as listed in Table 5-3.

NOTE

As a reminder, because all process inputs, tools and techniques, and outputs are shown in the *PMBOK*, I only discuss those that are new or have significant pertinence to the topics of discussion in this book. For a complete list of all processes and associated inputs, tools and techniques, and outputs refer to the *PMBOK Guide, Fourth Edition*.

Inputs   According to PMI, the two primary inputs for the Collect Requirements process are

- **Project charter**   Used to provide the high-level project requirements and high-level product description so more detailed requirements can be developed

- **Stakeholder register**   Used to identify stakeholders who have the skills needed to provide important information to help develop detailed product and project requirements

Inputs	Tools and Techniques	Outputs
Project charter	Interviews	Requirements documentation
Stakeholder registry	Focus groups	Requirements management plan
	Facilitated workshops	Requirements traceability matrix
	Group creativity techniques	

Table 5-3   Inputs, Tools and Techniques, and Outputs for the Collect Requirements Process

In the real world of project management, collecting requirements can occur at different times and may surface in different ways (casual conversations over coffee or lunch, in the hallway, during meetings, while reviewing processes, or as part of procedural documents). Therefore, it is important to listen more than talk during the requirements-gathering phase of the project. The information provided often becomes a valuable input and can be the difference between success and failure for the project.

Going back to the "Ready, fire, aim" dilemma, we need to make sure we know what and where the target is before we can ever hope to hit it. We must take the extra time to collect and verify project requirements (that is, we must aim before we fire).

Tools and Techniques   A number of tools and techniques are available to assist the PM and project team in collecting requirements:

- **Interviews**   As mentioned earlier in this chapter, there are many interviewing styles or techniques. Interviews provide a formal or informal way to collect information from stakeholders and are a great way to discover the "real" situation, the areas of concern, as well as what is working if the project is already underway.

- **Focus groups**   One form of interview is to form a focus group. This involves bringing together prequalified stakeholders or subject matter experts (people with similar and perhaps vested interest) in the project to learn their interests, preferences, concerns, and expectations from the project. For example, a company is planning to build a new fitness center in a particular location and wants to get input from the residents of the local community to see what they would like in the way of facilities, child care, pool (or no pool), tennis courts (indoor or outdoor), hours of operation, available classes, and so on.

- **Facilitated workshops**   These are sessions that bring a variety of people together to discuss options, help define product requirements, build trust/relationships on the project team, and most importantly improve communications. These workshops are sometimes called Quality Function Deployment (QFD) workshops, Joint Application Development (JAD) Design workshops, or Joint Application Requirements (JAR) Definition workshops.

- **Group creativity techniques**   One or more of the following group creativity techniques can be used to help collect requirements:

  - **Brainstorming**—A good way for a group to generate and collect many ideas (uses synergy, where one idea helps generate another).

  - **Nominal group technique**—Same as brainstorming, only a voting process is added to help rank the most useful ideas for further brainstorming.

- **Delphi technique**—Used to build a consensus of experts who participate anonymously. A request for information is sent to a select group of experts, their responses are compiled, and the results are sent back to the group for further review until consensus is reached.

- **Idea or mind mapping**—Ideas created through individual brainstorming are consolidated into single map to reflect the commonalities and differences in understanding to help generate new ideas.

- **Affinity diagram**—Allows large numbers of ideas to be sorted into groups for review and analysis.

- **Group decision-making techniques**—An assessment process with many alternatives to help prioritize requirements. Here are some of the methods in this process:

  - Majority: Support from more than 50 percent of the group.

  - Plurality: The largest block of the group decides, even if it's not a majority.

  - Unanimity: Everyone agrees on requirements or the course of action.

  - Dictatorship: One person makes the decision for the group.

- **Questionnaires and surveys**—A written set of questions designed to quickly collect information from a wider audience.

- **Observations**—Involves usability labs, job shadowing, or other types of viewing to collect needed information or requirements from end users.

- **Prototyping**—Involves putting the early release (prototype) product in the hands of the user to see how it works

Outputs

According to PMI, there are three outputs from the Collect Requirements process. The details of each are

- **Requirements documentation**   This details how requirements will meet the business need/opportunity or the solution to the problem the project is intended to address. The components of the requirements documentation include the following:

  - Acceptance criteria

  - Business need

  - Quality measurements and tracking

- Organizational impacts (for example, training and support)
- Assumptions and constraints
- **Requirements management plan**   Documents how requirements will be analyzed and managed throughout the project life cycle.
- **Requirements traceability matrix**   Typically a spreadsheet or table that shows requirements and the links to their source and traces them throughout the project life cycle.

Creating a traceability matrix helps ensure each requirement adds business value by linking it to the business and project objectives. Because requirements are so important to the Project Scope Management knowledge area, properly using a requirements traceability matrix can provide a structure for managing change to the product scope. The matrix can include the following:

- Requirements to business needs, opportunities, goals, and objectives
- Requirements to project objectives, project scope, and WBS deliverables
- Requirements to product design, development, and test strategy

Some of the attributes (components) captured in the traceability matrix include a unique identifier, a description of the requirement, the relationship to other requirements, as well as the owner, source, priority, version, and current status (for example, active, cancelled, deferred, added, approved, and date completed).

TIP

The *PMBOK Guide* refers to the requirements traceability matrix several times as both an output (of the Collect Requirements process) and input to two other processes (Verify Scope and Control Scope). Therefore, you are likely to see questions on the PMI exams related to this matrix.

Managing Requirements

Once the requirements are verified and approved, the job of managing the requirements should be focused—unless, of course, there is turnover in the project sponsors, team, project funding (budget), or overall expectations. There are times when a project has a long duration resulting in changes to the requirements or expected results. This is where the change control process is extremely important to combat scope creep or scope leap.

2. Define Scope Process

The Define Scope process involves the development of a detailed description of the project and the expected product, service, or result. This process is grouped with the Planning process group.

The scope definition may be an iterative (evolutionary) process, starting with a preliminary scope statement and growing in detail as the project progresses and more information is known. In fact, the approved scope definition is the baseline (point of reference) for the project and should not be taken lightly. Some project managers are a bit reluctant or shy about setting the project baseline for schedule, cost, or scope. If you are using Microsoft Project as a scheduling tool, the first question the application sometimes will ask when you save a file is, "Do you want to save this file as a baseline?" Unfortunately, the majority of the time we click No. Big mistake....

TIP

The quicker you establish an approved baseline, the easier it is to manage to that baseline. I have seen case after case where a customer complains the project is behind schedule, only to find there were many approved changes that moved out the target completion date and the PM didn't establish or update the baseline. The customer often only remembers the original target date, and so what if there were approved changes that moved the project end date? Because the PM didn't set the baseline, the customer viewed the original completion date as being missed.

Define Scope Inputs, Tools and Techniques, and Outputs

Note that the inputs to the Define Scope process (shown in Table 5-4) are the outputs of previous processes (shown previously in Table 5-3) and that the outputs for the Define Scope process become the inputs to the next process (Create WBS).

The inputs to the Define Scope process are similar to many of the processes in the *PMBOK*, except in this case the requirements documentation and project charter (which are outputs of previous processes) are key inputs to consider for this process.

Inputs	Tools and Techniques	Outputs
Project charter	Expert judgment	Project scope statement
Requirements documentation	Product analysis	Project document updates
Organizational process assets	Alternatives identification	
	Facilitated workshops	

Table 5-4 Inputs, Tools and Techniques, and Outputs for the Define Scope Process

The tools and techniques for the Define Scope process include expert judgment to help analyze the inputs. In this case, we should also take a closer look at the product analysis and any alternatives or workshop findings that should be considered prior to the scope statement being finalized.

The outputs for this process are straightforward. The primary output of the Define Scope process is the project scope statement. However, project management is all about realizing that as we go further into the project life cycle, we learn more. After almost every process comes more knowledge and a clearer view of what needs to be done on the project. With the clearer vision, it is important to review and update project documents as appropriate. This ties back to the PMI term *progressive elaboration,* which is a technique for increasing the accuracy of plan documents and estimates as more and more information becomes available.

NOTE

PMI is big on the concept of progressive elaboration as a way to effectively manage a project. If you are planning to take a PMI exam, take note of this concept.

Project Scope Statement

According to PMI, "The project scope statement describes, in detail, the project's deliverables and the work required to create these deliverables. The intent is to provide a common understanding of the project scope so there is no confusion between project stakeholders." [3]

The scope statement serves as a guide to the project manager and team during the execution of the project. It should be used as a "working document," not kept in a drawer or cabinet. It can be used for team member orientation to the project, to help answer questions, and for audits when they occur.

The project scope statement is also an agreement among the project team, the project sponsor, and key stakeholders. It represents a common understanding of the project for the purpose of facilitating communication among the stakeholders. The scope statement includes relating the project to business objectives, and defining the boundaries of the project in multiple dimensions including approach, deliverables, milestones, and budget.

The best way to develop a scope statement is to use a template from a previous, similar project or from an experienced PM source. A number of great templates are available on the Internet (for example: CVR/IT Consulting LLC at http://www.cvr-it.com/ PM_Templates/) to assist you in defining the scope of the project and ensuring you have the important components identified to render the scope statement useful in the scope management process.

Here are examples of some key components of a scope statement:

- **Executive summary**   A brief summary of the project using the project charter or work authorization as the basis for the summary
- **Business or project objectives (business need/opportunity)**   The purpose of the project
- **Project description**   What is in (and not in) the scope of the project
  - Proposed solution, deliverables, and completion criteria
  - Risks, constraints, dependencies, assumptions, and success factors
  - Roles and responsibilities (critical skills, high-level staffing plan)
  - Target date for completion
- **Project planned approach**   Methodology to be used and implementation strategy
- **Project estimates**   Duration, cost, resources, hours, and so on
- **Project controls**   How the project will be measured, tracked, and managed (change control, risk management, issue management, and communications)
- **Authorizations**   Project sponsor/owner, approvers, version control, and reviewers
- **Scope statement approval signatures**

TIP

In many cases the contract, work order, or statement of work (SOW) will have all the pertinent information needed to identify the project and its major deliverables, key contacts, and constraints, to the point where these documents may serve as (or replace the need for) a separate scope statement.

Case Study: Scope Statement

Let's look at our case study and how the scope of the project is defined and managed by BEC. They use a "Technical Data Sheet" sometimes called a "contract rider" that comes from the artist/performer/manager/agent. It is around 20 pages on average and details the requirements for the event, including dates, planned equipment needs, stage configuration, dressing rooms, and other special needs. These details are reviewed and, once accepted, are then put into the "Events Data Sheet," which serves many purposes, such as the all-in-one contract, scope statement, schedule of events, outline of special needs, and so on.

Figure 5-4, shown at the end of this chapter, provides an example of a scope statement for a "Rock On" concert event/project.

3. Create Work Breakdown Structure (WBS) Process

What is a WBS? The PMI answer is, it is a "deliverables-oriented" decomposition of the work to be performed on the project. In plain English, the WBS is a tool that helps the project team document the work (activities/tasks) needed to build or develop the identified and approved deliverables of the project.

The Create WBS process is located in the Planning process group and works best at the beginning of the project.

TIP

The WBS is a useful tool, and PMI views it as an important part of project planning and management. Therefore, you can expect a number of questions on the PMP exam regarding the WBS.

Here are some key points to remember about the WBS:

- It should be used on every project (and can be reused on similar projects).
- It identifies all the work of the project. (PMI feels that if the work is not in the WBS, it is not part of the project; therefore, you should view the WBS as the foundation of the project.)
- It shows the hierarchy of the project (groupings or categories).
- It is deliverables oriented (should be aligned and focused on project deliverables).
- It forces you and the team to look at all aspects of the project.
- It should *not* show dependencies (that comes later in the Project Time Management processes).

Creating the WBS

Creating a WBS is the act of subdividing (decomposing) the project into manageable chunks (or categories) of work, often called "work packages," to accomplish the defined and approved project deliverables. This is why the WBS is referred to as a "deliverables-oriented" hierarchical decomposition of the work to be performed on the project. It should be focused on and created around the project deliverables.

The WBS Work Package   The work package is considered to be the lowest level managed by the PM in the WBS. A work package may contain multiple activities. The benefit for the PM to manage at the work package level as opposed to the activity level is that they can better manage the summary work as packages. It requires less of the PM's time to manage at the work package level because many projects end up with hundreds if not thousands of activities. If you manage at the activity level, you are too deeply involved in the details to effectively manage the overall project. You also need to give the team members some credit and allow them to manage at the activity level and report status at the work package level.

At the work package level, it is also easier to schedule the work, assign owners, perform cost estimates, make duration estimates, and control the deliverables and phases throughout the life cycle of the project. Because the WBS is developed around deliverables, milestones, and progress, reporting is much simpler as well.

The WBS can be created and shown in a number of different ways:

- Using major deliverables of the project as the first level of decomposition

- Using project phases as the first level of decomposition, with product and project deliverables shown in subsequent (second and third) levels of the WBS

- As a listed WBS using a numbering system to show the relationship and hierarchy, as opposed to using a diagram view (which looks much like an organization chart)

- As a fishbone diagram, in the five process groups, as an outline, or other method

Example of a WBS and Work Packages

Figure 5-1 shows a high-level WBS with several work packages. Each work package can then be expanded later on by adding one or more activities.

Activities should be managed by the project team member assigned to a particular work package, and the project manager should focus on the status at the work package level (see Figure 5-2).

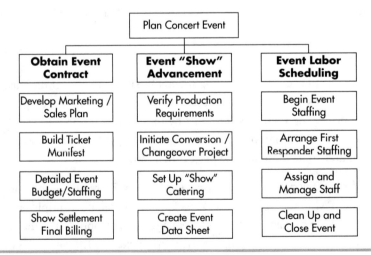

Figure 5-1   A WBS and work packages shown as a diagram

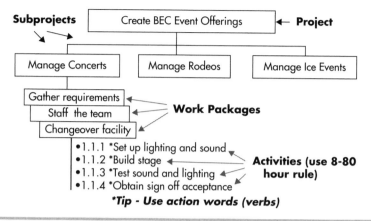

Figure 5-2 Sample WBS with activities

Many project management authors talk about the 8-to-80-hour rule (or simply the 80-hour rule), which states that work should be broken into activities or groups of activities that can be performed within 8 to 80 hours (which translates into one day minimum and not more than two weeks). This helps ensure work is grouped in a way that is easier to track, report, and manage. This heuristic method (rule of thumb) is simply a guide or recommendation to think about the work of the project in a way that allows you to group the work so that it is easy to assign, and easier to estimate duration and cost.

If an activity takes less than eight hours, it is being tracked to a level far too granular for the PM and perhaps even the team member responsible for the work. If it takes more than 80 hours, it will span a longer duration and potentially slip through the cracks if not tracked more closely (and therefore is not being monitored and managed in a responsive timeframe).

NOTE
Keep in mind the 80-hour rule is just a "rule of thumb" recommendation; if the activities take more than 80 hours or less than 8 hours, then use logic and assign the realistic estimated time needed and disregard this rule.

Creating the WBS Should Be a Team Sport
The best way to create the WBS is to get the team together and brainstorm using sticky notes, preferably placed on flip chart paper (you can tape several pages together if you need a larger space). This also makes the work portable as you can roll up the charts and take them with you.

Start with the deliverables from the scope statement, project charter, and/or contract. After the deliverables are listed, continue the brainstorming session to identify the work (activities) of the project for each of the deliverables. Group them in a logical order that will help you and the team better manage the work of the project. You can group by product, by project phase, or by function (for example, design, develop, test, implement, and project closure). If you are working on a construction project, you could create the WBS by stage, such as pour the foundation, frame the structure, install the plumbing, install the electrical, finish the trim, and so on.

The good news is, there is no set rule on how you create a WBS. The only recommendation is that you create it in a way that makes sense and works best for you and the project team.

Have Some Fun Creating the WBS

The process of creating the WBS can be fun and a great way to get to know the team in a relaxed environment.

One time on a project for a Fortune 50 company in Cincinnati, Ohio, we initiated the Create WBS process in a customer's home on his dining room wall. The day the contract was signed, several of the project team leads met for dinner and afterward went back to the host's home and created a WBS by filling his dining room wall with sticky notes. We even used different colors for the different key areas of the project. We had a good time and were able to get a great start on the project. We then captured the work from the dining room wall into a well-known scheduling tool (application software) for portability and for future updates.

Next, we showed the preliminary WBS to the team and rolled the work packages into the scheduling tool. We then worked the project from the scheduling tool. As a last step, we assigned the work packages and deliverables to the appropriate team leads and key subject matter experts. They agreed to add the activities to the work packages, track to the detailed activity level, and report to the PM weekly at the work package level.

Another WBS Story: Butterflies on the Floor

Several years ago, I was called in to help jumpstart a project in southern California. The lead project manager and I agreed the best way to start this project was by creating the WBS. We used sticky notes to identify the activities (work packages) needed on a new Strategic Outsourcing (SO) contract. We worked for about nine hours the first day and filled his office wall with the sticky notes and used a numbering system to identify the activities and deliverables. When we were at a good stopping place, we called it a day.

The next morning when we arrived, we found the sticky notes were all lying on the floor. As it turned out the paint on the office wall was old and the sticky part of the sticky notes was unable to hold. There was our work from the day before resting like butterflies on the floor. I could envision the notes slowly releasing in the night one by one and drifting to the floor. The only thing that saved us was the numbers on the notes, which allowed us to reconstruct the WBS in about an hour (this time, however, we used taped-together sheets of flip chart paper, so we could roll everything up and take it with us at the end of each day).

TIP

It is best to put the results of the Create WBS process into a scheduling tool or some other digital media prior to going home to ensure you don't lose the work. I have seen cases where the WBS was created on a white board or on a conference room wall and the cleaning people erased it that night (or in one case, they cleared the wall of sticky notes ... ouch!).

WBS Dictionary

The WBS dictionary is an output of the Create WBS process. Just as you would think, a WBS dictionary is a document generated by this process that supports the WBS. The dictionary provides a more detailed description of the activities in the WBS. It provides a clear description of the work to be done for each WBS work package and helps make sure the resulting work better matches what is needed. Therefore, the project manager uses this tool to prevent scope creep. Here are some of the components that can be built into the WBS dictionary:

- Number identifier and related control account (for tracking and cost)
- Work package description
- Resources assigned (who is responsible for doing the work)
- Deliverables for the work in the work package
- Assumptions, interdependencies, and expected duration
- Schedule milestones (major events)
- Due date and approved by signature field

The WBS dictionary includes work packages and control accounts. It can include account codes (numbering system or a chart of accounts) that identify work packages and a detailed description of the work; in some cases it even identifies the responsible organization, even though that component usually falls into the Organization Breakdown Structure (OBS). It may also have a list of schedule milestones, quality requirements, and technical references along with key contact information as it relates to the WBS.

Figure 5-3 shows the WBS dictionary relationship to the WBS.

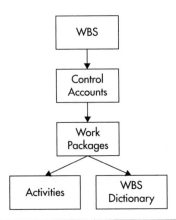

Figure 5-3 WBS dictionary relationship to the WBS

It has been my experience that the real-world applicability of the WBS dictionary is that it is used more often on larger, more complex projects with many different applications and the need for more detail at the work package level. However, the WBS dictionary can be used on projects of all sizes. According to *PMP Exam Prep, Sixth Edition,* by Rita Mulcahy, "It can be used as part of a work authorization system to inform team members of when their work package is going to start, schedule milestones and other information. It can then be used to control what work is done when, to prevent scope creep and increase understanding of the effort for each work package. The WBS dictionary helps the project by putting boundaries on what is included in the work package [and what is not]."[4]

4. Verify Scope Process

The Verify Scope process focuses on formalizing acceptance of the completed project deliverables. One important aspect is verification, which includes reviewing the scope and deliverables of the project with the customer or sponsor to ensure they are in agreement with what needs to be completed at the end of the project. PMI is really big on formal acceptance (and you should be, too). In many cases project completion letters are obtained with signed acceptance by the customer to show that they agree the project is officially ended and all deliverables have been met.

Once the scope is clearly defined, it is up to the project manager and team to verify it to ensure everyone is fully aware of the content. Scope verification is the process of comparing the work against the project management plan, the project scope statement,

Ask the Expert

Q: Everyone on our project team knows the scope of the project, so why do I need to bother with scope verification and formal signoff from the customer?

A: If the scope is clearly understood, then getting verification and signoff from the customer or sponsor should be easy. However, with the dynamics of most projects, there frequently are deliverables that were not clearly understood or communicated to the project manager. There may also be subprojects or activities that the customer is expecting from you that were not part of the original scope. These sometimes surface only when you ask for formal signoff or verification from the customer or project sponsor.

  The best way to approach the customer/sponsor to obtain scope verification is to set up a meeting when no one is rushed for time and in a comfortable location with minimal distractions. Be sure to have a concise project scope statement and report showing the status of the deliverables. It is also best to provide a signature and date line on the scope document. If you have done your homework, the customer should not raise any concerns and will be more than happy to sign off on the scope of the project. Note that you should retain this verification document to meet your company record retention or audit readiness requirements.

and the WBS, and then meeting with the customer and/or project sponsor to obtain formal acceptance of the scope. You would be surprised how often this step is not performed.

  Often we are either too embarrassed to ask for confirmation (it will make us look like we were not listening) or too busy to stop and confirm the scope of the project. Then if you add in changing or unrealistic customer expectations, it makes for a moving target. The result is a failed project due to unclear or unverified scope. We end up building the wrong product or the right product with the wrong features.

Verify Scope Inputs, Tools and Techniques, and Outputs

Table 5-5 lists the inputs, tools and techniques, and outputs for the Verify Scope process. Also note that the single tool and technique for this process is inspection. This is a simple word that can require significant time and resources, depending on the number of documents that need to be reviewed and verified prior to finalizing the list of accepted deliverables.

  The outputs are clear and extremely important, because if there is confusion, incomplete results, or poor documentation, you are wide open for scrutiny. The primary output is accepted deliverables. The best approach for this is to be organized and keep copious records

Inputs	Tools and Techniques	Outputs
Project management plan	Inspection	Accepted deliverables
Requirements documentation		Change requests
Requirements traceability matrix		Project document updates
Validated deliverables		

Table 5-5   Inputs, Tools and Techniques, and Outputs for the Verify Scope Process

on the status and acceptance of each of the deliverables and phase signoffs throughout the project. This is something you should do throughout the project life cycle, not just at the end of the project.

TIP

The PMP exam focuses more on situations rather than definitions and may describe a situation that relates to scope verification without actually using the term. With this in mind, it is a good idea to be familiar with alternative phrases that potentially describe scope verification—for example, conducting inspections, reviews, and audits; determining whether results or work products are completed according to (or conforming to) approved requirements; and gaining formal signoff.

It is also important to note that scope verification is a close cousin to quality control. The only real difference is that quality control tends to be more product specific, whereas scope verification is at the overall project scope level. There is a huge risk in not being able to successfully close the project if the Verify Scope process is not formally accepted—not to mention that you will likely miss the target unless you are clear on the scope and deliverables of the project (don't wait until near the end of the project and find out you missed the target).

5. Control Scope Process

The only way to effectively control a project is to control the scope of the project; these go hand-in-glove (you can't have one without the other). The Control Scope process is accomplished by monitoring the status of the project and product scope and then setting a baseline to measure against and manage to throughout the project phases. It involves constantly looking at the impact of changes to the scope of the project. As a project manager you need to be very proactive in controlling project scope.

The Control Scope process is grouped with the Monitoring and Controlling process group. If done properly this process helps ensure effective control of the project scope.

This is accomplished by managing all requested changes and taking or making recommended corrective or even preventative action as needed to keep the project scope aligned.

The project manager needs to focus on several key activities during this process. The best way to effectively manage and control scope is to make it part of the discussion and put it on the agenda during meetings and processes associated with the following focus areas:

- Steering committee meetings

- Monthly status reports

- Risk management

- Issue management

- Change management

- Communication management

Here's a sample communication plan for presenting scope management status:

1. The project manager presents the project scope status to the project owner on a weekly basis.

2. Ad-hoc meetings are conducted at the PM's discretion as issues or change control items arise.

3. The project manager provides a written status report to the project owner on a monthly basis and distributes the project team meeting minutes.

4. The project owner will be notified via e-mail on all urgent issues. Issue notification will include time constraints and impacts, which will identify the urgency of the request.

5. The project team will have weekly update/status meetings to review completed tasks and determine current work priorities. Minutes will be produced from all meetings.

6. The project manager will provide the project sponsors with project team meeting minutes and steering committee status reports.

Another consideration is to establish a project website (or team room) to provide access to the project documentation by anyone including geographically dispersed project members. Additional details on communications are covered in Chapter 10 of this book.

What Is Scope Creep?

If you have been around project management for even a short time, you have surely heard the term "scope creep." Scope creep is a seemingly silly yet frightening phrase that can turn the project manager's world upside down. This is when the scope of the project takes on a different size, shape, or complexity over time and requires changes in scope, schedule, or cost on the project.

Scope creep is often a result of uncontrolled change and in today's world, scope creep tends to grow quickly into "scope leap," which is the big brother of change on a project. Scope leap occurs when the final product, service, or result is significantly different from how it started out in the original scope. This is why clear project definition and effective change management are needed to manage scope on the project. Wikipedia.com offers the following definition of scope creep:

> "Scope creep (also called focus creep, requirement creep, feature creep, and sometimes kitchen sink syndrome) in project management refers to uncontrolled changes in a project's scope. This phenomenon can occur when the scope of a project is not properly defined, documented, or controlled. It is generally considered a negative occurrence that is to be avoided. Typically, the scope increase consists of either new products or new features to already approved product designs, without corresponding increases in resources, schedule, or budget. As a result, the project team risks drifting away from its original purpose and scope into unplanned additions. [...] Thus, scope creep can result in a project team overrunning its original budget and schedule."[5]

If, through change control, the budget and/or schedule are adjusted (up or down) along with the scope, the change is usually considered an acceptable change to the project, and the term "scope creep" is not used.

Scope creep can be a result of the following:

- Poor change management or scope control (or both)
- Lack of proper identification of what is required to meet project objectives
- Weak project management discipline or weak executive sponsorship
- Poor communication between the project's PM, sponsor, and other stakeholders

Scope creep is a very common risk in most projects, is difficult to overcome, and remains a difficult challenge for even the most experienced project managers.

How to Prevent Scope Creep (or Scope Leap)

The best way to prevent scope creep is to start with a clearly defined scope statement and have formal change control, as mentioned earlier. However, controlling scope creep is easier said than done. Change happens; projects are dynamic in nature and don't just stand still over the course of the project. Many PMs equate the attempt to manage scope much like trying to herd cats in an open field.

"Managing scope creep is one of the more difficult parts of a Project Manager's job, but solid documentation, clear communication and detailed information will minimize any risk to the project and the client relationship. When in doubt, draw on the expertise of your team to determine a few options your client can choose from. In the end, this will help ensure your projects are delivered on budget and on time." [6]

How Do You Identify Scope Creep?   In order to identity scope creep, a project manager must be able to prove that a given item falls outside the original agreement. The best way to do this is to reference the project plan, project charter, statement of work, or other similar documentation. This means project documentation needs to define the work effort of an initiative or deliverable in a very precise manner. More importantly, exclusions and assumptions will also support the identification of scope creep by clearly spelling out any items that are considered additional work (out of scope).[7]

What Do You Do When Scope Creep Occurs?   When you are confident that the client or project team has requested a change that is out of scope, it's important to immediately raise the flag by documenting the change and initiating the change process. This sends a message and sets expectations that the change must be handled as an out-of-scope change request.

As part of the documentation, you should clearly state the reason the request is out of scope and what the impact might be to the project if you move forward with the change. Note that the specific impact may require further evaluation and it could be costly to perform this analysis; therefore, as part of the change process, the client must agree to the additional time and cost to review and respond to the change request even if the change is not approved at the end of the review.

Ideally, you want to be able to go back to the requester and clearly articulate the impact of the requested change. You may also want to look at alternative solutions that might yield the same benefits with lower cost or schedule impact to the project. Another approach is to recommend a postponement of the requested change to a later date or phase of the project to allow you to stay focused on the deliverables and schedule at hand. Regardless of the solution, be very clear, and work with your team and customer to come to agreement on the solution. Then document the outcome in the change log and communicate the results to the team.

Seven Steps for Avoiding Scope Creep

Scope creep can originate from several sources and is a leading cause of project failure when handled poorly. You must take measures to control project embellishment and to ensure that you and your team don't fall victim to its unsavory results—deadline delay and budget shortage.

Controlling the scope of your project begins before the first line of code is written (or the first design document begins). Each development effort should have a corresponding project plan or project agreement, regardless of the situation. Even if you're just one developer trying to make the boss happy, you'll benefit greatly from documenting your efforts before you begin them. Use the following guidelines (from "Seven steps for avoiding scope creep" by Shelley Doll) to set yourself up to successfully control the scope of your project:

1. Thoroughly understand the project vision, objectives, and stakeholder expectations. Meet with the project sponsor and provide an overview of the project as a whole for their review and approval.

2. Understand project priorities. Make an ordered list for review throughout the project life cycle. Items should include budget, deliverables, target milestone dates, and completion date. Quality metrics (for example, features, functions, customer satisfaction measurement, and employee/team satisfaction) should also be used to determine priorities.

3. Define the deliverables with the project team. Deliverables should be descriptions of functionality and specific features of the product(s) to be completed during the project.

4. Break the approved deliverables into actual work requirements. The requirements should be as detailed as necessary and can be completed using a simple spreadsheet.

5. Break the project down into major and minor milestones. Whatever your method for determining activity duration, leave room for contingency, especially when working with an unfamiliar staff. If your schedule is tight, reevaluate your deliverables.

6. Once a schedule has been created, assign resources and determine your critical path. Your critical path may change over the course of your project, so it's important to

evaluate and reevaluate it fairly often. Manage the critical path to determine which deliverables must be completed on time (more details will be provided in Chapter 6).

7. Expect that there will be scope creep. Implement "change order" (request) forms early and educate the project stakeholders on the change process. A change order form will allow you to perform a cost-benefit analysis before scheduling changes.

"If you can perform all of these steps immediately, great, however, even if you start with just a few, any that you're able to implement will bring you that much closer to avoiding and controlling scope creep. That way, you are in a better position to control your project, instead of your project controlling you."[7]

TIP
There is a strong connection between scope control and integrated change control covered in Chapter 4. Also, keep in mind there are many types of changes and they tend to come from many different (and seemingly innocent) sources. The best bet is to run all changes through the change control process using the steps shown in the next section on change management. The change procedures, if used properly, will take out a lot of the emotion and personal decision making, putting final decisions in the hands of the change review board.

Additional Information on Change Management

The change management procedures (listed here) should be followed and should be consistent with your project management methodology and overall project integrated change control process:

1. A change request log should be established early to track all changes associated with the project effort.

2. All change requests should be assessed to determine possible alternatives and costs.

3. Change requests will be reviewed and approved by the project owner.

4. The effects of approved change requests on the scope and schedule of the project will be reflected in updates to the project plan.

5. The change request log will be updated to reflect the current status of change requests.

The best way to ensure formal change control procedures are enforced is to establish a Change Control Board (CCB).

Change Control Board

The CCB should be a mixed panel of organizational and project representatives and works best if it is made up of a small group of decision makers with appropriate authorization to approve change requests that can impact the overall project. It is also best if you have an odd number of CCB members because occasionally you will need a tie breaker to move forward on certain changes.

PMI defines a CCB as "a formally constituted group of stakeholders responsible for reviewing, evaluating, approving, delaying, or rejecting changes to a project, with all decisions and recommendations being recorded." [8]

The Importance of Solid Project Scope Management

Like the saying goes, "When it's right, you know it," and when you have a clearly defined and approved scope for your project, you know it and are more likely to hit the target. Managing scope effectively on your project is like getting a strike in the game of bowling—the points add up a lot quicker. I can't emphasize enough the importance of having clearly defined, documented and approved scope statement, completion criteria, and solid management of the scope of your project to increase your chances of success.

SAMPLE PROJECT SCOPE STATEMENT

Note: Any work not explicitly included in the *Project Scope Statement* is implicitly excluded.

Project Name:	Rock On Concert, featuring Suzy B. Singer	
Project Manager:	Mr. Rocky Road	

Version History (*insert rows as needed*):

Version	Date (MM/DD/YYYY)	Comments
1.0	6/1/2009	First draft completed and sent for review
1.1	6/7/2009	Review completed by Director of Events (Shane C.)

1. Executive Summary

The purpose of this project is to promote Suzy B. Singer, a national artist with outstanding rock music and crowd-pleasing entertainment, to the northern Colorado region. Ms. Singer has risen to new heights in the "Rock On" world of music, continues to draw "full-house" crowds, and will be a great addition to the BEC event schedule.

2. Business Objectives (Product and Project)

2.1 Product Description (Solution)

To provide a safe and exciting concert that will promote Rock On music to a broader audience and promote the BEC as a convenient and memorable entertainment venue for events of all types. This project will also produce a revenue-generating opportunity to assist in the annual operating budget.

2.1 Business / Project Objectives

To provide quality entertainment and sell the BEC to 100% capacity and showcase the facilities at The Ranch to attract repeat business by those attending. Also to provide excellent and efficient staffing and service as the host venue to the concert promoter and artist.

- Provide a unique, rock music genre quality oriented experience.
- Honor rock music genre heritage of Northern Colorado.
- Promote a sense of community (increase awareness of the BEC facility for future events).
- Conduct a safe, secure and comfortable environment (0 injuries and 0 incidents).

Additional details are available on the BEC website at http://www.budweisereventscenter.com/.

Figure 5-4 Sample Scope Statement for BEC Concert Event (*continued*)

3. Project Description

Rock On Concert Event

3.1 Project Scope

Includes:

Facilities, security, box office and merchandise sales, audio and lighting, fire and ambulance support

Does Not Include:

Transportation for the band, hotels, or "backline" (band-provided music gear and equipment)

3.2 External Dependencies

- Media partners (newspaper, television and radio), police officers, medical staff, and fire marshal
- Contracted staff for event security, parking attendants, stagehand labor, and post-event cleanup
- Production equipment vendors, concessions volunteers, and subcontracted concessions vendors

3.3 Assumptions/Constraints

All advancing to be initiated three weeks prior to the event start date of 7/3/2009 (right-to-left planning)

4. Project Milestones

4.1 Estimated Schedule

Project Milestone	Target Date (MM/DD/YYYY)
• Public advancement of the concert (no later than three weeks from event day)	6/12/2009
• Ticket "on-sale"	6/15/2009
• Advertisement/marketing campaign	6/15/2009
• Staffing, scheduling, event details planning, building conversion, and setup	6/19/2009
• Event day activities and closing/cleanup	7/3/2009

5. Project Approach

A phased approach is used to break the project into more manageable categories.

5.1 Primary Plans

The Event Data Sheet and marketing plan will serve as the primary plan documents to direct this project. The Advancing document (rider) from the artist serves as the project scope and deliverables document.

Figure 5-4 Sample Scope Statement for BEC Concert Event

5.2 Scheduled Meetings

Three weeks prior to the event, the event manager will lead a meeting with all building staff. This weekly meeting will provide all advanced information from the band, as well as all instructions on building requirements and setup for the concert. Review meetings will be held weekly for clear communications.

5.3 Status Reports

The primary status report and plans for BEC is the Event Data Sheet (EDS). This document provides very specific details regarding the particular concert, including show timeline, key contacts for each department, arena setup, power requirements, etc. Updated EDS to be reviewed in weekly status meetings.

5.4 Issue Management

Issues will be addressed as needed:

- Project-related issues will be tracked, prioritized, assigned, resolved, and communicated in accordance with the BEC event management process.
- Issue descriptions, owners, resolution, and status will be maintained in an issues log.
- Issues will be addressed with event manager and communicated in the weekly status report.

5.5 Change Management

The change control procedures to be followed will be consistent with the project management methodology and consist of the following processes:

- A change request log will be used by the event manager to track and manage changes.
- Change requests will be reviewed and approved by the event manager and the EDC updated to reflect changes.

5.6 Communication Management

The following strategies have been established to promote effective communications:

- The event team will have weekly update/status meetings to review completed tasks and determine current work priorities. Minutes will be produced from all meetings.
- The event director will provide a status report to the project sponsors on a monthly basis.

6. Project Scope Statement Approval / Signatures

Project Name:	Rock On Concert Event
Event Director:	Shane C.

I have reviewed the information contained in this Project Scope Statement and agree:

Name	Role	Signature	Date
Suzy B. Singer	Client / Artist		6/7/2009
Shane C.	Event Director		6/7/2009

Figure 5-4   Sample Scope Statement for BEC Concert Event

References

1. Evans, Gary. "Project Description—Scope Statement Template Instructions," CVR/IT Consulting LLC, section 3.1–3.3, page 4.

2. Morrison, Terri, Wayne A. Conaway, and George A. Borden, Ph.D. *Kiss, Bow, or Shake Hands* (Adams Media Corporation: Avon, MA), 1994.

3. *A Guide to the Project Management Body of Knowledge (PMBOK® Guide), Fourth Edition,* (PMI – Project Management Institute Global Standard: Newtown Square, PA), 2008, page 115.

4. Mulcahy, Rita. *PMP Exam Prep, Sixth Edition* (RMC Publications, Inc.), April 2009, page 165.

5. Wikipedia, http://en.wikipedia.org/wiki/Scope_creep.

6. Lijoi, Gina. "How to Manage Scope Creep," http://www.pmhut.com/how-to-manage-scope-creep.

7. Doll, Shelley. "Seven steps for avoiding scope creep," http://articles.techrepublic.com .com/5100-10878_11-1045555.html.

8. *A Guide to the Project Management Body of Knowledge (PMBOK® Guide), Fourth Edition,* (PMI – Project Management Institute Global Standard: Newtown Square, PA), 2008, page 420.

Chapter 6

Project Time Management

Key Skills & Concepts

- The true measure of success on a project

- The importance of time/schedule management

- The six time-management processes

- Managing the schedule (setting a baseline)

- The impact of constraints on a project

- Forward pass, backward pass, and float

- How to find the critical path (CP)

- Precedence diagramming method (PDM)

- Activity-on-arrow (AOA) network diagram

- Types of dependencies and relationships

- Types of reports and charts (PERT and Gantt)

When you read project management trade journals, magazines, and books, one true measure of success that's often discussed is bringing the project in "on time." The other measure of project success, as you may have guessed, is being "on budget" (a topic that's covered in Chapter 7). These two areas (time and cost) are tightly linked and are the primary constraints (or challenges) project managers encounter on a day-to-day basis.

It has also been said that the highest source of conflict on a project is the schedule. More projects miss their target schedule dates than anyone would like to admit. The misses are often due to changes to scope or deliverables that affect the project's scheduled completion date.

Time management, in a broad sense, involves both planning and execution. Time, unlike money, once spent, is gone and cannot be earned back. That is what makes time management an important knowledge area. The bad news is, there is no universally agreed-upon way to manage time. How time is managed and how activities are prioritized depend on the individual project manager. The good news is, there are some standard processes (discussed in this chapter) that, if followed, can help in this area.

To effectively manage time on a project, it is recommended that you use a time management (TM) system. A TM system is a designed combination of processes, tools, and techniques that allow the project manager and team to identify, analyze, sequence, and estimate the duration for all project activities. One of the important components is a network diagram. A network diagram can be created in a number of ways, as we will discuss later in this chapter. The important thing to remember is that the tool, type, and format you choose should make sense to you and the team and must help you with managing the schedule. Too often we try to fit the process to the tool. The tool you use must work for you, not against you.

Time Management System

A TM system usually includes a resource calendar, resource assignment matrix (RAM), and a network diagram to help identify the overall duration and critical path activities of the project (all of these components are discussed in detail throughout this chapter).

Time management as a knowledge area involves a significant number of concepts, tools and techniques, and methods that challenge even the more experienced PMs. This chapter is designed with both the beginner and the experienced PM in mind and will address real-world project management and tips to help if you are planning to pursue PMP certification.

TIP
For readers not planning to pursue PMI's PMP or PMI-SP (Scheduling Professional) exam in the near future, I recommend you scan this chapter as a high-level overview and not for detailed comprehension. You can always come back to this chapter later when you are ready to prepare for PM certification. The good news is, many of the calculations for time management are performed by today's high-tech PM software tools; however, it is still important to learn the concepts.

A couple of things to remember in time management: First, it is a team sport. Second, five of the six time-management processes are planning processes. (Remember that PMI is big on planning—20 of the 42 processes in the *PMBOK* are in the Planning process group.)

Managing the Schedule

To give you an idea of the potential size and breadth of schedule management, consider that PMI has a separate independent credential (with its own exam) called Scheduling Professional (PMI-SP) that focuses on developing and maintaining project schedules.

Even though there is a separate PMI credential for schedule management, don't be confused between time management and schedule management. The two go hand in hand—you can't have one without the other. They are synonymous in the eyes of PMI.

This chapter is about more than how to manage time on your project. It is all about how to manage the project schedule to bring your project in on time. What is the difference, you might ask? Most people think of time management as how to get better organized so they have more time in their day to do other things—how to focus on the "A-list" of to-dos and not get distracted by the small stuff that tends to eat up every spare moment. I submit to you that time management is about learning how to better manage the schedule of events and activities on your project.

Managing the schedule involves getting focused on the importance of supply-and-demand concepts. It is about making sure we have everything we need—resources, people, tools, materials—to get the job rolling and keep it rolling to bring the project in on time.

Project Time Management Processes

You have probably heard the saying "time is money." This saying is especially true when you are managing a project. Project time management is the area that is least understood by many project managers and most often missed (underestimated) when it comes time to manage the schedule.

Time management, as a key knowledge area, includes six processes that center around effectively managing the project's work packages and activities (the actual work of the project). The ultimate goal is to bring the project to successful completion on time according to the approved delivery date. One thing that makes time management difficult is that time is constantly moving, and like the many dynamics we face on our projects, the milestones and target dates can be moving targets.

Here are the six processes of the Project Time Management knowledge area:

- **6.1: Define activities (Planning process group)** This involves identifying specific activities needed to produce the approved project deliverables.

- **6.2: Sequence activities (Planning process group)** This involves identifying and documenting relationships (for example, predecessor and successor) between the project activities.

- **6.3: Estimate activity resources (Planning process group)** This involves estimating the type and quantities of material, people, equipment, or supplies needed to perform each activity.

- **6.4: Estimate activity durations (Planning process group)**   This involves approximating the number of work periods needed to complete individual activities with the estimated number of resources available.

- **6.5: Develop schedule (Planning process group)**   This involves analyzing the activity sequences, durations, resource requirements, and schedule constraints to create the project schedule.

- **6.6: Control schedule (Monitoring and Controlling process group)**   This is the process of monitoring the progress of the project to update status and manage changes to the schedule baseline.

This knowledge area has a significant number of inputs, tools and techniques, and outputs, and they are best shown as they appear in the *PMBOK* (in Figure 6-1 on page 131). In this chapter I show a few tables as they relate to the key processes in the time management knowledge area; however, I do not intend to duplicate the many detailed charts in the *PMBOK*.

TIP

PMP exam takers find time management one of the more difficult knowledge areas. The reason is usually lack of experience creating, planning, and executing network diagrams, including understanding the forward and backward pass, calculating float, and identifying activities on the critical path. We tend to rely on software tools to do the calculations for us. Well, it is time to smell the coffee because there are a few things you need to know before you take the PMI exam. Read on....

No matter the size or type of project, the one constant seems to be "time is of the essence." The feeling seems to be—especially in today's environment—to "get it done fast." After all, the faster we get the project completed, the less it will cost. Between our lack of patience, the ever-pressing concern of the budget going away (sometimes in the middle of the project), and the number of changes, project managers and team members alike seem to be running on "fast forward."

A project manager friend of mine from Australia flew to the United States to participate in a project planning session several years ago, and at the end of the week-long planning session I asked her what she thought of the U.S. Her response was abrupt but, not surprising, when she proclaimed, "You Yanks are so impatient, and you never want to take the time to plan the details of the project. You just want to jump in and start the activities even if you are not sure what needs to be done." Does this sound familiar? It sounds a lot like the "Ready, fire, aim" dilemma mentioned in Chapter 2.

To further investigate my friend's statement, I raised the same question to some of my project team members from Japan and a couple of my Asian students, their responses were the same. Most other countries actually spend time planning their projects (on average they said they spend around 60 percent to 70 percent of the project time planning, compared to less than 10 percent in the U.S.). To further substantiate this, Dr. Liker in the *Toyota Way Fieldbook* uses the phrase, "Ready, aim, aim, aim, aim, fire" to describe Japanese project teams. The Japanese approach tends to be the other extreme from that of the U.S., and it really shows the need for a happy medium when it comes time to plan our projects. Planning is essential to effective project management.

The following is from the section "How We Use Time" in the Wikipedia page for time management:

> "Time is similar to money in how we use it: We spend time; we save time; we invest time. When we spend time, there is no improvement in efficiency, productivity, or effectiveness. The time is gone without return. We save time when we perform tasks in less time or with less effort than previously. We use shortcuts and processes that streamline activities. We invest time when we take time now to save time later . . .

> Delegation is a valuable investment of our time. When we delegate, we teach someone to perform tasks we usually perform. While the training process takes time right now, the investment pays off later since we free our time to perform higher-payoff activities. The goal is to look for ways a person can save and invest time."[1]

1. Define Activities Process

Define Activities is the process of identifying the specific actions (activities) to be performed to produce project deliverables. The Create WBS process performed in Chapter 5 (if done properly) should have already identified the deliverables and the majority of the activities needed to complete the project successfully.

The best place to start with the Define Activities process, other than the WBS, is to go back to the scope baseline and other inputs such as organizational process assets and environmental factors. Activities from previous similar projects help provide great insight into the activities needed (why reinvent the wheel, right?). The resulting activity list is one of the important outputs of this process and is sometimes referred to as "activity attributes."

TIP

In the real world, the Define Activities process is often either bypassed or fast tracked (done in parallel) with or as part of the WBS-creation process. Many project managers prefer not to get involved with this process because the activities may be far too detailed and difficult to manage in a network diagram. The tendency is to go directly to the scheduling software and enter only the work packages, not all the activities. The best approach is to use what works best for you and the team to identify all the activities now rather than after project execution begins.

Some common mistakes or shortfalls when defining project activities include underestimating the time involved in managing the overall project. You should try to think outside the box to identify possible risks ("known unknowns" and "unknown unknowns," which will be discussed in more detail in Chapter 11).

Define Activities Inputs, Tools and Techniques, and Outputs

The inputs, tools and techniques, and outputs in the Define Activities process are listed in this section. Note that one of the key inputs is the scope baseline and that each of the tools and techniques is designed to assist us in clearly defining the project activities to deliver to the approved scope of the project.

Inputs:

- Scope baseline
- Enterprise environmental factors
- Organizational process assets

Tools and Techniques:

- Decomposition
- Rolling wave planning
- Templates
- Expert judgment

Outputs:

- Activity list
- Activity attributes
- Milestone list

Milestone Lists

The best way to organize the work of the Define Activities process is with a milestone list. A milestone, as you may recall from Chapter 5, is a major event on the project. Think of the milestone list as an outline (high-level view) of the deliverables of the project. The milestone list will help the team focus on the deliverables identified in the Create WBS process, and it helps promote discussion and synergy from the team to get you to the next level of detail (activities). It also serves as a very effective input tool for the PM to generate a monthly milestone report. The milestone report can be used to communicate success or concerns of overall progress on the project to upper-level managers. Additional details are provided on the milestone report and other reports in Chapter 10.

The milestone list should also identify whether the milestone is mandatory (such as those required by contract or by outside agencies) or optional (such as those based on similar projects or historical information).

Take a construction project as an example, where the milestone list ties to the major handoffs (changeovers) between the different subcontractors. It is important to be keenly aware of the scheduled completion of a major milestone, such as the foundation being complete and ready for the framer. In our example, such handoffs require city inspections and signoffs prior to the project going to the next phase. If you don't receive signoff from the inspector for the framework of the building, you cannot move onto the electrical and plumbing phases. You may lose valuable time, not to mention get a bad reputation, if you are not able to keep the project on schedule (see Table 6-1).

Milestone	Schedule date	Comments
Approved blueprints	April 15	Dependencies: Client/sponsor and city building permit office review and approval. (M)
Foundation complete	April 30	Dependencies: Land surveyed and marked, forms set, cement poured and cured, and city inspection (signoff). (M)
Framing complete	May 25	Dependencies: Materials available for crew to begin as scheduled. Building framed according to approved blueprints, rough plumbing installed, and all must meet building code inspection. (M)
Roof decked and frame structure "dried in" against weather	June 15	Dependencies: Roofing crew complete decking according to design, windows & doors installed, and signoff from city inspector. (M)
Electrical and plumbing complete	June 28	Dependencies: Wiring and plumbing installed according to design and building codes and signoff complete. (M)
Patio piped for gas grill	July 15	Dependencies: Customer signed work order. (O)

Table 6-1 Sample Milestone List (M=Mandatory, O=Optional)

ID	Milestone	March	April	May	June	July
1	Start	◆ 3/30/09				
2	Blueprints approved		◆ 4/15/09			
3	Foundation complete		◆ 4/30/09			
4	Frame complete			◆ 5/25/09		
5	Structure complete "dried in"				◆ 6/15/09	
6	Electrical and plumbing complete				◆ 6/28/09	
7	Finish work complete					◆ 7/10/09
8	Final Inspection (OC) complete					◆ 7/30/09

Figure 6-1   Sample milestone chart

TIP

Milestones are usually shown in the scheduling tool or on a network diagram as a diamond-shaped event that has zero time duration and uses zero project resources. For example, an inspection on your construction project is performed by a city or county employee who is not part of the project team and who doesn't charge time or money (well, not directly) to the project.

When reporting milestones, the PM often uses a milestone chart. Figure 6-1 shows the milestone chart for the construction project detailed in Table 6-1.

Activity List and Attributes

The finished activities list and the associated attributes should comprise a comprehensive list that includes all schedule activities required to successfully complete the project.

Activity List   The activity list is an output of the Define Activities process and includes all the work activities (and only the work activities) to be performed on the project. The list should be a logical extension of the scope statement and should be focused on what it takes to produce the deliverables of the project. Remember, as the project manager it is up to you to keep the team focused on the approved work during this process.

The creation of the activity list relies on the combined knowledge, skills, and experience of you and the team as well as all completed and approved documents generated thus far on the project to use as a guide. This includes documents (inputs) such as the following:

- The project charter
- The scope statement
- The WBS dictionary
- The project management plan
- Enterprise environmental factors (company culture, existing systems, building codes, and so on)
- Organizational process assets (procedures, templates, standard forms, company policies, and historical information)

Activity Attributes   Activity attributes extend the description of an activity by identifying the many components associated with the activity. Attributes are the characteristics of schedule activities, and they can be organized, sorted, or summarized according to the attribute categories. For example, a measure of the elapsed time required to complete an activity is an attribute.[2]

Other types of activity attributes are any measure of capacity, cost drivers, cycle time, and other such cost and performance characteristics, such as installing increased memory in a computer. The activity is installing the new memory chip, and the attribute is the size of the memory being installed (for example, 4GB of memory).

During the initial phase of the project, activity attributes may include the activity identification (ID) number, WBS ID number, activity name, activity codes, and logical relationships. As the project progresses, the attributes tend to evolve into more complex descriptions, resource requirements, locations of the work, and activity types, such as level of effort (LOE), discrete (independent) effort, and apportioned (spread over multiple activities) effort (AE).

The number of attributes varies by application area.

NOTE
According to the Wideman Comparative Glossary of Project Management Terms, *level of effort (LOE)* is usually "work that does not result in a final product (such as liaison, coordination, follow up, or other support activities) and which cannot be effectively associated with a definable end product process result. Level of effort is measured only in terms of resources actually consumed within a given time period."[3] Once you and the team have defined the project activities, the next step is the team beginning the "what needs to be done and when" relationship placement on the schedule. This is where the Sequence Activities process comes into the picture.

2. Sequence Activities Process

Now that you have identified the milestones, activities, and attributes, you need to start thinking about the sequence of the activities (that is, the order in which the work will be performed). Sequencing is when you start "connecting the dots" between which activities come first, second, third, and so on. Certain terms in this process tend to throw people for a loop—terms such as *predecessor* and *successor relationships, lead* and *lag time,* not to mention *float, total float, slack, PERT charts,* and more. All of this should be a lot clearer by the time you get to the end of the chapter.

The good news is, several great project management software applications are available that do a lot of the work for you. The bad news is, you still need to have a fundamental understanding of the terms and concepts to be able to effectively use these software products; otherwise, you'll fall back into the "garbage in, garbage out" situation.

TIP

Don't fall into the trap of thinking the scheduling tool takes the place of the overall project management plan. I have been asked by a number of PMs to review and provide suggestions on their "project plan" only to have them send me a project schedule. I will be the first to admit the scheduling tools today do a lot more than help track and manage the schedule, but they should not take the place of having an overall project management plan. The scheduling tool is part of the overall management plan.

What Is the Critical Path?

Before we get into the details of schedule activity sequencing and network diagrams methods, it is important to mention that the primary purpose for this effort is to be able to determine which activities are on the critical path. In other words, which activities, if not completed, will delay the overall project end date?

The critical path (CP) is defined as the longest path through the network that represents the shortest amount of time to complete the project. The most important element of determining the critical path is accurate activity duration estimates.

Why is it important to know which activities are on the critical path? Because this is where you get the most bang for the buck (return on investment) when it comes time to compress or adjust the schedule. Knowing the specific activities on the critical path gives you a direct line to where you need to focus to ensure against slippage (delays) in the schedule.

The best known method for finding the critical path on a project is called the *critical path method (CPM).* CPM is a schedule network analysis technique to determine the amount of flexibility (called *float* or *slack)* for each of the paths in the network diagram. Additional details on the history of CPM, how it is used, and definitions of float and slack are provided later in this chapter.

Methods Used to Draw Project Network Diagrams

A couple common methods are used to draw project network diagrams (PNDs):

- Precedence diagramming method (PDM), also known as *activity-on-node (AON)*

- Arrow diagramming method (ADM), also known as *activity-on-arrow (AOA)*

PDM is the most common and seems to be the method of choice in today's world of project management. It also tends to make more sense visually than ADM.

To develop a network diagram, start by getting the team together and then use the diagram from a previous similar project, standard templates, or the scheduling tools available from your organization process assets. The message here is: never reinvent the wheel if you can help it. You will save valuable time if you have tried-and-true work samples and templates from which to begin.

Precedence Diagramming Method   The precedence diagramming method displays the activities in nodes (boxes) to visually show the relationships between activities. PDM shows these relationships by using lines or arrows to depict which activity should come first (predecessor) and which are dependent activities (successors). PDM is also referred to as an *activity-on-node (AON)* network diagram (see Figure 6-2).

Any project network diagram drawn in such a way that the positioning and length of the activity represents its duration is also known as a *time-scaled network diagram.*

The precedence diagramming method is also used in what is known as the "critical path method," where the network diagram and activity duration estimates can be used to determine the activities on the critical path of the project.

PDM uses four different types of dependencies between activities (see Figure 6-3). These dependencies, listed next, are called "relationships":

- **Finish-to-start (FS)**   This is the most common logical relationship and shows that a predecessor activity (or "from" activity) must finish before the successor activity (or "to" activity) can start. This relationship is sequential in nature.

- **Start-to-start (SS)**   A predecessor activity (A) must start before the successor activity (B) can start. This relationship means the two activities can run in tandem; however, activity A must start before activity B can start.

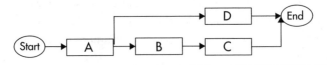

Figure 6-2   Sample precedence diagram method (PDM)

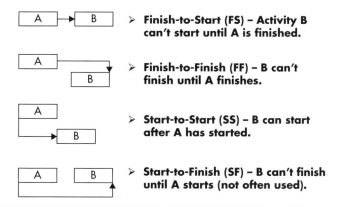

Figure 6-3 Sample activity relationships (dependencies)

- **Finish-to-finish (FF)** A predecessor activity (A) must finish before the successor (B) can finish. This relationship is often used at dinner time, when you would like all the food to be put on the table at the same time (finish-to-finish). This is tricky because each type of food (activity) takes more or less time to prepare and must be scheduled closely to complete at as near the same time as possible. Another example is a website for ordering tickets for an event. The website must be up and running at the same time the tickets are printed and ready to sell (finish-to-finish).

- **Start-to-finish (SF)** A predecessor activity (A) must start before the successor (B) can finish. This relationship is rarely used. It is also know as *just-in-time (JIT) scheduling* in manufacturing, event planning, and construction. For instance, for a concert event project, you would back into the activities' start times based on when the curtain goes up (finish time). For example, you must have the lighting and sound set up and tested prior to concert start time, so you start those activities early enough to allow the team adequate time to complete them prior to the "curtain up" time.

The best way to determine the relationship to use or to find the right link between two activities is to decide which one is driving or positioning the other activity. The driving activity (or task) is the predecessor; the other (driven) activity is the successor.

You also need to be aware of the following types of dependencies:

- **Mandatory (also known as hard logic)** Dependencies that are required by contract or inherent in the nature of the work. These often involve physical limitations; for example, the foundation (cement) must be set before the structure can be built.

- **Discretionary dependencies (preferred logic)** The project team determines which dependencies are discretionary (those that can wait or those that should proceed) and the preferred logic sequence for best results.

- **External dependencies** These dependencies include activities that are project related (for example, the testing of software is dependent on the hardware being received, installed, and running prior to installation of the software application). Or, in some cases, outside the project (for example, the project can't begin until the building materials are received onsite from the lumber yard). Other external dependencies might be government regulations that must be met or special reporting such as with regulatory organizations like the Occupational Safety and Health Administration (OSHA) or the Sarbanes-Oxley (SOX) Act (for financial reporting).

Arrow Diagramming Method The first thing to remember about the arrow diagramming method is that the activity is shown on the line (or arrow), not in a box (see Figure 6-4). AOA (activity-on-arrow) is less common than AON (activity-on-node). Also, AOA has no formal relationships other than the placement of the activities in the diagram. Unlike the AON network diagram, where you can show any relationships between activities (FS, SS, FF, and SF), the AOA network diagram can only show FS (Finish-to-Start) placement of activities.

The AOA approach is not as popular as AON but definitely has its place in certain industries or applications. As with AON, AOA can be created manually or via a software application tool or template in your Project Management Information System (PMIS).

Another feature of AOA (not found in AON) is the "dummy activity." A dummy activity indicates a dependency between two activities and is shown as a dashed (or dotted) line. Dummy activities carry zero time duration.

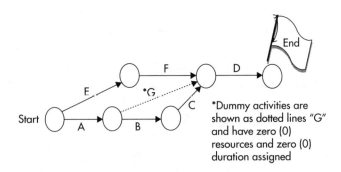

Figure 6-4 Sample arrow diagram method (ADM/AOA)

PERT and Gantt Charts

PERT and Gantt charts are tools commonly used by project managers to visually show activities and the time relationships of the activities for controlling and administering the project schedule.

The Gantt chart and the PERT chart are probably the two best known charts in project management. Each of these can be used for scheduling, but because Gantt charts don't illustrate task dependencies (relationship lines or arrows between activities), they can be confusing. Some PMs use both types of charts. The critical path can be found using CPM on either PERT or Gantt charts.

TIP

Network diagramming is a fairly simple process once you get the hang of it. According to Joseph Philips, in his book *PMP Project Management Professional Study Guide, Second Edition,* "Network diagrams may also be known as PERT charts, though this term may be slightly inaccurate. PERT, Program Evaluation and Review Technique, is a specific network diagram using weighted averages." [4] (Don't worry—PERT has been dropped from the *PMBOK.*)

PERT Charts   A PERT (Program Evaluation Review Technique) chart is a project management tool used to schedule, organize, and coordinate tasks within a project. PERT is a methodology developed by the U.S. Navy in the 1950s to manage very large, complex projects, such as the Polaris submarine missile program, which had a high degree of intertask dependency. A similar methodology, the critical path method (CPM), was developed for project management in the private sector at about the same time. Classical PERT charting is used to support projects that are often completed using an assembly-line approach. The PERT method extends the critical path method by considering the uncertainty in estimating activity duration in order to estimate the probability of finishing a project in a given time. [5]

TIP

Some scheduling softwares refer to the PERT chart as a "Gantt chart" (see Figure 6-5). This is not completely accurate because the Gantt chart is more of a bar chart and usually does not have relationship lines between activities. Also, it is important to know that even though PERT is similar to CPM, PERT uses Expected Value, which is calculated using the three-point (weighted value) estimate shown later in this chapter (in Figure 6-10).

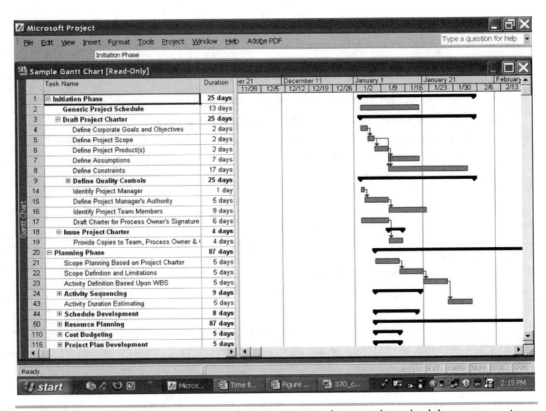

Figure 6-5 Sample PERT chart (referred to as a "Gantt chart" in this scheduling program)

Gantt Charts (Often Shown as Bar Charts)   The Gantt chart, developed by Charles Gantt in 1917, focuses on the sequence of activities necessary for completion of the project. Each activity on a Gantt chart is represented as a single horizontal bar on an X–Y chart. The horizontal axis (X-axis) is the time line of the project and the length of each activity (or task) bar corresponds to the duration of the activity. The Y-axis shows the list of WBS activities (see Figure 6-6). A Gantt chart is also a useful tool for planning and scheduling projects and is helpful when monitoring and reporting progress.

NOTE

Essentially, the Gantt chart is a "time-scaled network diagram" shown as a bar chart with no lines to indicate relationship between activities. As mentioned, some scheduling software tools inappropriately show Gantt charts with relationship lines between activities, much like a PERT chart.

Project Development Schedule

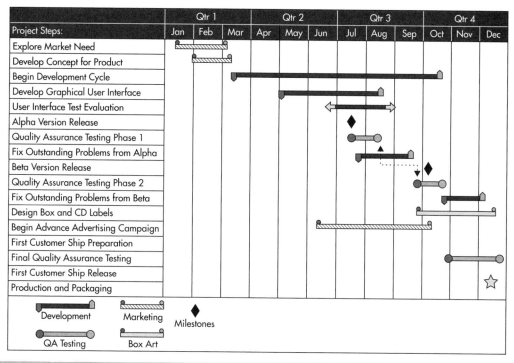

Figure 6-6   Sample Gantt chart

Other Charts Used in Schedule Management

A variety of other charts and methods are available to the project manager and project team for presenting schedule progress. In this section I introduce just a few of them:

- **Milestone chart**   As previously mentioned, these types of charts are great for project sponsor/executive-level reporting on schedule status (refer back to Figure 6-1 for an example of a milestone chart).

- **Dashboard**   Typically a single-page summary-level report of compressed project information usually displayed with "traffic light" (red, yellow, green) indicators. The indicators show overall status of the project and its key metrics (measurement components). The dashboard serves as a "heads-up display (HUD)" to sponsors on the schedule and other aspects of the project, such as cost, deliverables, and risk (see Figure 6-7). Using the dashboard report also requires a legend to clearly show criteria for each category (red, yellow, green) rating.

Weekly Status: Project Name
Executives: list sponsors names
Leads: other PMs you're working with in the program

Overall Status: (Y)
Last Updated: mm/dd/yyyy

Status Summary: Project objective and progress against that objective

Major Initiatives - Milestones/Deliverables	Due Dates		Dependencies on		Comments
Milestone #1	Target: Actual:	(G)	Dependency: Due date:	(G)	Reason for status: Issues:
Milestone #2	Target: Actual:	(Y)	Dependency: Due date:	(Y)	Reason for status: Issues:
Milestone #3	Target: Actual:	(G)	Dependency: Due date:	(G)	Reason for status: Issues:
Milestone #4	Target: Actual:	(R)	Track: Dependency:	(R)	Reason for status: Issues:
Milestone #5	Target: Actual:	(G)	Track: Dependency:	(G)	Reason for status: Issues:

Figure 6-7   Sample dashboard

- **Burn chart**   Shows the status and progress of the project and is the conceptual equivalent to earned value reports. These types of charts are commonly used in Agile project management methodologies such as Scrum and Extreme Programming (XP). Burn charts can be a useful addition or alternative to more conventional charts. (For more details on burn charts, Agile project management, or other terms mentioned here, I recommend you perform an Internet search.)

Regardless of the process or type of chart you use to report project schedule status, there are some basic terms and techniques you should be familiar with, such as lead time, lag time, and hammocks (not the kind you swing in).

Leads and Lags
Lead and *lag* are terms or techniques (including values) used to control the timing of activities. For example, if the work package is to paint the living room of your house, you must first prepare the surface to be painted by removing pictures, sanding, and so on.

Once the walls are painted, you must wait for the paint to dry prior to hanging the pictures back on the wall. This is lag time. Lead time is negative lag. For example, you might preheat the oven prior to cooking a turkey dinner; thus, the activity to preheat the oven involves lead time (starting the activity sooner than its associated activity—cooking the turkey).

If you need to alter the relationship between two work packages or activities, you would use lead or lag time. Lead time removes time from the start of the activity, allowing an acceleration of the successor activity, whereas lag time adds time to the start of the activity (allows a delay in the successor activity). Lead time is usually shown as a negative number, and lag time is a positive number (see Figure 6-8).

The concepts or techniques to manage time on your project schedule are better understood via examples.

First, let's use the BEC case study for an example of lead time. While finalizing the changeover project plan and staffing requirements to convert from a concert to a rodeo, the project manager needs the Event Data Sheet at least two weeks prior to the event. This would be shown as lead time on the network diagram. This commonly shows as a Finish-to-Start relationship with a two-week lead (FS – 2 weeks).

Second, lag time is best described as a forced or planned delay, such as in a construction project where we can begin restoring each room (hanging pictures, replacing the furniture, and so on) once the paint has dried (in assembly-line fashion). Lag time can be shown as a Finish-to-Start relationship, where the painting ends with one day lag time for the paint to dry prior to the room being restored. Another example often used is when pouring concrete; you must wait two days (lag time) to remove the forms after the concrete has dried (FS + 2 days).

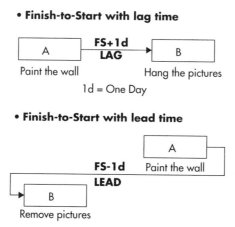

Figure 6-8   Sample lead and lag time relationship

Hammock Activity A hammock activity (also known as a "summary activity") represents a group or collection of related (or unrelated) activities aggregated at a summary level. It often groups subtasks or even subprojects that are not related in a logical sense of a dependency where one subtask must wait for another. For example:

- Grouping dissimilar activities that lead to an overall capability, such as preparations under a summary label; for example, "project initiation or construction site preparation"
- Grouping unrelated items for the purpose of a summary such as a calendar-based reporting period; for example, "First quarter plans"
- Grouping ongoing or overhead activities that run the length of an effort; for example, "project management"

TIP

Remember, change is inevitable. As you and the team are working the details of the Sequence Activities process, you will discover the need to make changes to the project plan, WBS, and perhaps other project documents. Requested changes can surface at any time by any stakeholder. Watch for the changes and manage them as part of the integrated change process, as mentioned in Chapter 4.

To emphasis the importance of network diagrams and how they can help you as a project manager, let's discuss their benefits.

Ask the Expert

Q: How does a network diagram help me as a project manager?

A: Network diagrams can help with schedule management in the following ways:
- They provide a visual relationship of the work to be performed on the project.
- They show interdependencies of all activities and the workflow from one to the next.
- They help in the project planning, organizing, and tracking progress of the project.
- They identify activities on the critical path for improved schedule awareness and control.
- They identify activities on the noncritical path (you can temporarily reassign resources to help expedite an activity on the critical path to potentially eliminate a schedule overrun).

3. Estimate Activity Resources Process

Now that you have identified the milestones and activities on your project, it is time to estimate the resources needed to perform the work. Remember that resources include not only the people (labor) but also materials (supplies) and equipment (tools).

The Estimate Activity Resources process involves the estimating of types and quantities needed to perform each activity. This process should be closely coordinated with the Estimate Costs process in the Project Cost Management knowledge area (Chapter 7).

This is the time where you start getting very much involved with the details of the types of skills and experience needed to complete the work of the project. Unique capabilities may be needed, and you must begin to look at the time and cost to acquire, train (if needed), and organize the resources to address the activities you and the team have identified. As you add more people to the team, your job as the PM gets more complicated, especially in the execution phase. On construction projects, you need journeyman-level skills, people familiar with the building codes, and a realistic view of the time it takes to move from one activity (or process) to the next.

Resource Calendars and Resource Leveling

In project management, the team is the number one asset. The only way to manage the team, the individuals on the team, and other key resources is with organized scheduling. Knowing who needs to be where and when is like being an air traffic controller. Without the scheduling tools of resource calendars and resource leveling, you will have conflicts.

Resource Calendars   As a project manager, you live and die by the calendar. You need to know who is available on your team at all times. A resource calendar is a great way to do this.

In a tight economy there may be overtime restrictions or team members on your project who are also working other projects. This can be especially true in matrix management and functional organization structures. The problem occurs when you need work done on your project and the team members are not available. There can be many distractions and constraints with getting and keeping highly skilled people focused on your project. The type of information that would go into a resource calendar includes, but is not limited to name, skill set, availability (time period available to the project), planned vacation schedule, backup person, and manager name.

Try This Who's on First? (Knowing the Schedule)

You are the PM on a global project that requires "all hands on deck" availability during a critical test of a new call center scheduled to go live after the Labor Day weekend (a holiday in the U.S. on the first Monday during the month of September). The majority of the project preparation work effort is to occur during the month of August. One of your team members in Asia casually mentions that most of the Asian team members will be out honoring religious holidays most of the month of August. What do you do? Take a few minutes to jot down possible solutions before reading the following answer.

Answer: If the schedule is set and the deliverable is firm, use team members from other countries who don't recognize the same holidays, or pay higher rates to the people who are available and willing to work over the holiday period to keep the project on schedule.

To effectively manage resources, you need to do your research ahead of time. You need to know that many countries in both Asia and Europe have major holidays/vacations during the month of August. Therefore, you should plan accordingly. Useful tools include a resource/responsibility assignment matrix (RAM) (see Figure 6-9) and, of course, a resource calendar for quick reference to see who is assigned to critical activities and whether they are available when needed.

The resource calendar can be used to identify risks, schedule duration, and needed backup skills. It also serves as a negotiation tool when critical path activities are at risk. This is where the PM needs to be focused and use all the resources available to the fullest extent possible. The PM must keep people informed, assigned, focused, engaged, and challenged as well as continue to reinforce the value of each person to the team and their roll on the project.

Resource Leveling   Resource leveling does not mean knocking people over (like on the football or rugby field), even though the large workload many of us face tends to knock us over at times. Resource leveling is when you balance the work across the workers and not overload our friend the overachiever.

Activity	Mary	Joey	Bob	Sue
Plan party	P			
Purchase food		P		S
Decorate office	S		P	
Serve the food		P	S	

Legend: P = Primary, S = Secondary

Figure 6-9   Sample resource assignment matrix (RAM)

From a project manager's perspective, resource leveling is a process used to examine a project for an unbalanced use of resources (usually people) over time and for resolving conflicts in worker availability or overallocation of work to help prevent "burnout." Wikipedia offers the following on resource leveling:

> "When performing project planning activities, the [project] manager will attempt to schedule certain tasks simultaneously. When more resources such as machines or people are needed than are available, or perhaps a specific person is needed in both tasks, the tasks will have to be rescheduled concurrently or sequentially to manage the constraint." [6]

During project planning, the PM and the team need to look closely at resource leveling to resolve potential conflicts early in the project life cycle. Note that this process is one that should be used over the course of the project; otherwise, you will likely impact one of the key constraints (time, cost, and scope).

When you use project scheduling software, resource leveling is a feature that can help you to calculate delays. However, don't let the scheduling software run amuck by making assumptions for you. Real resource leveling might require delaying tasks until resources are truly available.

In any case, leveling could result in a later project finish date, especially if the activities affected are on the critical path.

Try This The Overachiever ("Pick Me, Coach!")

During the project kickoff meeting, one of your team members who is known to be an overachiever (OA) keeps volunteering for more work. The OA has always been quick to sign up for extra work. You think to yourself, "What a team player!" As you quietly wish you had a whole team of OAs, you enter the assignments in the software scheduling tool and click the "Resource Leveling" button to verify the work is balanced across the team. Your heart stops when you see the OA has signed up for two years worth of work on a one-year project. What do you do now? Take a few minutes to jot down a possible solution before looking at the following answer.

Answer: You pull OA aside (one-on-one) and thank her for her willingness to take on the extra work. Then you have to explain there are not enough days in a year for her to complete all the work she signed up for. Lastly, you go through the work packages together to focus on the best use of OA's time and reassign the extra work to other team members as equably as possible.

Make-or-Buy Decision

Sometimes it is best to do the work internal to your project team or make a product in-house if you have the tools and the talent. Then there are times you need to go outside the project team to buy the expertise or products needed. The make-or-buy analysis is a way to help ensure you and the team are focused on those things you can do internally and allows you increased flexibility when you are better off going outside for the skills or products needed. This option can work well or may add risk to your schedule. This risk will be discussed more in the Project Risk Management and Project Procurement Management knowledge areas (Chapters 11 and 12, respectively).

4. Estimate Activity Durations Process

Congratulations. By this time, you and the team have identified the work, what needs to be accomplished, and who is going to do the work. Now it is time to get the team together again and perform the Estimate Activity Durations process for all the activities on the project.

I can't emphasize enough the importance of this process being a team sport. This is where the team has to provide their input and expertise in estimating the duration of the work activities. You will have a better chance of getting buy-in if you work this process as a team. Besides, two heads (or many heads) are better than one. The synergy and brainstorming will provide you a more complete package when the process is finished.

I should also mention that duration estimating is usually measured in days, as opposed to "effort," which is usually estimated in hours. Duration estimating is the length of time the activity will take, whereas effort is the labor applied to the activity. Duration estimating should take into account meetings, unscheduled interruptions, and project management activities other than hands-on work, which tends to always take longer than expected.

Effort (or level of effort) estimating is used more extensively in estimating cost, where you are only charged for the actual time spent on the project. These two types of estimating usually go out the window if the person is assigned to your project full time (dedicated) and you will be paying for them full-time, regardless of the specific hours spent in direct support of the project.

NOTE
Let's say we are working on our painting project. The team has determined it will take 80 hours to complete painting the house. Now if we have two people painting, we can complete the job in 40 hours. Therefore, the estimate based on resources available is 40 hours (or one business week). If we add two more people to the project, we should be able to complete the job in 20 hours duration; however, we are still expending 80 hours of effort.

Other dynamics need to be considered when estimating activity duration. For example, it has been my experience that the actual time to complete an activity goes up with the more people you assign to it. When you put more people on the project, there tends to be more distractions, the workspace may become limiting, and the workers can become counterproductive. Therefore, instead of 80 hours, the activity could very well take 100 hours.

Another common problem occurs when making the team work more overtime. At some stage, you reach the point (or law) of diminishing returns when throwing more overtime hours at an activity. The result of this dilemma is a decrease in quality, more mistakes, and potential injuries due to employee fatigue.

Estimate Activity Durations Inputs, Tools and Techniques, and Outputs

There are a large number of inputs, tools and techniques, and outputs associated with the Estimate Activity Durations process. Also notice the many types of tools and techniques (see Table 6-2) that can assist the PM and team in estimating activity durations. Let's take a closer look at some of them.

Types of Duration Estimating

PMI recognizes five tools and techniques for estimating the duration of the activities identified during the previous processes:

- **Expert judgment** This is the preferred technique, especially if you have worked with the project team before and you know who to call on for the best answers to certain questions. For example, if you are estimating how long it takes to change over from an ice hockey arena to a rodeo at the BEC, you call on Jake or Matt who have done this activity a hundred times or more to tell you how long it takes. You might also want to qualify the estimate based on skill level required (for example, the expert can do things quicker than a novice employee).

Inputs	Tools and Techniques	Outputs
Activity list	Expert judgment	Activity duration estimates
Activity attributes	Analogous estimating	Project document updates
Activity resources requirements	Parametric estimating	
Resource calendars	Three-point estimates	
Project scope statement	Reserve analysis	
Enterprise environmental factors		
Organizational process assets		

Table 6-2 Estimate Activity Durations Process Inputs, Tools and Techniques, and Outputs

- **Analogous estimating**   This is a form of expert judgment that's also called "top-down estimating." It involves taking historical estimates from previous, similar projects (an analogy). This estimation technique is used to determine the duration when the detailed information about the project is not available, usually during the early stages of the project.

- **Parametric estimating**   This type of estimating uses a "cost per unit" (quantifiable/ mathematical) model, such as cost per square foot (for a construction project), cost per line of code (for a software development project), and units per hour (for a manufacturing project) to determine how long an activity will take. You simply multiply the cost per unit (price) by the quantity (P*Q) to get the estimated amount of work to determine the overall cost.

- **Three-point estimate**   In the real world, the probability of completing a project on a set date (especially when change is inevitable) is pretty low. Therefore, the best way to determine the range of estimating accuracy is to estimate the probable date using a three-point estimate. A weighted average is used to estimate the three times (or costs). Here is how it works: A subject matter expert (SME) who is very familiar with the activity estimates the best (optimistic = O), worst (pessimistic = P), and most likely (ML) time or cost to perform the activity. Then you use the following formula to calculate the three-point estimate:

$(P + (4*ML) + O)/6$

Note that PMI refers to the three-point time estimate as a PERT estimate along with two other formulas that may appear on the PMP exam for activity duration and cost estimating (see Figure 6-10). It would be a good idea to memorize them. Also note that PMI has changed the look of the formula not the concept (see *PMBOK* page 150).

Three-point estimate for an activity:	Standard deviation of an activity:	Variance of an activity:
$$\frac{(P + 4ML + O)}{6}$$	$$\frac{P - O}{6}$$	$$\left(\frac{P - O}{6}\right)^2$$

Note: To estimate duration for the project, you need to add up the activity estimates on the critical path and because statistically you can't add standard deviations, you must calculate the variances for the activities.

Figure 6-10   Pert formulas

Try This Using Three-Point Estimate for Travel Time

You have driven the same route to work for the past three years, so you are the SME on how long the trip takes. You have determined it takes you 45 minutes to get to work on a good (optimistic) day (with good weather and minimum traffic). On a poor-weather or heavy-traffic day, it takes as long as 75 minutes. However, the most likely drive time is one hour (60 minutes). Plugging these numbers into a three-point formula results in the following:

(45 + (4 * 60) + 75)/6, or (45 + 240 + 75)/6, or 360/6 = 60

Therefore, knowing the three-point formula, what do you get?

Answer: It will take one hour (60 minutes) on average to drive to work.

●   **Reserve analysis**   This technique is used to estimate the cost of project activities. Depending on the results of the reserve analysis, dollars can be set aside (called contingency or management reserves) to be used to cover risk events that are likely to affect schedule and cost. This topic is discussed in more detail in Chapter 7.

5. Develop Schedule Process

Schedule development is where the rubber meets the road, so to speak. It's where the schedule management work really begins, and the results of this process will have a huge impact on your project management capability and credibility.

Once you have a network diagram and activity and resources estimates, it is time to put the information into a schedule. (The difference between a time estimate and a schedule is that the schedule is calendar based.)

Ask the Expert

Q: Is there a check list that can help me and my team develop a schedule for our project?

A: Yes, there is. This is one I have used that seems to work pretty well.

- Start with a clear understanding of the work required on the project (scope statement, charter, stakeholder priorities, expectations, time frame, deliverables, and so on).
- Clearly define the activities (WBS, WBS dictionary, and activity list) and alternatives.
- Have a clear idea of the order of how the work should be done (activity sequencing).
- Obtain an estimate of the resources needed (activity resource estimating).
- Obtain an estimate of the duration of each activity (activity duration estimating).
- Obtain a company calendar identifying working days and nonworking days (this varies by country) as well as key stakeholder (team members and sponsor) vacation days.
- Identify imposed dates (deadlines or major deliverable target dates).
- Identify and verify milestones and dependencies (internal and external agents).
- Identify and document assumptions (in scope and out of scope exclusions).
- Identify constraints (time, cost limitations, lead times, lag times, and dependencies).
- Identify other potential impacts to the schedule such as resource availability.
- Obtain formal stakeholder acceptance of the schedule.

According to PMI, the Develop Schedule process involves analyzing activity sequences, activity durations, resource requirements, and schedule constraints to create a project schedule.

So, how do you effectively develop the project schedule? This process starts with the outputs from other previous processes. With your team, focus on activity duration estimates to help ensure the schedule is both realistic and achievable.

The question that must be answered at the end of this process is, how long will the entire project take to complete? Armed with the activity duration estimates, your team, and the outputs already collected, you work very closely with all the stakeholders to develop the project schedule. As with all project management processes, it always helps to have a planned approach. Here are some things to consider when developing your project schedule:

- As always, first and foremost, remember to make this a team sport by getting all the information, constraints, and expert judgment you can. At the end of the process, you should have buy-in from the team and other key stakeholders.

- Next, you need to fully understand the requirements and stakeholder priorities (don't be afraid to ask and verify these key components).

- Be open-minded and look at various options. Also, document the options even if they are not used right away. This will give you a head start on risk management plan development (see Chapter 11).

- Look across the entire project (charter to close), as mentioned in Chapter 4, to see how the project can impact (or be impacted by) other projects—for example, limited resources, changes in priorities, and shift in sponsors (turnover) or budget dollars. To this end, you might want to get managers to provide you with "letters of commitment" for key resources to ensure the people will be available on your project for the time needed without interruptions from other work or projects.

- Lastly, when the schedule is developed, you must continuously manage it. Never put the schedule in a desk drawer or on a shelf. It should be a working document that's reviewed, worked, and revised (through change control) early and often, as needed, to be up to date and accurate.

Also, it is important for you to use progressive elaboration (iterative processing) to apply the things you have learned as you progress further into the project life cycle to update the schedule and other documents. As much as we would like to "lock in" on the schedule at the beginning, a phenomenon called "discovery" surfaces as we get deeper into the project. As we learn more about the project, we need to make updates to the schedule. This is often called "hindsight" (which people say is 20/20). This means historical information is a good thing.

TIP

Be very aware of project constraints, limitations, or barriers that can cause you and the team to stumble and fall. It is extremely difficult to see all the constraints at the beginning of the project. This is why you need to be aware of possible constraints and the possible impact to the project throughout the life cycle. Constraints can appear in many forms; some are self-inflicted and in some cases can be turned into real opportunities. A good example of a project with a schedule constraint is the Olympics: It doesn't matter whether or not the paint is dry on the stadium seats; the torch is to be lit at a specific time on a specific date.

Impact of Project Constraints

Constraints are imposed on projects from many sources—even from within (self-inflicted). Suppose you are putting activities into your scheduling software tool and you decide the date for a particular activity is fixed (for example, "must start on" or "must finish on"). What do you think this does to the scheduling software that works so hard to calculate float, overall duration, and the critical path of your project? It can really mess things up! I have seen this happen many times. When the dates don't make sense in the scheduling tool, chances are you or someone has set a constraint without fully understanding the impact to the overall project. Don't get me wrong—there are times when fixed date constraints are needed. Just be aware that when a date is fixed (constrained), it will likely force an override in the software tool and change the overall schedule.

Types of Schedule Constraints

The four common types of schedule constraints are listed and described in Table 6-3. The two used most often are:

- Start No Earlier Than
- Finish No Later Than

It is important to remember that constraints can be tied to individual project activities and/or the entire project. Also, constraints are often tied directly to a milestone, which may be outside the project team. Remember, milestones are major events on the project and require zero resources (from the project team) and carry zero duration.

Constraint	What the Constraint Does	Examples
Start No Earlier Than (SNET)	The constraint sets when an activity can begin based on a predetermined date or time, often because of a dependency (usually customer imposed).	Setting up the church for a wedding. This activity cannot begin until Monday after the Sunday evening church service has been completed. The electrician on a construction project can start no earlier than when the milestone of the building inspector signing off on the roof decking is complete.
Start No Later Than (SNLT)	The constraint indicates the activity must start prior to a predetermined deadline. This is also known as "right-to-left scheduling."	A changeover project to convert the events center from a rodeo to a concert takes two weeks; therefore, the changeover can start no later than June 1 to be ready for a June 15 concert date.
Finish No Earlier Than (FNET)	This constraint requires the activity to be in progress up until a predetermined date.	The tests for software are required to run continuously until June 15 to obtain adequate results.
Finish No Later Than (FNLT)	This constraint states that an activity or project must finish on a predetermined date.	Federal income taxes must be mailed (postmarked) no later than April 15.

Table 6-3 Schedule Constraints

Reporting Schedule Status

Different styles for different stakeholders is an easy way to think about the type of report to use (as well as format and frequency) when reporting the project schedule. This topic will be discussed in more detail in Chapter 10. There are a few things to think about before you set up your status reports.

Some project managers when asked, "Are we on schedule?" are so detail oriented they are quick to tell you how to build a watch rather than just tell you the time of day. Too often we feel the need to tell the whole story rather than the only-the-facts version. This is especially true on project status reports—keep them short and to the point. This is where milestone charts are great for reporting status to middle- or executive-level managers.

Remember there are times when "less is more." Less information—as long as it is the right information—is often more than enough detail to get the message across. The key is to know your audience—know what their interests are and be sure to work on providing the right information, as needed, in a suitable format. For example, a "dashboard" report provides a great way to show high-level status.

It is difficult to stay focused on the overall project schedule if you are trying to manage time only. You must be able to manage both time and the overall project sequence of activities to bring the project in on schedule.

Types of Schedule Reports

As you know, a number of report types and styles are available to present the status of a project schedule. Most PMs send the current copy of their project schedule as a Microsoft Project (.mpp) file. This is easy to do; however, not everyone on the team or your sponsors will have licensed software to view Microsoft Project files. This or any other scheduling software can be expensive. Fortunately, most software products today allow you to save the file in HTML or other viewable formats, such as exports to Microsoft Excel or other software that allows you to view files from other applications.

Ask the Expert

Q: When should I baseline the project schedule?

A: The sooner you baseline, the better (as mentioned in Chapter 5). The longer you wait, the more changes will likely occur, thus making the schedule end date a moving target. When there are many changes, you need to document, verify, and obtain formal acceptance of the target date. Once the target date is approved, you should baseline the schedule and use change control, which will give you an opportunity to renegotiate a new adjusted target date and re-baseline the schedule when changes are likely to move out the project completion date.

Critical Path Method (CPM)

As mentioned earlier, the critical path (CP) is defined as the longest path through the network that represents the shortest amount of time to complete the project. The activities on the CP have the biggest impact on the project end date. The way to calculate CP is by using the critical path method.

The critical path method (CPM), as part of the precedence diagramming method, helps you determine where the flexibility (or lack of flexibility) resides. The CPM involves calculating the earliest start (ES) date, earliest finish (EF) date, latest start (LS) date, and latest finish (LF) date for each activity in the network diagram. Sounds pretty ominous. However, it is much easier done as a team exercise, and adds validity (buy-in) to the time it takes to complete the project.

In Chapter 5, we discussed creating the WBS and the use of sticky notes to identify activities. For a recommended layout of CPM activities and how to use a sticky note to assist with the calculation of forward and backward pass and float, see Figure 6-11.

It is also important to remember that activities on the critical path typically have zero float. Float (or slack) time is determined by performing a forward and backward pass through the network and calculating the amount of time an activity takes in relationship to the other activities. The goal is to identify activities that will potentially impact other activities or the overall project end date if delayed (details and examples will be discussed later in this chapter).

You should also be aware that the critical path can change if delays occur, or if milestones or dependencies are missed. Also, an approved scope change or a triggered risk may cause you to have to recalculate the critical path.

Basic Scheduling Terms

Here are several terms you should be familiar with prior to calculating the critical path:

- **Forward pass** and **Backward pass**   These terms are related to ways of determining the early or late start (forward pass) or early or late finish (backward pass) for an activity. Forward pass is a technique to move forward through a diagram to calculate activity duration. Backward pass is its opposite.

- **Predecessor**   An activity (A) that exists on a common logic path that occurs before another activity (B).

- **Successor**   An activity (B) that exists on a common logic path that occurs after another activity (A).

- **Free float**   The amount of time an activity can be delayed without delaying the early start of any immediately following (successor) activities.

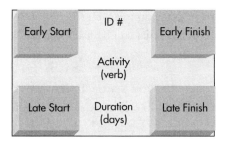

Figure 6-11   Sample sticky note layout

- **Float**   Also called "total float" or "slack." The amount of time an activity can be delayed from its early start without delaying the project finish date.

- **Near critical path**   The path through the network with the lowest total float (if changes occur to the network, the near critical path may become the critical path).

- **Lag time**   Fixed delay between the start and finish of one activity and the start or finish of another (for example, letting the paint dry before hanging the pictures).

- **Lead time**   Modification of a fixed relationship to accelerate the start of a successor activity (for example, preheating the oven prior to the "cook the turkey" activity).

- **Dangler**   An unintended break in the network path or an activity in the network diagram that is missing a dependency from its predecessor or successor activity.

- **Loops**   Circular relationships that won't allow an activity to end (for example, a software test cycle that continuously identifies corrections and enhancements that are never ending).

Calculating the Critical Path

To determine the critical path duration of a project, you must first perform a forward pass and then a backward pass. This process will allow you to calculate the float of each activity. The activities that have zero float are those activities that determine the critical path. You simply add the duration of every activity with zero float across the network, and that will confirm the overall project duration. This means that any activity, if changed, that impacts the project end date is likely to be on the critical path.

By identifying all paths in the network and adding the activity durations along each path, you can determine which path is the longest duration—and that is the critical path. This process will also help identify if you have more than one critical path. (Yes, you can have more than one CP on a project.) It is also important to know the path that is nearest to the critical path in case the CP changes for some reason.

There are several steps in determining the critical path of the network diagram. The following summary level checklist can be used as a guide to help you through this process:

1. All network diagrams should have a start activity (zero duration) and can start at day zero or day one (most PMs like to start at day one; however, there is no hard rule on this).

2. Identify all activities that can begin immediately. These may become the different paths.

3. Identify the next dependent or associated activity to continue the logical relationship of the network path.

4. Complete the process until all predecessors and successors have been identified (with no danglers).

5. Identify the activities that signify completion of the project (always have an "end" activity).

6. Calculate the forward pass. Note that when multiple activities converge into a single activity, you should select the activity with the highest early finish (EF) to carry forward to the early start (ES) of the successor activity (see details and Figure 6-12, later in this chapter).

7. Find the latest early finish dates of the project. This will give you an idea of the overall length of the project.

8. Calculate the backward pass. Note that when multiple activities converge into a single activity, you should select the lowest late start (LS) to carry over to the late finish (LF) single-predecessor activity (see details and Figure 6-13, later in this chapter).

9. Calculate the float. Note that the total float is within the box, and free float is outside the box (on the line between activities).

10. Identify the critical path (or critical paths) and the near critical path.

11. Validate the network to ensure that it is correct and complete.

12. Become familiar with the characteristics of the network.

13. Verify that the work can be done with the available resources.

14. Take actions to adjust the schedule as needed.

15. Be sure to include project management activities.

Activity Convergence and Divergence

Other terms you need to be aware of when calculating the forward and backward pass are activity convergence and activity divergence:

- **Activity convergence**   Occurs when deliverables of two or more predecessor activities are required for the start of a single activity (successor). On a forward pass, when converging activities into a single activity, you should always use the largest of the early finish dates of the predecessor activities as the early start date of the successor activity. On a backward pass, always use the smallest late start date as the late finish date of the successor activity (see Figure 6-12).

- **Activity divergence**   Occurs when deliverables of one activity are required for the start of two or more activities. On a forward pass, when diverging a single activity into multiple activities, you should use the early finish of the predecessor activity as the early start date of each of the successor activities. On a backward pass, when diverging a single activity into multiple activities, use the late start of the predecessor activity as the late finish date of each of the successor activities (see Figure 6-13).

TIP

Here are a couple tips to help when you are running the forward and backward pass:
"Mind the line," which means pay close attention to the relationship lines (convergent paths, finish-to-start, and so on).
"Mind the sign (+/−)," which means watch for lead and lag times. Lag is a delay (+ time) going forward; however, it's a minus sign (−) coming back on the backward pass. Lead time is "negative" lag—that is, minus sign (−) on the forward pass and a plus sign (+) on the backward pass.
These tips will make more sense as you work through your own network diagrams.

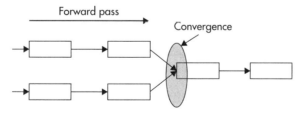

Figure 6-12   Sample converging paths

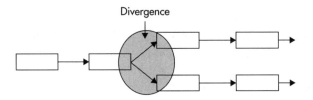

Divergence

Figure 6-13 Sample diverging paths

Steps to Calculate the Forward Pass

The forward pass is where the activity duration estimate comes in and is crucial to the accuracy of the critical path calculations. The detailed steps to calculate the forward pass are as follows:

1. Calculating the forward pass will determine the early start (ES) and early finish (EF) days for each activity. The ES and EF numbers go in the upper-left (ES) and upper-right (EF) corners, respectively, of each activity (refer to Figure 6-11).

2. The ES for the first activity (A) is usually zero (place that number in the ES corner of the sticky note).

3. The EF of Activity A is calculated by adding the duration of A to its early start (early start + duration = early finish). Place this number in the EF corner of the sticky note.

4. The early finish of Activity A then becomes the early start for the next activity.

5. Add the duration of the activity you are calculating to the ES number to get the EF number for that activity, and so on.

6. Complete the forward pass for the entire project to determine the total project duration (this number, once confirmed, represents the overall expected duration of the project).

Table 6-4 is used as input to help demonstrate the forward and backward passes. Using the information in Table 6-4, Figure 6-14 shows how the forward pass might look.

Steps to Calculate the Backward Pass

The backward pass, if calculated properly, should get you back to the original starting day (0 or 1, depending on which you used at the start box). The backward pass provides the numbers to help you calculate float. To perform the backward pass, use the late start (LS)

Activity	Predecessor	Duration
Start	—	0
A	Start	7
D	A	2
C	A	8
B	D	3
H	D	5
E	C	5
F	B, H	6
G	E	1
I	F, G	9
End	I	0

Table 6-4　Sample Table Used to Calculate Forward and Backward Pass

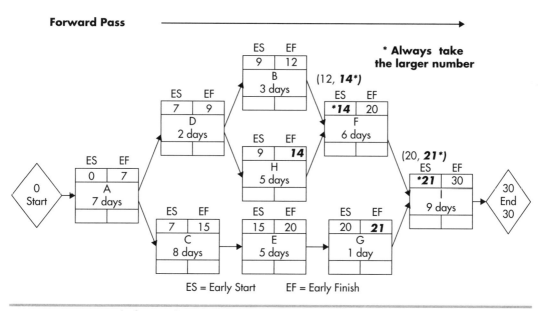

Figure 6-14　Sample forward pass

in the lower-left corner box and the late finish (LF) in the lower-right corner box of the sticky note for each activity (see Figure 6-15).

- **Late start (LS)**   The latest date an activity may begin as logically constrained by the network

- **Late finish (LF)**   The latest date an activity may finish as logically constrained by the network

The detailed steps involved with calculating the backward pass are as follows:

1. Doing the backward pass will determine the late start (LS) and late finish (LF) duration times for each activity in the project.

2. Starting with the final activity and working backward (right to left), subtract the duration of the last activity from its LF to arrive at its LS time (Late Finish – Duration = Late Start).

NOTE

Always take the lowest number when multiple paths converge going back through the network diagram.

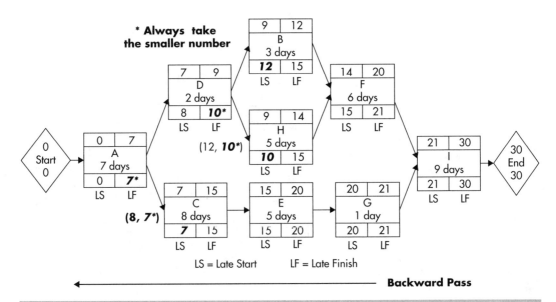

Figure 6-15   Sample backward pass

3. When more than one activity succeeds a given task, the earliest of the LS dates of the successor activities is selected to become the LF date.

4. The LF is the latest that a given activity may finish without delaying the completion of the project.

5. Complete the backward pass for the entire project and calculate float to determine the critical path.

Float and Slack

The good news is, most project management software will calculate float (synonymous with "slack"). To make sure you have an idea of what is going on (or should be going on) in the software and to be able to check the software results, you should have at least a fundamental understanding of these calculations (see Figure 6-16).

- **Total Float (slack)**   The amount of time an activity can be delayed without delaying the project end date or an intermediary milestone. To calculate a task or activity's float, use the following formula:

  (Late Start – Early Start) or (Late Finish – Early Finish) = Float

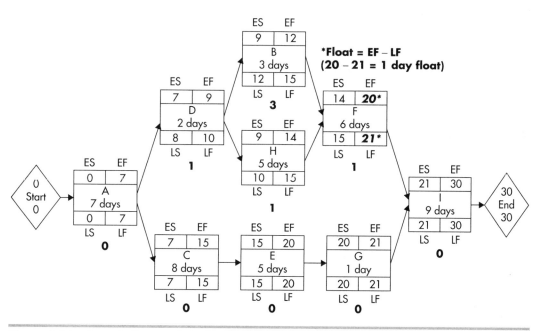

Figure 6-16   Sample float and slack calculation

- **Free float (slack)** The amount of time an activity can be delayed without the early start date of its successor. Here's the formula to use:

    (Early Start B – Early Finish A) = Free Float of A

- **Project float (slack)** The amount of time a *project* can be delayed without delaying the externally imposed project completion date required by the customer or management or the date committed to by the PM.

As an important reminder, activities on the critical path have zero float. After float has been calculated, you take the activities with zero float, and those are the activities on the critical path (see Figure 6-17).

6. Control Schedule Process

The Control Schedule process involves monitoring the status of the project and reporting progress on the schedule toward project completion. Remember, all projects have an end date (or they should), so controlling the schedule is the only way to get the project to successful completion.

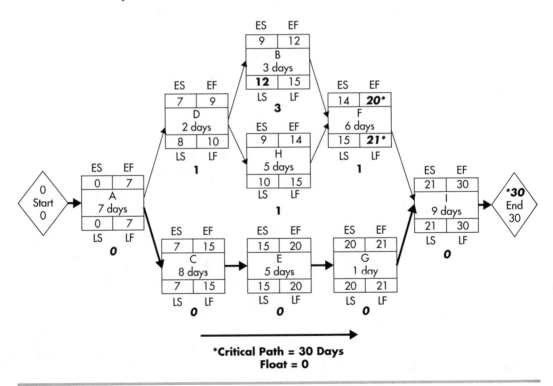

Figure 6-17 Sample critical path

Progress Reporting

Many forms and templates are available to report progress. I recommend performing an Internet search on "project progress reports" for a plethora of real-world examples.

TIP

For reporting high-level progress to top and middle managers and executives, you should use a dashboard or milestone charts to show major accomplishments without all the details. Also, there are ways to produce summary-level charts directly from your PM software tools using filters and such. For example, Microsoft Project has reporting options such as Overview, Current Cost, Assignments, Workload (Resource Leveling), Earned Value (EV), and Custom Reports.

A progress report is a useful method to control the schedule and costs. Many project managers determine how much work has been accomplished by asking team members for an estimate of "percent complete" for each work package or activity. On projects where work cannot be measured, this estimate is a simple guess. This is time consuming and almost always a complete waste of time because a guess does not provide a confident estimate of the actual percent complete.

If a project has been planned using a WBS, and work packages require about 80 hours of work, there are alternatives to percent complete. Because work packages will be completed faster and more frequently, we can forget percent complete and use one of the following rules:

- **50/50 rule**   An activity is considered 50-percent complete when it begins and gets credit for the last 50 percent only when it is completed.

- **20/80 rule**   An activity is considered 20-percent complete when it begins and gets credit for the other 80 percent only when it is completed.

- **0/100 rule**   An activity does not get credit for partial completion, only full credit when complete.[7]

TIP

The PM must work with the team to get consensus to ensure that all team members have the same expectation of what 20 percent or 50 percent complete really means so that schedule updates are reported consistently throughout the project.

Managing the Schedule (Compression)

There are two ways to manage (compress) the project schedule. One is "fast tracking" (doing things in parallel) and the other is "crashing" (bringing in additional resources). Both methods help get you back on schedule. As with any form of compression, there are increased risks and/or tradeoffs, such as increased cost (for example, the cost of rework or training if the added resources are not experts in the activity).

With fast tracking, you add risk by doing multiple things at the same time (a form of multitasking), and when you bring more people on the project (crashing) you add cost. Therefore, you might want to use a combination of compression techniques, as needed, to minimize cost and risk whenever possible.

One way to remember "crashing" is to think of a party. Someone who arrives uninvited is said to "crash" the party (likely eating up more food than the host had planned). Although silly, this memory tickler usually works (according to my students). Therefore, remember that crashing the schedule involves bringing more people to the party, and it usually always costs more than planned.

Try This Out-of-Control Schedule

The customer comes to you (the PM) in the hallway and says, "The date for the rock concert has been moved up (sooner) by two weeks and they want additional pyrotechnics and lighting changes. I need to know if there is any way you can move this project ahead to meet the new date and additional requirements." What do you say?

A. Sure, we can do that! No problem.

B. I will need to get with the team and see what our options are and the level of risk if we compress the schedule by two weeks. Give me a day or two to work this out.

C. I will be happy to work with you to better understand the changes to the schedule and will help initiate the request as part of our urgent change control process.

D. Sorry, if we move the schedule ahead, the team will have to work overtime. We are coming up on vacation time and will be short on staff.

Answer: C. You should always manage the schedule by using a documented and approved change control process.

Work the Plan (Project Execution)

At the end of the day, it is all about execution. You can have the best plan and the best schedule ever, but if you can't effectively execute (work) the plan, you might as well update your résumé and move on. The primary job of project managers is to be able to put our money where our mouth is and deliver what we said we would, on time and on budget. Effective time management enables you to perform your job as the PM with confidence and successful results.

References

1. Wikipedia, http://en.wikipedia.org/wiki/Time_management.

2. Answers.com, http://www.answers.com/topic/activity-attributes.

3. Wideman Comparative Glossary of Project Management Terms, http://www.maxwideman .com/pmglossary/PMG_L01.htm.

4. Philips, Joseph. *PMP Project Management Professional Study Guide, Second Edition* (McGraw-Hill, San Francisco), 2008, page 222.

5. SearchSoftwareQuality.com at: http://searchsoftwarequality.techtarget.com/sDefinition/ 0,,sid92_gci331391,00.html

6. Wikipedia, http://en.wikipedia.org/wiki/Resource_Leveling.

7. Mulcahy, Rita. *PMP Exam Prep, Sixth Edition* (RMC Publications, Inc.), April 2009, page 240.

Chapter 7

Project Cost Management

Key Skills & Concepts

- The role of the project sponsor

- The importance of cost management

- The three cost management processes

- Managing the budget

- Types of estimates

- Range of accuracy

- Earned value management (EVM)

- Tips on how to remember EVM formulas

- Reserve analysis (contingency)

- Types of reports

- Life cycle cost

Cost management is one of the key project management measurements. Remember the project constraints? Cost is one of the primary focus areas when managing projects.

In any economy, managing cost can mean the difference in whether or not a project can survive. Companies are sometimes forced to cut budgets (or move to other suppliers or markets) to stay competitive. The projects that cost the most or are not moving as quickly as the company feels they should are the ones that are frequently terminated. The end result is, projects live and die by the almighty dollar (or peso, euro, yen, and so on).

If you have managed projects, even briefly, chances are you have had one terminated due to budget problems. I was caught by surprise five months into a six-month project in New York when my boss called and informed me the project I was working on was just cancelled due to budget cuts. It is a fact of life, so what can you do? The answer is pretty clear: You manage the budget as closely as you can. You must get (and stay) cost conscious and manage the budget as if it were your own money. If the project goes away, your paycheck may go away with it if you don't manage cost wisely.

If managing a budget was easy, anyone could do it. After all, it is like balancing your checkbook, right? You have a budget, and you have costs and expenses that bleed down the budget. In the world of finance, we call this a "two-line chart" (budget versus actual cost). In the world of project management, you need to be familiar with additional tools and techniques to more effectively estimate, manage, and report progress against your project budget.

One of the tools for managing cost as a project manager is *earned value (EV),* which in PMI terms is the value of the work performed. I like to call it a "three-line chart" because EV looks beyond the budget and actual dollars spent. EV takes a real look at the work that has been completed and allows you to put that accomplishment into dollars and cents so you can show the true financial health and performance of your project. The objective is to give you a better understanding of the benefits of performance tracking as opposed to just looking at the dollars spent.

Many project managers are either unfamiliar with earned value or simply choose not to use it because it takes some time to incorporate and manage it. Another reason PMs shy away from the financial aspects of a project is a lack of a financial background. For example, how much finance or accounting experience do you have? If not that much, don't worry. This chapter provides some easy tips and tricks to help you manage cost on your project and to help you remember the formulas needed to answer the earned value management (EVM) questions on the PMP exam. More details are provided on EVM later in this chapter.

TIP

There are usually only a few questions (approximately 6–10) on earned value on the PMP and CAPM exams and the formulas are pretty easy to remember.

An Offer I Couldn't Refuse

In 1984 I was invited to interview for a big promotion in Chicago, and the company truly made me an offer I couldn't refuse. I accepted the promotion as a Technical Program Manager. After the move, and with only one month on the job, my boss came into my office and introduced me to my new manager in the finance department.

I was stunned and promptly made what could have been a career-limiting announcement: "I never, ever wanted to be a bean counter," I declared. "Well," my boss said, "you are one." The reason I received this "opportunity" was because I had personal computer (PC) experience. I had, in fact, purchased a PC in 1983, only two years after PCs were introduced in 1981. The one I bought didn't even have a hard drive (only dual floppy 5 ¼" disks). Because I had taken the time (with mentoring from my previous branch manager who had said, "The PC is the wave of the future!") to learn how to set up basic spreadsheets and graphs, I was now a "Financial Analyst."

It turns out that getting involved with finance for the company's 26 branch offices and two regional offices in the Chicago area was one of the best things that happened to me. It forced me to learn about the world of finance and how to set budgets as well as track and report performance more effectively. I also believe this experience helped me manage my projects and my own financials more effectively. Thanks, boss.

How Do You Spell "$ponsor"?

Of all the stakeholders on a project, the most important is the sponsor. I tell my students that when they think of the sponsor, they should visualize a dollar sign as the first letter of the word to help remember who the real customer is and who is funding the project.

In my Chicago days, I often said, "Funding is fun." Not that the process is fun, but without funding the project doesn't exist. Thus, no funding equals no project, and that is no fun!

The project selection process and how projects are born was discussed in Chapter 3. Well before the first diaper is purchased for a new project, you need a sponsor. Money is what makes the project emerge. Someone, somewhere is authorizing the project, and that takes money.

How Cost Management Ties into Time Management

Assuming at this point your project is part of the business strategy and has been recognized as essential (and is therefore funded), let's look at how cost management ties into the work you just completed in the previous chapter on time management.

We left off in Chapter 6 on the topic of controlling the schedule, which is the last process in time management. The good news is, all the time and work you and the team invested in estimating the resources and duration of each activity (or work package) will be a key input in converting these items into costs.

Cost estimating is a simple process in most cases. You take the activity duration (usually in number of days) and further decompose this into estimated hours of work effort by activity. Once you assign the activities to different people you can use this simple formula

$$P * Q$$

where the quantity (Q) of hours is multiplied by the price (P) or hourly rate of the different people working on the project to determine cost of labor.

Notice that I started with labor in the cost estimating process because it represents the highest source of cost to your project. There are exceptions (equipment and materials can be high-dollar costs), but almost always the cost of labor is the top of the list (usually around 80 percent of the overall cost to the average project).

The rest of the cost estimating can be pretty easy because the cost of material, equipment, leases, supplies, and such are what they are. You can shop around and negotiate for the best prices for these things (even labor rates in some cases), but the amount quoted is usually straightforward. Clearly, other factors need to be considered in cost estimating and management, and these other factors can come at you in many ways. For example; changes in project scope as well as unexpected events and delays (such as bad weather on a construction project) may drive up overtime or cause a turnover in personnel (which in turn drives training costs up). Also, natural disasters such as hurricanes can drive up the cost of building materials and supplies. If any of these cases mentioned occur, the original cost estimate goes out the window. This is why you also need to plan for risk (see Chapter 11 for more details on risk management). Many dynamics must be considered when planning, estimating, and managing the costs for your project.

Project Cost Management Processes

Project cost management includes the processes needed to estimate, budget, and control costs so that the project can be completed within the approved budget. Cost management is primarily concerned with developing a plan and sticking to it by tracking actual spending and the impact to the budget. Three primary processes are associated with cost management:

- **7.1: Estimate costs (Planning process group)**   The process of developing an estimation of the monetary resources needed to complete project activities.

- **7.2: Determine budget (Planning process group)**   Aggregating the estimated costs of each activity or work package to establish an approved cost baseline.

- **7.3: Control costs (Monitoring and Controlling process group)**   Monitoring project status to update the budget and manage changes to the cost baseline.

In the real world of project management (and especially on smaller projects), cost estimating and cost budgeting are tightly linked and may be viewed as, or even combined into, a single process.

As you may have noticed, two of the three cost management processes are Planning processes, with the last one falling into the Monitoring and Controlling process group. Clearly, the focus is on planning the cost, how to track and manage it, and the tools and methods available to ensure the project is on track to come in at or under the approved budget.

In order to create an accurate cost estimate, you need to consider the inputs (which are often outputs from previous processes). These include the project scope statement, WBS, project constraints, the schedule, company policies, existing systems, standard tools or procedures, and lessons learned from previous or similar projects. Historical information is always a great place to start. You also need an approved, documented plan.

A cost management plan cannot be complete without measurements and rules of engagement, such as procurement; preferred vendors (suppliers or sellers as well as purchase order processing procedures); and tracking tools, techniques, and methods. The cost management plan should be part of the overall project plan and needs to have a clear set of estimates, measurements to be tracked, and reporting status to show that you

- Are in control of the project cost and budget.
- Can demonstrate your overall capability through accurate forecasting to bring in the project at or below the approved budget.

As a project manager, you may have the authority to negotiate for resources (people, equipment, and materials). However, many of us work in a centralized procurement organization, meaning we have to engage and work closely with purchasing and accounts payable departments. These departments may have strict rules that you need to be aware of prior to spending (or committing) money to obtain goods and services.

As part of the planning process, you and the team should, as early as possible in the project life cycle, determine which processes or tools you will use to manage cost on your project. Once you decide how you are managing the project costs and how you are going to track and report progress, you need to include these components in your project cost management plan. The cost management plan should address the following areas:

- Type of estimate used. (More detail on specific types will be shown later in the chapter.)
- Level of accuracy needed for estimates (for example, ±10 percent within budget or within delivery schedule).
- Units of measure (hours, currency, cost per square foot, number of widgets produced in an hour, cost per widget, hours per day worked, cost per hour of labor, and so on).
- Type of tracking (for example, plan versus actual, milestones, trends, and earned value).

- Type of reporting (for example, format, frequency, and distribution of reports).

- Record retention (where they are stored and for how long) and who has access.

These are only a few of the things you might include in a cost management plan. It can be formal or informal, provide lots of detail, or just be basic. At the end of the day, however, the plan needs be in place to help you manage the cost of the project with an acceptable level of control based on the needs of the project. The plan needs to meet the needs of the stakeholder requirements for capturing and reporting project costs.

When planning for cost, keep in mind that it is common to see a lot of money being charged to a project at the beginning without much to show for it. Unless the PM manages the startup carefully (using entrance criteria, with a good orientation on what is needed versus what they may have done on similar projects), they can go over budget very quickly.

TIP

It is important to tie the cost of the project to its expected life cycle. As you can imagine, the lowest costs will be at the ends (starting and closing), with the highest cost occurring during the execution phase, when you are fully staffed and using the most equipment and materials. Also, you want to plan for some residual costs after the project is shut down for "punch list" or warranty corrections.

1. Estimate Costs Process

The one question that comes up for every project (especially new projects) is, How much will it cost? The only thing that can make this question easier to answer (unless you have a really clear and accurate crystal ball) is to utilize a similar project that has been completed recently for an actual cost comparison. This is called top-down or analogous estimating. We talked about it in Chapter 6 and will discuss it further in this chapter—it is one of several estimating tools and techniques for determining the estimated cost to run your project.

The cost-estimating process involves developing a best guess (approximation) of the resources needed to complete project activities and their associated costs. The estimates should be refined during the course of the project as more information becomes known through progressive elaboration.

As you progress through the project life cycle, you learn more about the project, so the accuracy of your cost estimate will increase accordingly. The cost estimates should be refined based on the additional information you have gained (this is an iterative process from one phase to the next).

Range of Estimating Accuracy

According to PMI, the two primary ranges of accuracy, which can be used at different times during the project life cycle, are rough order of magnitude (ROM) and definitive estimate (see Table 7-1).

The decision of when to use each range depends on the degree of confidence in the data available and the timing of the estimate during the project life cycle. For example, during the initiating phase (early in the project life cycle), there are many unknowns and a lot of uncertainty concerning the cost and information. The project team may be new or the project may be unique; this is the time to use a rough order of magnitude (ROM) estimate.

NOTE
ROM is sometimes called order of magnitude (OM) and carries a wider range of accuracy to estimate the cost of a project early in the life cycle.

As you get further into the project life cycle, you should have more accurate information and your confidence level will increase to the point where you may choose to use a narrower range (definitive or budget level) of accuracy. In either case, the decision is up to you and your team as to the range of accuracy you feel is appropriate for your estimate.

The main thing to remember when determining the type of estimate and range of accuracy is to document the assumptions made, the type of estimating you used, and the percentage of expected accuracy (can be ±10 percent, ±30 percent, or ±50 percent). It is your call. Once the team agrees, you document and communicate the information to the appropriate stakeholders to minimize any confusion as to the degree of confidence in the range chosen.

TIP
There are times when a project sponsor will come to you and say, "I just need a best guess as to the estimated cost before I can agree to start the project." And far too often the number you provide gets "poured in concrete" and the sponsor wants to hold you accountable for that guess without giving you time to conduct a proper estimate. This would be a great time to use a ROM estimate and document the type of estimate used and the range of accuracy you predict based on your (and the team's) confidence level.

Type of Estimate	Accuracy Range	When Used
Rough order of magnitude (ROM)	±50 percent	Early in the project life cycle or when confidence is low concerning the information available (for example, for a new and unique project)
Definitive estimate (sometimes a budget-level estimate can be used from -10 to +25 percent).	±10 percent	Later in the life cycle or when confidence is high concerning the information available (for example, for a repeat project)

Table 7-1 Range of Estimating Accuracy

As always, the best place to start the cost-estimating process is to look at the work (inputs and outputs) collected and created thus far from previous processes. However, you need to look at the information from a slightly different perspective—for example, dollars and cents as they tie to work (time, resources, deliverables, and so on) as opposed to descriptions. For example, instead of looking at the scope statement as a way to define the deliverables, look at it for signs of the cost of the deliverables to the project. You should also look for language that translates into a direct or indirect cost to your project, such as "Security services will continue to be provided by Watchdog, Inc." This means you are forced to use a security resource and are likely bound by an existing contract for predetermined cost to the project. While reviewing the contract for Watchdog, Inc., you also see it is a five-year contract with 5 percent cost of living adjustment (COLA) increases every year over the life of the contract. See what I mean? Now you are looking at the dollars and cents of cost management. This makes a big difference.

TIP

More and more companies are requiring that the project manager calculate the project costs and factor the ROI (return on investment) and other cost benefit models into the project product. The goal is to see the value of the project once its deliverables are in operation.[1]

Cost vs. Pricing   Keep in mind that cost and pricing are two different things. *Cost* is an expenditure of money, time, and labor to acquire or provide goods and/or services whereas *pricing* is the cost plus profit margin.

Profit Margin   Profit is important to a company's ability to stay in business. Profit margin (or net profit) is a measure of profitability that is calculated by finding the net profit as a percentage of the company's revenue (see Figure 7-1).

A low profit margin indicates a low margin of safety: The risk is higher that a decline in sales will erase profits and result in a net loss.

For example, suppose a company produces a product that sells for $10. The cost to produce the product is $6, and the company also has to pay $2 in taxes. That makes the company's net income $2. Because the revenue is $10, the profit margin would be (2/10) or 20 percent.

$$\text{Net profit margin} = \frac{\text{Net profit (after taxes)}}{\text{Revenue}} \times 100$$

Figure 7-1   Net profit margin formula

Wikipedia provides the following definition:

> "Profit margin is an indicator of a company's pricing policies and its ability to control costs. Differences in competitive strategy and product mix cause the profit margin to vary among different companies."[2]

Estimate Costs Inputs

Six inputs are identified for the Estimate Costs process:

- **Scope baseline** The focus here is on the costs to the project.
- **Project schedule** Specifically the activities and work packages converted from duration in days (most likely) to hours and cost.
- **Human resource plan** Staffing is key to labor costs, including subcontractors, vendors, suppliers, hourly rates, cost of employee benefits (sometimes called a burden rate), cost of office space (occupancy), and equipment (phones, desks, PCs, and so on).
- **Risk register** The cost to mitigate risk events, should they occur, and the cost of inspection to ensure against risk.
- **Enterprise environmental factors** The cost of information, impact of market conditions, and so on.
- **Organizational process assets** Cost-estimating policies, templates, historical information, and cost to store the project documents.

Types of Estimates

The cost of work (activities) should be estimated using the same tools and techniques introduced in Chapter 6, such as one-cost, analogous, parametric, and three-point estimates, with an additional type called bottom-up estimating.

Things to Know about Estimating Cost

As project managers, we love checklists; here is a list that I find especially helpful (excerpted from Rita Mulcahy's *PMP Exam Prep, Sixth Edition*):

- The cost estimates should be based on the WBS to improve accuracy.
- The cost estimates should be done by the person (or persons) doing the work (get accuracy and buy-in).
- Use historical information when available from similar projects.
- A cost baseline should be set and only changed after approved changes.

- The budget should be managed to the cost baseline for the project.

- Estimates are more accurate if tied to work packages rather than at higher levels.

- Corrective action or preventive action should be recommended when cost problems occur (as with other types of problems around scope, schedule, quality, and so on).

- A project manager should always analyze requirements and not just accept them as delivered by management (they should be realistic and achievable).

- Padding is not an acceptable project management practice.

- The project manager must meet any agreed-upon estimates (need to keep estimates realistic).[3]

Types of Cost

A number of different types of cost can be associated with project management. This is also consistent with other real-world applications besides project management. The categories are listed next. It is recommended you study them and be able to differentiate one from the other for the PMP or CAPM exam:

- **Variable costs**   Costs that change with the amount of work or production (for example, the cost of salaries, supplies, equipment, and materials).

- **Fixed costs**   Fixed costs don't usually change (for example, fixed monthly fee for maintenance agreement on computers, monthly lease payments, and rent).

- **Direct costs**   Costs that are directly associated with the project (for example, material, project labor, travel, cell phones, or other discretionary costs).

- **Indirect costs**   Costs that are incurred across multiple projects. This can include facilities, Project Management Office (PMO) costs, employee benefits, and overhead costs.

Things to Consider When Estimating Costs

Value analysis and risk are often not considered when costing a project. As mentioned earlier, project managers usually do a good job at estimating direct cost; however, they often underestimate (or miss altogether) some of the key ingredients (components), such as the following:

- Cost of managing the project (the PM's time, meetings, documentation, and so on)

- Cost of quality (cost of nonconformance; rework, scrap cost, and so on)

- Training or company-related meetings not related to the project
- Office expenses for space, phones, computers, raised floor, and network costs
- Estimated profit and ROI (return on investment), ROA (return on assets), or ROS (return on sales)
- Overhead (indirect costs)

Estimate Costs Tools and Techniques

The list of tools and techniques for cost estimating are similar to the Estimate Activity Durations process from Chapter 6, with just a few differences. We will focus on a few of the items in the following list in greater detail in this section:

- Expert judgment
- Analogous (top-down) estimating
- Parametric estimating (unit of measure)
- Bottom-up estimating
- Three-point estimating
- Reserve analysis
- Cost of quality (COQ)
- Project management estimating software
- Vendor bid analysis (covered in Chapter 12)

Bottom-up Estimating Bottom-up estimating is considered very accurate because the estimate is provided by the subject matter expert (SME) or person doing the work. The estimates collected from the team are then rolled up to make the aggregate cost estimate for the project. The accuracy of the cost can be influenced by the size and complexity of the individual activity or work package.

Parametric Estimating Parametric estimating uses a statistical relationship between historical data and other variables to calculate an estimate for activity parameters, such as cost, budget, and duration. This technique usually provides a high degree of accuracy because you have historical information to draw from. As always, you can use this estimating method with other methods, as needed, to reach a level of confidence in the accuracy of your cost estimate for the entire project.

Parametric Estimating

Your manager is aware of a "Green Data Center" in Boulder, Colorado, and asks you to contact the company (IBM) to obtain a cost estimate to set up five mainframe systems and 300 servers in their center. What do you do?

Answer: You contact IBM and ask the Data Center Manager for a parametric cost estimate (cost per square foot) for hosting your systems and servers. When you receive the cost estimate, you provide this and other pertinent details to your boss.

Three-Point Estimates   Introduced in Chapter 6, the three-point estimate adds a degree of accuracy over the one-point estimate (which is the most common). You may recall the three-point estimate is a PERT (Program Evaluation and Review Technique) that takes input from a subject matter expert (SME). Based on the SME's understanding of an activity (in this case, the cost), they apply their best estimates for optimistic (O), pessimistic (P) and most likely (ML, sometimes shown as M) and work through the formula to determine expected cost. The PERT formula can be shown in different ways, Figure 7-2 duplicates how it is shown in the fourth edition of the *PMBOK*.

Reserve Analysis   Contingency: What is it and why do we care? Contingency is a reserve accomplished by setting aside money either inside the project budget (called "contingency reserves") or outside the project budget (called "management reserves"). Contingency reserves are used to cover those risk events that you and the team have identified (known) that are likely to occur on the project. Management reserves are held at the management level (outside the project budget for many companies) for unknown risk events that are not identified or foreseen at the specific project level. Management reserves are not usually project specific and can be used across multiple projects, as

$$C_E = \frac{C_O + 4C_M + C_P}{6}$$

Legend
  C_E (Cost Estimate)
  C_O (Cost Optimistic)
  $4C_M$ (4 × Cost Most Likely)
  C_P (Cost Pessimistic)

Figure 7-2   Three-point estimate formula

needed, and at management's discretion. An example of this would be FEMA (Federal Emergency Management Agency) funds for disaster recovery.

Cost of Quality (COQ)   Cost of quality (COQ) is the cost of work needed by the PM and team to ensure quality management is part of the project. In the real world, COQ is also a measurement used for assessing the waste or losses from some defined process (machine, production line, plant, department, company, and so on).

The COQ measurement can track changes over time for one particular process, or it can be used as a benchmark for comparison of two or more different processes (for example, two machines, production lines, sister plants, competitor companies, and so on).

Most COQ systems are defined using categories of costs. The information in Table 7-2 comes from Process Quality Associates, Inc.

COQ systems are sometimes assisted by specially designed COQ software and are helpful in the identification and tracking of COQ.

COQ Category	Typical Descriptions (May Vary Between Different Organizations)	Examples
Internal	Costs associated with internal losses (for example, within the process being analyzed).	Off-cuts (waste), equipment breakdowns, spills, scrap, yield, and productivity
External	Costs external to the process being analyzed (for example, occur outside, not within). These costs are usually discovered by or affect third parties (for example, vendors or customers). Some external costs may have originated from within or have been caused, created by, or made worse by the process being analyzed. They are defined as "external" because of where they were discovered, or who is primarily or initially affected.	Customer complaints, latent defects found by the customer, warranties
Preventive	Costs associated with the prevention of future losses (for example, unplanned or undesired problems, lost opportunities, breakdowns, work stoppages, and waste).	Planning, mistake-proofing, scheduled maintenance, and quality assurance
Assessment	Costs associated with measurement and assessment of the process.	Key performance indicators (KPIs), inspections, quality checks, dock audits, third-party audits, measuring devices, reporting systems, data-collection systems, and forms

Table 7-2   Categories of Cost of Quality (COG)

Ask the Expert

Q: How is cost estimating and cost management done in the real world?

A: A project manager in the real world first must ask one very important question of the project sponsor: "How accurate do you want me to be?" The answer should be based on the time allotted, the information and resources available, and the degree of accuracy the sponsor needs to sell the project (for example, getting the funding/budget approved). Then the PM should look at the scope and deliverables to determine which estimating tools and techniques to use based on the type and complexity of the project. It is also important to know if a similar project has been done before. Then the PM takes all this information into consideration and usually rolls the details into a software estimating tool, if one is available.

TIP

If you are planning to take the PMP exam, not only should you know the different types of estimating tools and techniques, but you should also be able to identify the advantages and disadvantages of each. Examples are provided in Tables 7-3 and 7-4.

Estimate Costs Outputs

Here are the three key outputs from the Estimate Costs process:

- **Activity cost estimates** Quantifiable assessments of the probable cost required to complete the work of the project. The cost estimates can be presented in various forms—for example, at the summary level or in a bill of materials (BOM) with cost broken down into details of labor, facilities, equipment, materials, IT, travel, and so on. It can be in a spreadsheet distributed over time by month, by process group, or phase of the project life cycle.

Analogous Estimating Advantages	Analogous Estimating Disadvantages
Quick and easy	Less accurate than bottom-up estimating
Don't need to estimate at activity level	Less detail based on limited information
Less costly to create	Requires higher experience to do well
Higher level of management expectation	Difficult for projects with a lot of uncertainty
Based on historical information of similar previous projects	Doesn't consider project differences and requires accurate history from previous projects

Table 7-3 Analogous Estimating

Bottom-up Estimating Advantages	Bottom-up Estimating Disadvantages
More accurate than most other methods	Takes more time to create and is more expensive.
Gains buy-in from the team members because they create the estimates	There is a tendency for team members to "pad" the estimates to provide a comfort zone.
Developed based on detailed analysis	Requires the scope and activities to be clearly defined and understood by the team members.
Provides a level of detail that should be easier to monitor and control	Requires more time to perform the details as they relate to the WBS activities and work packages.

Table 7-4 Bottom-up Estimating

- **Basis of estimates** This is where you should show the type of estimating tools and techniques used as well as other supporting details, such as the following:

  - Documented basis of how the cost estimate was developed—bottom-up, top-down (analogous), parametric, and so on—and a clearly documented range of expected accuracy (for example, ±50 percent or -10 percent to +25 percent).

  - The list of assumptions made by you and the team to come up with the estimate.

  - The known constraints (time, cost, resources, permits, compliance, and so on).

  - An indication of the confidence level of the final estimate (for example, high, medium, or low) and the reasons for your conclusion.

- **Project document updates** Updates to the scope statement, WBS, WBS dictionary, schedule, risk register, and communications plan based on findings during this process.

Reporting Formats and Frequency of Delivery

The format and frequency used to report progress should be applicable to the type and complexity of your project. The reports and when they are presented (and in what format) must meet the needs and expectations of the sponsor and other key stakeholders. You should fit the report to the need. For example, for executive-level reporting, keep it simple and concise. I recommend using a milestone report for middle- to high-level managers and customers just to show the status and progress on major events.

Weekly status reports should provide adequate details for the team to understand the specifics needed and potential delays due to dependencies and so on.

For monthly financial reports, such as earned value measurements and other sponsor-level interests, keep the format focused on dollars and cents and show accurate forecasts if possible (with supporting assumptions and justification data).

2. Determine Budget Process

The Determine Budget process is where you combine all the estimates from the Estimate Costs process into one overall project cost budget. You also add in any cost contingency, usually in conjunction with risk management (for example, those risk events that have a high probability of impacting the project if they occur). Remember, contingency reserves should be included as part of the overall project budget. Collectively the project budget should consist of the approved funds to begin executing the project.

TIP

There will be times when only a portion of the project budget will be authorized for a particular phase; for example, the concept phase may be funded to cover the costs of prototyping the solution so you can demonstrate the solution will work prior to the total project being funded.

Once the budget is authorized, you need to establish and confirm the key measurements. These measurements will need to be tracked and reported on a regular basis (usually monthly) to the project sponsor(s) to demonstrate you are managing the project budget.

Budget Estimating and Measuring Project Health

The project status (that is, the health of the project) can be measured in a number of ways. To perform any "health checking," you must first have an agreed-upon cost performance baseline. You should remember baselines from Chapter 5. Earned value (EV) is a good way to measure progress and the overall health of your project. It will be covered in more detail later in this chapter.

Cost Performance Baseline

The cost performance baseline is an authorized time-phased budget at completion (BAC). BAC is one of the key components in calculating earned value (EV).

In setting the cost performance baseline, you must first look at the scope baseline to ensure the cost is aligned with the scope. The cost baseline should also take the scheduled activities and work packages into consideration because this is where the budget will be spent.

Other key considerations should be the project contract, the SOW, and specific performance requirements of these documents.

Sample Cost Performance Baseline Overview

Each project should have a formally approved and communicated performance baseline (PB) that describes the integration of the technical objectives and requirements with the schedule and cost objectives.

Here are the main reasons for establishing, approving, controlling, and documenting a performance baseline:

- To ensure achievement of project objectives
- To manage and monitor progress during project execution
- To define the project for approval and authorization by the office of management
- To ensure accurate information on the final configuration (as-built drawings, specifications, expenditures, and so on)
- To establish performance-measurement criteria for projects

According to "Performance Baseline Development and Validation," by the U.S. Department of Energy, "Development of the PB begins with the planning cost, schedule estimate, and the preliminary scope included in the mission need statement, and is further defined in conceptual design documents."[4]

3. Control Costs Process

Now that you have an approved budget, which is the main output of the Determine Budget process, you need to be thinking about how to control costs.

The key to effective cost control is the management of the approved performance baseline and the changes to that baseline. It is common to reset the performance baseline, especially on larger projects, and this should only be done through proper change control.

Project cost control includes the following:

- Ensuring all change requests are responded to in a timely manner
- Reviewing possible impact to the project (cost, time, scope, risk, and so on)
- Managing the actual changes when and as they occur (document and communicate)
- Preventing unapproved changes from impacting the project and budget
- Managing the cost expenditures to not exceed the approved funding by period and in total for the project
- Monitoring cost performance to isolate and understand variances
- Monitoring work performance (value of work performed, or EV) against approved budget and time

- Accurately reporting to appropriate stakeholders all approved changes and costs

- Managing any cost overruns within the acceptable limits (consistent with approved contingency reserves)

The bottom-line intent of project cost control is to effectively manage the approved budget and seek out potential impact variances (both positive and negative) against the budget. The best way to ensure cost control is through effective change management and close monitoring and reporting of earned value.

TIP

For readers not planning to pursue PMI's PMP exam in the near future, I recommend you scan this section for a high-level overview and not for detailed comprehension. You can always come back to this chapter later when you are ready to prepare for PM certification.

Control Costs Tools and Techniques

PMBOK, Fourth Edition shows six tools and techniques for this process, which will be discussed in this section. The first to be discussed is earned value management (EVM). EVM is growing in popularity, especially in large companies and on government projects. Some companies even have an earned value analyst (EVA) working with the project managers and teams across multiple projects, tracking and reporting on their EV status using a consistent format and frequency.

NOTE

Earned value management involves a number of concepts, calculations, and methods that are performed by today's high-tech PM software tools. Even the more experienced project manager is often not completely comfortable with EV tracking because it requires extra time and a degree of judgment on when/how to report the completion and progress of activities.

Earned value management can be used in various ways. EVM is most often used as a method of measuring project performance in dollars and cents. The principle of EVM is used to develop and monitor three key dimensions (components) for each work package (or at the control account level). To manage EV, you collect key data at regular intervals (for example, weekly or monthly, depending on the size and duration of the project) to establish a checkpoint (snapshot) in time to measure progress on your project. The key dimensions of EVM are as follows:

- **Planned value (PV)**   This is the authorized budget assigned to the work planned to be accomplished based on historical or expert knowledge for activities or work packages. Planned value is the amount you planned to spend at a given time on the project. If nothing changes, the original PV adds up to be the budget at completion (BAC) at the end of the project.

- **Actual cost (AC)**   The total cost actually incurred and recorded for the work performed.

NOTE
Tracking and reporting actual cost can be somewhat elusive in the case of delayed invoices from suppliers, allocated costs that are apportioned across multiple projects, and missed or hidden charges.

- **Earned value (EV)**   The value of the work performed (for example, those activities or work packages that are complete and should receive appropriate credit for the expected dollar value they are assigned). EV must be compared to the PV baseline and actual cost (AC) to determine schedule and cost variance.

TIP
Earned value should clearly show not just how much of your budget has been spent (AC) against what you thought you were going to spend (PV), but it should also show the value of work completed (EV). EV is becoming more widely used, especially in large companies and government projects.

When reporting the progress of work performed and EV in dollars and cents for a particular activity or work package, use the progress-reporting rules introduced in Chapter 6:

- **50/50 rule**   Fifty percent credit for the value of an activity when it begins and 50 percent when complete

- **20/80 rule**   Twenty percent credit for the value of an activity when it begins and 80 percent when complete

- **0/100 rule**   Zero percent credit when the activity begins and 100 percent credit when it is complete

NOTE
It is important to discuss and ensure a clear understanding of which rule (or rules) you plan to use when measuring and reporting EVM with the team to minimize any confusion.

Acronym	Term	Interpretation
PV	Planned Value	As of today, what is the estimated value of the work planned to be done?
EV	Earned Value	As of today, what is the estimated value of the work actually accomplished?
AC	Actual Cost	As of today, what is the actual cost incurred for the work accomplished?
BAC	Budget at Completion	How much did we budget for the total project?
EAC	Estimate at Completion	What do we currently expect the total project to cost (a forecast)?
ETC	Estimate to Complete	From this point on, how much more do we expect it to cost to finish the project (a forecast)?
VAC	Variance at Completion	As of today, how much over or under budget do we expect to be at the end of the project?

Table 7-5   EVM Terms and Interpretations

Earned Value Formulas

You should be familiar with several formulas (especially if you are planning to take the PMP or PMI Scheduling exam) to enable yourself and the team to effectively perform and understand EVM. You should also be familiar with the definition or interpretation of each of the key components of EVM, as detailed in Tables 7-5 and 7-6.[5]

How to Remember the EVM Formulas

A few tips are going around the PM world concerning how to remember the EVM formulas. They are as follows:

- *Variances* are always "minus." For example, EV minus (–) either cost (AC) or schedule (PV).

- *Indexes* (CPI, SPI and TCPI) are always "divide." Think "I = divide."

- *EV* is almost always first in the formula (the exceptions are EAC, ETC, and VAC).

Name	Formula	Interpretation and Tips
Schedule Variance (SV)	$SV = EV - PV$	Ahead or behind schedule. Minus (negative) is behind schedule, and plus (positive) is ahead of schedule (good).
Cost Variance (CV)	$CV = EV - AC$	Ahead or behind budget. Minus (negative) is over budget (bad), and plus (positive) is under budget (good).
Schedule Performance Index (SPI)	$SPI = \dfrac{EV}{PV}$	The project is currently progressing at _____ % of the rate originally planned. (Note: < 1.0 is good.)
Cost Performance Index (CPI)	$CPI = \dfrac{EV}{AC}$	Currently getting $_____ worth of work out of every dollar spent. Budget is or is not being spent wisely (> 1.0 is good). CPI is an index showing the efficiency of the utilization of the resources on the project.
To-Complete Performance Index	$TCPI = \dfrac{(BAC - EV)}{(BAC - AC)}$	Projection of cost performance needed to achieve the original budget. **Note:** If the resultant number is higher than 1.0, the chances of getting back to the original budget (BAC) is extremely difficult.
Estimate to Complete (ETC)	$ETC = EAC - AC$	How much more do we expect the project to cost from this point forward?
Estimate at Completion (EAC)	There are several ways to calculate EAC, depending on the assumptions made.	At this time, how much do you expect the total project to cost? (See the formulas to the left and below.)
	$EAC = AC + \text{Bottom-up ETC}$ **Note:** This formula is most often asked for on the exam.	This formula calculates actual plus a new estimate for the remaining work.
	$EAC = \dfrac{BAC}{\text{Cumulative CPI}}$	Used if no variances from BAC have occurred or if you plan to continue at the same spend (burn) rate.
	$EAC = AC + ETC$	Actual cost plus the new estimate to complete remaining work. Used when original estimate is not appropriate.
	$EAC = AC + (BAC - EV)$	Actual to date plus remaining budget. Used when current variances are thought to be atypical (it is essentially AC plus the remaining value of work to be performed).
	$EAC = AC + \left[\dfrac{(BAC - EV)}{(\text{cumulative CPI} \times \text{cumlative SPI})} \right]$	Actual to date plus remaining budget modified by performance. Used when current variances are thought to be typical (representative) of the future. EAC is the manager's projection of total cost of the project at completion.
Variance at Completion (VAC)	$VAC = BAC - EAC$	How much over or under budget do we expect to be at the end of the project?

Table 7-6   EVM Formulas

Ask the Expert

Q: **How do we know where we are in the project? Can you show an example?**

A: Earned value management is a good way to tell where you are on your project. The important thing to remember if you are planning to use EVM is that you need to set it up early in the project life cycle. You need to determine which progress-reporting rule (or rules) mentioned earlier in this chapter you plan to use. Also, you need to be consistent in how you credit the work performed and how you report the progress. This may take some education for both you and your project team. See Figure 7-3 for an example of how the earned value key components would map out in a chart.

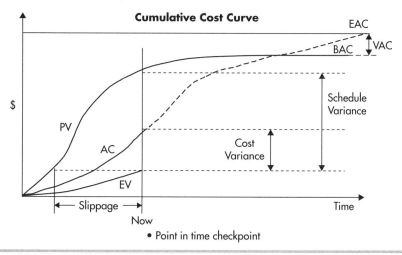

Figure 7-3   Sample earned value chart

An important aspect of calculating earned value is that it is typically a point in time checkpoint, and to be effective it should be checked on a regular basis (early and often). Let's take the chart shown in Figure 7-3 and do the math.

Try This Earned Value Example Using BEC Case Study

You are the PM on a new project to build the sidewalls (protective barrier) for an ice hockey game. The assumptions used to calculate EV for this project are as follows:

- You have four days to build four walls for the ice arena.
- The duration estimate indicates it will take one day to build each side of the arena.
- The estimated cost (planned value) is $1,000 per wall.
- A checkpoint at Day 3 shows you have only completed two-and-a-half sides of the ice arena.

  The information in the questions, tables, and answers that follow will guide you through the process of determining earned value on this project.

Question 1: What are the earned value management key component values? (For the answer, see Table 7-7.)

EVM Component	Formula or Results	Comments
Planned Value (PV)	$3,000 PV = Day 1 PV + Day 2 PV + Day 3 PV **or** PV = $1000 + $1000 + $1000	Checkpoint at Day 3 of a four-day project. Planned value/cost at $1,000 per day is as follows: PV = 3 * $1,000 = $3,000
Actual Cost (AC)	$2,900 AC = dollars spent at this time. For example: Labor ($1,500) + Materials ($800) + Equipment ($600)	You would only know this from the hours worked by the team times, the cost per hour, and of course the actual cost of equipment and building materials spent.
Earned Value (EV)	$2,500 EV = Day 1 EV + Day 2 EV + Day 3 EV (EV = $1000 + $1000 + $500) **or** EV = 2.5 * $1,000 = $2,500	Two and a half sides of the ice arena are completed by Day 3. Therefore, the value of the work performed (completed) is $2,500.
Budget at Completion (BAC)	$4,000 Four sides at $1,000 per side, BAC = 4 * $1,000 = $4,000	The BAC is usually set at the beginning of the project and can only change through approved change control.

Table 7-7   Key Components for Earned Value Management

Earned Value Variances	Formula and Results	Interpretation
Schedule Variance (SV)	SV = EV − PV $2,500 − $3,000 = −$500	Negative means you are behind schedule (the project is delayed) or the schedule was not estimated accurately.
Cost Variance (CV)	CV = EV − AC $2,500 − $2,900 = −$400	Negative means your have overspent the budget or underestimated the cost of the project.

Table 7-8   Schedule and Cost Variance Calculations

Question 2: Is the project on schedule and on budget? (See Table 7-8 for the answers.)

Answer: In this case, the project is behind schedule and the budget is overspent.

Other key components of EVM are CPI and SPI; these indexes help you forecast the remaining cost to your project. Using the information provided in the preceding earned value case study example, calculate the run rate (CPI and SPI) to see if you are getting your money's worth of performance for the money spent on setting up the walls at the ice arena.

Question: What are the CPI and SPI for the ice arena project, and are you receiving the work performance or cost performance you had planned for? (See Table 7-9 for the answer.)

Answer: Based on the results in the table (and the interpretation), the answer is "no" on both counts, which means you will miss your target to complete as well as missing your budget.

Earned Value Variances	Formula and Results	Interpretation
Schedule Performance Index (SPI)	SPI = EV / PV SPI = 2,500 / 3,000 = 0.83 (Note that 0.83 is rounded. If the calculation uses more decimal places, the results will vary.)	Less than 1.0 means you are getting less performance than planned against the schedule; in other words, you are performing at a rate that is 83 percent of your target schedule.
Cost Performance Index (CPI)	CPI = EV / AC CPI = 2,500 / 2,900 = 0.86 (Note that 0.86 is rounded. If the calculation uses more decimal places, the ETC results will vary.)	Less than 1.0 means you are getting less cost performance for each dollar spent (for example, in this case, you're getting 86 cents for every dollar spent).

Table 7-9   SPI and CPI Calculations

Now that you have key information about your project, you can use the results of the EVM calculations to apply the results of CPI and SPI toward the future. Here are the key questions that need to be answered before you forecast the future cost and schedule performance for the remainder of the project:

- Is the CPI (sometimes called "run rate" or "burn rate") representative of what the project will cost?

- Is the SPI a true representation of the performance you can expect as you go forward with the project?

The answer to these questions will help you decide if you need to adjust the schedule or cost due to unforeseen problems or if you need to take correction action to get the team and budget back on target.

The next tool and technique in the Control Costs process is forecasting. It is important to forecast the future cost and performance early and throughout the project life cycle. The components of earned value for forecasting are

- **Estimate to compete (ETC)**, which answers the question of "what is the remaining cost from this point forward to finish the project?"

- **Estimate at completion (EAC)**, which answers the question of "what will be the total cost of the project be based on our new ETC?"

- **Variance at completion (VAC)**, which answers the question of "what is the amount over or under the original budget at completion (BAC) based on the latest cost information?"

See Table 7-10 for the forecast calculations for the ice hockey arena wall project.

EVM Component	Formula or Results	Comments
Estimate at Completion (EAC)	EAC = BAC / CPI $4,000 / 0.86 = $4,651	The new estimated budget at the completion of the project based on EVM at this time. **Note:** There are several ways to calculate EAC (see Table 7-5), and the decision should be based on the level of confidence in the actual cost (AC) and other factors.
Estimate to Complete (ETC)	ETC = EAC − AC $4,651 − $2,900 = $1,751	How much do you anticipate you need to spend to complete the project?
Variance at Completion (VAC)	VAC = BAC − EAC $4,000 − $4,651 = −$651	Based on the information available, you expect to be $651 over budget at the end of the project. Again, minus is bad.

Table 7-10 Estimating Future Cost (ETC, EAC, and VAC)

In the case of our ice hockey project, with the estimated cost to complete (ETC) of $1,751 added to what we have already spent (AC) of $2,900, we can forecast the new estimate at completion (EAC) for the entire project to be $4,651. The overrun variance at completion (VAC) is $651 dollars.

The next step is to present the status and forecast amounts to the project sponsor along with your action plan to either get back on track or the justification for additional funding. As you would expect, the project's forecast gets more and more accurate the closer to the end of the project. (Go figure. There goes that progressive elaboration again.)

TIP

Accurate forecasting is essential to managing the costs on your project. Some companies go so far as to hold the PM accountable for an accurate project forecast (within ±10%, for example). The reason is clear—the more accurate the forecast for each project, the more accurate the financial department can forecast across all their projects. You can see this at the corporate level each quarter when stock analysts predict (forecast) a company's earnings. It doesn't matter if the company made a profit and grew their revenue, if they missed the analysts' forecasts (expectations), especially if the number is lower than expected, then the company's stock will often go down.

To-Complete Performance Index (TCPI)

The next tool and technique in the Control Costs process is TCPI. Basically, TCPI provides a way to calculate how much work it would take (future required cost efficiency needed to achieve the original approved budget at completion). If the TCPI calculation is greater than 1.0 late in the project life cycle, this means the chances of being able to get back to the original baseline budget are not likely.

As shown in the previous Table 7-6 this can be calculated using the following formula:

$$TCPI = \frac{(BAC - EV)}{(BAC - AC)}$$

Performance Reviews

Performance reviews compare cost performance over time as well as schedule activities or work packages that are either running over or under the budget. They also estimate the funds needed to complete the work in progress. The performance review is another tool in the Control Costs process. If used with EVM, it applies the following information:

- **Variance analysis** Compares actual project performance to planned or expected performance. Cost and schedule variances are the most frequently analyzed.

- **Trend analysis**   Examines project performance over time to determine whether it is improving. Many graphical tools are available that can visually show trends on the project.

- **Earned value performance**   EVP compares the baseline plan to the actual schedule and cost performance and looks at the value of work performed to show the true status of the project.

Variance Analysis

The last of the tools and techniques in the Control Costs process focuses on cost performance measurement (CV, CPI) and is used to assess the extent of variation to the original cost baseline. The results of variance analysis provide the PM and team valuable information on cost performance and help them decide if correction or preventative action is required.

As always, PM software can be used to assist with the many tools and techniques to help you control costs on your projects.

Other Terms and Concepts in Cost Management

A few other terms and concepts are associated with cost management that you should be familiar with. I will only briefly touch on these topics because they are not used extensively in project management, unless you are on a project selection board, for example, voting on which projects should be selected and funded.

Ask the Expert

Q: What are the real goals of cost management? And how do I know if the cost is the norm or an anomaly (one-off)?

A: The goals of cost management are simple:

- Focus on the end cost results (deliverables, scope, schedule, products, and so on).

- Use the tools and resources available to determine what the project should cost.

- Work as a team to ensure you are controlling cost to the best of your ability and are reporting it accurately.

I am not sure I have ever seen a project that is "normal." After all, that is what makes each project unique. Therefore, watch for the anomalies because there tend to be many; be sure to adjust accordingly. Note that these three goals should sound familiar (they align with the three takeaway points from Chapter 2).

Present Value   Present value (PV) is the value today of future cash flows and can be found by using the following formula:

PV = FV / (1 + r) n

where

- PV = Present value
- FV = Future value (see FV formulas, next)
- r = interest rate
- n = number of time periods

You can think about PV as "how much money do you need to put in the bank today (PV) at r percent interest if you want to reach a future cash flow of FV in n years?"

TIP

The good news is present value is usually only mentioned once or twice on the PMI exam and you will not likely have to remember the formula. You should know that present value is "less" than the amount of cash flow you receive in the future. In other words, if you see a question that asks for PV of $300,000, the answer would be a number less than $300,000.

Net Present Value (NPV)   NPV is used in capital budgeting to analyze the profitability of an investment or project. FinAid.org offers the following definition of net present value (NPV):

> "Net Present Value (NPV) is a way of comparing the value of money now with the value of money in the future. A dollar today is worth more than a dollar in the future, because inflation erodes the buying power of the future money, while money available today can be invested and grow.... Calculating NPV is difficult, in part, because it isn't clear what discount (interest) rate should be used, nor is it clear how to project future changes in the discount rate."[6]

TIP

For the PMP exam, you will not likely have to calculate NPV. You just need to know that the project with the highest NPV provides the more favorable financial investment. In addition to the formula, net present value can often be calculated using tables and spreadsheets.

Generally, if NPV is positive, the investment choice is a good one. NPV in simple terms is the sum of PV for the period measured minus the investment costs for those same periods.

For example: To calculate NPV on a project (project A), use the sample data in Table 7-11. First, calculate the present value for income/revenue based on the interest rate as shown in the third column. Then, calculate the present value of cost over the number of periods as shown in the fifth column. Last, take the total present value of income/revenue minus the total costs and you get the net present value. In this example, NPV = 481 – 290 = 191.

Here's how this helps in the project selection process. Take the example where the NPV of project A is 191 and compare this to another project (B) that has an NPV of 120. Which project has the most favorable NPV? Even though they are both positive NPV, you would recommend project A to your sponsor; it has the higher value, if all other things are equal.

Future Value Future value is the value of an asset or cash at a specified date in the future that is equivalent in value to a specified sum today. There are two ways to calculate FV:

- For an asset with simple annual interest:

    original investment * (1 + (interest rate * number of years))

- For an asset with interest compounded annually:

    original investment * ((1 + interest rate) ^ number of years)

Time Period	Income/ Revenue	Present Value of Income/ Revenue at 10% Interest Rate	Costs	Present Value of Cost at 10% Interest Rate
0	0	0	200	200
1	100	90	100	90
2	200	166	0	0
3	300	225	0	0
Total		481		290

Table 7-11 Sample NPV Calculation

Consider the following examples from Investopedia.com:

- $1,000 invested for five years with simple annual interest of 10 percent would have a future value of $1,500.
- $1000 invested for five years at 10 percent, compounded annually, has a future value of $1,610.51.[7]

These calculations demonstrate that time literally is money—the value of the money you have now is not the same as it will be in the future, and vice versa. Therefore, it is important to know how to calculate the time value of money so that you can distinguish between the worth of investments that offer you returns at different times.[8]

Internal Rate of Turn (IRR)   The internal rate of return (IRR) is a capital budgeting metric used by firms to decide whether they should make investments. It is also called discounted cash flow rate of return (DCFROR) or rate of return (ROR). IRR is an indicator of the "efficiency" or quality of an investment, as opposed to net present value (NPV), which indicates value or magnitude.

Here's an easy way to relate this to project management: Say, for example, you have to choose between projects A and B. Project A has an IRR of 20 percent, and project B has an IRR of 10 percent. Which do you choose?

Answer: You would choose project A because it has a higher efficiency (internal rate of return on the dollars invested).

Payback Period   Payback period is the number of time periods it takes to recover your investment in a project before you start making a profit. For example, project A has a payback period of ten months, and project B has a payback period of 24 months. Which would you choose to fund?

Answer: You would choose project A because it has a shorter payback period (sometimes known as "break-even point").

Opportunity Cost   Opportunity cost analysis is an important part of a company's decision-making process but is not treated as an actual cost in any financial statement.

Here's an example of opportunity cost: If a person invests $10,000 in a particular stock, they are denying themselves the interest they could have earned by leaving the $10,000 in a bank account instead. The opportunity cost of the decision to invest in stock is the value of the interest they would have made by leaving the money in the bank.

Note that opportunity cost is not the sum of the available alternatives when those alternatives are, in turn, mutually exclusive to each other. The opportunity cost of the city's decision to build a hospital on its vacant land is the loss of the land for other venues, such as an events center, or the money that could have been made from selling the land, because use for any one of those purposes would preclude the possibility to implement any of the other opportunities.

Here's another way to look at opportunity cost: It is the cost spent (given up) by selecting one project over another. The good news is, no calculations are needed. For example, project A has an NPV of $45,000, and project B has NPV of $85,000. What is the opportunity cost of selecting project B?

Answer: $45,000.

Sunk Costs Simply put, these are project costs that have been expended (spent). Be aware that according to general accounting standards (and they say this is usually true in project management as well), sunk costs should not be considered when deciding whether to continue or terminate a troubled project. This is a hard one because clearly you don't want to throw good money after bad.

Say, for example, your company has approved $10,000 to fund a project to build a prototype medical product called Heart Beat II (HB2). Two months later you see a competitor has just announced the very same product for a lower per unit price than you were estimating to sell yours. No matter the outcome of the project, the money already spent is "sunk cost." The logical decision might be to terminate the project. However, your company sees a way to reduce production cost and anticipates very high demand for HB2. The decision to continue building the product should not be made based on sunk cost but rather on the business need, the marketability and potential benefits to your customer, the law of diminishing returns, and of course profit.

Depreciation Most people are familiar with the different types of depreciation, but just in case let's talk about a couple as a refresher.

In simple terms, we can say that depreciation is the reduction in the value of an asset due to wear and tear, obsolescence, depletion, or other factors.

In accounting, depreciation is a term used to describe any method of spreading the purchase cost of an asset across its useful life, caused by normal wear and tear.

Straight-line depreciation is the simplest and most often used technique, in which the company estimates the salvage value of the asset at the end of the period during which it will be used to generate income (useful life). It will expense a portion of the original cost in equal increments over that period. The salvage value is an estimate of the value of the asset at the time it will be sold or disposed of; it may be zero. Salvage value is also called "scrap value."

Another type of depreciation is *accelerated depreciation*. It has two forms, and both decline faster than using traditional straight-line depreciation:

- **Double declining balance**   The most common rate of accelerated depreciation used is double the straight-line rate. For this reason, this technique is referred to as the double declining balance method.

  To illustrate, say a business has an asset with $4,000 original cost, $100 salvage value, and five years of useful life. First, calculate the straight-line depreciation rate. Because the asset has five years of useful life, the straight-line depreciation rate is 20 percent per year (100% / 5 years). With the double declining balance method, as the name suggests, you would double that rate (40-percent depreciation rate) for the first two years and 20 percent is used the third year. You might use an accelerated depreciation on an asset that has a shorter life span.

  Book value at the beginning of the first year of depreciation is the original cost of the asset. At any time book value equals original cost minus accumulated depreciation.

  > Book Value = Original Cost – Accumulated Depreciation

  Book value at the end of one year becomes the book value at the beginning of the next year. The asset is depreciated until the book value equals the salvage value (or scrap value).

- **Sum of the years digits**   Sum of years digits is a depreciation method that results in a more accelerated write-off than straight line, but less than the double declining balance method. Under this method, annual depreciation is determined by multiplying the depreciable cost by a schedule of fractions.

  Depreciable Cost = Original Cost – Salvage Value

  Book Value = Original Cost – Accumulated Depreciation

  For example, if an asset has an original cost $1000, a useful life of five years, and a salvage value of $100, how do you compute its depreciation schedule?

  First, determine the years' digits. Because the asset has useful life of five years, the years' digits are 5, 4, 3, 2, and 1. Next, calculate the sum of the digits (5 + 4 + 3 + 2 + 1 = 15).

  Depreciation rates are as follows:

  5/15 for the first year, 4/15 for the second year, 3/15 for the third year, 2/15 for the fourth year, and 1/15 for the fifth year.[9]

Cost Management Summary

As mentioned at the beginning of this chapter, cost management is one of the primary constraints on projects, and costs should be managed as if your own money was being used.

Studies show that cost overruns average over 45 percent of original budgets!

According to a *Software Magazine* article, cost overruns in 1994 equaled 189 percent over the original estimate. This was reduced to 69 percent in 1998 and further reduced to 45 percent in a 2000 study.[10] Some of the likely reasons are poor initial cost estimates, unrealistic budgets, poor financial management, and changes in scope, any of which will likely yield a lower than expected return on investment (ROI).

The good news is that a lot of good tools and techniques are available to help you manage cost. The best way to manage cost on your project is to

- Stay alert and focused on project costs.

- Use the tools and resources available to effectively estimate, monitor, report and manage costs.

- Work with the project team to ensure everyone is doing their part to provide accurate cost estimates, develop and monitor budgets, and help manage cash flow.

Also, you want to use earned value analysis (EVA), when possible and as appropriate, to ensure that the project's return on investment (ROI) is achieved.

One thing that is painfully clear is that if you and the project team are not diligent in managing cost and reporting status in a timely manner, you are at risk when it comes to cost management. Another thing to remember is, as a project manager you need to look beyond identifying potential cost problems and make sound recommendations to keep the gaps (misses) from showing up in the future.

References

1. Phillips, Joseph. *PMP Project Management Professional Study Guide, Second Edition,* (McGraw-Hill, San Francisco), 2008, page 267.

2. Wikipedia, http://en.wikipedia.org/wiki/Profit_margin.

3. Mulcahy, Rita. *PMP Exam Prep, Sixth Edition* (RMC Publications, Inc.), April 2009, page 232.

4. U.S. Department of Energy. "Project Management Practices: Performance Baseline Development and Validation," June 2003, http://oecm.energy.gov/Portals/2/PBDevValidation.pdf.

5. Mulcahy, Rita. *PMP Exam Prep, Sixth Edition* (RMC Publishing, Inc.), April 2009, pages 241–242.

6. FinAid, http://www.finaid.org/loans/npv.phtml.

7. Investopedia, http://www.investopedia.com/terms/f/futurevalue.asp.

8. "Understanding the Time Value of Money," Investopedia, http://www.investopedia.com/articles/03/082703.asp.

9. Wikipedia, http://en.wikipedia.org/wiki/Depreciation.

10. Johnson, Jim, Karen D. Boucher, Kyle Connors, and James Robinson. "Collaboration: Development & Management: Collaborating on Project Success," *Software Magazine* (February/March 2001), http://www.softwaremag.com/archive/2001feb/collaborativemgt.html.

Chapter 8

Project Quality Management

Key Skills & Concepts

- Definition of quality

- How to measure quality

- The importance of managing project quality

- Plan-Do-Check-Act (PDCA) cycle

- Introduction to Six Sigma and Lean

- Three quality-management processes

- Continuous improvement

- Cost of quality conformance and nonconformance

- Types of reports and charts

- Determining whether a project meets the requirements and expectations

- Quality terms

- Statistical sampling

How do you really know what a quality product or service is? As a project manager, how do you know you have delivered a quality project?

The answer is simple: Quality is in the eyes of the customer. After all, the customer is paying for the product, service, or result of the project. The customer needs to feel the project is delivered to their specifications and that the project does what it was intended to do.

The tough part of measuring quality at the project level is that it tends to be elusive and in many cases is a moving target. Some things are extremely difficult to measure because the qualities are intangible. If you ask 100 project customers what their idea of quality is, you will likely get well over 100 different answers because their current views or expectations vary depending on when and how you ask the question (face-to-face interview, survey, e-mail, by phone, and so on).

Early in the project life cycle the customer might simply say they want a "full-function website to promote their products or services." In the middle of the life cycle when the customer sees what functions and features are being developed, they are likely to change their mind regarding the look and feel of the website. They may end up wanting something totally different at the end of the project.

As you work the project, you and the team will gather more details from the customer and reach a higher degree of understanding as to what they want the website (the product of the project) to look like. This should be accomplished through close communications and documented acceptance criteria.

Once you have an approved acceptance criteria based on what the customer wants, the team can begin to develop or prototype the website. This prototype will give the customer an opportunity to test the site to see how it responds and where the links take them. The closer you get to the end of the project, the more the product should align with the customer's needs and expectations.

As a project manager, the ideal solution is always to get a clear understanding of what the customer wants as early in the life cycle as possible. This is easier said than done, especially when the customer is not completely sure what they want or what they expect at the end of the project.

I am sure you have experienced an unclear scope definition on one or more of your projects. The situation usually goes something like this: Your boss or the customer simply says, "Build a new website so shoppers can buy our products online quicker and easier." Or maybe they say, "We have had too many problems on our database servers lately. Put a team together to fix the problems."

Occasionally you get more precise project direction, such as "We need to reach a 15-percent increase in systems availability of our database servers" or "To reach our revenue goals we need to increase ticket sales by 10 percent." As clear as the expected results may be, the actual detailed requirements are usually as clear as mud. The reason is that when it comes down to the actual requirements, in most cases the customer doesn't know how to articulate their needs and expectations. That is why they are paying you as the project manager to "just fix it."

At the end of the project, the only way you will meet the expected results is if the requirements are clear, verified, documented, and most importantly approved. And, of course, that is just the starting point (the price of admission, so to speak). The next important step is to get a "qualified" team together and keep them focused on the approved scope. All of these steps are essential to achieve project quality.

How to Achieve Customer Satisfaction

The only way to achieve customer satisfaction is to interview the customer and gain an understanding of their needs and expectations. When you think you are crystal clear on what the customer wants, document it. Take the documented requirements back to the customer for verification. Customer verification can be conducted by simply asking them, "Is this what you had in mind?" Once verified, you now have "formal acceptance" from the customer on what the project should deliver.

Once you have formal acceptance (agreement) of the requirements from the customer, you take these requirements to the project team to be evaluated for "do-ability." That is, can the project deliver what the customer wants according to their specifications?

If the customer expectations are realistic, the project team is capable of meeting those expectations, and the project is officially accepted (chartered), then the work of managing the project can begin. When I say "managing the project," this includes managing customer expectations so their requirements (needs and expectations) are met. This necessitates a combination of conformance to requirements (so the project produces what it is intended to produce) and fitness for use (the product or service must satisfy the customer's needs).

Because quality is in the eyes of the customer, the best thing to do as the project manager to help deliver quality on your project is follow these five steps:

1. You must have a clear understanding of what the customer wants.

2. You must ensure the deliverables of the project are reasonable (doable), documented, and approved by the customer.

3. You must clearly communicate the customer expectations and deliverables to the project stakeholders (especially the performing project team).

4. You must have realistic measurements to allow for tracking and reporting the progress of the project.

5. You must effectively manage changes on your project.

NOTE
Following the five steps above will help you achieve customer satisfaction on your project.

How Do You Measure Quality?

For an accountant, the measure of quality is pretty clear—the ledger books must be balanced. What does it mean to say the books are balanced? It means all book entries (debits and credits) are in order and properly coded in accordance with approved accounting practices. All receipts are filed properly and available in case of an audit. The bank statements match the tracking reports (spreadsheets, financial statements, and so on). The client receives reports in a timely manner and is clear on the account balances and potential financial exposures.

Ask the Expert

Q: What is a good measure of quality when managing projects?

A: If the product of the project meets the specified (approved) requirements and if the product does what the project definition says it should do (fitness of use), then you have met the quality standards for the project.

When you're managing projects, what you measure and when you measure it are not always as clear as they are in accounting. So, what is a good measure of quality in project management?

Any time you measure quality, you must have a baseline or reference point to measure against. A simple approach I like to use is what I call the "Texas Three-Step." After you have a baseline, you ask yourself and your team these three questions:

- **Where are we today compared to where we should be?** You remember earned value management (EVM) from Chapter 7; this is a good way to confirm current status, but you also need to look in real terms, not just dollars and cents.

- **How did we get here?** Take a look at "the road just taken." Was it the road or path you had planned to take? Or did you have road bumps (pot holes) that impacted the project and had to take a different path? Lessons learned are a great tool for helping you understand what worked and what didn't work the way it should have (we must learn from our actions and/or our mistakes).

- **Where do we go from here?** Looking forward, what course corrections do you need to take to keep the project on track (or to get it back on track)?

When it comes to measuring quality, the problem is and always will be, "what is important to the customer?"

Case Study: Sample Quality Measurements

For a real-world example of quality measurements, let's take a look at our BEC case study. For ice skating events (such as ice hockey and performance shows on ice), the ice has to be set up to meet very rigid specifications to be considered safe for the skaters. If the ice is too warm, it becomes spongy and slow, and the skaters have a difficult time making turns and stops. If the ice is too cold, it becomes brittle and is susceptible to cracking, and sprawls or holes form.

Quality Requirements and Measurements:

- The paint is to be applied as close to the concrete as possible without drips, drifting lines, and "pearling" of the white base coat.

- Ice "slab" temperature must be maintained at 18–19 degrees Fahrenheit (F).

- Surface temperature at 1" must be maintained at 21 degrees F.

- The ice has to be at a depth that's thick enough so the skaters can't dig down to the concrete (for example, 2 ½ inches for ice hockey).

- Edges are to be conditioned to eliminate rough edge surface.

Quality Assurance and Control:

- Dry and wet cuts must be used to keep the ice conditioned and smooth after practice.

- Depth checks are performed and recorded daily after each Zamboni conditioning to track and control quality of the ice.

- Protective glass (barriers around the ice) is to be walked prior to every game to ensure it's secure, thus reducing the chance of glass popping out during a game.

Importance of Quality

How important is quality? Most people would say it is extremely important. In fact, the word is often used in advertising slogans. Here are some examples of classic slogans that begin with "quality":

- Quality at your feet (Brown Shoe).

- Quality first... from America's first pen maker (Esterbrook Pen).

- The quality goes in before the name goes on (Zenith).

- The quality name in refrigeration and air conditioning (York).

- Quality runs deep (Rustoleum).

- Quality toys with a purpose (Tinkertoy).

- Quality you can trust (Crown Central Petroleum).[1]

Sometimes talk is cheap. The main question is, does the company really know what we as customers want when it comes to quality? Do they know what is broken and what to do to fix it?

What Is Broken and How Do We Fix It?

Throughout the years, many of us woke up to the following news:

- Ford recalled 10,000 1999 Cougars because of a door problem, and 3,800 Mercury Villager minivans because of a problem with fuel tank retention straps.
- Ford's Volvo division announced a recall of more than 122,600 1998 models for a glitch with passenger-side airbags and an additional 114,850 1998 and 1997 cars for a faulty headlight switch.
- DaimlerChrysler recalled 227,283 1991–94 Shadows and Sundances because of a risk that the driver's seat could suddenly break.
- General Motors recalled 6,584 1999 Chevy Cavaliers and Pontiac Sunfires because of the possibility of an instrument panel light malfunction.
- More than 11,000 1999 Land Rover Discovery sport utility vehicle (SUV) owners were having problems with the Antilock Brake System (ABS) alarm.[2]

One recall in particular was the gas tank on the Ford Pinto (1971–1980). The following is from CNNMoney.com:

> "The issue wasn't just the car itself, however, but the alleged decision-making process within Ford Motor Co.... The company was willing, it seemed, to let a certain number of people die rather than spend a few dollars per car to make the repairs.... In retrospect, it turns out that about as many people died in fiery crashes in Pintos as in other popular cars of that time, although crash tests indicated the gas tank problem was genuine."[3]

In response to these quality problems, Ford renewed their focus on quality in the 1980s. You probably remember their slogan "Quality Is Job 1." Ford recently dropped this slogan after 17 years because of the perception that in today's marketplace, high quality is a given and is no longer an important marketing variable. Quality is expected, it is not an option.

As always, other influencing factors are at work when it comes to ensuring quality. Could it be that even though quality is important (a given), the real focus on cost overrides quality? In the interest of being competitive, companies seem to be more concerned with the cost of quality than they are with providing quality in their products or services.

No one goes to work in the morning wanting to do a bad job. However, how many people do you know who go to work each day and just do enough to get by? It seems people just want a job and are not as interested in a career like in the old days. I have seen entire departments of people who "jumped ship" from one company to another for a few bucks more per hour or for a signing bonus. It seems the loyalty of the workforce has diminished the last few years. Most unhappy employees feel it is the shift of work to other countries or companies that outsource work to the lowest bidder that has caused this drop in employee loyalty.

With the shift of work or work reduction, there tends to be an increased level of uncertainty among the employees. Uncertainty causes distractions on the job and will affect the quality of work being performed. This can be seen in many industries, even in professional sports, where athletes are traded from one team to another, causing a drop or change in performance. If you don't know where you will be working (or playing in the case of an athlete) next month, or next year, it is much harder to establish a sound attitude toward quality. People want to do a good job; however, the priorities seem to have shifted, and doing quality work is not as high of a priority in today's workforce (in many cases). The following is from an article titled "Quality Is Job...?" by Gary S. Vasilash:

> "There are no easy answers to any of this [situations described previously]. If there were, then there wouldn't be the problems. But at an individual level we should all understand that getting by isn't getting ahead, and that quality still counts, even if those doing the numbers may have forgotten."[4]

Even in Japan, where the "job for life" concept went out the window several years ago, the quality of work is still there. Quality is an attitude.

How Do We Fix the Quality Problems?

Everything we say and do affects our reputation. There is an old saying that it takes a lifetime to build a reputation, and one second to destroy it. Perfection may not be fully attainable; however, we can perform our jobs with excellence. To do so, it just takes a little more focus, a few extra minutes. For example, try reviewing a note one more time before you send it out or try verifying the spreadsheet totals before distributing a report. How many times have you spent hours doing "damage control," or having to explain what you meant to say or why your e-mail said the meeting was at 2:00 A.M. instead of 2:00 P.M.

You may save a lot of time and have a much better chance of maintaining a good reputation for quality if you plan ahead and don't rush. Always double-check your work. At the end of the day, quality is a matter of time and attitude.

TIP

It is no surprise we are not at our best after working long hours "burning the midnight oil." It has been my experience that if I send an e-mail after midnight, the quality is not as good as when I am rested. Therefore, my recommendation is, do not send an e-mail after midnight. Wait until the next morning and read it one last time before you send it (especially if the note is to your customer or your boss). You should always double-check for errors before you send important documents—maybe have a friend, coworker, or even your spouse (if they are willing) read over the e-mail to check for errors. This could save the day and your reputation.

Definition of Quality and How It Changed

The definition of quality has changed through the years, depending on who you talk to. PMI's definition in the first edition of the *PMBOK* was, "The totality of characteristics of an entity that bear on its ability to satisfy stated or implied needs." My wife almost fell out of her chair when I read that to her in 1998 as I was preparing for the PMP exam. The good news is, in the latest edition of the *PMBOK* the definition is much easier to remember and more applicable: Quality is "the degree to which a set of inherent characteristics fulfills requirements."

According to BusinessDictionary.com, quality is a "measure of excellence or state of being free from defects, deficiencies, and significant variations. The ISO 8402-1986 Standard defines quality as 'the totality of features and characteristics of a product or service that bears its ability to satisfy stated or implied needs." In manufacturing, quality is "strict and consistent adherence to measurable and verifiable standards to achieve uniformity of output that satisfies specific customer or user requirements."[5]

Gurus of Quality

There are many quality theorists (or gurus, as they are often called) in the world of project management. The gurus you need to be familiar with who have made significant contributions to quality in project management (and may appear on PMI exams) are the following:

- **Joseph M. Juran**   Dr. Juran defined quality as "fitness for use," and developed the 80/20 principle and advocated top management involvement. He made many contributions to the field of quality management in his 70+ active working years. He was the first to incorporate the human aspect of quality management, which is referred to as Total Quality Management (TQM). His classic book, *Quality Control Handbook,* first released in 1951, is still the standard reference work for quality managers. Table 8-1 outlines the major points of Dr. Juran's quality management ideas.[6]

Quality Categories	Steps
Quality Planning	• Identify who are the customers.
	• Determine the needs of those customers.
	• Translate those needs into our language.
	• Develop a product that can respond to those needs.
	• Optimize the product features so as to meet our needs and customer needs.
Quality Improvement	• Develop a process that is able to produce the product.
	• Optimize the process.
Quality Control	• Prove that the process can produce the product under operating conditions with minimal inspection.
	• Transfer the process to Operations.

Table 8-1 Juran's Quality Trilogy

- **W. Edwards Deming** Dr. Deming advocated quality improvement using the Plan-Do-Check-Act (PDCA) cycle and developed 14 Steps to Total Quality Management. According to the Wikipedia entry for Dr. Deming's management training, he "taught that by adopting appropriate principles of management, organizations can increase quality and simultaneously reduce costs (by reducing waste, rework, staff attrition and litigation while increasing customer loyalty). The key is to practice continual improvement and think of manufacturing as a system, not as bits and pieces."[7]

- **Philip Crosby** Popularized the concept of "Do it right the first time." He believed management should take primary responsibility for quality, and workers should follow their managers' example. He defined the Four Absolutes of Quality Management:

1. Quality is conformance to requirements.
2. Quality prevention is preferable to quality inspection.
3. "Zero defects" is the quality performance standard.
4. Quality is measured in monetary terms—the price of nonconformance.[8]

Key Quality Terms

Before we get into a lot of details surrounding the quality processes, there are some terms and distinctions that are important for you to know (especially if you are planning to take the PMI exam).

Quality vs. Grade

Quality and grade are not the same:

- Quality is the degree to which the characteristics of the product meet its specified requirements. Take meat, for example. Several factors go into determining the quality of the meat, including maturity, firmness, texture, color, and the amount and distribution of marbling.

- Grade is a category assigned to products or services having the same functional uses but with different technical characteristics. Looking at meat again (can you tell it is getting close to meal time?), there are different applications (uses) and different grades (for example, Prime, Choice, Select, and Standard). See the following table for a description of beef quality grades according to Meat Quality and Safety, Purdue University Animal Sciences: [9]

Grade	Characteristics	Suggested Use
Prime	Has abundant marbling and is generally sold in restaurants and hotels.	Prime roasts and steaks are excellent for roasting, broiling, and grilling (dry heat methods).
Choice	Has less marbling than Prime grades, but is still high quality.	May be cooked with dry heat. Be careful not to overcook roasts from rump, round, and blade chuck. A meat thermometer can be helpful in cooking to a safe temperature.
Select	Leaner than the higher grades. Fairly tender but may lack some juiciness and flavor of higher grades.	Only the loin, ribs, and sirloin should be cooked with dry heat. Other cuts should be marinated before cooking or cooked with moisture.
Standard	Has no marbling. Will lack juiciness and flavor of higher grades.	May be sold as ungraded or "store brand" meat.

Precision vs. Accuracy

Precise means that the product is exact, as in performance. It is repeatable and gets the same measure every time. *Accuracy,* on the other hand, means the measured value is very close to the true value (hitting the bull's eye on a target), meaning a measurement is accurate if it correctly reflects the size of the thing being measured. Precision measurements are not necessarily accurate. A very accurate measurement is not necessarily precise. See the following examples:

- In target shooting, a high score indicates the closeness to the bull's eye and is a measure of the shooter's accuracy.

- In target shooting, precision is the tightness of the pattern (cluster) when bullets hit the target close together. If the pattern is scattered (lots of space between the hits on the target), it is not precise. The smaller (or tighter) the pattern, the higher the precision, even if the bullet hits are not close to the bull's eye.

Prevention over Inspection

Many quality experts feel that quality has to be "built in" (prevention) through planning and design, not "inspected in." There is usually a large cost (not just monetary) associated with inspection. If quality is built in, you are likely to save a lot of time and money (and your reputation) over the cost of inspection.

Inspecting quality means that you are not fixing the root cause of the problem. If you are relying on inspection to ensure quality, for example, if you are spot-checking car parts on an assembly line, how many parts go through the line that are nonconforming? You can't inspect every part, so in this case you are letting bad parts get to the customer.

If you fix the part by building quality in, you eliminate the waste, scrap, and rework, which will save time, effort, and materials and improve your reputation as well as the profit margins.

You have probably heard the statement "Do it right the first time," from Phillip Crosby, many times before. To ensure you have long-term quality products, processes, or services, you need prevention. Prevention goes far beyond just "doing it right the first time." The PM and team need to constantly look for ways to improve the project over its life cycle.

Continuous Improvement

The Plan-Do-Check-Act (PDCA) cycle is the basis for quality improvement, as defined by Walter Shewhart and later modified by W. Edwards Deming. The PDCA cycle is about creating a continuous long-term improvement cycle. The details of the cycle are as follows:

1. **Plan**   From the top of the organization (or even across companies, as they do in Japan), establish the objectives and processes necessary to deliver results in accordance with the expected output. The goal is to ensure consistency in project management tools and methods.

2. **Do**   Implement the new processes. Everyone on the team is encouraged to look at innovative ways to improve the process flow, identify problems, and implement solutions (for example, stop to fix the problem when it occurs).

3. **Check**   Measure the new processes by collecting actual process data and compare the outcome against the expected results to verify that the target is being met.

4. Act Analyze the differences to determine their cause. Then make necessary adjustments to solutions and update action plans as needed. Also, identify future steps to make sure the problem doesn't resurface. Then you start the cycle again, thus continuing improvement.

NOTE

Each PDCA step will be part of either one or more of the other PDCA steps.

ISO (International Organization for Standardization)

An organization you should be familiar with that helps ensure quality is the International Organization for Standardization (ISO). Founded in 1946, ISO is an international organization composed of national standards bodies from over 75 countries—for example, American National Standards Institute (ANSI) is a member of ISO. ISO has defined a number of important computer standards, the most significant of which is perhaps OSI (Open Systems Interconnection), a standardized architecture for designing networks. Although ISO defines itself as a nongovernmental organization, it has the ability to set standards that often become law.

Here are some examples of ISO standards:

- ISO 9000 refers to a set of three standards (ISO 9000, ISO 9001, and ISO 9004). All three are referred to as "quality management system standards." For example, ISO 9004 provides a set of guidelines and is used to develop quality management systems.

  The ISO 9000 standards apply to all kinds of organizations across many industries, including manufacturing, processing, forestry, electronics, steel, computing, legal services, financial services, accounting, banking, recycling, aerospace, and construction.

- The ISO 14000 family of standards addresses various aspects of environmental management. The very first two standards (ISO 14001:2004 and ISO 14004:2004) deal with environmental management systems (EMS).

The other standards and guidelines in the family address specific environmental aspects, including labeling, performance evaluation, life cycle analysis, communication, and auditing.

Six Sigma, Lean, and Kaizen Initiatives

Six Sigma and Lean are two quality initiatives that have emerged at higher levels of interest in government and commercial organizations. These new initiatives, combined with the previous focus on Kaizen (continuous improvement), tend to add confusion to

Ask the Expert

Q: **Is this a Six Sigma, Lean, or Kaizen project? Which concept should I use?**

A: According to the article "Is This a Six Sigma, Lean, or Kaizen Project?" by Terence T. Burton, "This is a familiar question that is often [raised] by organizations. In fact, it's the wrong question. These concepts are nothing more than tools in your management toolbox. You don't fix a watch with a hammer, and you get the same results when you deploy Six Sigma, Lean, and Kaizen incorrectly. The fact is, a business problem is a business problem, and it needs to be fixed. Understanding the application of these tools to various improvement opportunities is the key to success."[10] With any tool, the application or use depends on the size and complexity of the project as well as the availability and affordability of the tool or model to use.

Before anyone can accurately answer the question of which initiative or tool to use on your specific project, you need a better understanding of the definition of each. Otherwise, you run the risk of seeing each quality issue as a nail, thus limiting yourself to using only one tool (a hammer).

people trying to improve project or product quality. A question that often comes up from clients and students alike is, "Which concept (or initiative) should we use to improve quality on our projects?"

What Is Six Sigma?

Six Sigma is a management-driven companywide business initiative to generate breakthrough (innovative) results in business performance. Six Sigma is a focus on quality that strives for near perfection. It is a disciplined, data-driven approach and methodology for eliminating defects by driving toward six standard deviations between the mean and the nearest specification limit of a product or process. Six Sigma can be applied across businesses and industries from manufacturing to services. Here are a couple of examples:

Ford Motor Company began its Six Sigma push in 1999 when the director of quality for Ford's global truck business began looking for new ways to improve quality. Other companies were quick to jump on the bandwagon.

According to an IBM Business Value Study, "At Caterpillar, stagnant revenue growth prompted the company to undertake a massive transformation in January 2001. Through its Six Sigma initiative, the company developed a strategic vision that outlined a roadmap for change based on fact-based analysis. Caterpillar's initiative also led to product innovations like its phenomenally successful low-emissions diesel engine and to redesigned processes including a streamlined supply chain. By 2005, revenues had grown by 80 percent." [11]

The work processes tied to Six Sigma are Define, Measure, Analyze, Improve, and Control (DMAIC). It is important to note that Six Sigma is a business initiative, not a quality initiative. The theory is that if you improve business processes and work flow, then quality will follow.

What Is Lean?

Lean (the term) was first coined in the late 1980 (or 1990, depending on which article/ book you read). Lean is a system (or set of tools) that thrives on change and flexibility and focuses on reducing waste in the workplace. Lean can be used for organizing and managing projects, product development, ongoing operations, and supplier services. Many companies and organizations use Lean principles to reduce defects, streamline processes, reduce manufacturing space, and improve employee performance.

Specifically, Lean seeks to eliminate wait time between production stations, over processing (for example, too many steps in the process), and reduce excess inventory. Lean also seeks out employee creativity to help solve problems and increase productivity.

According to the Lean Enterprise Institute website, "Many of the key principles were pioneered by Henry Ford, who was the first person to integrate an entire production system, under what he termed 'flow production.' Following World War II, the Toyota Motor Company adapted Ford's principles as a means of compensating for its challenge of limited human, financial, and material resources. The Toyota Production System (or TPS), which evolved from this need, was one of the first managerial systems using lean principles throughout the enterprise to produce a wide variety of products at lower volumes and many fewer defects than competitors."[12]

Try This Go Lean Project

Your manager comes to you and says he wants his department to "Go Lean," and you have been selected to be the project manager to implement the quality initiative. The very next question from your manager is, "What is the expected completion date for this project?"

What is your answer?

A Six months from today.

B You need more information. For example, is this project part of an overall companywide initiative?

C One year from today.

D On the Monday after Easter.

Answer: B. You need more information because Lean must have top management sponsorship with companywide operational-level commitment, not just commitment from a single department. Lean implementation looks at quality problems throughout the operation. It requires systemwide focus and should be implemented across the entire organization.

Lean should be viewed as a culture change (developed over time). Lean is the set of "tools" that assist in the identification and steady elimination of wasted time, lost productivity, scrap, or rework. When waste is eliminated quality improves while production time and cost are reduced. Examples of other "tools" are Value Stream Mapping, Five S, and Kanban (pull systems).

Note that Lean can only happen with planning, organization, and high-level management commitment to provide the resources needed to succeed.

What Is Kaizen?

Kaizen is a Japanese word meaning "continuous improvement." It comes from the words *kai*, which means "change," or "to correct," and *zen,* which means "good." Kaizen is used in Lean manufacturing, the Toyota Production System (TPS), Just In Time (JIT) inventory, and other effective manufacturing strategies.

For Kaizen to work correctly it should involve every employee—from upper management to the cleaning crew. Everyone is encouraged to come up with improvement ideas (no matter how small) and make suggestions on a continuous basis. The ideas are based on making small changes along the way to improve productivity, safety, and efficiency to reduce extra steps and waste in the work place.

Another quality program you may be aware of (so far not on the PMI exam) is the Five S program found predominantly in manufacturing and other types of businesses such as retail, warehouses, and even hospitals. The Five S program, usually part of Kaizen, is designed to a establish a clean Visual Workplace. The Five S program focuses on having visual order and standardization. The Five S's are

- **Sort** The first step in making things cleaned and organized
- **Set in Order** Organize, identify, and arrange everything in a work area
- **Shine** Regular cleaning and maintenance
- **Standardize** Make it easy to maintain—simplify and standardize
- **Sustain** Maintaining what has been accomplished

The results you can expect are improved profitability, safety, and efficiency.

Project Quality Management Processes

Quality management must be planned into the project from the beginning. Quality must be ensured by the team. This means quality must be clearly defined and documented in both qualitative and quantitative terms, and it should be reviewed by all the stakeholders to make sure it will satisfy the needs for which it was developed. Once this is defined and agreed to by the project team, quality measurements must be implemented according to the approved guidelines. And last but not least, the team must continue to monitor quality to ensure the project deliverables meet the planned quality performance requirements.

Monitoring quality to meet requirements is one thing; however, the PM and entire team should also continually seek ways to improve quality on the project. To help accomplish this continuous improvement, the PM and team need to be aware of and exercise quality management processes.

Quality management, according to PMI, includes the processes and activities to enable the project manager and team to effectively manage the quality of the products (deliverables of the project), and the overall project results using proven project management processes, tools and techniques, and outputs. True quality is achieved when the PM and team demonstrate proven results through tracking, reporting, and managing quality over the entire project life cycle.

Here are the three project quality management processes, according to PMI:

- **8.1: Plan quality (Planning process group)**   Includes identifying quality requirements and standards for the project, determining the product of the project, and managing the documentation to ensure quality compliance.

- **8.2: Perform quality assurance (Executing process group)**   The process of inspecting or auditing quality requirements and the results from quality control measurements to ensure appropriate quality standards and operational definitions are being used.

- **8.3: Perform quality control (Monitoring and Controlling process group)**   Involves monitoring and recording results of the execution of quality activities to assess performance and make necessary corrective actions through the change control process.

TIP

An easy way to remember the three processes for quality is to think of them as coming in a "three-PAC" (Planning, Assurance, and Control). When you're preparing for the PMP exam, acronyms like this often make the memorization a little easier.

1. Plan Quality Process

The purpose of the Plan Quality process is to identify requirements and standards for the product of the project and to provide and document how the project will comply with the defined quality requirements.

As with many of the PM processes, the Plan Quality process should be performed in parallel with other key project planning processes, especially risk and the change control processes. Many tools and techniques are useful during the Plan Quality process. Here's a summary list of them (many of these will be discussed in further detail later in this chapter):

- Cost-benefit analysis
- Cost of quality (COQ)
- Control charts
- Benchmarking
- Design of experiments (DOE)
- Statistical sampling
- Flowcharting
- Proprietary quality management methods
- Additional quality planning tools

Cost-Benefit Analysis

Most projects require a business case or cost case to help justify the need for them. Cost-benefit analysis is a relatively simple and widely used technique for deciding whether to make a change (for example, staying with an existing process or tool or going with one project versus another). As its name suggests, you simply list the benefits of a particular course of action as well as the savings or improvements realized and then subtract the costs associated with that action. Hopefully the benefits far outweigh the cost, thus making the project an easy sell. Cost-benefit analysis really helps decision makers choose the projects they want (or need) to sponsor.

Details of Cost of Quality (COQ)

Cost of quality (COQ) refers to the total cost of all efforts related to quality throughout the product life cycle. The decisions made during the project can impact the operation costs of quality as well (for example, the type of equipment or material used to build the product may not have a long life cycle or may require higher maintenance in the long run).

When calculating COQ, you also need to consider failure cost (cost of poor quality), potential cost of rework, cost of scrap, lost productivity (work stoppage), and so on. Costs can usually be broken into one of two categories: cost of conformance or cost of nonconformance.

Here are some examples of the cost of conformance:

- Prevention costs (money spent during the project to avoid defects or failures)
  - Training
  - Document processes
  - Equipment
  - Time to "do it right the first time"
- Appraisal costs (to assess quality of the product)
  - Testing
  - Destructive testing loss (for example, car safety testing)
  - Inspections

And here are some examples of the cost of nonconformance:

- Internal failure costs (failures found by the project)
  - Rework
  - Scrap
- External failure costs (failures found by the customer)
  - Lost business
  - Warranty work
  - Liability

Control Charts

Control charts are a great tool to determine if a process or product is performing to expected levels. They can be used to track a variety of products, repetitive activities, cost and schedule variances, volume of output, and even the impact of changes to the project. Control charts or graphs can be used to show specific targets with upper and lower control limits tied to the acceptable requirements of the product.

If the product is not meeting the acceptable range (within approved control limits) in the specifications, there may be fallout (throwaway) parts and/or penalties associated with the out-of-limit parts or products. The control (specification) limits usually represent three standard deviations on either side of the centerline (or mean) of a normal distribution of data plotted in the control chart (see Figure 8-1).

When a process is within acceptable (control or warning) limits (generally ± 3 sigma), it is said to be "in control" and doesn't need to be adjusted. When the process is outside the control limit, it should be monitored. If you see a "run" (seven consecutive points or events outside, above or below, the control limit), that indicates the process is out of control and adjustments may be required.

Standard Deviation

When managing quality on a project, you may encounter the term "standard deviation." People who have taken a statistics class in school are familiar with the term and might even understand it. Standard deviation (or sigma) is a measure of the range or area of a normal distribution (bell curve) from the mean (average). Sigma is taken from both sides of the mean and shows as a minus (–) on the left side and a plus (+) on the right side (see Figure 8-2). The following explanation comes from Wikipedia:

> "In statistics, standard deviation is a simple measure of the variability or dispersion of a data set. A low standard deviation indicates that the data points tend to be very close to the same value (the mean), while high standard deviation indicates that the data are "spread out" over a large range of values. For example, the average height for adult men in the United States is about 70 inches, with a standard deviation of around 3 inches. This means that most men (about 68%, assuming a normal distribution) have a height within 3 inches of the mean (67 inches–73 inches), while almost all men (about 95%) have a height within 6 inches of the mean (64 inches–76 inches). If the standard deviation were zero, then all men would be exactly 70 inches high. If the standard deviation were 20 inches, then men would have much more variable heights, with a typical range of about 50 to 90 inches."[13]

TIP

Remember that half of a normal distribution curve is on the left side of the mean and half is on the right side of the mean. If you are planning to take the PMP exam, you should memorize the following ranges:
   ±1 sigma (or standard deviations) = 68.26%, which is the percentage of data points (occurrences) that fall between the two control limits
   ±2 sigma (or standard deviations) = 95.46%
   ±3 sigma (or standard deviations) = 99.73%
   ±6 sigma (or standard deviations) = 99.99985%

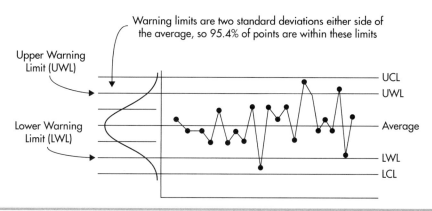

Figure 8-1 Sample control chart

Benchmarking

Benchmarking is a process that uses standard measurements for comparing various things such as the cycle time, quality of a process or procedure, or method against an industry standard or best practice. Benchmarking provides a snapshot of how your business or organization's performance compares to these standards.

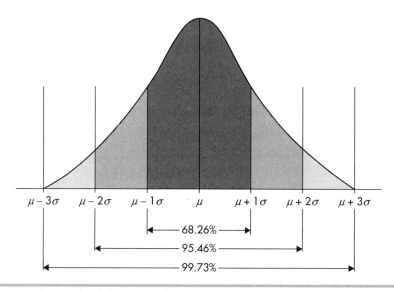

Figure 8-2 Sample standard deviation chart

Certain groups conduct research and provide industry standards that can be used for benchmarking. These include The Gartner Group, Benchmarking Partners, and the Benchmarking Network, Inc., just to name a few.

Design of Experiments (DOE)

Design of experiments (DOE) is a statistical method or framework for identifying which factors may influence variables of a product or process. This is generally used during the quality-planning process to determine the number and type of tests that may need to be run to ensure quality and the potential cost or outcome associated with the tests.

An example of DOE could be the study of rain, sun, and fertilizer on agricultural products for best growing conditions, or when a drug company conducts a series of tests on volunteers representing a sample group meeting certain criteria (for example, age group, and level of fitness) using different doses, different frequencies, or even placebos to collect results and to determine which design of experiments yields the most favorable results for treating an illness.

Statistical Sampling

Statistical sampling is a way to obtain data without spending the time and money to observe, or survey an entire population. Wikipedia offers the following definition:

> "Typically, the population is very large, making a census ... of all the values in the population impractical or impossible. The sample represents a subset of manageable size. Samples are collected and statistics are calculated from the samples so that one can make inferences or extrapolations from the sample to the population. The best way to avoid a biased or unrepresentative sample is to select a random sample [...].
>
> A random sample is defined as a sample where the probability that any individual member from the population being selected as part of the sample is exactly the same as any other individual member of the population."[14]

Survey weighting factors are often applied to the data to adjust for the sample design or to normalize the data in some way. The sampling process is comprised of several steps:

- Defining the population of interest
- Selecting a sampling set of items or events possible to measure
- Determining a sampling method (for example, interviews, observations, surveys, and so on)

- Determining the sample size
- Implementing the sampling plan
- Sampling and data collecting
- Reviewing the sampling process

Flowcharting

A flowchart is a graphical representation of a process usually showing relationship between steps, thus the term "flow." Different design techniques and software tools are available to make this process easier. The flowchart can be used to show activities on the project, decision points (shown as a diamond-shaped image), and the order (or sequence) to follow. The use of arrows helps direct the viewer down the path based on decisions or answers to certain questions. Figure 8-3 shows a sample flowchart.

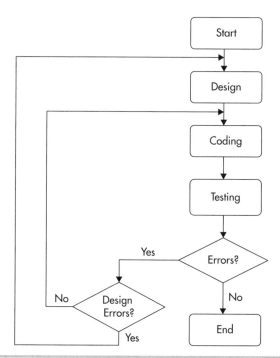

Figure 8-3 Sample flowchart

Outputs of the Plan Quality Process

Here are the five primary outputs from the Plan Quality process:

- **Quality management plan (QMP)** Describes how the project team will implement the approved quality policies. The QMP is a key component of and provides inputs to the overall project management plan. The QMP can be formal or informal, and it can be very detailed or a high-level summary, depending on the needs of the project.

- **Quality metrics** Describes operational details in very specific terms as to the product of the project as well as its features, functions (sometimes called "product attributes"), allowable tolerances, and so on. The quality metrics are used as inputs to the Perform Quality Assurance and Perform Quality Control processes. Examples of quality metrics are failure rates (mean time between failure) of parts, budget or schedule control, on-time performance, defect frequency, and response time to fix problems.

- **Quality checklists** Usually very specific and used to verify that a set of requirements is being met. The checklist can be complex or simple, again depending on the size, type, and complexity of the project.

- **Process improvement plan** A subset of the overall project management plan that details the steps for analyzing the process or activities to streamline or reduce redundancy or wasted steps. The improvement plan answers the question "What are we going to do to make the process better (faster, more efficient, or more productive)?"

- **Project document updates** As always, you want to use progressive elaboration to ensure the project plan and output documents are updated along the way when new information is learned or as changes occur. Examples of documents that might need to be updated are the responsibility assignment matrix (RAM) and the risk registry.

2. Perform Quality Assurance Process

The Perform Quality Assurance process is in the Executing process group and uses data created during the Perform Quality Control process. It involves auditing the quality requirements and the results from the quality control measurement to ensure all appropriate quality standards are being met.

A lot of companies and organizations have a quality assurance representative or department as part of their management structure. The benefit of this person or department is that they help reduce waste and help ensure that quality measures are accurate and communicated to the project stakeholders.

Quality assurance processes should be clearly documented and included in the quality plan as well as the overall project management plan.

Quality Control Measures

Quality control measures, along with quality metrics, the process improvement plan, and performance information, are all things that need to be considered as inputs during the quality assurance process.

Quality control measures are the results of quality management activities. They are used to analyze and evaluate quality standards as established and approved at the project management office (PMO) and at the organizational level.

Quality Audits

One of the tools and techniques used in the Perform Quality Assurance process is quality audits. Audits typically are structured, independent reviews to determine whether project activities comply with organizational and project policies, processes, and procedures. Here are the reasons for quality audits:

- To identify best practices that can be shared across the organization

- To identify gaps or shortfalls for follow-up action

- To proactively assist in improving the implementation of approved processes

- To strive for continual improvement by identifying ways for the team to increase efficiency and performance

3. Perform Quality Control Process

The Perform Quality Control process involves monitoring and recording the results of project execution. Quality control should be performed early and often throughout the project life cycle. This process is often performed by a quality control representative or department within an organization. Their goal is to help ensure quality is being performed to the approved tolerances, according to the specifications. This team is in place to prevent errors from reaching the customer. They perform this function through oversight and sampling, inspections, and other techniques to help ensure quality is controlled.

The project team is responsible to comply with all quality standards, processes, and procedures. Quality control (QC) is accomplished through the implementation of regular testing procedures according to the approved project definitions of quality and more specifically the refinement of these procedures by the project/quality control team using the following steps:

- Planning structured tests

- Following approved documented specifications/requirements

- Conducting formal controlled testing according to standards

- Acting on the results of the tests (lessons learned)

- Updating documentation, processes, and procedures

- Using Quality Circle or similar review/implantation forums

- Following up to ensure continuous improvement (Plan-Do-Check-Act)

Successful companies and project managers place great emphasis on quality control. In "Quality Management Principles," Krister Forsberg states the following:

> "With growing global competition, Quality Management is becoming increasingly important to the leadership and management of all organizations. Quality Management Principles provide understanding of and guidance on the application of Quality Management. By applying following eight Quality Management Principles, organizations will produce benefits for customers, owners, people, suppliers and society at large."[15]

Here is a summary of Forsberg's quality management principles:

- **Principle 1: Customer-focused organization** Organizations depend on their customers and therefore should understand current and future customer needs, meet customer requirements, and strive to exceed customer expectations.

- **Principle 2: Leadership** Leaders establish unity of purpose, direction, and the internal environment of an organization. They create an environment in which people can become fully involved in achieving the organization's objectives.

- **Principle 3: Involvement of people** People at all levels are the essence of an organization and their full involvement enables their abilities to be used for the organization's benefit.

- **Principle 4: Process approach** A desired result is achieved more efficiently when related resources and activities are managed as a process.

- **Principle 5: System approach to management**   Identifying, understanding, and managing a system of interrelated processes for a given objective all contribute to the effectiveness and efficiency of the organization.

- **Principle 6: Continual improvement**   Continual improvement is a permanent objective of the organization.

- **Principle 7: Factual approach to decision making**   Effective decisions and actions are based on the logical and intuitive analysis of data and information.

- **Principle 8: Mutually beneficial supplier relationships**   Mutually beneficial relationships between the organization and its supplier enhance the ability of both organizations to create value. Act promptly to resolve customer concerns. Enclose a brief survey form with the final invoice requesting information on the customer's opinions and expectations. Listen with great care to every one of your customer's ideas and suggestions, and thank them for their input.

For these principles to be effective, all business executives and managers have to first understand and then agree that quality management is essential to the success of the business. Once that agreement has been reached and you have full sponsorship at the highest level in the organization, the commitment must be communicated and enforced all the way down to each and every employee. All employees and managers must be involved in the process. All too often, employees are reluctant to report quality problems, feeling that they would be "rocking the boat" or seen as criticizing coworkers (whistleblowers) to management. Every employee must understand that their job and the prosperity of the company depend on quality products and services, and that teamwork and cooperation are essential to ensure quality.

Tools and Techniques for Performing Quality Control

Many tools and techniques are used for quality control. Some of them are listed in this section. Check sheets are sometimes referred to as a tool used for quality control as well; they are simple sheets used for collecting data in real time. The seven tools listed next are known as Ishikawa's seven basic tools of quality control:

- **Cause-and-effect diagrams**   These are also known as Fishbone or Ishikawa diagrams.

- **Control charts**   Walter Shewhart began using control charts in 1924.

- **Flowcharts**   These are used to identify failing process steps and used in risk analysis.

- **Histograms**   These are vertical bar charts, where the total area of a histogram always equals 1.

- **Pareto charts** These charts use the 80/20 principle and show the number of defects by type or category.

- **Run charts** These are line graphs similar to control charts, only without control limits.

- **Scatter diagrams** These show the relationship between two variables.

Here's a list of some quality control techniques:

- Statistical sampling

- Inspection

- Approved change requests review

Pareto Diagram (Pareto's Law)

Named after Vilfredo Pareto, this diagram is used in quality assurance and is a special type of bar chart where the values being plotted are arranged in descending order. The graph is accompanied by a line on the graph that shows the cumulative totals of each category from left to right.

Pareto diagrams are conceptually related to Pareto's Law (you have probably heard of this as the 80/20 Rule or Principle), which states that a relatively small number of causes (20 percent) will typically produce the majority (80 percent) of the problems or defects. The Pareto diagram is a form of histogram (see Figure 8-4).

Lessons Learned

With every project, we learn more about what worked and what didn't. A good project manager will document those lessons and use the information gained to improve on the next project and the next, which is why lessons learned are such a vital component in quality control.

14 Principles of the Toyota Way

We have learned a great deal from the pioneers of quality, the theorists and gurus mentioned in this chapter, and from the many quality references shown as well. Another great reference for lessons learned is *The Toyota Way: 14 Management Principles from the World's Greatest Manufacturer,* by Dr. Jeffrey K. Liker (McGraw-Hill, 2004). These principles exemplify quality and have propelled the Toyota Motor Corporation into the

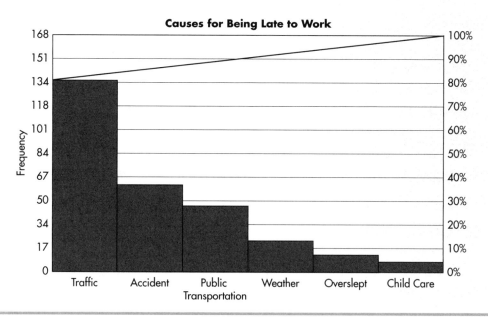

Figure 8-4 Sample Pareto diagram

"world's largest automobile manufacturer," as reported January 22, 2009 by Bloomberg News Service:

1. Base your management decision on the long-term philosophy, even at the expense of short-term financial goals.

2. Create continuous process flow to bring problems to the surface.

3. Use "pull" systems to avoid overproduction.

4. Level out the workload (*hijunka*). (Work like the tortoise, not the hare.)

5. Build a culture of stopping to fix problems, to get quality right the first time.

6. Standardized tasks are the foundation for continuous improvement and employee empowerment.

7. Use visual control so no problems are hidden.

8. Use only reliable, thoroughly tested technology that serves your people and processes.

9. Grow leaders who thoroughly understand the work, live the philosophy, and teach it to others.

10. Develop exceptional people and teams who follow your company's philosophy.

11. Respect your extended network of partners and suppliers by challenging them and helping them improve.

12. Go and see for yourself to thoroughly understand the situation (known as *genchi genbutsu*).

13. Make decisions slowly by consensus, thoroughly considering all options; then implement decision rapidly.

14. Become a learning organization through relentless reflection *(hansei)* and continuous improvement *(kaizen)*.

Managing Change Requests

You have heard me say this several times before, but when it comes to quality control, it is worth repeating: "Change is inevitable, except from a vending machine." In quality management, change, if managed properly, can be your friend. However, if it's not controlled, it can be your number-one enemy. Therefore, plan for change, monitor it, and manage it to the best of your ability.

Quality Management Summary

As mentioned, quality is an attitude; it is not optional if you and your company intend to be successful. When you truly listen to the customer and understand what's important to them, you have a much better idea of what to measure. When you measure the right things and match the product of the project to the customer's needs and expectations, you are demonstrating that you and the team are focused on quality. When you are focused on quality results and using all the tools and resources available to produce quality products and services on your project, it should be clear that you have the right priorities and the right attitude.

References

1. Sticky Slogans, http://www.stickyslogans.com/qualityslogans.html.

2. Vasilash, Gary S. "Quality Is Job...?" Field Guide to Automotive Technology, http://www.autofieldguide.com/columns/1299stic.html.

3. "Tagged: 10 cars with bad reputations," CNNMoney.com, http://money.cnn.com/galleries/2007/autos/0708/gallery.questionable_cars/3.html

   (This website has other links. For example, see http://www.cs.rice.edu/~vardi/comp601/case2.html and http://www.fordpinto.com/blowup.htm.)

4. Vasilash, Gary S. "Quality Is Job…?" Field Guide to Automotive Technology, http://www.autofieldguide.com/columns/1299stic.html.

5. BusinessDictionary.com, http://www.businessdictionary.com/definition/quality.html.

6. SkyMark, http://www.skymark.com/resources/leaders/juran.asp.

7. Wikipedia, http://en.wikipedia.org/wiki/W._Edwards_Deming.

8. SkyMark, http://www.skymark.com/resources/leaders/crosby.asp.

9. Purdue University Animal Sciences, Meat Quality and Safety, Beef Quality Grades, http://ag.ansc.purdue.edu/meat_quality/consumer_grading.html.

10. Burton, Terence T. "Is This a Six Sigma, Lean, or Kaizen Project?" http://www.isixsigma.com/library/content/c020204a.asp.

11. IBM Institute for Business Value Study, Driving operational innovation using Lean Six Sigma http://www-935.ibm.com/services/uk/index.wss/ibvstudy/igs/a1027370?cntxt=a1006791.

12. Lean Enterprise Institute, http://www.lean.org/WhatsLean/History.cfm.

13. Wikipedia, http://en.wikipedia.org/wiki/Standard_deviation.

14. Wikipedia, http://en.wikipedia.org/wiki/Sample_(statistics).

15. Forsberg, Krister. "The Quality Management Principles," http://www.kristerforsberg.com/qmp/about.html.

Chapter 9

Project Human Resource Management

Key Skills & Concepts

- Definition of human resource management

- The importance of the team

- The role of the PM in HR management

- Four HR management processes

- Stages of team development

- Types of teams (including virtual)

- Skills needed to manage project teams

- Managing conflict

- Problem solving

- Management and leadership styles

- Negotiation skills

- Five key people skills

Until now, we have spent most of our time in the Planning process group (refer to Table 3-1 in Chapter 3). We are now shifting gears, and this chapter is where the execution work of the project really begins. Most (three of four) of the HR management processes are in the Executing process group.

Before we jump too deep into the Executing process group, allow me to set the stage a bit. You may recall the first process in the Executing process group from reading Chapter 4. As a reminder, Project Integration Management is the only knowledge area in the *PMBOK* that crosses all five process groups. The specific process I am referring to is "4.3: Direct and manage project execution." The purpose of this process is to carry out the project plan. This is when you begin project execution (working the plan), and the only way to do that is with people (often referred to as "human resources"). It is safe to say that people are the heartbeat of the project. They perform the activities, and they interact to come up with ideas and solutions. As a project manager, you will need to direct and manage these extremely important resources in order to succeed.

A good place to start is with a brief definition of what project HR management is. So let's roll up our shirt sleeves and get started.

What Is Project Human Resource Management?

According to PMI, human resource management (HRM) includes the processes that organize, manage, and lead the project team.

HRM in many cases has replaced the term "personnel management" and is considered the planned strategic approach to managing an organization's most valued assets—the people working on projects to meet the objectives of the business. HRM, by definition, includes the processes involved in managing people to meet business and organizational needs.

TIP

Most of the questions on the PMP exam regarding HR management come from everyday PM experiences. It is worth noting that PMI views HR management as falling into two general groups:

Administrative   People who help organize the communications and documents of the project.

Behavioral management   Management of team members. This group is covered in more detail later in this chapter.

Role of the Project Manager in HR Management

When you have a team of any kind, you are likely to have conflict or at least differences of opinion. This can be healthy if handled properly; for example, it can facilitate constructive alternatives, the sharing of ideas, and open-mindedness. But it can also be disruptive, distracting, and counterproductive.

The success of the project is directly tied to the PM's ability to lead and bring individuals together to form a cohesive, productive team. The PM lives and dies by the team; this means you, as the PM, need to demonstrate strong organizational and communication skills. You need to be supportive (a cheerleader, a den mother, a coach, and an advocate) for the team.

Keeping the team focused on the deliverables of the project and working together to ensure against distractions and confusion is an extremely important role of the PM.

As the project manager you need to do the following:

- Be keenly aware of the importance of the team.

- Identify the team members and other key stakeholders on the project.

- Develop the HR and staffing plan (including skills and scheduling).

- Negotiate for skilled resources on the team as needed.

- Obtain funding, adequate workspace, and tools for the team.

- Get to know each team member's strengths and weaknesses.

- Establish trust and confidence with team members.

- Evaluate team member performance and provide feedback.

- Recognize and reward good performers.

- Help develop the team through strong leadership and guidance, including mentoring, education, and on-the-job training.

As the project manager, it is your role and responsibility to effectively obtain, develop, and manage the team. To do this well, you need to understand the processes that will assist you in this effort.

Project Human Resource Management Processes

Four processes are used most often to manage human resources on a project. Even though these four processes seem independent, they, in fact, overlap. Developing the team is an ongoing process, and, of course, there is always turnover in staff. On average, depending on the project, you should plan for at least 10-percent turnover in project team members. This means the cycle begins again and again as new team members rotate on and off your project. It is up to you to get the new members up to speed quickly so they can become productive contributors to the team.

The four HR management processes according to PMI are as follows:

- **9.1: Develop human resource plan (Planning process group)**   Identifying and documenting project roles and responsibilities, required skills, organizational relationships, and creating a staffing plan.

- **9.2: Acquire project team (Executing process group)**   Verifying the availability of the project team human resources and acquiring the team necessary to successfully complete the project.

- **9.3: Develop project team (Executing process group)**   Improving the interaction and the team's competency to perform better as part of the overall project team.

- **9.4: Manage project team (Executing process group)**   Tracking individual team member performance, providing feedback, managing and resolving issues, and managing changes to optimize the team's performance.

1. Develop Human Resource Plan Process

The HR planning process is very important because if you don't plan properly for the right skills, in the right place and at the right time, you will end up missing the boat. You'll experience schedule slips, people will be overworked, or the quality of the work will suffer due to lack of proper skills or fatigue.

Planning includes determining the five W's (who, what, when, where, and why). The why is especially important because you will need to justify why you need 15 people instead of 10, or you may have to prove why you need one person over another, especially if they are in a higher pay grade or are working on another project.

Equally important to the five W's is the age-old question, How much is the project expected to cost? Typically, HRM and labor account for the highest cost on the project (an average of 80 percent). This is where HR management overlaps with scope, schedule, and especially cost management.

The cost of the people assigned to the project is determined by several things, such as when the team members come onboard, at what salary rate, and when will they need to cycle off the project. HR or labor planning usually is measured in hours of effort at first, and will vary depending on the type and size of the project. For example, on a small project you have fewer people to spread the work among, and they end up being cross-functional. They become less specialized and have to perform work in many different areas (maybe even outside their area of expertise). Later, the PM often has to translate the hours into dollars and will fall back to cost management (discussed in Chapter 7) to determine the overall cost of project labor and other costs to ensure adequate funding for the project budget.

You'll recall that three of the four HR management processes are in the Executing process group. This means the bulk of the work occurs during the execution phase and therefore the lion's share of the budget will typically be spent during this phase. The reason for the higher cost is because the full project team is onboard and performing the activities of the project (full speed ahead). The cost of labor (number of people and types of skills) typically comes with an added cost for the tools and equipment needed to allow the team members to perform their duties on the project (for example, workspace, computers, software licenses, phones, and so on). These costs are at full flow during this phase to keep the team productive.

TIP

You will likely see a question on the PMP exam similar to the following: During which phase of the project is the majority of the budget spent? The best answer should be "During the execution phase of the project."

Ask the Expert

Q: I am the project manager on a new project and have quickly pulled a team of 12 highly skilled people together and have flown them to the customer's office to jumpstart the project. The team arrived safely, but the laptop computers and software that were ordered for them did not. What do I do?

A: I suggest you approach the customer and confidently suggest that because the project team will be working at the customer location and will need to communicate with the customer's employees, the team should use the customer's standard equipment tools and configuration. Ask if the customer can provide a dozen loaner laptop computers loaded with the customer's standard software so the team can plug into the project immediately. Try it. It never hurts to ask—it has worked for me.

Nothing is more frustrating than having the project team onboard, ready to work, and not having the right tools they need to do the job. As part of the HR management plan, you need to ensure you have all the right people and right tools to get the job done properly. This is where the staffing management plan fits in.

As the project manager you need to get the team productive immediately; otherwise, they are sitting around, the schedule slips, and extra costs are incurred.

Staffing Management Plan

The best way to determine the staffing needs and ultimately the cost of the resources is first to develop a responsibility (or resource) assignment matrix (RAM). The RAM will help identify the skills needed and help with work assignments. You can start with the job roles or skills needed to develop the RAM and then add the names of the people performing or filling the roles as they are assigned. In the real world of project management, you will likely hear team members referred to in a number of different ways—resources, staff, heartbeats, headcount, person months, or full-time equivalents (FTEs). What matters the most is that whatever you call the project team members, you must treat them with respect and as individuals.

When calculating labor hours per month of the work needed or performed on the project, most PMs use a monthly estimate of somewhere around 140–160 hours per month/per person. The hours will vary depending on the productivity rate (expected time worked) assumed for the project, country labor laws, overtime expectations, and so on. The best way to sort out who is doing what on your project is to create a responsibility assignment matrix.

Developing a Responsibility Assignment Matrix

The RAM is one of the many tools used for HR management as well as risk and communications management planning. The good news is there is no fixed rule on how to create a RAM. You can use a spreadsheet or table available in the many available software tools or you can even use a notepad, just as long as the tool and format works for you and the team.

The responsibility assignment matrix shown in Table 9-1 is for the BEC case study. It's for an ice event based on an estimated attendance of 2,400 people.

NOTE

A responsibility assignment matrix can be turned into a resource assignment matrix to include the names of people next to their assignments.

Another RAM table often used is the RACI format (Responsible, Accountable, Consulted, and Informed). This is shown in Table 9-2.

To clarify the difference between *responsible* and *accountable*—you may have one person doing the work who is responsible for the activity; however, another person may be held accountable for the results of the work (for example, the PM is accountable in that if the work fails, the project will fail).

Clearly the RAM/RACI chart approach works best if the project team is identified and already assigned to the project. If the project team is not already assigned, you will need to acquire the project team.

2. Acquire Project Team Process

As mentioned earlier in this chapter, HR management includes the processes that organize, manage, and lead the project team. If you had to narrow the project down to a single most important asset, what would it be? Consider the following statement from *PMP Project Management Professional Exam Study Guide, Second Edition,* by Kim Heldman et al.

> "Projects are performed by people, and most projects require more than one person to perform all the activities. If you have more than one person working on your project, you've got a team. If you've got a team, you've got a wide assortment of personalities, skills, needs, and the mix."[1]

The project manager (no matter how good they are) cannot successfully complete the project without the project team. This means the number-one asset on a project is the *team*.

There Are Teams, and Then There Are Teams

Teams come in all sizes and types. For purposes of project management, we will focus on two types of teams: the project management team and the project team.

Responsibility	Primary	Secondary/ Backup	Number of Staff Needed	Comments
Staff	1 supervisor	3 leads	25	Various services.
Zamboni drivers	1	1		Ice events only.
Event crew	2 for first show and 1 for second show	1		1 staff to stay for 1–2 hours after each show for performer practice and lights.
Fire panel	1	1		Fire alarm monitoring and reset.
Sound/lights	1 supervisor	1	21	6 carpenters, 3 properties, 4 wardrobe, 1 house light operator, and 7 spotlight operators.
Cleaning	1 during event		10	10+ post-event.
Security	1	1	7 for each show	Staff will provide 1 loading dock, 2 dressing rooms.
First responders (security)	1 sheriff		5 traffic 2 EMT	Local law enforcement and medical team.
Runners	1 lead		3 to 6	Depends on event.
Show call	1 steward		1 house electrician	Depends on event.
Setup & catering	1	1	5	Food service for crew only.
Audio/video mixers	1	1	2	Depends on event.
Load-out (loading and unloading trucks)	8 riggers	1 floater	4 loaders and 8 electricians	Breakdown: 6 up riggers and 2 down riggers.
Parking	1	1	10 (contract labor)	
Pyro shooter	1	1		For ice and concert events.
Merchandise	1 supervisor	1 lead	2 to 3 per booth	Stands open 1 hour before and 1½ hours into show time.
Box office	1	1	3	Varies by event.

Table 9-1   Sample RAM

Activity	George	Pam	Candy	Dawn	Maverick
Collect requirements	A	R	C	I	I
Define code	R	A	I	I	C
Design code	I	A	R	C	I
Develop code	C	I	I	R	A
Code testing	I	I	A	I	R
Promote to production	R	A	C	I	I

Table 9-2   RACI Chart

The project management (PM) team is comprised of a subset of the overall project team and includes the people who directly perform the management activities on the project. They are sometimes referred to as the core team, the executive team, or the leadership team. They are responsible for the overall management of the project, including the five process groups' various phases of the project. The project management team is everyone specifically responsible and accountable for the outcome (deliverables) of the project.

The project team, on the other hand, extends beyond the project management team and includes all stakeholders. You may recall from Chapter 2 that the definition of a stakeholder is anyone or any organization that is positively or negatively impacted by the project. The project team can be extensive, even on a small project, when you consider the end users, suppliers, support managers, executives, the community, government, and even other companies.

The number and mix of stakeholders depends on the specific needs of the project. Because projects (and project managers) are unique, many factors should be considered when building your project team. The PM's leadership style is one of the many factors, as well as existing or new relationships, that play an important role in the success rate of the project.

Before we talk about leadership styles, let's take a look at the typical role of the project manager when it comes to managing human resources.

Where Do Project Teams Come From?

A key role of the PM is to establish the project team. On newer projects the PM may have full ownership and responsibility to build or acquire the team. When forming a team, strong negotiation skills are a plus to ensure the best skills necessary for a productive team are acquired. In the case of existing projects, the project team (or at least the core PM team) may already be staffed/assigned.

Many companies have a centralized HR department or project management office (or even virtual project management offices) that handles HR staffing and project assignments. In a centralized HR environment, the PM may have little control over who is assigned to the project.

For purposes of this chapter, we will focus mostly on the project management team. As a project manager it is your responsibility to identify the project management team (even if some members are preassigned), and with assistance from the core leadership team you can further identify the overall project team—vendors, suppliers, and other key contacts, as necessary—to get a clear picture of the people involved (directly and indirectly) in the support of your project.

Another form of team that has emerged in recent years is the virtual team.

What Are Virtual Teams?

The answer to this question is fast becoming the norm for projects all over the world. Virtual teams are groups of people who are geographically dispersed and work across time, space, and organizational boundaries.

With the advent of the Internet, emerging software, and networking technology, the ability to work from anywhere in the world is not only possible but preferred by companies and employees alike. According to the "Computing and Information Technology" section of the "Virtual" entry on Wikipedia, "These technologies build the environment for virtual work in teams, with members who may never meet each other in person. Communicating by telephone and e-mail, with work products shared electronically, virtual teams produce results without being co-located."[2]

Working at home can save money and increase productivity. For example, in 1988, I was working in downtown Chicago and living in Hoffman Estates, Illinois, a mere three-hour (roundtrip) commute each day. I was working on a project that required a lot of computer time, and even though I had a PC at home, I was expected to be in the office every day. When I found out I needed surgery that required five weeks of recovery time, my boss was less than excited.

As it turns out, a couple technical gurus in my office had started playing around with software that would allow remote access to our office computer and internal mail system. I asked if I could be their test subject, because this would enable me to work from home during my recovery period. We tested it, and it worked. Therefore, I was one of the first employees in our office to work from home on what we later called "The Home Office" program. My boss liked the idea a lot, and I was able to keep up with my project and work from the comfort of my home, saving hours of travel time.

Most companies now embrace partial or full-time home office employees. This practice saves office space and allows people to collaborate on projects at any time from anywhere in the world. Even though these new channels of communications make virtual teaming possible, they are often more difficult to manage than an onsite (co-located) team because of time zone differences, language barriers, and lack of oversight management.

Negotiation Skills

When acquiring a project team, you often need to put your negotiation skills to use.

TIP

You are likely to see negotiations referred to frequently on the PMP exam related to obtaining resources, reducing cost, improving quality, improving schedule, collecting input/requirements from the team, customer, and so on.

When it comes to negotiation skills, the project manager should be aware of the following items:

- The purpose and priority of the project

- The needs of the organization, the team, and the customer

- Using the tools and resources available to analyze and prove needs before the negotiations (including picking a suitable location at an acceptable time)

- The relationship between parties and how to approach and negotiate accordingly

- The importance of working with decision makers

- Not asking for the best resources if they're not needed

- Understanding the influencing factors in negotiations

Once you have acquired the team members, you need to develop their skills to help bring them together into a productive full-functioning team.

3. Develop Project Team Process

This is the process where you don't want to spin your wheels. By this I mean you don't want turnover in personnel on your project. A high turnover rate is an indicator that something is wrong on your project. There may be extenuating circumstances why people move between projects—reorganizations, retirements, or resource actions (RAs) where people are released from their jobs. However, turnover can be directly related to a bad project or bad project manager. Either it sucks the life out of a project (with lost time, lost money used to train the new team members, and lost productivity) or it revitalizes the project team with new skills, new experience, new ideas, and a newfound energy. Hopefully, you experience the latter on all your projects.

Here are the true benefits of solid team development:

- Less turnover
- Happy "campers" (happy project team members)
- Team spirit (good communications, collaboration, and camaraderie)
- Efficient results

Ways to Develop Your Team

Teamwork is a critical success factor on projects. It all starts with good communications (more on this topic in Chapter 10). It is up to the PM to communicate effectively to minimize confusion and maximize results. The PM is responsible for building a sense of teamwork (team spirit) and for motivating the team members so they want to work together for the greater good of the project. Here are some things you can do that will help build and develop your team members:

- Get to know your team members (including their strengths and weaknesses) and be there for them if they have questions or need support or assistance.
- Use a kickoff meeting to set the tone, communicate expectations, and get everyone on the same page.
- Schedule and manage regular team meetings to keep the team informed (not just meetings for the sake of meetings; they must be meaningful and informative).
- Set up and communicate your recognition, award, or reward program (where the incentives may include on-time delivery of activities under the person's control.
- Allow time for one-on-one discussions and for team brainstorming for new ideas.
- Set the tone for open discussions and listen to your team (verbal and nonverbal cues).
- Consider a team charter (to set the ground rules or rules of engagement for team members). This can include how team meetings will be conducted, voting (if appropriate), and escalations (if there are disagreements or disputes).
- Provide timely team and individual evaluations and feedback so there are no surprises.
- Praise good performance through your established awards and recognition program.
- Be willing to change if things are not working as planned. For example, don't hold on to an employee just because he has been there forever and is a "good guy." Such a decision can't be personal; it has to be based on project performance.

Ask the Expert

Q: There is a guy named Jack on my project who has been a manager for many years and has decided to step down in rank while remaining on the project team. He is not used to actually doing the work, let alone taking directions from someone who is much younger in age. He is very resistant to change. What can I do to get him onboard?

A: You need to first sit down in a quiet place and think through how best to approach Jack. It is important to have a one-on-one meeting to sort this out; make sure you conduct the meeting in a suitable (undisturbed) place. Picking the proper time, place, and approach is essential to a better outcome. Don't try to rush a meeting while Jack is driving you to a customer location (like a fellow PM friend of mine did). You could be let out of the car to walk back to the office! During the meeting, take the time to get to know Jack to better understand his concerns or his situation and then ask for his assistance on the project by appealing to his knowledge and experience. If that doesn't work, you may have to take more aggressive measures.

Develop Project Team Inputs, Tools and Techniques, and Outputs

The inputs, tools and techniques, and outputs that need to be considered as part of the project team development process are pretty straightforward yet very important.

Inputs

- Project staff assignments
- Project management plan
- Resource calendar

Tools and Techniques

- Interpersonal skills
- Training
- Team-building activities
- Ground rules
- Co-location (when possible)
- Recognition and rewards

Outputs

- Team performance assessments
- Enterprise environmental factors updates

Personally, I feel the outputs should include high team morale, effective collaboration, and team spirit, which lead to improved project results.

One way to ensure the team has the proper focus and the tools needed to perform their jobs well is to provide the right training and education to the team members.

Importance of Training and Education

Projects tend to be dynamic; they move quickly. (I once had a project manager say he could feel the earth move beneath his feet because his project was experiencing change almost daily.) The only way to keep up with change is through training and education. With all the new technology, updated software tools, new processes, and techniques, change is constant. In fact, I like to say that the only constant is "change." This is one reason PMI requires professional development units (PDUs) as part of their continuing certification requirements (CCRs). Other organizations have similar types of credentials and require continuing education units (CEUs), to ensure we are keeping up with the changes in the profession. Staying current and connected with the latest tools, techniques, and methods is essential to your ability to manage your project team effectively.

Consider training and education an investment in the future. Your team members will appreciate being viewed as important enough that their company is willing to spend the money (and allow them time off from the project) to stay current on new technology, tools and techniques, and process improvements. Unfortunately, education is sometimes the first thing that is cut when times are tough financially.

Team Building and the Five Stages of Team Development

Team building not only involves the forming of the team but also motivating the team members into a cohesive functioning group with the tools and talent needed to deliver the project successfully.

Several of the tools and processes already discussed are, in essence, team-building activities—for example, the WBS, scope definition and management, time management, cost management, and especially risk management (more details on risk management can be found in Chapter 11).

We talked earlier about the role of the PM in HR management. The PM's role in team building and skills development is also extremely important. The PM should start with obtaining top management support, gaining team member commitment by creating a team identity, promoting trust and confidence, and fostering frequent open communications. The single most important step above communications is to establish strong leadership skills.

TIP

The true measure of success on a project is when team members come to you (the PM) at the end of the project and say they enjoyed working with you and offer to work with you on future projects. When they have trust and confidence in you as a project leader, you have a good solid team relationship.

One of the most important skills in developing a team is how to handle project team problems. Problems, issues, and conflicts are a reality and need to be handled in different ways, depending on when they occur and the stakeholders involved. Problems tend to surface at different times and to varying degrees of impact on the team. In some cases conflicts are normal when building teams, so it is important for the project manager to be aware of the five stages of team development.

A number of theorists have conducted extensive research on the topic of team development. However, one that tends to stand out is Dr. Bruce Tuckman and his five stages of team development:

> "Dr. Bruce Tuckman published his Forming Storming Norming Performing model in 1965. He added a fifth stage, Adjourning, in the 1970s. […] Tuckman's model explains that as the team develops maturity and ability, relationships establish, and the leader changes leadership style. Beginning with a directing style, moving through coaching, then participating, finishing, delegating, and almost detached. […] This progression of team behavior and leadership style can be seen clearly in the Tannenbaum and Schmidt Continuum—the authority and freedom extended by the leader to the team increases while the control of the leader reduces."[3]

Let's take a closer look at Dr. Tuckman's five stages of team development.

Stage 1: Forming   High dependence on the project leader for guidance and direction; individual roles and responsibilities are unclear. The project leader must be prepared to answer lots of questions about the team's purpose, objectives, and external relationships. Processes are often ignored. Members test tolerance of the system and the team leader.

Stage 2: Storming   Decisions don't come easily within groups. Team members vie for position as they attempt to establish themselves in relation to other team members and the leader. There may be power struggles. The team needs to be focused on its goals to avoid becoming distracted by relationships and emotional issues. Compromises may be required to enable progress. Conflict among the team members is not uncommon in this stage.

Stage 3: Norming   Roles and responsibilities are clear and accepted. Big decisions are made by group agreement. Smaller decisions may be delegated to individuals or small teams within the group. Commitment and unity is strong. The team may engage in fun and social activities. The team discusses and develops its processes and working style. There is general respect for the leader, and some leadership is shared by the team. The project leader facilitates and enables the team.

Stage 4: Performing   The team is more strategically aware; the team knows clearly what it is doing and why. The team members have a shared vision and are able to stand on their own feet with no interference or participation from the leader. Disagreements occur but now they are resolved within the team positively. Necessary changes to processes and structure are made by the team. The team is able to work toward achieving the goal of the project and the members look after each other.

Stage 5: Adjourning (Added in 1975)   Adjourning, also referred to as the Deforming and Mourning stage, is very relevant to the people in the group and their well-being. Adjourning is the break-up of the group (hopefully when the project is completed successfully). Team members prepare to move on to new projects and may feel a sense of insecurity or threat from this change.

Skills Needed to Manage Project Teams (Including Virtual Teams)

Because the number-one asset on a project is the team and because the team is made up of people, it is worth investing in understanding and developing people management skills. The following is from the article "Key People Skills for Virtual Project Managers," written by Dr. Ginger Levin and Dr. Parviz Rad:

> "Effective and successful project managers and leaders must be extremely people oriented. They need to create an environment that is conducive to innovation, productivity, and high performance by using their human skills, along with their technical skills in areas such as scheduling, procurement, cost estimating and budgeting, monitoring and controlling, and risk management. Accordingly, they must maintain their technical and functional skills at the highest possible level, while enhancing their softer skills to meet the challenges of today and tomorrow."[4]

Social skills take on greater importance with virtual teams, and PMs need to facilitate and encourage successful interaction. It represents a dramatic change in how we work on projects and creates new challenges for the project team. When managing project teams, especially virtual teams, the PM needs the following important skills:

- **Networking**   The ability to assess and build the quality of working relationships.
- **Building trust and rapport**   Developing a positive attitude.
- **Motivation skills**   Ensuring that everyone is motivated on the team.
- **Communications (especially listening)**   One of the most important skills to have.
- **Organizational skills**   Shows order and allows for higher productivity.
- **Counseling skills**   Used to overcome personal issues.
- **Appropriate use of power**   Power needs to be used appropriately.
- **Delegation**   A basic management skill and vital in project management.
- **Conflict management and problem solving**   Conflicts can be a good thing when managed properly.
- **Negotiation**   It takes negotiation skills to make necessary changes.

All of us have had situations where we let our emotions run wild, only to find we didn't have all the facts. That is why it is important to be sensitive, stay open-minded, and listen to your team. The signs may not be clear, so don't be too quick to judge.

The best way I have found to get people's attention and to help inspire creativity and improved performance is by providing recognition and rewards.

Recognize and Reward the Project Team and Individuals

Even if it is just a pair of new socks (you read that right), you need to find a way to recognize and reward good performance. You are probably thinking, "What a cheapskate!" Well, it worked in one situation on one of my more difficult projects.

The story goes like this: Once upon a time, there was a computer programmer (named Mark) working for me on a large project in Portland, Oregon. Mark was staying at a hotel for the duration of the nine-month project and had put in so many hours one week he didn't have time to drop his laundry off at the front desk for cleaning. One day he was getting dressed and had no clean socks, so Mark came in to work wearing no socks. We all kidded him a bit and at the end of the project I presented him with a new pair of socks for his dedication to the project and included a nice check as well. He was a great sport, and the team got a huge, endearing laugh out the socks.

Ask the Expert

Q: What should I do as the project manager when a team member is distracted, sometimes falls asleep in meetings, is not taking the work seriously, and is talking back?

A: Pull the individual aside (one-on-one) and calmly and professionally ask the person to please explain the reason for their behavior. If there is no logical or acceptable response, you will need to be firm and explain this action is not acceptable. Give specific examples of how it is disrupting team meetings and is distracting the team. Have an action plan documented and in hand with acceptable options in mind to present to the individual. Here are some sample options for the distracted team member:

- An open apology to you and the team in the next meeting
- Additional work because this person appears to have spare time on their hands
- Possible performance rating reduction
- Moved off the project or fired

Be aware there are times when the person may have a good reason for their actions, or at least they think they do. Therefore, be patient and listen. You may find they have a medical condition, are going through a personal situation, or have a work-related reason that may require your compassion or assistance.

TIP

Don't be too quick to judge. I once had a student who dozed off in class and would snore, which I found distracting and rude. I was getting upset and was considering how to reprimand him in class. Then I decided instead to give the class a 15-minute break so I could approach this student one-on-one. He explained to me that he was on heavy medication to prepare for a liver transplant. He was on the top of the recipients list and was expecting a call at any time to go to the hospital. Imagine how embarrassed I would have felt if I called him out in class and then learned the news. I am glad I didn't make a fool of myself by jumping to the wrong conclusion.

Rewards and recognition can come in many forms or flavors. I know an outstanding project manager who received a large award (of several thousand dollars) for successfully completing a challenging project ahead of schedule and under budget. His manager asked him to set up an award dinner for the whole team. At the dinner his manager gave out awards to everyone on the team but failed to announce the project manager's award, the largest of them all. The PM didn't get the team recognition, only a check. Even though the award was sizable, it was anticlimactic when it came without an announcement to the team. Some would say, "Don't give me applause, just send money." But at the end of the day we all like the open team recognition, even if its just a pair of socks (given in the right situation).

Another example is of a team member (Jim) who was in a project meeting where I handed out commemorative, uncirculated coin sets to several of the team members. After the second one was handed out, Jim counted the face value of the coins and boldly announced the set was worth only a few dollars. His tune changed when *he* received a coin set, announcing that the coin set was truly priceless and would be worth a lot of money some day!

The moral to the story is, you can get great results by handing out recognition and awards even if the dollar value is low, as long as the recognition is meaningful and can be appreciated by the recipient and the team. Also remember that the high-dollar awards can seem meaningless if not presented in a favorable manner.

4. Manage Project Team Process

The Manage Project Team process is in the Executing process group. It involves being involved with the team activities, having open communications, and making sure the team members are focused and productive.

Management and Leadership Styles

Managing people and being a leader are two different things. They have slightly different motivations and require slightly different approaches.

For example, managers tend to look at the daily operations and are focused on the following:

- The short-term perspective
- Did everyone show up for work today?
- What have you done today?
- How are we going to accomplish this?

Leaders, on the other hand, look for ways to develop the team members and focus on the following:

- The long-term perspective
- Is there a better way to do things?

- Coaching and mentoring the team

- Working with the team for best results

Management Styles   Even though these are not in the *PMBOK,* you should be familiar with the different types of management styles:

- **Autocratic**   The manager makes all the decisions.

- **Democratic**   The team is involved in the decision-making process.

- **Laissez-faire**   The team is self-led (as in Agile project management).

- **Exceptional**   Looking at only the top and bottom 10 percent of performers (that is, who is doing well and who is not).

Much like project management skills, the general management skills needed to effectively manage people are as follows:

- Strong communications skills

- Organizational skills

- Negotiating skills

- Problem-solving skills

- Leading and influencing people

Being a good manager doesn't mean the manager is a good leader. Strong leaders demonstrate slightly different styles.

Leadership Styles   Leadership styles are not in the *PMBOK* either. However, you need to be familiar with the different types of leadership. Your style will likely be slightly different from other project managers (or totally unique). You need to incorporate the style that works best for you and the team. Be aware that different situations and different team members will call for different leadership styles. It is best to be flexible and "mix it up" to meet your needs and the needs of the team.

Here are a few leadership styles you may already be familiar with:

- **Directing**   Telling others what to do ("my way or the highway")

- **Autocratic**   Same as management styles (making decisions without outside information)

- **Facilitating**   Coordinating input from others to help solve problems or make decision

- **Coaching**   Instructing or inspiring others
- **Supportive**   Being an advocate and providing assistance to the team and individuals
- **Consultative**   Inviting ideas from others and assisting in the decision process
- **Consensus**   Group decision-making process based on group agreement

As project manager, you will likely use different styles at different times. You will probably exhibit more management style on the front end of the project and more coaching style further into the project life cycle. A lot will also depend on the relationship and history you have with your team members.

Know the Capabilities of the Team Members

Know you team members' skills, experience, capabilities, and any limitations they may have. It can be embarrassing to assign someone to perform certain activities and then find they don't have the knowledge, skills, or education to perform these duties.

Problem Solving

When you effectively use strong project management skills, you may be able to avoid many problems. However, problems will occur. There are various ways to solve problems, and the first step is always to take the time to identify and understand the problem. Make sure you are focused on the problem and not a downstream result of the problem. Here is the recommended process to help solve problems:

1. Identify the cause of the problem (focus on the cause and not the symptom).

2. Understand and analyze the problem (use available tools and resources to help).

3. Work out an agreeable solution (it may be a temporary workaround at first).

4. Solve the problem to the best of your ability using the resources available.

5. Monitor the situation after the problem has been resolved to ensure it doesn't reoccur.

TIP

For those of you planning to take the PMP exam, you can expect approximately 100 questions that require you to look at a situation (cost, schedule, HR, and so on) and make the best decision to help solve the problem.

Manage Project Team Inputs, Tools and Techniques, and Outputs

There are a number of inputs to consider during the managing the project team process. Keep in mind the main focus is on the team. When you have the staff assigned according to the project management plan, it's time to manage the team through use of the various tools and techniques available (see the list that follows). As mentioned earlier, when you have a team, you tend to have conflicts. Sources of conflict include resource constraints, interpersonal relationships, and competing demands.

Inputs

- Project staff assignments
- Project management plan
- Team performance and reports

Tools and Techniques

- Observation and conversation
- Project performance appraisals
- Conflict management
- Issues log
- Interpersonal skills

Outputs

- Change requests
- Project management plan updates
- Updates to other project documents

How to Motivate the Team

To help you solve problems and conflicts on your project, it is always helpful to know how to motivate your team. This is a good place to look to professional sport coaches and people who have proven success in team motivation. They can provide great examples of ways to get the team to focus on the end results, to work together as a team, and to use all the tools and resources available. (Sound familiar? It should, because this goes back to my three takeaway points in Chapter 2. By the time you get to the end of this book, you should be able to recite these in your sleep.)

Being a project manager is like being a coach, teacher, or mentor. Here are some quotes I pulled from the Internet to help you coach and motivate your team:

- "The achievements of an organization are the results of the combined effort of each individual." –Vince Lombardi

Ask the Expert

Q: Pam writes, "I am a new project manager, and my boss, coworkers, and team are constantly stopping by my office at all hours of the day just to introduce themselves and talk. I enjoyed this attention at first, but now it is becoming distracting and taking time away from my project. I don't want to be rude, but what can I do to minimize the distractions?"

A: The first question I ask myself in such a situation (and it has happened often) is, "Do I have a candy dish or other snacks on my desk?" The answer in most cases has been "yes." I hate to say this, but people can see candy as an open invitation to come by your desk. If this is the case with you, I recommend one of two things: Take away the candy dish, or have some work folders handy with tasks that need to be done and when someone stops by give them the work. After a short period of time, people won't stop by as often. Try it—you'll be surprised how well it works. You may also want to consider the location of your guest chairs. Too close to the door invites people to come in and sit. Further away requires them to ask permission, at which point you can say, "Would you mind coming back in 15 minutes? I will finish what I'm working on and then I will be able to concentrate on your question."

- "Practice Golden-Rule 1 of Management in everything you do: Manage others the way you would like to be managed." –Brian Tracy

- "Coaches have to watch for what they don't want to see and listen to what they don't want to hear." –John Madden

- "Probably my best quality as a coach is that I ask a lot of challenging questions and let the person come up with the answer." –Phil Dixon

- "People will exceed targets they set themselves." –Gordon Dryden

- "Coaching is 90 percent attitude and 10 percent technique." –Author unknown

- "A good coach passes on information quickly. They do not hold back information that affects my job." –Byron and Catherine Pulsifer, from "People's Expectations of a Coach"

- "You get the best effort from others not by lighting a fire beneath them, but by building a fire within." –Bob Nelson[5]

From personal experience I will add a couple of tips on coaching as well.

- Take time to listen. (This one is very difficult, as we tend to be busy formulating our thoughts for the answer and we don't fully hear the question.)

- Look at the situation from the other person's point of view. (This gives you a new perspective.)

- Think positively and be open-minded to new ideas and suggestions.

- Trust your team—give them room to grow. (People tend to rise to your level of expectation.)

- Recognize even the little things and offer praise early and often. (Rewards are good.)

Try This Take Me Out to the Ball Game: Networking the Project Team

You are the PM for a large Information Technology (IT) systems support team. The team is so large and physically dispersed across several states and countries that you are experiencing difficulty getting the team members focused on the project activities and schedule. A critical date has been missed, and the customer is very upset. What do you do?

Answer: Take the team (including the customer) to a baseball game. That is exactly what a good friend of mine (and fellow project executive) did. He invited as many of the project team members, including the customer, that were within a short traveling distance to the local baseball stadium. He reserved a club room that enabled the project team to not only enjoy the game, but intermingle, talk, relax, and get to know one another. The results were amazing.

Granted, getting the team together, even on the phone, is not easy if they are spread out in different locations and different time zones, especially if you don't have the budget to allow everyone to travel to a baseball game. However, maybe you can coordinate a similar get-together for the other locations concurrently so everyone can participate at some level. It is also good to give out T-shirts or baseball hats with a team slogan or logo. I have seen this approach work time after time, and it goes a long way toward helping build the team spirit.

Types of Power

As leader of a team, the PM needs to be aware of different types of power. Getting team members and stakeholders to cooperate is sometimes difficult, especially when managing virtual teams. Here are the different types of power you as the PM can use (or be aware of in case others are using these powers on you):

- **Formal (legitimate)**   Based on a person's position or level in the company.

- **Reward**   Giving people awards to get things done or in recognition for a job well done.

- **Penalty (coercive)**   The opposite of reward.

- **Expert**   Recognized for knowledge and experience.

- **Referent**   Referring to the authority of someone in higher position (name dropper). "The vice president has made it clear this project takes top priority."

There is always more than one way to get things done. Before we exercise our power as a PM, it is good to be aware of the different motivational theories.

Motivational Theory

One way to get the team motivated is to understand what drives them. Many behavioral science tools and techniques are available to assist you in better understanding what motivates individuals or teams. Here are a few that are not in the *PMBOK* but you should still be aware of them if you are planning to take a PMI exam.

Maslow's Hierarchy of Needs   According to the article "Abraham Maslow's Hierarchy of Needs motivational model" at BusinessBalls.com, "Abraham Maslow developed the Hierarchy of Needs model in 1940–50 USA, and [his] theory remains valid today for understanding human motivation, management training, and personal development."[6]

The article goes on to explain his theory:

> "Each of us is motivated by needs. Our most basic needs are inborn, having evolved over tens of thousands of years. Abraham Maslow's Hierarchy of Needs helps to explain how these needs motivate us all.
>
> Maslow's Hierarchy of Needs states that we must satisfy each need in turn, starting with the first, which deals with the most obvious needs for survival itself.

Only when the lower order needs of physical and emotional well-being are satisfied are we concerned with the higher order needs of influence and personal development.

Conversely, if the things that satisfy our lower order needs are swept away, we are no longer concerned about the maintenance of our higher order needs."[7]

For example, if a person has reached the top (that is, has accomplished/self-actualized) and then is stranded on a desert isle, they immediately go to the bottom of the needs hierarchy pyramid to seek food, water, and shelter. Figure 9-1 shows Maslow's Hierarchy of Needs.

Herzberg's Motivator-Hygiene Theory Frederick Irving Herzberg (1923–2000) was a psychologist who was also influential in business management. He is most famous for introducing the Motivator-Hygiene theory, which is also known as the Two-Factor Theory of Job Satisfaction. According to this theory, people are influenced by two factors: motivation factors and hygiene factors.[8]

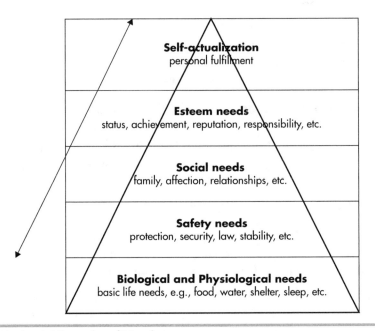

Figure 9-1 Maslow's Hierarchy of Needs

Here's a list of motivation factors according to Herzberg's Motivator-Hygiene Theory:

- Achievement
- Recognition
- Work itself
- Responsibility
- Promotion
- Growth

And here's a list of some hygiene factors:

- Pay and benefits
- Company policy and administration
- Relationships with coworkers
- Physical environment
- Supervision
- Status
- Job security
- Salary

Hygiene factors relate to how people respond to their environment. Because workers in certain countries have come to expect a safe and suitable working environment, we are more often dissatisfied by a bad environment and seldom satisfied by a good environment. Wikipedia states the following about motivation and hygiene factors:

> "Hygiene factors operate independently of motivation factors. An individual can be highly motivated in his work and be dissatisfied with his work environment.
>
> All hygiene factors are equally important, although their frequency of occurrence differs considerably. Hygiene improvements typically have short-term effects. Any improvements result in a short-term removal of, or prevention of, dissatisfaction.
>
> Hygiene needs are cyclical in nature and come back to a starting point. This leads to the 'What have you done for me lately?' syndrome."[9]

McGregor Theory X and Theory Y In his book *The Human Side of Enterprise* (published in 1960), Douglas McGregor examined theories on the behavior of individuals at work and formulated two models, known as Theory X and Theory Y.[10] Theory X is based on managers who believe that people need to be watched every minute; they are incapable and avoid work whenever possible. This is opposed to Theory Y, where managers believe people are self-motivated and work without supervision. Here's a list of assumptions for these theories:

Theory X Assumptions

- The average human being has an inherent dislike of work and will avoid it if they can.
- Most people must be controlled and threatened before they will work hard.
- The average person prefers to be directed and dislikes responsibility.

Theory Y Assumptions

- People are self-motivated, and work is as natural as play or rest.
- If a job is satisfying, the result will be commitment to the organization.
- The average person not only accepts but seeks responsibility.
- Workers use imagination, creativity, and ingenuity to solve work problems.

Expectancy Theory

Another theory to be aware of is the Expectancy Theory. This motivation theory was first proposed by Victor Vroom of the Yale School of Management and is based on the expectation by employees that their work efforts will lead to results and that they will be rewarded for their effort. Expectancy Theory is about choice. It explains the processes that an individual undergoes to make choices.

Expectancy Theory predicts that employees in an organization will be motivated when they believe the following:

- Putting in more effort will yield better job performance.
- Better job performance will lead to organizational rewards, such as an increase in salary or benefits.

Theories like the Expectancy Theory help us better understand what motivates people; however, the only way to know how your team is performing is to assess their results.

Team Performance Assessments

Team performance assessments can be informal or formal. The goal is to evaluate the team's performance to make the members aware of what is working and what is not.

Overall results of the project are influenced by each and every individual on the team and should be looked at from both the team perspective and the team member perspective.

The performance of a successful team is measured in a number of different ways, depending on the nature of the project. For example, if the project is time constrained (schedule dependent), then clearly a measure of team success is whether the project is being delivered on time.

Team assessment is used to determine team effectiveness, and the results can be detailed and specific or general. In either case, the assessment should show how the team is measuring up to the agreed scope, cost, and schedule of the project. Here are some examples of team evaluation points:

- Is the team working together in a productive and cohesive manner?

- Are the improvements a result of a joint team effort or individual effort?

- What is the overall project team turnover rate? (Remember, this is a risk indicator as to whether or not things are going well on the project. If people are not happy, they will want to move on.)

- Is the team showing respect for the PM and project team leads/members?

- What is the quality of the products being delivered by the project team?

The results of the team performance assessment should be used to analyze the situation and make improvements, as needed, to help ensure quality work. Any action taken should be documented with cause-and-effect details, including action plans for improvements. Examples of action items include suggesting specific education or training, mentoring, and the assistance of other team members.

Extra care should be given in assessing a virtual team because you can't see the team members face-to-face. You may also have contract performance clauses, country privacy issues, or other laws that must be considered when managing virtual project teams.

Understanding how your team is performing will also help in managing your customer's expectations.

Managing Customer Expectations

The customer is a part of the project team and in most cases part of the project management team. They provide review and approval for changes. They are also involved in risk management and communications management. They should provide requirements of what they expect from the project, the target completion date, and what specific results they want to see at the end. As part of the team, they are privy to information that can cause concerns or conflicts. So, how do you manage customer expectations and conflict?

Note that conflict is not always bad; it can sometimes raise opportunities to improve the way you do things. You can enhance the relationship with your customer and your team by looking at conflict as a healthy way to learn new things. The main thing to remember is to be open-minded. Ask the customer questions. Make sure you understand what is important to the customer and what their expectations are at the end of the project. You may be surprised, but better to find out sooner than later and lose valuable HR resources, time, and cost going down the wrong path.

Ask the Expert

Q: I am the PM on a small project. My customer called recently with a request to mail a survey and invoices to their clients. The additional mailing requests are out of scope of the project. Therefore, I set up a meeting for 8:00 A.M. the next morning to discuss their requests. During the meeting, the customer demanded the survey go out immediately. I calmly explained the request was not in scope and that if the team was pulled off the project to perform the extra work, it would delay the overall project by one week. The customer was very upset and threatened to cancel the entire project. A shouting match ensued. How could I have handled this situation better?

A: When things heat up, I suggest you try taking a short break and have some coffee and rolls or donuts to calm the situation. It might make all the difference in the world. The customer could become more agreeable once you both take a minute to relax and get something to eat. (Perhaps the customer is a single parent with a sick child, was running late for the 8:00 A.M. meeting, and had skipped breakfast.) After you have your break, you can then pursue settling your differences in a more professional manner.

Signs of a Conflict

How do you know when conflict is looming? Some characteristics or triggers are listed here:

- Team members are working excessive hours (for example, 15+ hours per week of overtime for long periods of time).

- The customer or team members are defensive during meetings or discussions.

- Relations are strained (the customer or team members are avoiding you).

- Tempers flare (outbreaks of emotions in meetings or one-on-ones).

- The customer is micromanaging the team (loss of confidence).

- High turnover of team members (as mentioned earlier).

- Lots of extra meetings (meeting to prepare for meetings).

- Significant number of changes (dissatisfaction or disorganization).

Conflict Resolution

Now that you know some of the signs or triggers of conflict, the question is, How can you resolve conflict? The best way to resolve conflict is to understand it—what it is and how it will impact the project. Conflict, like change, is inevitable in the project environment. Conflict is a state of disharmony or opposition between people or forces when they, with perceived incompatible goals, seek to undermine each other's capability or objectives.

There are many sources of conflict, including lack of skilled resources, scheduling conflicts, cost constraints, different management and leadership styles, communications problems, change, and risk events.

When conflict is managed properly, the results are improved productivity, higher team morale, and higher quality product and project deliverables.

Here are a few things to remember when it comes to managing conflict:

- Don't take yourself too seriously.

- Don't take the conflict personally.

- You need to know conflict is normal and helps you look at the options.

- It is a team issue and needs to be resolved early.

- Keep the conflict to problems and issues, not personalities.

- Be aware of the relative importance and impact of the conflict on the project.

- Be aware of the downstream results (ripple effects).

- Focus on the root cause of the conflict and not the symptoms.

- Help the team stay focused and motivate them to help resolve conflict.

Techniques to Help Resolve Conflicts

One way of analyzing and understanding a problem is by interviewing the customer or parties involved. There are a number of techniques you can use to help resolve conflicts, as listed here:

- **Withdrawing/avoiding**   Retreating from the actual or potential conflict situation.

- **Smoothing/accommodating**   Emphasizing areas of agreement rather than areas of difference.

- **Compromising**   Searching for solutions that bring some degree of satisfaction to all parties. This is often viewed as a lose/lose situation as everyone gives up something.

- **Forcing**   Pushing one's view on others (someone wins and someone loses).

- **Collaborating**   Looks at multiple views from different perspectives (leads to consensus).

- **Confronting/problem solving**   This is a win/win situation because it treats the conflict as a problem to be solved by looking at alternatives (requires give-and-take approach by all parties).

TIP

PMI views confronting/problem solving as the best approach to resolve conflicts. You may even see a question or two concerning this technique on the PMP exam.

No matter what resolution approach you take, the end results depend on your ability to apply sound judgment and good interpersonal skills, including leadership and the ability to influence others to help solve conflicts. Conflict resolution is a team sport; the PM can't succeed without the team, and the team must be productive and fully functional to provide results. However, it is up to the PM to set the stage and to lead by example.

It is important to note that conflict resolution begins at home in your project team first. This is what HR management is all about. Here are the other key steps:

1. Make sure you have sponsorship for the project (turnover in executive sponsors can change the focus, funding, and fun on the project).

2. Make sure you have a clear and confirmed understanding of scope, target dates, and expectations from all key stakeholders (especially the customer).

3. Ensure clear communications, including listening at all times (no news is not always good news, and it leaves room for speculation and uncertainty in the ranks).

4. Manage your human resources (all the people on your project) with respect.

5. Be flexible and open-minded. Be firm when needed, but be compassionate as appropriate.

I realize there are many variables when it comes to HR management. Any time you deal with people, you have feelings and emotions to consider. The good news is, you can find lots of help in the way of courses, mentors, coworkers, family, and friends to collaborate with. The thing to remember is, you want to invest in this skill to help you and your team grow.

HR Management Summary

HR management is truly the life blood of the project. Many organizations have found teaming to be an extremely effective way to accomplish project goals and objectives.

As a project manager, having the knowledge and skills to effectively acquire, develop, and manage teams is a necessity. With the uniqueness of projects and team members, there is clearly a challenge for the PM to keep everyone focused on the end results. Deal with problems head on, quickly, yet with compassion and respect for all parties involved. Remember, the problem won't go away on its own and will likely grow the longer you allow it to remain unresolved.

When asked what I like most about project management, I have to say it's the people. Working with project teams from all over the world has opened my eyes to the benefits and barriers of managing diverse projects. The true measure of success is the size and breadth of your network, and your network is what makes the world of project management go round.

References

1. Heldman, Kim, Claudia Baca, and Pattie Jensen. *PMP Project Management Professional Exam Study Guide, Second Edition* (Wiley Publishing Inc.: Indianapolis, Indiana), 2007, pages 336 and 353.

2. Wikipedia, http://en.wikipedia.org/wiki/Virtual.

3. "Bruce Tuckman's 1965 Forming Storming Norming Performing team-development model," http://www.businessballs.com/tuckmanformingstormingnormingperforming.htm.

4. Dr. Levin, Ginger and Dr. Parviz Rad. "Key People Skills for Virtual Project Managers," http://www.allpm.com/modules.php?op=modload&name=News&file=article&sid=440.

5. Coaching Quotes.com, http://www.wow4u.com/coaching/.

6. "Abraham Maslow's Hierarchy of Needs motivational model," http://www.businessballs.com/maslow.htm

7. Ibid.

8. Wikipedia, http://en.wikipedia.org/wiki/Frederick_Herzberg.

9. Ibid.

10. "Human Relations Contributors," http://accel-team.com/human_relations/hrels_03_mcgregor.html.

Chapter 10

Project Communications Management

Key Skills & Concepts

- Importance of communications

- Four communications management processes

- Identifying stakeholders

- Managing stakeholder expectations

- Communications model

- Communication channels (including formula)

- Percentage of time PM spends communicating

- Communication blockers (barriers)

- Information distribution

- Project management reports

There's communication, and then there's (or should be) *effective* communication. Communication is the simple exchange of information between two or more parties. Basically there's the sender of the message, the receiver of the message, and the message itself. These are three of the seven components that make up the communication model.

For the communication model to be effective, we must add a few more elements. For example, the information needs to be *encoded* (translated into thoughts or ideas that can be understood by others) by the sender. The sender then needs to select the appropriate method (or vehicle) to send (convey) the message—for example, a *medium* such as e-mail, letter, text message, touch, or phone call. Then the receiver needs to *decode* the message (translating it back into understandable meaningful thoughts and ideas). Ideally the receiver then provides feedback to the sender in the form of either an acknowledgement or additional questions to clarify the message. The intent is to have a communication circle of a clearly understood actionable exchange of information, ideas, or directions that produce the desired results (see Figure 10-1).

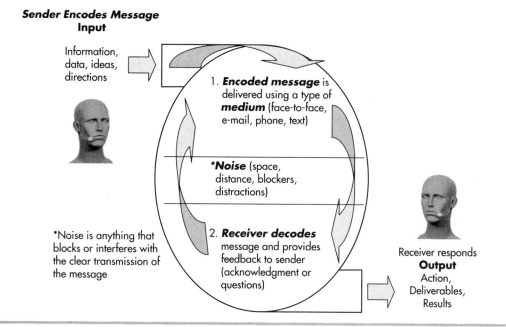

Figure 10-1   Communication circle

Now let's talk about effective communications on which the project manager needs to focus. Communications instructor Michael Starling offers the following insight (from a 2009 webcast):

"Effective communications is a connection between people that allows for the exchange of thoughts, feelings, and ideas, which leads to understanding."[1]

For the communication to be successful, it also helps if all parties have a common language and similar knowledge of the topic. For the message to be clear and understood, there should be minimal *noise* (or interference) with the transmission of the message. Examples of noise include unfamiliar terms, lack of background information, distance (temporal or physical), and environmental factors (phones ringing, crowed room, and so on).

Because communication is so important in managing projects, you are likely to see several questions on the PMP exam concerning communication in areas such as risk management, scope management, and status reporting.

The Importance of Clear Communication

I saw a cute birthday card recently that really says it all about communication. The card shows three elderly men walking along the beach. The first man says, "It's a windy day." The second man says, "No, I think it's Thursday." And the third man says, "I'm thirsty, too. Let's go have a beer."

This kind of conversation happens far too often. We only hear half of what is said, and we retain even less.

To recap, here are the seven components of the communication model:

- Sender
- Encoding
- Message (including the feedback message)
- Medium
- Minimal noise
- Decoding
- Receiver

The PM's Role in Communications

Communications is an important tool in project management. Effective communications is a skill that helps the PM to inform the team and stakeholders about all aspects of the project. The PM must develop this skill to successfully employ the tool as part of the Project Communications Management knowledge area.

The good news is, the communications model is simple to use; in fact, we use it from the time we learn to talk. The bad news is, if the model is not used effectively, you will send or receive the wrong message. Thus, the team is off building the wrong widget at the wrong time, or they are so confused they don't know what you want and may just choose to ignore you.

As simple as the communication model is, communicating is one of the more difficult activities in managing a project. Talking is easy; communicating is a challenge!

Being able to communicate effectively is a skill that is developed and honed your entire life. Communicating is not just about the *sender.* It is an interactive, two-way session where both sender and receiver continuously influence each other as messages are cycled back and forth, on sometimes nonverbal, barely perceptible levels.

TIP

To be prepared for your PMP exam, you need to know that PMs spend an average of 90 percent of their time communicating and that any questions on communications management will likely be intermingled with other topics. For example, the WBS is a communications tool, and scope and risk response strategy has to be clearly communicated to the team. As a PM, you communicate to yourself internally—and even in your sleep. During light sleep is when some of the best ideas come to mind, so keep a pad and pencil next to your bed to capture those great ideas or reminders.

There are a multitude of reasons for good, clear, two-way communications. Here are some examples:

- To improve our working relationships
- To be able to adapt to change and enable prompt action
- To understand different communication styles and to take advantage of the right style to eliminate confusion and influence positive results
- To increase the overall quality of the project team and the deliverables

As you probably already know, there are two primary types of communication: verbal and nonverbal. Verbal (or auditory) communication includes talking, singing, tone, and the pitch of your voice. Paralanguage (sometimes called *vocalics*) is the nonverbal cues of the voice. Paralanguage may change the meaning of words.[2] Nonverbal communication includes body language, sign language, touch, and eye contact.

The Medium (How We Deliver the Message)

Have you ever heard a person telling a joke mess up the punch line or put the emphasis on the wrong syllable? Or they nailed the punch line but hesitated at the wrong time or used the wrong word? When this happens, the receiver will likely say, "I don't get it," or they may get the joke but will think it wasn't funny. The only way to improve the delivery of a joke or any other communication is through practice.

Some of the more common communication delivery methods are face-to-face, written, and virtual. Virtual is a whole new ballgame, as we adapt to a new generation of highly interactive, fast-paced, multitasking project managers.

The delivery method can be formal or informal, both of which will affect the way you deliver the message. An important thing to remember is that your message is likely to be received incorrectly or the meaning lost depending on your delivery method, the timing, or the mood in which you deliver the message. This is especially noticeable in the face-to-face delivery method. For a summary of delivery methods, see Table 10-1.

Virtual Communications (Wave of the Future)

A new medium that has emerged with the advent of computers is virtual communications. Some examples include the virtual classroom or virtual "worlds" such as *Second Life*. In these virtual worlds, a person can choose an avatar (a virtual alter ego) and walk,

Delivery Method	When Used	Advantages	Comments
Face-to-face	For important meetings or conferences	Shows importance of the meeting or event and is great for networking, building trust and confidence, as well as improving relationships	Be aware of expressions and gestures; they can be distracting or even insulting. Generally, 55 percent of a message is conveyed by body language and only 7 percent in what is said; the remaining 38 percent is in tone, pitch, and volume
Written	For formal or informal, depending on the type of medium used	Works well in many ways to communicate to a broad diverse audience	Generally, two categories: formal (letters, contracts, and so on) and informal (e-mails, and texting, which is a whole new language in itself)
Haptics (nonverbal touching such as a handshake, hug, slap on the back, and so on)	Close proximity as appropriate	Can show sincerity and friendship	Not always accepted and can be offensive in some cultures
Virtual (more detail provided later in this chapter)	Physically dispersed team members or when travel is not possible	Broader team skills, allows for "follow the sun" coverage in different time zones, and saves on travel and other expenses	Can be challenging and can be distracting for some especially with language or other barriers

Table 10-1 Communication Delivery Methods

talk, or even fly around in virtual settings. According to the SecondLife.com website, "*Second Life* is a free online virtual world imagined and created by its Residents. From the moment you enter *Second Life,* you'll discover a fast-growing digital world filled with people, entertainment, experiences and opportunity."[3]

Project Communications Management Processes

According to PMI, five processes are associated with communications management:

- **10.1: Identify stakeholders (Initiating process group)**   The process of identifying all the people and organizations impacted by the project and documenting relevant information pertaining to their interests, level of involvement, and impact to the success of the project

- **10.2: Plan communications (Planning process group)**   Determining stakeholder information needs and approach to project communications

- **10.3: Distribute information (Executing process group)**   The process of making relevant information available to project stakeholders as planned

- **10.4: Manage stakeholder expectations (Monitoring and Controlling process group)**   Working with all stakeholders to meet their communication needs and addressing issues as they occur

- **10.5: Report performance (Monitoring and Controlling process group)**   Collecting and distributing performance information, including status reports, progress measurements, and forecasts

1. Identify Stakeholders Process

This is a new process just added in the fourth edition of the *PMBOK* that is extremely important to managing projects in the real world. It is critical to identify the stakeholders early in the project life cycle (see Figure 10-2). You need to know who the stakeholders are and their level of interest or influence on the project (for example, funding sponsor, end users, or managers). If you need a refresher on who the project stakeholders are, see Chapter 2.

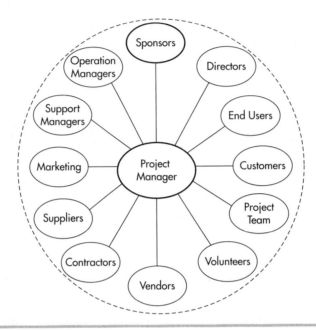

Figure 10-2 Identify stakeholders

Try This How to Plan Communications for Key Stakeholders

Say for a moment you are the events center manager for an upcoming concert. How do you plan for the communications needs of the stakeholders, (sponsors, team, and so on) for this event?

Answer: The best way to plan for communications is to brainstorm. Get the core project management team together and make a list of who will be affected by this project. I like to use a spreadsheet or table (refer to Figures 9-1 and 9-2 in Chapter 9) for the project team and then add to it for additional stakeholders, including their level of interest or power (that is, decision maker, end user, support manager, or customer).

Stakeholder Management Strategy

Once you identify the stakeholders, you need to have a strategy to help guide the team and yourself in managing those stakeholders. Stakeholder management strategy is an output of the Identify Stakeholders process, and it should provide direction on how you plan to effectively manage all the stakeholders affected by the project.

Because projects are unique and stakeholders change, one thing is certain: You can't treat all stakeholders alike. For example, you would treat the sponsor of the project differently than a meddling manager (who, for some reason, wants extra deliverables added to the project even though they are not a decision maker and have no authority to make these kinds of demands or changes). To get an idea of the different stakeholder interests and the flow of communication to the various stakeholders, see Figure 10-3.

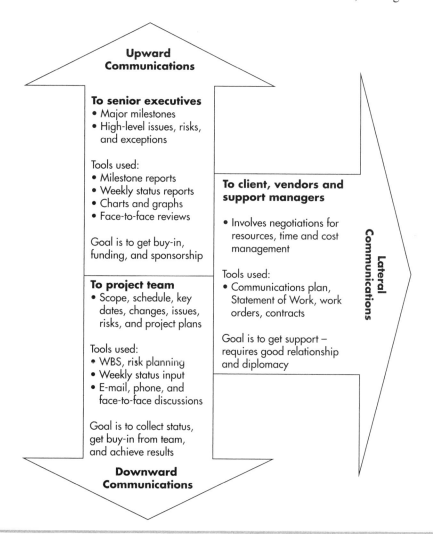

Figure 10-3 Communications flow

Identify Stakeholders Tools and Techniques

One of the more important tools and techniques for identifying stakeholders is stakeholder analysis. Three primary steps are involved:

- Identify all potential project stakeholders, including their roles, departments, level of knowledge, and influence on the project or information (or funding) needed on the project. Are they decision makers or subject matter experts that can help technically?

  A good way to do this is to interview the stakeholders and expand your list based on the new information gained.

- Identify the potential impact or support of each stakeholder and prioritize the key stakeholders to ensure communications flow appropriately.

  An effective tool in this case is a power/interest grid (see Figure 10-4). This allows you to group the stakeholders based on their active involvement or level of influence (power). This is a simple grid with quadrants; on the Y axis is Power (from low to high) and on the X axis is Interest (from low to high). Then as a team, you determine where your stakeholders should be placed on the grid. For example, from left to right in the bottom quadrants, insert Monitor (Minimum Effort) and Keep Informed. In the top two corners, put from left to right Keep Satisfied and Monitor Closely. Then, it

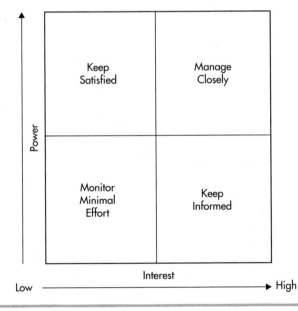

Figure 10-4 Sample power/interest grid

is a matter of coming to some agreement as a team on an agreed placement of each stakeholder.

- Assess how key stakeholders are likely to respond in different situations in order to better plan how to influence them in their support and to mitigate potential negative impact to the project.

Identify Stakeholders Outputs

Here are the two outputs in the *PMBOK* from the Identify Stakeholders process:

- **Stakeholder register**   A log that should include each stakeholder's name, organization, position (title), role on the project, contact information, and assessment information (such as expectations or level of influence)
- **Stakeholder management strategy**   How you plan to manage the stakeholders

2. Plan Communications Process

The PM and team need to work together when planning communications for the project. You need to start with the stakeholders identified in the previous process. This list will help you determine the level of communications needed, the frequency, the format, the reports needed, and so on.

Sample Project Communications Plans

A well-planned project has a well-planned communication strategy. The following tables provide examples of two project management communication plans.

The detailed sample communications plan shown in Table 10-2 is a modification of Princeton Project Communication Plan.[4]

What	Who/Target	Purpose	When/Frequency	Type/Method(s)
Initiation meeting.	All lead project management team members.	Gather information for initiation plan.	First. Before project start date.	Meeting (co-located if possible).
Distribute project plan.	All key stakeholders.*	Distribute plan to alert stakeholders of project scope and to gain buy in.	Before kick off meeting. Before project start date.	Document routed via hardcopy or electronically. May be posted on project team room or website. PM templates: Project Scope "Lite" and Initiation Plan

Table 10-2   Sample Communications Plan (*continued*)

What	Who/Target	Purpose	When/Frequency	Type/Method(s)
Project kickoff.	All key stakeholders.*	Communicate plans and stakeholder roles/ responsibilities. Encourage communication among stakeholders.	At or near project start date.	Meeting.
Status reports.	All stakeholders and project office.	Update stakeholders on progress of the project.	Regularly scheduled. Monthly is recommended for large/midsize projects.	Distribute electronically and post in team room or via Web. PM template: Status Report.
Team meetings.	Entire project team. Individual meetings for subteams, technical teams, and functional teams, as appropriate.	To review detailed plans (activities, resource assignments, and action items).	Regularly scheduled. Weekly is recommended for the entire team. Weekly or biweekly for subteams, as appropriate.	Meeting PM template: Detailed project plan and key project documents, as appropriate.
Project advisory group meetings (may apply only to larger projects).	Project advisory group (steering committee), PMO, and project manager.	Update project advisory group on status and discuss critical issues. Work through issues and change requests here before escalating to the sponsor(s).	Regularly scheduled. Monthly is recommended.	Meeting.
Sponsor meetings.	Sponsor(s) and project manager.	Update sponsor(s) on status and discuss critical issues. Seek approval for changes to the project plan.	Regularly scheduled. Recommended biweekly or monthly, or as needed when issues cannot be resolved or changes need to be made to the project plan.	Meeting.

Table 10-2 Sample Communications Plan

What	Who/Target	Purpose	When/Frequency	Type/Method(s)
Executive sponsor meetings (may apply only to larger projects).	Executive sponsor(s) and project manager.	Update sponsor(s) on status and discuss critical issues. Seek approval for changes to the project plan.	Scheduled as needed when issues cannot be resolved or when changes need to be made to the project plan.	Meeting.
PO audit/ reviews.	Project office, project manager, select stakeholders, and possibly sponsors, if necessary.	Review status reports, issues, and risks. To identify and communicate potential risks and issues that may affect the project.	Monthly. Scheduled by the project office.	Meeting/report. The project office will produce the report using their (auditors) template.
Post-project review.	Project office, PM, and key stakeholders (including sponsors).	Identify improvement plans, lessons learned, what worked, and what could have gone better. Review accomplishments.	End of project or end of major phase.	Meeting/report. The PM or project office will produce the report.
Quarterly project review.	Project office, project manager, and key stakeholders.	Review the overall health of the project and highlight areas that need action.	Quarterly, depending on size and criticality of the project. Scheduled by the project office.	Meeting/report. The project office will produce the report using an internal template.
Other.	To be determined by the project manager and team.	General communications.	As needed.	Group meetings, Lunch-n-Learns, e-mails, webinars, webcasts, postings in project team room or website, and so on.

* A key stakeholder is defined as a person whose support is critical to the project—if the support of a key stakeholder is withdrawn, the project may fail.

Table 10-2   Sample Communications Plan

Case Study: BEC Sample Communications Plan

For projects that are similar in nature and can be repeated, it is good to streamline the communications plan. Take our BEC case study for example. Weekly meetings are conducted to streamline the flow and frequency of communications from the director of events to the operations managers. In these meetings, the director uses an Event Data Sheet showing all the key information needed—dates, times, expected seating capacity, security and lighting for the event, and so on.

Based on the scope statement, here is a brief overview of the communications strategy, followed by a table showing when each communication should occur, who the assigned owner is, and a brief description of the communication activity.

- The event team will have weekly update/status meetings to review completed tasks and determine current work priorities. Minutes will be produced from all meetings.

- The event director will lead weekly meetings to review the previous event's lessons learned and the upcoming events for team awareness. A customized Event Data Sheet will be used and distributed to the project team to show all pertinent information about the events with timelines, department assignments, key contacts, and other requirements for each event.

For the purpose of this example, we will focus on our "Rock On" concert, introduced in Chapter 5. A streamlined communications plan for BEC is shown in Table 10-3.

Frequency of Meeting	Owner / Tool Used	Description
As needed for project initiation (varies by event)	Event director and artist's agent or sponsor / contract	This is the initial meeting to finalize the event contract and requirements.
Three weeks prior to event	Event manager / Event Data Sheet (EDS)	Meeting with all building staff to provide advanced information from the band and building requirements for the event.
Two weeks prior to event	Event manager / EDS	Distribution of the Event Data Sheet to start the planning.
One week prior to event	Operations manager / EDS	Review requirements and begin staffing and facility changeover staging for event week.
Week of event	Project or changeover manager / EDS	Use the Event Data Sheet as a guide for setup of the venue.
One week after event review	Full team / EDS	Review lessons learned.
Close the event communications	Sign-off by the project team and event manager	Document the results of the event, tickets sold, issues, and so on.

Table 10-3 Sample Communications Plan for BEC

Plan Communications Tools and Techniques

Four tools and techniques are associated with the Plan Communications process. They are discussed in detail in the following subsections.

Communication Requirements Analysis   To establish a communications plan, the PM and team often need to perform a communications requirements analysis. The analysis varies depending on the project and will be more detailed for new/first-time projects.

One thing we tend to overlook as PMs is the complexity of the communications required. Even on a small project, you can have dozens or even hundreds of stakeholders to consider during communications analysis. The number of lines of communication grows exponentially as the size of the project team grows.

Say, for example, you have four team members on your project. The formula, then, is

$$(n * (n - 1))/2$$

where *n* represents the number of stakeholders. For the sample project, the formula would look like this:

$$(4 * (4 - 1))/2, \text{ or } (4 * 3)/2, \text{ or } 12/2 = 6$$

Therefore, you have six communication channels on your project. The number of lines of communication between the four team members is shown in Figure 10-5.

Now suppose you have ten people on your team. The calculation now is

$$(10 * (10 - 1))/2, \text{ or } (10 * 9)/2, \text{ or } 90/2 = 45$$

This means you have 45 different communication channels (or paths) among the ten team members. That's a lot of lines of communication. The more lines you have, the more room there is for a breakdown in communication, where someone is not clear and does the wrong thing. This could be devastating to the project. Now just imagine if you have 50 or 100 people on the project team!

Communication Technology   Various methods are used to transfer information among project stakeholders. You also have a number of factors to consider when selecting the technologies or tools for this process:

- The urgency of the needed information
- The availability of the technology (both physically and from an affordability perspective)

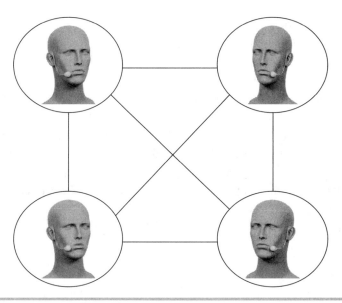

Figure 10-5 Communication channels

- Telephony needs (for example, phones, systems, and technology compatibility)
- The duration of the project and project environment (for example, short or long term and virtual or co-located team) and, of course, the size of the team.

Communication Model   We covered the communication model earlier in this chapter. Do you remember the seven components of the communications model? If not, go back now and review.

The one point I want to reemphasize here is the noise factor. Don't let noise get in the way of clear communications. This includes physical noise, temporal distance, language barriers, poor phone connections, and distractions.

On one of my projects on the West Coast, the project office team room was a storage closet of just over 50 square feet. At times there were six to eight people in the room, and for meetings we often had to gather in the cafeteria, with all the traffic and distractions. Talk about lots of noise/interference in trying to communicate with the team in this environment. It was difficult at best.

Ask the Expert

Q: Can you provide an example of the type of question the PMP exam asks regarding calculating the number of communication channels?

A: The PMP exam will likely ask a question similar to the following:

"There are four new team members added to your existing team of five. How many additional communication channels have been added?"

When answering a question like this, you will need to remember the formula used to calculate the number of communication channels, which is $(n * (n - 1))/2$, and you will need to read the question closely. To arrive at the answer, first calculate the current number of existing communication channels: $(5 * 4)/2 = 10$. Then calculate the new total number of team members if four more are added: $5 + 4 = 9$. Plugging this number into the formula gives you the following:

$(9 * 8)/2$, or $72/2 = 36$

Then you simply need to subtract your starting number of channels (10) from 36, and you get $36 - 10 = 26$. Therefore, 26 additional communication channels are created by adding four new team members to this project.

Communication Methods   You need to be aware of several communication methods. Here are just a few:

- **Interactive communications**   Communication occurs between two or more parties (one-on-one or in meetings).

- **Push communications**   Information is sent to specific recipients or in broadcast messages.

- **Pull communications**   Used for very large volumes of information or large audience. The information is downloaded from a central repository when needed.

How to Conduct Effective Meetings

Most projects that fail are doomed before 20 percent of the work has been completed. One reason, among the many possible, is poor communications. One way to communicate to a group of people is through meetings. How will you run meetings as a project manager (both internally and externally)? See the following sample list of things to consider when conducting meetings. Remember, PMs spend an average of 90 percent of their time communicating, and meetings are a big part of project communications.

- Preplan the meeting. What is the purpose/objective? Who should attend? Who will facilitate? Who will present? Where will the meeting be held? (Is the meeting room scheduled? Is the room large enough? Do you have the room properly set up for the type of meeting you are going to run?) Are distractions minimized? Who will document the minutes of the meeting? And who will follow up on "to-dos" or action items from the meeting?

- Always set an agenda (clearly document who will present, what they will present, and when). Make sure the presenters are clear on the timing and provide prompts or cues if they are about to run over their allotted time.

- Always send the agenda out to the attendees ahead of time (usually at least a day or two ahead of the meeting). This can be used as a reminder to attendees and to the presenters that they are scheduled.

- Preview the presentations if time allows (depending on sensitivity of material and audience) just so there are no (or fewer) surprises.

- Allow time for networking (keep this between five and eight minutes at the beginning or end of the meeting).

- Maintain meeting integrity. It should start on time and end on time.

- Manage the meeting. If there are disruptions, such as someone spending too much time on a topic or getting carried away in the discussions, flag the topic for follow-up. Be sure to capture the discussion item and be sure to follow up; otherwise, you lose credibility.

- Take control of the meeting if things get off track and reschedule it if necessary.

- Publish the minutes in the project team room in a timely manner (usually one or two days after the meeting).

- Consider putting caveats (qualifiers) in the minutes, such as "If anything has been omitted or misstated in the meeting minutes, please let me (host of the meeting) know within five business days. *No response to this note implies acceptance of the minutes as written.*"

3. Distribute Information Process

All of us at one time or another have received a message or e-mail that was not meant for us. Oh well, you simply delete it and move on. How about receiving an e-mail that is to a cast of thousands and is about a meeting that has already taken place? Again you mumble to yourself and delete the message. But, what about the real slipups? You know the ones....

- **Clicking the "Reply to All" button**   The RTA button is a powerful tool. Talk about instant gratification. It's a quick-and-easy way to tell a lot of people that a meeting has been rescheduled or the new contract has been signed. But be very careful with your reply. It can get you into an embarrassing situation.

- **Responding with a message that doesn't match the question**   This is a result of not reading the whole e-mail. I am guilty of this one myself. I have answered e-mails too quickly, only to find I missed the real question and had to send follow-up messages to clear things up.

- **Sending streaming (cascading) e-mail**   These are e-mails containing notes from several people that are forwarded to person after person. Half the time the message gets so convoluted that by the time it comes to you, it makes no sense at all. This happens far too often and can be quite counterproductive. Often the e-mail is ignored altogether.

The Distribute Information process involves making relevant information available to project stakeholders. This process occurs throughout the project life cycle and can come in many forms, such as formal requests for information from an auditor or sponsor, or informal requests from anyone at any time.

So how do you effectively distribute information? The main thing is to do your homework. You should also make sure you have a good idea of who the stakeholders are

Ask the Expert

Q: How do I tell a top executive they resurfaced an old e-mail and are asking for the status of a problem on a project that was already resolved?

A: Read the e-mail (all of it) carefully. Tactfully summarize the problem and the solution to the requesting executive with assurance that the issue has been resolved.

This situation actually happened to me. I received an e-mail from a top executive asking me to set up a meeting with several VPs to report the status of a certification project that had already been closed. In my case, as I read down through the cascade of eight messages that had been sent and forwarded and responded to, I noticed something very peculiar. The original note was sent over a year ago, and the question had already been addressed by the person's manager. The problem was already solved, and here we were about to generate a lot of work and tie up a lot of high-powered executives because the sender didn't carefully read the original message. That was embarrassing and could have even been worse had I done what the top executive asked me to do. Therefore, always read the entire e-mail before responding and respond in a professional manner.

and their level of interest in the project. Finally, have a clear communication plan. Always remember the communications model. Make sure you are clear on who the specific senders and receivers are, the message that needs to be received (actions to take, response needed, and so on), and how to ensure open communication channels for the feedback loop to ensure the message is in fact getting through as intended.

Now you need to think about how you are going to distribute the information—what format to use, what delivery method to use, and the frequency of the distribution. Here are some tips to keep in mind:

- Tell the recipient up front the purpose of the communication (FYI only, project status, decision required, input needed, and so on).

- Write the message as a news reporter would. Start with the most important information first, followed by deeper levels of detail or background.

- Have a clear communications plan and stick to it.

- Keep the message simple and concise. Use active voice instead of passive voice, and pay attention to your writing style. For example, all capital letters seems like you are yelling, all lowercase seems like you are either uneducated or don't care.

- Send the information only to the person who needs to take action, and copy only those people who have a need to know.

- Avoid streaming (or stacking) e-mails that have been forwarded and replied to several times already. Delete the previous unnecessary messages when you reply to keep your response clean and to the point.

- Use an action word or phrase in the subject line of the e-mail: Action Required, FYI Only, At Your Convenience, Response Due By, and so on.

- Avoid using the Reply to All button unless you are sure everyone should know.

- Avoid sending and responding to e-mails after midnight. They will likely miss the point or be confusing.

- Use effective meeting management techniques by sending out agendas, staying on time, and capturing and posting the minutes to the meeting. (This is very important.)

- Work on your presentation skills and facilitation techniques to be effective when running meetings.

- Remember that anything you send becomes public record instantly—even if you've sent it confidentially to one person.

Be sure you set some ground rules, communicate them to the team, and then make sure you follow these rules to set a good example. You should be familiar with the many dimensions of the communication activity, which include the following:

- Internal (within the project) and external (clients, other project team members, the public)

- Formal (reports, memos, briefings) and informal (e-mails, open discussions, phone calls)

- Vertical (up and down the organization) and horizontal (to peers, vendors)

- Official (newsletter, annual report) and unofficial (off-the-record communications)

- Written and oral (or texted)

- Verbal and nonverbal (voice inflections, body language)

I talked earlier about building your skill to help you improve communication. Here are some communication skills you may want to develop or refine:

- Active listening (effective two-way communications)

- Questioning by probing ideas and situations so they are better understood and more effective (keep asking "Why?" until you have a clear understanding)

- Education, training, and mentoring to increase knowledge and awareness

- Fact-finding to identify or confirm information

- Setting and managing expectations

- Resolving conflict to prevent disruptive impact on the project

- Summarizing, recapping, and identifying the next steps

Distribute Information Tools and Techniques

The *PMBOK* lists only two tools and techniques in this process:

- **Communication methods** For example, individual and group meetings, conferences, computer chats, texting, IMing, and other remote methods

- **Information distribution tools** For example, hard copy, soft copy (electronic), reverse 911 calls, and websites

Distribute Information Outputs

Outputs from this process include project reports, presentations, records, feedback from stakeholders, and lessons learned documentation.

4. Manage Stakeholder Expectations Process

This process, if not done properly, tends to come back to haunt you. I have managed a lot of projects in my 30 years in project management, so I know this is an area that on some projects takes the most time.

Especially in today's world, we tend to expect or demand instant gratification. Managing stakeholder expectations is not easy. The only way to help make managing stakeholder expectations easier is to establish a good working relationship with the key stakeholders (remember, the team is your number-one asset on the project). You want to keep them happy. Also, don't forget the sponsors who are funding the project. They may need special care as well. Therefore, you need to learn how to play well with others, even when emotions run high and mood swings occur. Always keep your responses friendly and professional. Don't raise your voice, get cynical, or sarcastic. In Asia and other countries, raising your voice or showing emotion is a sign of weakness. You want to stay in control in all situations.

Try This Managing Unrealistic Expectations

Imagine for a moment you are a new project manager for a six-month transition of IT services from the customer's location (West Coast) to Boulder, Colorado. The project is to mirror the computer system as is by simply setting up a clone of the current system's operating environment in Boulder, copying the system image over to the new system, and then running the tests. Sounds pretty simple, right?

Now throw in a little change in the customer expectations. For example, the client decides (after equipment has already been ordered based on original approved and priced configuration) to add new human resource and financial applications that require a significant increase in the system's processing power (double the usage). A larger computer system is needed and will cost another $500,000 and the software licenses will cost over $1 million. The impact to make these changes will extend the schedule by two to three months.

So the question is, How do you manage unrealistic expectations?

Answer: Meet with the customer to fully understand their reason for the change. Then, armed with all the facts and figures, explain to them in a professional manner the impact to the project both in time and cost. Hopefully, the client will be reasonable and allow the extra time and additional pricing to match their new expectations. I have seen this go both ways, but in all cases it strained the relationship. Therefore, always work on establishing a good relationship with stakeholders as early as possible. That is the key to success.

Managing stakeholder expectations involves frequent interaction, negotiations, regular meetings, and status reports to keep them in the loop. The old saying "No news is good news" doesn't hold true here. If you are not communicating with the stakeholders, they begin wondering who is in charge and whether you are hiding something. Therefore, it is best to communicate early and often. Even if the news is bad, you need to keep the stakeholders informed. The key is to stay connected, communicate any problems, and most of all have an action plan. The key stakeholders have a right to know what is going on and how you are managing problems.

Manage Stakeholder Expectations Tools and Techniques
The tools and techniques that can be used for this process are

- Communication methods (how you plan to communicate with the stakeholders)
- Interpersonal skills (build trust, resolve conflict in a timely manner, actively listen)
- Management skills (work on negotiation, writing, and presentation skills, even public speaking techniques and style)

As you can see, these are closely tied to relationship building.

Here are some tips to ensure success when managing stakeholders:

- Demonstrate integrity and honesty.

- Actively manage their expectations (interactively and proactively).

- Address concerns before they become larger issues or problems.

- Clarify and track issues using an issue-tracking log and resolve them quickly.

What Happens When We Don't Communicate Clearly?

Have you ever said something and didn't get the reaction you thought you would? Or have you said something that didn't come out clearly as planned? We have all experienced those embarrassing moments.

Here are a few tips from Michael Starling to help you avoid classic communication blunders. The following are things you don't want to do:

- *Say too little.* The "I'm the leader, just trust me" line doesn't work these days. People usually do trust you, but they want to hear your thinking and reasoning.

- *Say too much.* You don't have to give every detail to every person. For most people, keep the discussion at a high level.

- *Talk to the wrong people.* You have to target your communication. For example, you don't want to tell the sponsor about the technical details (how to build the watch); all they want to hear is the current project status (on schedule and on budget).

- *Lose sight of emotional impact.* Remember, when things are changing, emotions run high. Statements can be made that have lots of energy. Give people time to emotionally adjust to the change.

- *Rush the process.* Because you are the leader, you probably have processed the information before anyone else. Your grief or excitement or passion is behind you. It's easy to rush others expecting them to catch up. Give them time.

- *Look away or look uninterested.* Your nonverbal actions must be consistent with your spoken message. Ralph Waldo Emerson said it well: "What you do speaks so loudly that I cannot hear what you say."

- *Have bad timing.* Delivering the right solution at the wrong time can get you in trouble. It is like telling a joke: The punch line has to be in the right place at the right time for it to be funny. The same is true in when and how you communicate.[5]

- *Use unconscious or distracting body language.* See the sidebar "Five Body Language Tips from the Presidential Debates."

Five Body Language Tips from the Presidential Debates

The information in this sidebar comes from the article "Five Body Language Tips from the Presidential Debates," by Carol Kinsey Goman, Ph.D. (http://hodu.com/debates.shtml).

Watching political debates provides an opportunity to learn from body language dos and don'ts. Here are some tips from presidential debates that you can apply to your role as a PM.

Tip 1: With nonverbal communication, it's not how the sender feels that's most important; it's how the observer perceives how the sender feels. A famous debate signal occurred in 1992 when incumbent President George H. W. Bush looked at his watch while his opponent, Bill Clinton (who would win the election) spoke. Why he looked at his watch doesn't matter. What does matter is that to the viewing audience, President Bush's gesture conveyed boredom.

Tip 2: Watch those facial expressions! In the 2008 presidential debates, both candidates made facial expression errors. In most of the debates, Senator Obama minimized his emotional reactions and reinforced the impression that he is remote and "cold." Senator McCain's forced grins and eye rolling in the third debate sent a negative signal (for example, insincerity) that was reflected instantly in polls rating likeability.

Tip 3: Don't underestimate the power of touch. While Senator Obama shook hands with audience members after the 2008 debates, only Senator McCain touched anyone during a debate. Toward the end of the second debate, McCain walked into the audience and patted a U.S. military veteran on the back and then shook his hand, which produced a genuine smile from the veteran. McCain's gesture was exquisitely done and worked very much in his favor.

Touch is so powerful and effective that clinical studies at the Mayo Clinic show that premature babies who are stroked grow 40 percent faster than those who do not receive the same amount of touching. A study on handshakes by the Income Center for Trade Shows showed that people are twice as likely to remember you if you shake hands with them. (Thus the reason for candidates to get out in public and shake a lot of hands and kiss a few babies.)

Tip 4: When your body language is out of sync with your words, people believe what they see. Anytime Senator McCain was speaking in the first debate of the 2008 campaign, Senator Obama oriented his body toward McCain and looked

(continued)

directly at him. In doing so, he sent a nonverbal signal of interest and respect. McCain's decision to avoid looking at Obama during that debate was not only dismissive, it was counter to McCain's stated position that Democrats and Republicans need to work together on behalf of the American people.

Tip 5: Remember that you are never "off camera." When the second presidential debate of 2008 was over, and their wives were on stage, Senator McCain tapped his rival on the back. Senator Obama turned around to offer his hand, but it was not reciprocated. McCain, instead, pointed to his wife, Cindy—an action that many viewers took for a nonverbal brush-off.[6]

Communication Blockers/Barriers

According to a fellow instructor Michael Starling, "Vague terms are deadly to effective communication. People are free to interpret things according to their own frames of reference (everyone has different filters)."[7]

The vague words in Table 10-4 can create huge misunderstandings and conflict.

How do you avoid using vague words, terms, or phrases? Practice thinking about what you say and how you say it; then work on ways to say it without the use of vague terms.

5. Report Performance Process

The Report Performance process involves collecting and distributing performance information, including status reports, measurements, and forecasts.

Performance reports need to provide the stakeholders with an appropriate level of information according to their level of involvement in the project. One size doesn't always fit all when it comes to project reports.

Soon	Often	A Lot	Many	Better
Worse	Bad	Good	Like	Similar
Later	Difficult	Easy	More	Less
Faster	Efficient	Timely	Always	Never
Nice	Stuff	Things	Everyone	Guys

Table 10-4 Vague Words

Ask the Expert

Q: My client continues to ask for more and more reports, more details, and in various formats. This has required me to assign a full-time person to generate all the reports for my project. What can I do to get this under control?

A: I recommend meeting with the key stakeholders and determine which reports are essential and which are just nice to have. If there are mixed results, take a vote or, worst case, stop sending what you and the team view as nonessential reports and see who complains. Another option is to determine the impact to the project (for example, extra time and cost) and write a proposal to charge more for the additional reports. That should get someone's attention. If the stakeholders are not willing to pay extra, then reduce the number of reports and the problem is solved.

TIP

Performance reports are essential to the success of the project. Their importance is evident in the number of times performance reports show up in the PMBOK (49 times). Performance reports are referenced as inputs and outputs to many processes in many knowledge areas, such as integration management, risk management, HR, and communications. Therefore, you can expect a number of questions on these reports in the PMP and CAPM exams.

Report Performance Outputs

The primary output from the Report Performance process is the actual performance reports. Reports are created and distributed at different intervals and to different stakeholder audiences. (See the list of report types shown later in this section for details.)

The reports you create and distribute on your project will more than likely be customized to meet your needs and the needs of the stakeholders.

There is an old saying that goes something like this: "A job is never done until the paperwork is complete." The paperwork makes the finding or results real and auditable; it is the glue that keeps the project together.

Types of Performance Reports

The type of reports that go to the various stakeholders depend on a number of factors, including the size of the project, level of criticality, and impact to the community.

Reports come in many types, and the following list shows only a few areas of focus for performance reports (according to PMI):

● Current status for project progress (usually reported on a weekly basis)

● Previous project performance analysis (trends, lessons learned, and so on)

● Risk and issue logs to know where the threats and opportunities might be

● Work completed during the period (earned value reports, percentage complete, and so on)

● Summary of changes reviewed, approved, and implemented during the period

● Specific approved measurements or metrics (for example, schedule and budget results)

● Plan versus actual charts with variance analysis against the approved baseline

● Forecast reports, such as ETC (estimate to complete) and EAC (estimate at completion)

● Other relevant information, as needed, for review and discussion

Forecasting Methods

Forecasting involves dusting off your crystal ball to look at the future and determine if the current status is going to affect the future outcome of the project.

Several methods can be used to forecast your project:

● **Time series methods**   These methods involve the use of historical data as the basis for estimating the future (for example, earned value, moving average, extrapolation, trend estimating, and various growth curves).

● **Causal/econometric methods**   These methods make the assumption that it is possible to identify the underlying (root cause) events that may affect the outcome. For example, the sales of ski passes are affected by the amount of snowfall at any given time. Some examples include linear and nonlinear regression, autoregressive moving average (ARMA), and econometrics.

● **Expert judgmental methods**   These methods use the intuitive judgments of subject matter experts for cost estimates, probability and impact estimates, time estimates, and so on. Some tools/techniques used in this type of forecasting are the Delphi method, technology forecasting, and analogy forecasting (top-down from similar previous projects).

Other methods include simulation modeling, probabilistic forecasting, and ensemble forecasting.

Summary of Communications Management

Remember the importance of good two-way communications. Also remember that project managers spend about 90 percent of their time communicating. In the world of real estate, the famous motto is "location, location, location." In the world of project management, the motto should be "communication, communication, communication."

And don't forget the importance of listening. To be better communicators we have to learn to listen. After all, you were given two ears and only one mouth, so you should listen twice as much as you talk.

When I first became a PM, I felt that I was not contributing to the work of the project. Sure, I was busy scheduling meetings, talking to stakeholders, preparing reports, running the numbers, and keeping track of the budget and schedule, but this didn't feel like real work. Then one day a team member said, "This project would fall apart without the work you do to organize, coordinate, and communicate what needs to be done." It was then I realized my worth on the project and accepted the fact that true project management involves managing the flow of communications, like a conductor of an orchestra.

So raise your baton and direct your team to success through effective communications management.

References

1. Michael Starling 2009 webcast on communications.

2. Wikipedia, http://en.wikipedia.org/wiki/Nonverbal_communication.

3. Second Life, http://secondlife.com/whatis/.

4. "Princeton Project Methodology—Project Communication Plan" (rev. 10/03/03), http://web.princeton.edu/sites/ppo/PMCommunicationPlan.doc.

5. Michael Starling 2009 webcast.

6. Carol Kinsey Goman, Ph.D. "Five Body Language Tips From the Presidential Debates," http://hodu.com/debates.shtml.

7. Michael Starling 2009 webcast.

Chapter 11

Project Risk Management

Key Skills & Concepts

- Project risk management process
- Definition of risk (uncertainty)
- Six risk management processes
- Three key components of risk
- Threats and opportunities
- Risk identification techniques
- Risk response strategy
- Probability and impact analysis
- Risk tolerances and thresholds
- Expected monetary value
- Monte Carlo analysis
- Risk types and categories
- Contingency plans

Risk is often defined as *uncertainty* (a lack of knowledge about a potential event that can cause a positive or negative impact to the project). As mentioned previously in this book, risk management must be done early and often. Risk is always considered to be in the future. It can have one or many causes, and often has a cascading effect on other elements of the project. Risk management should be conducted as a team. It should be planned thoroughly because risk comes in many different flavors and most of the time can leave a very bad taste in your mouth (by costing you the project). The upside is you can minimize risks by following a few simple processes.

When is the last time your project team sat down and talked about risk? We are so focused on specific events and activities on the project that we rarely just talk about risk in general. The bad news is, risk is all around us; it is lurking in every corner and can happen at any time. Yet, for some reason, proactive risk management is often not formally practiced in projects; it is only discussed after a risk event has occurred.

TIP

Risk management is viewed as one of the toughest areas of the PMP exam. This is true for a couple reasons. This first reason is that PMI assumes you and the team are managing risk (it is a given). However, the reality is only a small percentage of projects in the real world actually have a risk management plan. The second reason is lack of experience. We hope we never encounter serious risks so we tend to ignore or avoid them. Therefore, there are not a lot of experts in this field. Paying close attention to the material in this chapter will help you manage risk more effectively and score higher on the PMP exam.

When you get up in the morning and start down the stairs for that first cup of coffee, you probably aren't thinking about whether the kids forget to put away their toys or whether the dog is fast asleep on the top step as you stumble and fall. Threats are everywhere. The really good news is, our brains and senses are constantly scanning (like radar) and will pick up potential danger without us even realizing we are doing it. A large number of accidents are avoided due to this internal radar and our quick reactions during times of danger.

The same is true on projects. A good project manager is constantly on the lookout for risk events, probability, impact, timing, gaps, or potential threats (or opportunities) in managing risk.

Risk Factors

To be better risk managers, we need to better understand risk factors. Here are the primary factors to risk that always need to be considered on your project:

- The risk event itself (R)
- The probability (P) of occurrence
- The range of possible outcomes (impact [I] or amount at stake)

Other key considerations are *timing* and anticipated *frequency* of occurrence. Timing is an important consideration because the probability and impact change dramatically, depending on time of year (for example, weather is a bigger risk for outdoor events such as picnics and weddings).

Threats, Opportunities, and Triggers

It is important to know that PMI views risk as not just a *threat* (negative event) but as an *opportunity* (positive event). With proper planning, risk can be managed effectively with substantially reduced impact to the project. This means we have to think and talk about risk. We must plan for it, train for it, and be proactive about managing risk.

Most people have a pretty good idea about threats. A threat is a risk that has a negative impact on the project if it occurs. But how can a risk be an opportunity? Opportunities are risks that have a positive impact on the project should they occur. Here's a list of opportunities that can arise from risk:

- A supplier is out of stock for the building materials you ordered and they upgrade the order to a higher quality product.

- A team member retires and his replacement has more experience at less cost.

- A meeting is postponed and moved to a new location at a local branch office instead of at an expensive hotel.

- An ice hockey event is cancelled because the team doesn't make the playoffs and a professional rodeo agent calls to schedule the events center for the same dates that had been reserved. The rodeo event draws a large crowd in what would have been an empty arena.

NOTE
It is said that up to 90 percent of threats that are identified and analyzed by the project team during the risk management processes can be eliminated.

How can you predict when a risk is about to happen? The best way is to look for risk triggers. A trigger is a symptom or an early warning sign that indicates a risk has a high probability of occurring. A trigger can simply be noise around the water cooler (that is, people talking and then stopping when the project manager or customer walks by) which may be a sign that there are staffing or other problems. Other triggers include market trends, foreclosures on housing having a ripple effect on the banking industry, or a series of budget cuts or resource actions (RAs) that might signal a company is thinking about a merger or reorganization. Any of these triggers should raise suspicions about the budget, staffing, or support on a project.

In 1984, I was assigned to participate on the project team to set up and maintain a number of computer systems to score the Olympic Summer Games at 26 venues in the greater Los Angeles area. One of the first things we did was to sit down as a team (remember, risk is a team sport) and start identifying risks, such as traffic jams, communications and power blackouts, equipment failure, weather, and so on. The list was long, but we went through the risk management processes to make sure we had a plan for if (or when) the risk events occurred.

The project team felt that we did a pretty good job of identifying the risks, who would own the response strategy, the action items, and how we were going to ensure backup plans so the Olympic scoring could go on. But we missed acting on a simple trigger—a damp musty smell in a storage room (see the following "Try This").

Try This ## Don't Rain on My Project

You are a project manager working at the Olympics. You come in one morning after a long steady rain the night before to find that the storage building where your computers, tools, and other equipment are stored is soaked. The roof leaked and water is all over everything. What do you do?

A Look at your project risk plan to see who was assigned to this risk event and then work with the risk owner to respond to the risk based on their documented response plan.

B Look for someone to blame.

C Gather the team to discuss a recovery plan.

D Order new equipment, fast.

Answer: A. If you have planned properly, the risk event will have been identified, the owner assigned, and a response strategy will have been documented and approved.

Watching for triggers (such as the damp musty smell in the storage room) and having a good mitigation plan would have helped reduce the risk probability or negative impact to the project. A good proactive mitigation plan would be to cover the equipment in the storage room with plastic in the event of rain or other potential contamination.

The project team in 1984 missed the trigger and didn't identify or mitigate this risk event. The team used hair dryers to blow dry the equipment in the storage room. We learned our lesson.

Be Proactive (Plan for Risk and Mitigate Wherever Possible)

Talk about being proactive. Let's look at a risk event that could have cost 155 lives. It is hard to believe a few birds could take down a 170,000 pound airplane, but they did. I am sure you remember the 2009 incident dubbed the "Miracle on the Hudson." Liana Stanley,

Ask the Expert

Q: I am the PM on a project to mitigate the risk of bird strikes to airplanes at my local airport. What do I do first?

A: You start by doing your homework by first identifying the problem. You would find that bird strikes occur mostly around airports. Since 1990, about 82,000 wildlife strikes have been reported to the Federal Aviation Administration, and the number of strikes is growing steadily each year. In 1997, the number of reported strikes was 3,458, and in 2007 that number had risen to 7,666. You also find that reports estimate that only 20 percent of all wildlife strikes are reported to the FAA.[2] Therefore, the problem is bigger than the reports show.

Next, as a short-term solution, you recommend the airport use an integrated approach, with habitat modification such as maintaining a consistent low grass height as well as using noisemakers and other scare devices. Additionally, you would want to verify pilots have a minimum number of hours spent in a simulator to practice how to deal with bird strike situations. Lastly, you might want to get a team of engineers together to determine ways to design deflectors of sorts to minimize the probability and impact to the airplane. Risk management is the key.

in the *New American* article "Heroics Behind the 'Miracle on the Hudson'" describes it as follows:

> "When US Airways Flight 1549 was forced to make a splash landing in the Hudson River on Thursday, January 15, cool heads [Captain Chesley Sullenberger III] prevailed and what could have been an immense tragedy turned into 10 minutes of teamwork that has awed the nation."[1]

Risk Averse or Risk Prone (Which Are You?)

The sample project about mitigating bird strikes at an airport is a project that needs a project manager who is "risk averse." You want a perfectionist when it comes to people's lives. A person who is risk averse is someone who doesn't want to take risks.

On the other side of the coin are the people/companies that are willing to take risks. Thrill seekers who perform extreme sports (skydivers, race car drivers, and so on) or project managers that don't take the time to plan for risk are risk prone.

Even though airline pilots train for emergency situations in simulators, when you lose both engines in a real airplane just minutes after takeoff, the odds are against you. On Flight 1549, the pilot's training and experience really paid off. That is risk response at its finest.

Risk Tolerances and Thresholds

Risk tolerances are the areas of risk that are either acceptable or unacceptable. For example, a risk in health or safety for a company in the food-processing or drug-manufacturing business is totally unacceptable. There are some risks we are not willing to tolerate.

Risk thresholds, on the other hand, refer to the degree of risk a person or company is or is not willing to accept. In some cases, a company's secret to success is tied to its willingness to take risks. This is especially true in the technology sector, where the name of the game is to push the envelope on new product development to be the first to market whenever possible to gain market share. In this case, risk threshold must be high to ever expect higher success and innovation. In the article "On The Edge: Setting the Thresholds," Carl Pritchard states the following:

> "In establishing project plans (and more specifically, risk plans), project managers need to recognize the importance of elements that go beyond basic risk identification and assessment. One critical issue we often miss out on is the notion of the risk threshold. How much can we stand? How much of a schedule delay is too much? How much of a cost overrun can the organization tolerate? The formal, pat answer is often 'no overruns are acceptable.' But that's not realistic. Most projects can withstand some small overruns in terms of schedule or cost, or some small shortcomings in terms of requirements. Those represent our thresholds."[3]

Another way to show thresholds for identified risks is to determine their risk scores. You simply multiply probability by impact and then compare the risk score to the approved thresholds.

Approved thresholds for risk should be set depending on the size, type, and criticality of the project. There are many risk tools that assist in determining the risk score based on certain criteria. Often the scores are set in risk priority categories such as high/medium/low, red/yellow/green, or a numerical range from 1–10 or even 1–100 for more complex scoring. No matter what scoring system you or your company uses, the key is to have clearly defined thresholds and response strategies to align with the score.

Project Risk Management Processes

Project Risk Management includes six processes, according to PMI, and includes conducting risk planning, identification, analysis (qualitative and quantitative), response strategy, and monitoring and controlling the project risks.

The majority of the processes (five of six) are in the Planning process group, as you would imagine. (The Monitor and Control Risks process is in the Monitoring and Controlling process group.) Be careful to not let this preponderance of emphasis during the planning phase dull you to the critical importance of managing risks throughout the life of your project. You should plan to have at least weekly meetings to review your risk log. Otherwise, you will suffer a common fate: out of sight, out of mind equals missed risks and a higher probability of project failure!

- **11.1: Plan risk management**   Define how the team will conduct risk management.

- **11.2: Identify risks**   Determine which risks could occur and may affect the project.

- **11.3: Perform qualitative risk analysis**   Analyze the risks identified and prioritize them to see which risks need further review or action based on probability and impact.

- **11.4: Perform quantitative risk analysis**   Analyze the risks in numerical terms to see which ones potentially have the highest impact on project objectives.

- **11.5: Plan risk responses**   Look at options and actions to reduce threats and increase opportunities when the risk event occurs.

- **11.6: Monitor and control risks**   Make sure you have a risk strategy plan in place that can be effectively measured and tracked to ensure there are no surprises (always be looking for new risks or the ripple effects from existing risks should/when they occur).

These processes are interactive with other processes in other knowledge areas. Risk management crosses all boundaries and can affect scope, schedule, cost, quality, and so on.

TIP

By now I am sure you get the importance of risk management, and with something this important you can expect many questions on the PMP exam. The best way to lock in on the processes is to memorize the order and how they tie to the process groups. You should remember the inputs, tools and techniques, and outputs to the processes, the risk factors, and response strategies as well (all covered later in this chapter).

1. Plan Risk Management Process

The first process in the Project Risk Management knowledge area is risk management planning. The Plan Risk Management process involves deciding how to approach, define, plan, and execute the risk management activities for the project. As with many other processes, this one is definitely a team sport. With this process, the more stakeholders you have involved, and the earlier in the life cycle the better. Key players such as the project manager, sponsor, team, customer, and subject matter experts should take part in the planning process.

The amount of time spent and the number of resources involved in this process will vary based on a number of variables, such as the priority of the project, the overall size and complexity of the project, and the potential impact to the company, team, or community.

TIP

You might see a question on an exam someday that goes something like this: "The highest level of risk is encountered during which process group (or which phase of the project)?" Answer is the Initiating group. The earlier you are in the project life cycle, the higher the degree of uncertainty and the higher the risk.

Risk Categories (or Sources of Risk)

There are several categories of risk (sometimes referred to as sources of risk):

- **Internal**   Risks inside the project or organization (staffing/resource availability, other constraints, changes to the project, lack of proper planning, and so on).

- **External**   Risks outside the project team or organization (environmental factors, regulatory agencies, weather, shift in consumer demand, and so on). These risks can be predicted or unpredicted (see Table 11-1).

- **Technical**   Risks due to changes in technology, system upgrades, configuration, infrastructure, and support.

- **Unforeseeable**   Even though most risks can be identified, there is always a small percent (approximately 10–15 percent) of risks that cannot be predicted.

External Predictable	External Unpredictable
Market risks	Government or regulatory compliance
Operational risks	Unusual natural disasters
Environment impacts	Vandalism and sabotage
Inflation or currency exchange rates	Political unrest and labor strikes
Taxes	Supplier availability (bankruptcy, mergers, and so on)

Table 11-1   External Risk Examples

Another way to help identify or categorize risk is by source. Looking at risk from its source (from the customer, supplier dependencies, poor working conditions) might help you align the risk specifically with the potential impact to your project (cost, schedule, scope). A risk may also cross categories; for example, a lack of skilled resources can affect cost, quality, and schedule. The bad news about risk is the ripple effect an event can have both inside and outside the project. The ripple effect can be felt both upstream and downstream from the project and can impact the team, customer satisfaction, milestones, delivery dates, and so on.

During the planning process, you must understand that risks are either *known* or *unknown*. Risks that are known are those you can identify from previous projects or from common sense. Bird strikes, for example, are a known risk for the airlines. They do happen, and frequently. Therefore, airlines plan for this risk and train how to recover when it occurs.

In the United States, the "Great Flood of 1993" caused a number of levies to fail in Louisiana. This was a known risk. Agencies had performed Monte Carlo computer simulations (explained in more detail later in this chapter) and hundreds of "what-if" scenarios, but the planners determined that it would take a "perfect storm" (multiple events with high intensity) for such an event to happen. Well, it happened. The following is from "The Great USA Flood of 1993" by Lee W. Larson:

> "The magnitude and severity of this flood event was simply over-whelming, and it ranks as one of the greatest natural disasters ever to hit the United States. Approximately 600 river forecast points in the Midwestern United States were above flood stage at the same time. Nearly 150 major rivers and tributaries were affected. [...]

> "Tens of thousands of people were evacuated, some never to return to their homes. At least 10,000 homes were totally destroyed."[4]

There will always be risks that catch us by surprise. They are considered to be *unknown* risks and are usually events that haven't happened before or were not even considered during the planning process. Because risk happens, we should plan for both the known and unknown risks. This involves going into the planning process (brain storming session) open-minded and think of things that can go wrong, both inside and outside the box.

Unknown risks cannot be managed proactively, which means the project team should create a contingency plan—an estimated budget amount (often referred to as "management reserves") that is usually held outside the project budget at the management or government level. An example is the Federal Emergency Management Agency (FEMA) emergency funds.

Plan Risk Management Data Flow

When planning for risk and how to manage it on your project, it is best to start with a documented risk management plan. The plan should include the interaction and dependencies across the various knowledge areas, people, departments, and organizations to ensure a clear picture of how you plan to identify, analyze, and manage risk on your project.

To get a better look at the way data should flow and the various inputs into the Plan Risk Management process, see Figure 11-1 (note that the box numbers tie to the *PMBOK*).

Plan Risk Management Inputs, Tools and Techniques, and Outputs

You have a large number of inputs to consider during the Plan Risk Management process, but only one tool and technique and a single output. You may recall that inputs to a process are usually the outputs from the previous process, so a common thread exists between processes. This should help you when it comes time to study for the exam.

Inputs As important as inputs are for any process to be successful, inputs to risk management are essential. Note that in the case of risk management, there are inputs to the overall process as well as to each internal process. For example, historical information and

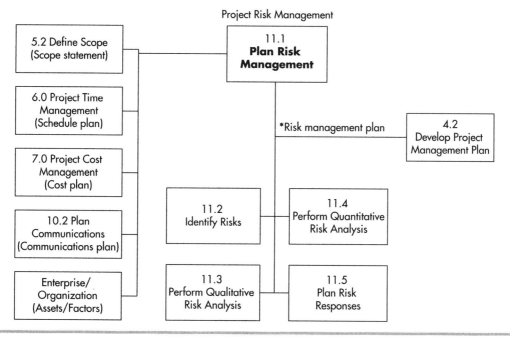

Figure 11-1 Plan Risk Management data flow (*output is the risk management plan)

lessons learned from previous projects are needed inputs to the overall risk management process. They should be reviewed prior to beginning the specific project planning process.

Remember that inputs should answer the following question: "What information, data, and resources do I need before I can begin this project (or process)?" All current and previous plans for the project should be considered when planning for risk management. Here's the list of inputs for this process:

- Scope statement
- Cost management plan
- Schedule management plan
- Communications plan
- Enterprise environmental factors, including attitude toward risk, tolerances, and the degree of risk (thresholds) the team or organization can accept
- Organization process assets (risk categories specific to the project, common definitions, templates, standards, concepts, and terms (potential penalties) of the contract)

Tools and Techniques   The only tool and technique for this process is planning meetings and analysis. This includes determining the frequency and format of meetings and when they should occur. The team comes together to share ideas about what could go wrong on the project, the probability of risk happening, and the potential impact if or when the risk occurs (analysis).

Outputs   As you should recall outputs are the deliverables (finished products or results) of the process. Outputs in all cases should answer the question, "What should we have when the process is complete?" The only output for this process is the risk management plan itself, which includes a number of components. Here are just a few:

- **Methodology**   Defines the approach your team plans to take in managing risk, including risk scoring, tracking tools, and other data sources used in performing risk management on your project.
- **Roles and responsibilities**   Defines who the key team members are for risk identification and analysis as well as risk owners for each identified risk in the plan.
- **Budget**   The approved cost management plan and baseline, risk contingency reserves, and so on.
- **Timing**   Describes when and how often risk review meetings and such should occur.

- **Risk categories**   This can be a simple or detailed list of risks by category that you and your team select to document and track risks. A great way to do this is by using a Risk Breakdown Structure (RBS) to show risks by category or source. A sample RBS is shown in Figure 11-2.

- **Risk analysis**   This can be by category and high-level at first or it can be detailed by work package; in either case it's designed to show the risk, probability, and impact. A matrix usually works best, and you can use a numbering system (1–10) or rating system (high, medium, low) to show the level of risk in a particular area in the matrix. (A sample matrix is shown later in this chapter in Table 11-2.)

- **Revised stakeholder tolerances**   As you work through this process, you learn more about the stakeholder tolerances, so you may need to revise the plan accordingly.

- **Reporting formats**   How the outcomes of the process will be captured and documented for use in the analysis and ultimately communication of the risk management plan.

- **Tracking**   How the risk activities will be tracked and recorded. This also shows how the results will be used for future projects (lessons learned, record-retention media, location, duration to store data, and how data is retrieved).

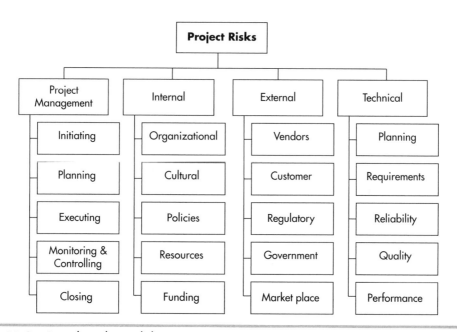

Figure 11-2   Sample Risk Breakdown Structure Categories

Some great templates are available to assist you in creating your risk management plan. See Figure 11-4 at the end of this chapter for a sample template from CVR/IT Consulting LLC.

2. Identify Risks Process

In this process the work of the team (all stakeholders) comes together; they should plan to put their heads together and brainstorm about what can go wrong and which risks may affect the project. This session (not a meeting) should be planned well, facilitated if possible by someone who can help capture the many potential risks that are identified. You should allow an adequate amount of time; sometimes these sessions go for hours. Also, as mentioned before, this process should begin early (at the onset of the project life cycle) and should be monitored throughout the entire project.

The reason I say the risk identification process session should be facilitated is because ground rules must be clear (no such thing as a bad idea or input, everyone has a voice, and so on). The intent is to think outside the box to collect *all* possible risks but to not evaluate any of them at this point. This process should be iterative, meaning there should be synergy where one idea leads to another. Don't worry about the prioritization or overall chance or impact of the risks; this will all come out during the analysis process. Analysis (both qualitative and quantitative) will separate out those risks that are high priority, medium priority, and low priority (based on probability and impact). Therefore, you should collect a long list to begin with and narrow it down from there.

TIP

If you see a question on the PMP exam that asks who should be involved in the Identify Risks process, the answer should be all stakeholders, including the customer, sponsor, project team, and so on.

How Do We Identify Risk?

The operative word is "we" in this question. And the answer is to use whatever tools and techniques you and the team can come up with that help to identify risks on your project.

The best way I have found to identify risk is through the facilitated brainstorming session mentioned previously, but I especially like the interview process as well. There are times when people are not open and candid in a workgroup session; therefore, one-on-one interviews tend to work really well in this situation. If possible, conduct the interview in a quiet, uninterrupted location and take time to put the person at ease. When people feel comfortable and in a "no-penalty" environment, they are more likely to open up with existing issues, concerns, and problems that you need to be aware of during the risk identification process. I have found that a quiet lunch or off-site meeting at a neutral location will help the person feel more at ease and willing to share any perceived and potential risks.

Another way to identify risk is to do your homework by reviewing all project-related documentation. The first thing you should do when assigned to a new or existing project is to review all the documentation available (including the documentation for similar previous projects). Keep in mind that PMI is big on lessons learned (and so am I).

Types of Risks

According to PMI, risks fall into one of two primary classifications:

- **Business risks**   These are usually risks that result in a gain or loss to the business.

- **Pure (insurable) risks**   These risks only apply to a loss (theft, fire, personal injury, and so on).

There are times when risks have a ripple effect; they ricochet around and have a residual impact on the project. The project team should be aware of these types of risks and plan accordingly. Here are some examples:

- **Residual risks**   Risks that remain even after the original risk has been responded to (for example, water damage that causes mildew or rust).

- **Secondary risks**   Risks that have side effects or cause other risks to occur (for example, the risk of electrical shock due to a leaky roof).

- **Risk interaction**   Risks that don't play well together. For example, the interaction of two chemicals to clean a storage tank can cause toxic fumes, even resulting in death. Now there is a risk event you don't want to have to deal with.

Identify Risks Inputs, Tools and Techniques, and Outputs

Like the previous risk management process, this one has many inputs (11 according to PMI). Also, there are many (PMI shows seven) tools and techniques that can be used to help you and the project team identify risk, but still just a single output (in this case, the risk register).

To get a better idea of all the areas that may cause risk on a project, look back at the risk management data flow diagram shown in Figure 11-1.

Inputs   Remember, when it comes to risk identification, you should look all around for anything that may jump up and impact (hurt or help) the project. Here's a sample list of inputs that should be considered, at a minimum:

- **Risk management plan**   This includes all the key areas of the plan, such as scope, schedule, communications plans, and so on.

- **Activity cost estimates**   Remember, cost is one of the key components of the project constraints and is often a major risk on projects (for example, budget cuts, overspending, and rising cost of materials).

- **Activity duration estimating**   This is another big risk on a project. Things seem to take longer than expected. For example, the Sydney Opera House ran nine years over the approved schedule.

- **Scope baseline**   The assumptions found in the scope statement that are approved as the baseline (including the WBS) are great sources of input to help identify risk.

TIP

The best time to start the risk identification process is during the creation of the WBS (see Chapter 5). By doing these activities together, you may be able to combine two processes into one at the very start of the project.

- **Stakeholder register**   Information about the stakeholders, their risk tolerances and thresholds, their expectations, their level of support, and even their attitude toward the project can help you identify stakeholder risks.

- **Cost management plan**   Understanding the overall budget and level of priority the project has at the upper management level will help you identify risks in this area. Look for indicators such as delays in order processing and delayed accounts payable, which can mean no management approval or financial issues may exist in the company or department.

- **Schedule management plan**   Another great place to look for potential risks. Remember that the schedule is a key component of the project constraints and is often the highest source of conflict on the project.

- **Quality management plan**   Quality requirements pose threats. Therefore, this is a great place to look for potential risks on your project.

Tools and Techniques   Here are a few of the tools and techniques used or places to look in the Identify Risks process:

- **Checklist analysis**   Using historical information, the checklist provides a simple way to capture the risks for review and analysis to make sure the risks are identified.

- **Assumptions analysis**   The assumptions should be documented and reviewed to see if they are valid. They are used for the purpose of identifying future risks.

- **Diagramming techniques**   Various diagrams can be used for risk identification: cause and effect diagrams (also known as Ishikawa or fishbone diagrams), system or process flow charts (show interrelationships), influence diagrams (graphical representations of situations or time-ordered events on the project), and mind mapping.[5]

- **Expert judgment**   Direct and effective use of subject matter experts is one of the more effective ways to identify risks.

- **Information gathering**   You have a multitude of ways to gather information about your project. Some of these have already been discussed, but for clarification I list a few of them here:

  - **Brainstorming**   One idea prompts another (synergy).

  - **Interviewing**   Also may be called "expert interviewing" on the exam.

  - **Delphi technique**   This technique provides a way to reach a consensus of experts. Experts participate anonymously through the use of a questionnaire or survey. A facilitator conducts an iterative process to narrow the field of possibilities until a consensus is drawn based on the results from the participating experts.

TIP

You should remember the Delphi technique if you are planning to take the PMP exam.

- **Root cause analysis (RCA)**   The use of tools to drill down to the core of the problem.

- **Strengths, weaknesses, opportunities, and threats (SWOT) analysis**   Looks at the overall project to determine where the strengths and the possible weaknesses may exist as well as the opportunities and threats.

NOTE

SWOT analysis examines the project itself as well as the project management processes, various plans, resources, and organizational structure to help identify future risks.

Ask the Expert

Q: What are the advantages of creating a risk register?

A: The advantages provided by creating a risk register start with the ability to organize the identified risks in a fashion that will assist in the analysis of those risks. The risk register should document the identified risks, the category (scope, quality, schedule, staffing, and so on), risk triggers (if known), and response strategies as well as the assigned owner, who will monitor and respond to the risk. The risk register is also a great way to demonstrate your project management control to stakeholders.

Outputs   The only output to the Identify Risks process is the risk register, which is a list of the identified risks and specific information about the risks. It is usually created in list or table format and contains the following information:

- **List of identified risks**   The risks should be described in as much detail as needed and should include the event, probability, impact, expected cause, and priority (to be determined during the analysis processes).

- **List of potential responses**   The responses should be determined by the assigned owner of the risk event and responses should be focused on the high-priority risks found during the risk identification and analysis processes.

3. Perform Qualitative Risk Analysis Process

Performing qualitative risk analysis involves assessing the probability and impact of the identified risks. Remember to always use the work performed in previous processes to help develop each downstream process. (PMI calls this "progressive elaboration." Remember this term.)

TIP

Remember that qualitative analysis is subjective analysis, which depends on judgment to determine or qualify the probability and impact to your project. You should also know that PMI (as does the real world) refers to the terms "probability" and "impact" in a number of different ways (refer to Table 11-3, later in this chapter).

The Perform Qualitative Risk Analysis process involves an understanding of the stakeholder tolerances and thresholds discussed earlier. As with all risk management processes, this analysis should be performed early and often throughout the project life cycle.

Probability and impact can be determined in many different ways:

- Expert judgment (using people who are subject matter experts and are experienced with the risk)
- Cost and time estimates as well as tools such as Monte Carlo analysis (computer simulation)
- Use of previous similar project risks (historical information or lessons learned)
- Delphi technique (mentioned earlier in the discussion of the Identify Risks process)

Probability and Impact Matrix

To determine the probability and impact to the project of the various risks, it is helpful to use a matrix (see Table 11-2). The matrix provides a good way to rate, sort, and rank (in order of priority) the risks that have been identified. The goal is to determine which risks will have the biggest impact on the project and should have an owner assigned and response strategy created. Table 11-2 is an example of a risk probability and impact matrix.

Be aware that risk probability and impact can be referred to using different terms (see Table 11-3) and you are likely to see these terms on the PMI exam.

Risk	Probability	Impact	Priority	Owner
Staff availability	High	High	1	PM
Scheduling issues	High	High	2	PM and team
Obtain budget	Med	High	3	Financial analyst
Procure equipment	Med	Med	4	Asset manager
Create training materials	Low	Low	5	Course developer

Table 11-2   Risk Probability and Impact Matrix

Probability	Impact
Likelihood	Consequence
Chance	Effort
Possibility	Outcome
Odds	Results

Table 11-3   Other Terms Used for Probability and Impact

Perform Qualitative Risk Analysis Inputs, Tools and Techniques, and Outputs

The inputs, tools and techniques, and outputs for this process are listed next.

Inputs Here's a list of some of the inputs that should be considered when performing qualitative risk analysis:

- **Risk register** Output from the previous process

- **Risk management plan** Including other project plans

- **Project scope statement** From the risk perspective (for example, new technology)

- **Organizational process assets** Standard templates, common terms, and so on

Tools and Techniques Here are a few of the tools and techniques used in this process:

- **Risk probability and impact assessment matrix** Discussed earlier in the "Probability and Impact Matrix" section.

- **Risk data quality assessment** Data needs to be accurate and unbiased for best results.

- **Risk categorization** Categorized by source of risk (use the RBS) or other categories.

- **Risk urgency assessment** Near-term response strategy for higher impact risks.

Outputs The only output of this process is updates to the risk register, based on any new information acquired. The risk register can also include causes of risk, near-term risk response activities, trend information that may be an indicator or trigger for potential risks, and any "watch lists" of lower priority risks.

4. Perform Quantitative Risk Analysis Process

The Perform Quantitative Risk Analysis process is the numerical view of the effect of the (prioritized) risk events. You assign a numerical rating to only the highest impact risks (sometimes referred to as the "amount-at-stake risks").

The purpose of a numerical rating is to determine which risks warrant a response. The list of risks should get shorter and shorter after each wave of analysis. Clearly, you don't have enough time or money to respond to all the risks identified. The qualitative and quantitative analysis helps narrow the field to a manageable number based on priority.

This process presents a quantitative (less subjective) approach to making decisions in the presence of uncertainty.

Quantitative Risk Analysis

Depending on the nature or lack of complexity of the project, you may not focus on this process as a separate activity. It may be consolidated with the qualitative analysis (or at least during the first wave of the process).

Quantitative analysis includes the following:

- Additional investigation of risks that are rated high for probability and/or impact

- Further definition of the type, source, or category of risk

- Determining the type of quantitative analysis to be used—the type of probability distribution (normal, triangular, beta, and so on), statistical data, how the data is collected, how the data is tested, and so on.

- Sensitivity analysis—determining which risks have the biggest impact (amount at stake)

- Expected monetary value (EMV) or the results of Monte Carlo simulations (or other computer simulations) to determine the possible cost/impact to the project.

Expected Monetary Value (EMV)

One of the big questions that always comes up when attempting to manage risk is, "What's it going to cost?" One estimate that can be used to determine this is *expected monetary value* (EMV). The formula is simple: EMV = P * I (probability times impact). EMV should be estimated for each work package on the WBS (see Table 11-4 for an example).

Work Package	Probability	Impact	Expected Monetary Value (EMV)
A (Zamboni failure)	20%	$10,000	$2,000
B (inaccurate painting of the sub-floor for ice hockey)	30%	$28,000	$8,400
C (failure of the cooling system to freeze the ice)	50%	$12,000	$6,000

Table 11-4   EMV Calculations

Monte Carlo Analysis

Monte Carlo analysis is a computer simulation used to determine possible outcomes by using random numbers. Many insurance and financial institutions use this software to run actuarial tables and "what-if" scenarios for the cost of premiums, retirement, and investment forecasts.

The Boeing 777 was tested extensively using Monte Carlo simulation software for everything from wing strength to flight capability after a bird strike to the engines.

For information only (as these steps are built into the software application), here are the basic steps involved in the Monte Carlo simulator:

1. Assess the range for the variables and determine the probability distribution.

2. Select a random value for each variable.

3. Run a deterministic analysis.

4. Repeat steps 2 and 3 many times to obtain probability distribution.

TIP

You should know the following regarding Monte Carlo analysis for the PMI exam:

- Computer-based software used to quantify the overall risk to the project
- Evaluates the overall risk for the project shown in a probability distribution
- Can provide probability estimates for the project to complete on time or on budget
- Provides the probability of any activity being on the critical path
- Takes into account path convergence
- Translates uncertainties into impact probability on the total project

Perform Quantitative Risk Analysis Inputs, Tools and Techniques, and Outputs

The inputs, tools and techniques, and outputs for the Perform Quantitative Risk Analysis process are as follows.

Inputs   Here's a list of some of the inputs that should be considered when performing quantitative risk analysis:

- Risk register
- Risk management plan
- Cost management plan
- Schedule management plan
- Organizational process asset (risk databases, studies on similar risks, and so on)

Tools and Techniques Here are a few of the tools and techniques used in this process:

- **Data gathering and representative techniques** Interviewing, data mining, probability distributions, and so on

- **Quantitative risk analysis and modeling techniques** Sensitivity analysis, EMV, Monte Carlo analysis, and so on

- **Expert judgment** The use of subject matter experts who specialize in quantitative analysis

Outputs The only output to the Perform Quantitative Risk Analysis process is the updates to the risk register (same as Perform Qualitative Risk Analysis process) based on any new information acquired. The updates to the risk register in this process might include statistical trends, updates to the prioritization list, and probabilistic analysis supported with facts and figures (for example, the schedule contingency shows the project is in the 78th percentile and is expected to complete on time).

Decision Tree Analysis

Decision trees are primarily used to assist the PM and team in making informed decisions about the risks and the alternatives being considered on the project (see example in Figure 11-3). Airline B has a lower fare but rates lower in on-time arrival.

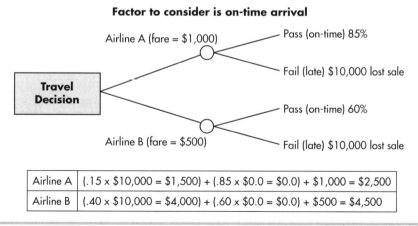

Figure 11-3 Decision tree diagram

A decision tree typically has the following attributes:

- A model of a real situation
- Takes into account future events to help you make a decision today
- Can be used to help calculate the expected monetary value (probability times impact)
- Involves mutual exclusivity (where two events are exclusive)

5. Plan Risk Responses Process

Planning risk responses involves developing options and actions to reduce the impact and probability of threats and to enhance opportunities. This process answers (or should answer) the following questions:

- What are we going to do if/when a particular risk event occurs?
- What can we do to decrease the probability and/or impact of the event occurring?
- What can we do to increase the opportunity should the event occur?

This process is also where the risk owner (the person assigned the risk) will document a response strategy and action for the risk event should it occur.

Risk Response Strategies

Sometimes called "risk mitigation strategies." Regardless of the name, the goal is clear: Keep things from breaking and fix them quickly so they don't break again in the future. If something breaks, the question becomes "How can we make it better?"

Risk response strategies are different for threats and opportunities (see Table 11-5).

Response Strategies for Threats	Response Strategies for Opportunities
Avoidance (do what you can to eliminate the threat)	Exploit (reverse of avoidance—take advantage of the risk should it occur)
Mitigation (reduce probability or impact)	Enhance (increase likelihood)
Transfer (deflect or allocate; for example, by purchasing insurance)	Share the risk (reverse of mitigation by writing joint responsibility in the contract or agreement)
Accept the risk (do nothing)	Accept the risk (do nothing)

Table 11-5 Risk Response Strategies

NOTE

Transferring risk doesn't mean transferring all the ownership and accountability. For example, outsourcing work to a vendor or third-party supplier doesn't let you off the hook for schedule delays or poor workmanship. You are still responsible for the quality of the work. Also, remember that accepting risk may be appropriate for either threats or opportunities.

Risk response strategies vary from case to case and should be adapted to the project situation to the best of your ability. Say, for example, you have two team members who are not showing up on time to meetings and are not meeting your expectations for performance on the project. In one case (Joan), it appears her performance is affected by a lack of experience and training. In the other case (Joey), it appears he is not interested in working on the project. The response strategy you choose will likely be different for each. You may decide to release Joey from the project and provide additional training and mentoring for Joan. For more examples of risk response strategies, see Table 11-6.

Plan Risk Responses Inputs, Tools and Techniques, and Outputs

The inputs, tools and techniques, and outputs for the Plan Risk Responses process are as follows.

Inputs   Here's a summary of the inputs that should be considered for this process:

- Risk register (output from previous process)
- Risk management plan (including other project plans)

Description of Risk Event	Response Strategy
Remove a poor performer from the project team	Avoid
Train a team member to improve their performance	Mitigate
Seek additional funding to cover increased cost of materials	Accept
Adjust the schedule to allow the use of more experienced person	Exploit
Hire a vendor/subcontractor to perform some of the work	Transfer
Order equipment early to take advantage of better pricing	Enhance
Work with the customer to ensure requirements are clear and dependencies are met	Share

Table 11-6   Sample Risk Response Strategies

Tools and Techniques   Here are a few of the tools and techniques used in this process:

- Strategy for dealing with negative risks and threats.
- Strategy for dealing with positive risks and opportunities.
- Contingent response strategies (designed for certain events that will be initiated only if a specific event occurs). For example, the loss of a highly skilled expert may require a unique response to obtain a specific-skilled resource replacement.

Outputs   The output shown below is unique for this process. The other three outputs (risk register updates, PM plan updates, and project document updates) are similar to outputs from other processes, so I will only discuss the risk-related contract decisions output here.

- **Risk-related contract decisions**   The information collected from inputs, and tools and techniques for the Plan Risk Responses process will influence the type of contract selected, the extent of shared risk, amount of insurance needed, or other key decisions.

NOTE

The output from this process (contract decisions made) becomes the input to the Plan Procurements (Section 12.1) process and potentially other processes as well.

Regardless of whether you are responding to threats or opportunities, there are some guidelines that should always be followed:

- Reponses should be timely and well communicated.
- Responses must be appropriate to the significance of the risk.
- Responses should be cost effective (if possible).
- Responses must be realistic in nature.
- Response can address multiple risks with a single root cause.
- Responses should involve the team and other stakeholders

6. Monitor and Control Risks Process

After the risks have been identified and analyzed, the owners assigned, and the response strategies documented and communicated, it's time to monitor and control the risks. This is an on-going process and needs to be reviewed and updated frequently. I recommend a weekly review, but what you choose depends on your project's length, complexity, and condition (troubled, stable, critical, and so on).

The Monitor and Control Risks process involves implementing the approved risk response plan, tracking those risks that have been deemed high priority, watching out for all risks (even lower probability threats in some cases), monitoring residual and secondary risks (ripple effect), and watching for new risks that may surface. To effectively control risks, you must be diligent in monitoring all risks, even though the majority of the focus is on those risks identified as most likely to occur or with high impact to the project.

Several tools and techniques are available for monitoring and controlling risks, such as trend analysis to look into the future for changes in risk probability and impact. Here are some of the questions that need to be asked, answered, and reviewed often:

- Are the assumptions for a particular risk event still valid?

- Has anything changed on the project, such as scope, schedule, cost, staffing, expectations, type of materials, and requirements?

- Are the risk policies and procedures documented and up to date?

- Is the risk management plan being followed and reviewed regularly?

- Are contingency reserves still appropriate and sufficient if needed?

NOTE
The Monitor and Control Risks process requires all team members to keep a close eye on their area of the project. It is important to use good management skills to weigh the situation and make decisions about all risk events in a timely manner. The alternatives and options (risk response strategies) have to be clear and must be implemented as needed to meet the challenge of risk management on your project.

Risk Assessment (Reassessment) and Audits

There is a saying that has floated around in the world of project management that goes like this: It is not a matter of *if* your project will be audited, but *when*. This means that at some time in your PM career, you *will* be audited. Risk audits are specifically directed toward how you and the team are managing (or managed) risk. The auditors will want to see your risk register; they will want to see how you identified and analyzed risks. Did you assign owners to the top risks? Did you collect documented risk response strategies for the top risks from the assigned owners?

Ask the Expert

Q: How does the PM and team ensure they are prepared for an audit?

A: Through risk assessment, reassessment, and audit preparedness. It is important to stay focused on risk by keeping your risk register log up to date and making sure you are effectively tracking and managing project risk (both internal and external to the project as appropriate).

This also requires that you and the team get (and stay) up to date on all regulatory compliance requirements that may apply to your project. The key is to do your homework, research those areas that apply to your project/industry, and find someone to assist in this process. You do not want to fail an audit.

Regulatory Authority and Agencies

Regulatory authority is a government or public authority responsible for exercising autonomous power over some area of human activity in a supervisory or governing capacity. An independent regulatory agency is usually separate from other branches of the government.

Regulatory agencies deal in the administrative law enforcement, regulation or rulemaking (such as code enforcement over building codes), and audit and regulatory compliance supervision. They provide oversight or governance for the benefit of the public at large.

The following is a short list of regulatory agencies that are sometimes involved with auditing projects in their areas of responsibility. For more details go to the Code of Federal Regulations (CFR) website[6] or perform an Internet search on "regulatory agencies."

- The Code of Federal Regulations (CFR) is a compilation of regulations issued by federal departments and includes the following:

    - The Federal Communications Commission (FCC) is the U.S. government agency that regulates and enforces the use of radio transmission frequencies (Title 47 CFR).

    - Title 21 is the Department of Health and Human Services (DHHS) regulations.

    - Title 29 is the Department of Labor regulations.

    - The Canadian Standards Association (CSA) is a private company that drafts standards for use in certifying product safety.

- The Security and Exchange Commission (SEC) oversees stock transactions and protects investors; maintains fair, orderly, and efficient markets; and facilitates capital formation.

- The Office of the Comptroller of the Currency (OCC) provides advice to help prevent borrowers from becoming victims of foreclosure rescue scams.

- The U.S. Food and Drug Administration (FDA) protects and promotes health and safety.

- The Sarbanes-Oxley (SOX) Act of 2002 affects how any accounting firm does business. Auditors and accountants pay close attention to the SOX Act when advising any business, large or small, on financial tracking and reporting.

- The Interstate Commerce Commission facilitates the transportation of products and services from one state to geographic points in other states.

- The Occupational Safety and Health Administration (OSHA) of the United States Department of Labor facilitates workplace safety and health by issuing and enforcing standards to prevent work-related injuries, illnesses, and deaths.

TIP
The code of regulations and list of regulatory agencies is for reference only and will not likely be on the PMI exam.

Reserve Analysis
Part of risk management is analyzing the reserves needed to respond to or mitigate risk. We talked about reserves in cost management (Chapter 7). As a reminder, there are two types of reserves:

- **Contingency reserves**   Used for known (possible) risks. Estimated funds are typically held inside the project budget. The response strategy and estimated cost should be clearly documented, monitored, and controlled.

- **Management reserves**   For unknown (unplanned) risks. Estimated funds are typically held outside the project budget and can normally only be accessed with management approval.

Case Study Example
Matt and Jake are seasoned changeover project managers for the Budweiser Events Center (BEC), and even though the Event Sheet clearly directs the work of the project, there are times when they are forced to make decisions "on the fly" in order to get the job completed in the most efficient way possible.

For example, during the changeover from indoor football to ice hockey, one of the two forklifts breaks down. It is a key piece of equipment involved in removing the indoor football field and pads, removing the insulated flooring, and hauling in heavy loads such as hockey glass, dasher boards, and so on. It is midnight, so getting the forklift repaired in time to complete the changeover is out of the question. Every minute that the crew is standing around waiting on the next step in the changeover process is costing time and money. The complete ice hockey setup must be finished by 6 A.M. to give the technicians enough time to prep the ice for practice that day.

This is one of those times when it is important to have a contingency (fallback) plan with backup options available. In this instance, although the options seem limited, the PMs have planned well; they have established a couple response strategy options to ensure that the project gets completed on time. The options are as follows:

- **Option A**   Line up a rental company that can provide the needed equipment at any time, day or night, and to make sure the estimated cost of the rental is held in the contingency reserve fund.

- **Option B**   Use temporary labor to provide late-night assistance to help complete the changeover in time (again, using contingency reserve funds).

Matt and Jake decided to use Option A to complete the changeover on time. Their risk management, solid project management, and contingency planning saved the day.

Monitor and Control Risks Inputs, Tools and Techniques, and Outputs

The inputs, tools and techniques, and outputs for the Monitor and Control Risks process are as follows.

Inputs   Some of the inputs for the Monitor and Control Risks process are the same as previous processes (risk register and project management plan) and the outputs from the Plan Risk Responses process. The two unique inputs for this process that should be considered are

- **Work performance information**   Deliverable status, schedule progress, and costs
- **Performance reports**   Look for trends, forecasting data accuracy, and so on

Tools and Techniques   The tools and techniques used in this process are unique and are as follows:

- **Risk reassessment**   Involves looking for secondary or new risks.
- **Risk audits**   Review effectiveness of risk responses, action taken, and so on.

- **Variance and trend analysis**   Statistical data that helps answer the questions: Were the expected results achieved? Where do we go from here?

- **Technical performance measurement**   Requires objective quantifiable measurements.

- **Reserve analysis**   Compare the plan to the actual use of reserves and future needs.

- **Status meetings**   Regular status reviews are used to ensure proper focus and action.

Outputs   The outputs to this process are as follows:

- **Risk register updates**   From reassessments, risk audits, and reviews.

- **Organizational process assets updates**   Information from the six risk management processes will produce information that can be used for current and future projects.

- **Change requests**   Change is inevitable. As a result, change requests may need to be initiated to put the project back on track (this includes recommended correction and preventive actions).

- **Project management plan updates**   Progressive elaboration yields new information, new situations, and new risks, which all tend to drive updates to your project plan.

- **Project document updates**   The ripple effect requires updates to various project documents as the project progresses.

Reporting Status—Early and Often

Nothing is more embarrassing than the customer knowing something before you do when it comes to your project. You need to be the air traffic controller, the conductor of your project. You need to be the person reporting the status of a risk event, the expected impact to your project, and the action plans (fallback or back-out plans) you are taking to ensure everything is under control.

TIP

Timely and accurate reporting is essential to risk management. Information is power when it comes to managing a project. Making sure you collect meaningful, accurate, and timely information can mean the difference in whether or not you meet your project objectives on time and on budget. There isn't a project manager alive who hasn't wished they would have known more about a situation sooner than later. Our actions and reactions are totally dependent on timely and accurate reports (verbal or written) so we can make prompt informed decisions.

Updates to Project Documents

For peace of mind and for audit purposes, you need to keep the project plan documents up to date and accurate. I recommend a Wiki (electronic, easy-access team room) or a similar central repository to hold the master project control book (PCB). No matter what tools or techniques you choose, they must be managed effectively; otherwise, they will get outdated and may cause misinformation or confusion, all of which is counterproductive on the project.

Summary of Risk Management

Risk happens, so plan for it! Make sure you have identified and analyzed the risks. You also need to have assigned risk owners and a documented action (response) plan for the top risks. Report status promptly and with conviction. Be diligent in looking for future risks.

Wouldn't it be great if all the risks that occurred on your project were identified, analyzed, assigned, and addressed as planned? When a risk event happens, nothing is more satisfying than being able to report, "The risk was identified in our plan, the owner assigned to the risk has implemented the approved response according to the plan, and everything is under control." The best motto for risk management is, "Be prepared for anything." No one likes surprises on their project.

Remember the definition of risk is "uncertainty," so even if the risk is a known risk, we don't always know if or when it will occur. The following list represents some common pitfalls and errors made in the area of risk management:

- Not conducting a thorough risk identification process with all stakeholders
- Not assigning owners to high-profile risks (and having a backup plan)
- Not documenting the risk response strategy clearly
- Not communicating the probability or impact to the project in a timely manner
- Not having adequate reserves to cover risks when they occur
- Not doing risk assessment early or often enough (and completely)
- Missing categories of risks (such as market impact, cultural risks, and customer risks)
- Conducting risk management with an unclear objective, scope, or target schedule

- Not obtaining project sponsor commitment to the project and the risk plan
- Not involving the team and all stakeholders in the risk management process
- Not monitoring your risk register regularly

When it comes to managing risk on your project, the best approach involves the same three takeaway points mentioned in other chapters:

1. Stay focused on the end results (especially on risk management).

2. Use the tools and resources available on your project to ensure effective risk management, such as the summary level sample shown in Figure 11-4 at the end of this chapter. (For the latest and complete risk management template from Dr Gary Evans at CVR/IT Consulting LLC, go to http://www.cvr-it.com/Samples/XRisk_Management_Plan_Template.pdf.)[7]

3. Work as a team. This is especially true when managing risks.

References

1. Stanley, Liana. "Heroics Behind the 'Miracle on the Hudson'" New American (January 20, 2009), http://www.thenewamerican.com/culture/family/698.

2. DeVault, Travis. "ISU alumnus works to cut down bird strikes," Indiana State University (January 29, 2009), http://www.indstate.edu/news/news.php?newsid=1613.

3. Pritchard, Carl. "On the Edge: Setting the Thresholds," ProjectConnections, http://www.projectconnections.com/articles/063000-pritchard.html.

4. Larson, Lee W. "The Great USA Flood of 1993," http://www.nwrfc.noaa.gov/floods/papers/oh_2/great.htm.

5. Wikipedia, http://en.wikipedia.org/wiki/Mind_map.

6. Tyco Electronics. "Regulatory Agencies and Compliance Requirements," http://www.elotouch.com/Products/agencies.asp.

7. CVR/IT Consulting LLC, http://www.cvr-it.com/Samples/XRisk_Management_Plan_Template.pdf.

Project Name:	
Prepared by:	
Date (MM/DD/YYYY):	

Risk Management Strategy

1. Define the risk management methodology to be used: Section 1 of this table defines your risk management process. The process is scalable to ensure that the level, type, and visibility of risk management on your process.

- **Risk Identification:** Identify risks through discussion with all major stakeholders. Also use the *Risk Assessment* and *Project Planning Assessment Checklist*, and other project-specific risks, as appropriate.

- **Risk Categorization:** Group the risks into categories by using the *Risk Assessment*. The project manager can create additional categories, as required.

- **Risk Probability and Impact Assessment:** Enter all risks into the *Risk Response Plan* document. For each risk identified, assess the risk event in terms of likelihood of occurrence (Risk Probability) and its effect on project objectives if the risk event occurs (Risk Severity = Impact Score).

- **Risk Prioritization:** Risks that meet the threshold criteria will be so noted in the *Risk Register*.

- **Risk Response Planning:** For each risk in the *Risk Register* that is above the Risk Threshold:

  - Determine options and actions to reduce the likelihood or consequences of impact to project objectives.
  - Describe the actions to be taken to mitigate the risk, and actions to be taken when risk event occurs.
  - Assign responsibilities for each agreed-upon response, and "due date" where risk responses are time sensitive.
  - Determine impact on project budget and schedule and make appropriate changes to the project plan.
  - Incorporate this information into the *Risk Register*.

- **Risk Response Tracking:**

  - Dates and the actions taken to mitigate the risk.
  - Actions taken when the risk event occurred (contingency plan).
  - Incorporate this information into the *Risk Register*.

Figure 11-4 Sample Risk Management Plan template

- **Risk Monitoring:** Establish systematic reviews and schedule them, ensuring the following reviews:
  - Ensure that all requirements of the *Risk Management Plan* are being implemented.
  - Assess currently defined risks as defined in the *Risk Register.*
  - Identify status of actions to be taken, and evaluate effectiveness of actions taken.
  - Validate previous risk assessment (likelihood and impact) and assumptions (state new assumptions).
  - Identify new risks, track risk response, establish communications.

- **Risk Control:**
  - Validate mitigation strategies and alternatives, and take corrective action when actual events occur.
  - Assess impact on the project of actions taken (cost, time, resources).
  - Identify new risks resulting from risk mitigation actions.
  - Update the *Project Plan* and *Risk Management Plan.*
  - Ensure change control addresses risks associated with the proposed change.
  - Revise the *Risk Assessment* and other risk management documents to capture results of mitigation actions.
  - Revise the *Risk Register* and establish communications.

2. Define assumptions that have a significant impact on project risk:
• Risk Assumptions:

3. Define the roles and responsibilities unique to the risk management function:	
• Risk Management Team:	• <Team Members>

4. Define risk management milestones (insert rows as needed):

Milestone	Date (MM/DD/YYYY)
• *Risk Management Plan* approved	
• *Risk Assessment* and *Project Planning Assessment Checklist* complete	
• *Risk Management Reviews* scheduled	

5. Define risk rating/scoring techniques: The project will rate each identified risk (e.g., Impact Score = High, Medium, Low) based on the likelihood that the risk event will occur and the effect on the project's objectives if the risk event occurs. This will be a subjective evaluation based on the experience of those assigned to the project's risk management team.

Default rating/scoring system is as follows:

Impact score can be rated as 1, 3, 5, 7, or 9 (1 = Very Low, 9 = Very High).

Probability can be rated as 0.1, 0.3, 0.5, 0.7, or 0.9 (0.1 = Very Low, 0.9 = Very High).

Figure 11-4   Sample Risk Management Plan template (*continued*)

6. Establish risk thresholds: Modify the text below to show how the project team will plan for risk events (for example, "The project will establish risk responses for risk events that have been determined to have a rating of High").

Risk priority is determined by calculating a Risk Score (= Impact * Probability) and then comparing that Risk Score to priority thresholds.

Based on the scoring system, the lowest possible Risk Score is $1 * 0.1 = .01$. The highest possible Risk Score is $9 * 0.9 = 8.1$.

7. Define risk communications: Describe the type and frequency of communications for risk management.

8. Define risk-tracking process: Describe how the risks will be tracked and reported.

Project Risk Management Plan Approval / Signatures

I have reviewed the information contained in this Project Risk Management Plan *and agree:*

Name	Title	Signature	Date

The signatures above indicate an understanding of the purpose and content of this document by those signing it. By signing this document, they agree to this as the formal Project Risk Management Plan *document.*

Figure 11-4 Sample Risk Management Plan template (*continued*). Reprinted with permission from CVR/IT Consulting LLC

Chapter 12

Project Procurement Management

Key Skills & Concepts

- Procurement management process
- Definition of a contract
- Elements of a legally binding contract
- Role of the project manager (buyer or seller)
- Make-or-buy analysis
- Buyer and seller relationship
- Source selection process
- Terms and conditions
- Privity of contract and contract waiver
- Types of contracts and who bears the burden of risk
- Project procurement documents: RFPs, RFQs, and RFBs
- Bidder's conference and vendor selection process
- Statement of work (SOW)
- Contract change control
- Administrative closure
- Force majeure

This chapter covers the difference between contracts and procurements and how they fit together when it comes to managing these important elements of a project.

Most project managers are familiar with contracts, and many project managers are involved with procurement of goods and services, so the information in this chapter may simply serve as a refresher. However, you'll encounter tips and terms along the way that you will need to be familiar with, especially if you are planning to take the PMI exam.

TIP

Knowledge of how to manage contracts as well as key terms and conditions is important to project managers in the real world. However, you should note that PMI tends to focus mostly on procurement management. You'll encounter a few exam questions regarding the types of contracts, who bears the burden of risk between the buyer and seller on the different contracts, and even some calculations. Therefore, you should be familiar with these key aspects of contract management.

Definition of a Contract

A *contract* is a legal, mutually binding document, agreement, or exchange of promises between two or more parties to provide goods or services in exchange for something of value. Contracts usually have terms and conditions and can be used for a wide range of purposes—sale of property, terms of employment, settlement of disputes, ownership protection (when it comes to licensing, intellectual property, or copyright protection), and even tickets to a sporting event. That's right. A ticket to a baseball game, for example, has terms and conditions ("Holder is admitted on the condition of...").

In the entertainment world, a contract may be referred to by various names: technical contract, appearance agreement, booking agreement, and even engagement contract. Whatever you decide to call this piece of paper, it is essential. It provides protection to both the performer and the venue/event center. The goal of the agreement is so that everything is laid out on the table and that both parties remain in total agreement. Once the contract or agreement is signed and dated, it becomes a legal binding document.

Contract Terms and Conditions

Terms and conditions (T&Cs) set the rights and obligations of the contracting parties. These include "general conditions," which are common to all types of contracts, as well as "special conditions," which are peculiar to a specific contract (for example, contract change conditions, payment conditions, price variation clauses, and penalties).

T&Cs also define the business relationship between the buyer and seller, the roles/ responsibilities of each party, and how the activities will be carried out throughout the established period of contract performance.

- **Terms**   Necessary statements that make the contract legally valid (for example, "The total term duration of the project, including all approved deliverables, shall not exceed 12 months").

  Another contract term is for payment. In the entertainment world, for example, a contract term may state the following: "All payments (including performance amount plus 5 percent of ticket sales) will be in cash and to be provided within 30 days following the concert."

Other terms should include what happens if the event is canceled due to low ticket sales, weather, flight delays, and so on. These terms need to be spelled out.

- **Conditions** Defined events that must happen in order for contingent terms in a contract to become fixed (for example, "Late payment penalty of 10 percent of the total invoice will be added to the statement for payments not received by the 10th business day of the month following the date of the invoice").

Conditions should include any specific restrictions or expectations for the performer that the venue or hosting party has set. This can include the performer's expected attire, language, and music selection. This condition varies from place to place. The performer has the right to lay out their own personal restrictions and expectations, such as guest lists, guest passes, dressing rooms, backstage refreshments (for example, blue M&Ms), and other hospitalities. The conditions depend on the individual performer and the venue's willingness/ability to meet the conditions of the contract.

The following list represents some items you might see in the terms and conditions of a contract:

- **Acceptance** Clearly defined project milestones and deliverables as well as what will be measured, reported, and deemed formally acceptable at completion.

- **Agent** Who specifically represents the buyer and seller.

- **Arbitration** A method that describes how disputes, escalations, or issues will be handled as well as how this process will be assigned and billed (and who does it).

- **Assignment** Describes the circumstances where one party or the other can assign their rights and obligations to another party (like to an agent or manager).

- **Authority** Who holds the power in a contract and under what conditions.

- **Bonds** If bonding (performance assurance) is required by one party or the other.

- **Breach/default** Failure of the seller to perform/deliver as promised in the contract.

- **Contract change process** Defines the process, who will serve on the CCB (change control board), and the tool used to track and manage changes.

- **Incentives (if appropriate)** To reward achievement of objectives on the contract.

- **Indemnification (liability)** Who is liable under what conditions and how this is handled.

- **Personnel**   Key personnel involved or who have been requested to remain for a specified period of time to provide services on a contract.

- **Reporting**   Format, frequency, distribution list, tool, and so on.

- **Termination**   Stopping the work before it is complete.

- **Waivers**   How or if rights can be waived. As a project manager, you need to understand how you may waive certain rights intentionally or unintentionally (for example, allowing changes to occur without going through the change process).

- **Warranties**   Measure of quality and duration of coverage.

No wonder people develop headaches while reading contracts! They can be quite complex. What's more, legal jargon and even the placement of a comma can change the meaning of a contract.

Unless you speak "legalese," the best thing you can do is get a lawyer or subject matter expert involved to help ensure you and the other parties understand the language of the contract. The good news is, many great forms, templates, and software applications are available to make this easier.

Ask the Expert

Q: What's a real-world example of a contract misinterpretation that provides a good lesson learned?

A: Try this one on for size: On a contract long, long ago, the PM was reviewing the service level agreements (SLAs) for computer support (for example, hours of support, system availability, and the financial penalties associated with missed SLAs). The contract language was not clear, and when the PM asked the contract manager to explain it, he simply said, "Don't worry. There will never be penalties against the SLAs because of the way the contract is worded." Well, the first time a critical server went out of operation due to a failure, the client came to the PM and said, "You owe several thousand dollars in penalties for the outage!" The customer had interpreted the contract language in one way, whereas the PM and team interpreted it totally different. After heated discussions, the legal team was called back to rewrite the language around SLAs and penalties. A penalty was paid and the contract rewritten to ensure there was no confusion in the future. The moral to this story is that unclear language is not good and when left to interpretation can create a lot of confusion and ill feelings in the end.

Elements of a Legally Binding Contract

Under normal circumstances, a contract must contain certain key elements to be legally binding and enforceable:

- **Offer and acceptance**   The contract must include an *offer* to provide goods or services and *acceptance* of the offer.

NOTE

A counteroffer is not an acceptance and will normally be treated as a rejection of the offer.

- **Mutual consideration**   The mutual exchange of something of value. In order for the contract to be valid, the parties to a contract must exchange money or something of value. (In the case of the sale of an event ticket, the buyer receives something of value in the form of attendance to the game, and the seller receives money.)

- **Legal purpose**   A contract cannot violate legal, government, or public policy. For example, if a contract is for the sale of illegal drugs, the contract is not enforceable.

- **Legal capacity**   Buyer and seller must have legal capacity to enter into contract for exchange of products or services. For example, someone trying to sell something they don't own does not have legal capacity.

Other elements of a legally binding contract are

- **Good faith**   It is implicit in all contracts that the parties are acting in good faith. For example, if the seller of a "bike" knows the buyer thinks he is purchasing a motorcycle instead of a bicycle, the seller is not acting in good faith and the contract will not be enforceable.

- **Performance or delivery**   In order to be enforceable, the agreed-to action of the contract must be completed (for example, the tickets have to be delivered as promised and payment received to complete the transaction).

- **Mutual consent**   There must be mutual consent between the buyer and seller (a "meeting of the minds") over products, services, or results to be provided and received.

- **Mutual understanding**   There must be a clear understanding by all parties to the contract of what is being provided and received. For example, in a contract for the sale of land the buyer may think he is buying a lot to build a house on when the seller is actually contracting to sell a pad of land for commercial use (zoned commercial use only). There is no meeting of the minds, and the contract will likely be held unenforceable.

Is an Oral Agreement Legally Binding?

There is an old saying "an oral contract isn't worth the paper it's written on," which is so true. It can be very difficult to prove an oral contract exists without documented proof of the agreement. With an oral agreement or "handshake," one party may be unable to enforce the agreement or may be forced to settle for less than the original bargain. The solution is to draft a contract (or agreement). It is good practice to always make some sort of written document, signed by both parties, to clarify the key terms of an agreement.

Definition of Procurement

Procurement is the acquisition of goods and/or services. Generally, procurements are acquired via a contract or agreement. A simple procurement however, may not require contracts, formal agreements, or purchase orders. Complex procurements should involve finding vendors or suppliers who are willing to establish a long-term buyer/seller relationship.

Almost all purchasing decisions include factors such as price, shipping, and delivery, quality of goods and/or services, benefits, and payment processing. Procurements may also involve making buying decisions that make use of economic analysis methods such as cost-benefit analysis, cost-utility analysis, and risk analysis:

- **Cost-benefit analysis**   Involves looking at the total costs and all the benefits of a decision, then weighing the pros and cons to determine before the decision is made if the planned action is beneficial.

- **Cost-utility analysis**   This method is often used as a basis for procurement decisions using a common unit of measure (for example, quality of life in health care, or money). This method tends to provide a more in-depth analysis of total benefits over cost-benefit analysis.

- **Risk analysis**   This method identifies and reviews the factors that may jeopardize the success of a project. It can also help the project team identify preventive measures to mitigate the risk (reduce possibility and the probability or impact) should the event occur.

Contracts and procurement processes can be performed by the project manager, a centralized department, or organization, or may be divided or spread over a number of

Centralized Contracts/Procurement		Decentralized Contracts/Procurement	
Advantages	**Disadvantages**	**Advantages**	**Disadvantages**
Standard processes	Less flexibility	More PM flexibility	Unclear processes
Volume discounts	Rigid bid process	Quicker acquisitions	Higher prices
Consistency	Bureaucracy	Less bureaucracy	Inconsistency
Support experts including legal	Administrative cost	Less overhead cost	Limited support, increased liability

Table 12-1 Differences in the Procurement Organizational Structures

different resources in the project organization. The most common organizational structure for managing contracts and procurement is through either a centralized structure or a decentralized structure. In the case of a centralized structure, the processes are managed within a specific department or group within the organization that specializes in the processes needed to carry out this role. In a decentralized structure, the work is often performed by the project manager. Clearly, there are advantages and disadvantages to both structures. Table 12-1 lists some of the differences.

Role of the Project Manager (Buyer or Seller)

The project manager can perform the role of either (or both) the buyer or the seller in a procurement transaction. For example, the PM may be the seller of project management services to a project sponsor (customer) and in turn contract for outside services from another group or company (in which case the PM is also a buyer of vendor/supplier services). Regardless of which side of the fence you are on, it's always a good idea to understand the other side's perspective and responsibilities from a PM standpoint.

TIP

PMI tends to view the project manager as the buyer in the buyer/seller relationship. Also, note that on the PMP exam the Project Procurement Management knowledge area can be difficult for people who have little experience in dealing with contracts or procurement. It is good to have real-world experience; however, you need to look at this knowledge area from PMI's perspective as covered throughout this chapter.

As a project manager, you will need to determine which products/goods/services will be needed from outside the project team. As always, the procurements needed are totally dependent on the size, type of project, and staffing requirements (skills and people available) on the project.

The best approach for determining what you will need to successfully administer the project deliverables is to pull the project management team together and conduct a brainstorming session. Start with the WBS and make a list of products, equipment, and/or services needed. Then initiate the make-or-buy analysis (discussed later in this chapter) to see whether or not your team can provide cost-effective products or services.

A PM needs to clearly understand labor requirements and related costs. Labor includes not only the people and their availability, but the skills, education, and experience they bring to the table to deliver the project (for example, programmer, construction manager, financial analyst, team leader, or contract manager). Then you must determine if your project team can perform these functions or if you will need to obtain (or procure) them from outside the project team. As for related cost, frequently labor rates are "loaded" or "burdened," which means that the rate includes overhead, benefits, profit, and other costs of doing business. Direct labor is generally the employee's salary or pay rate, whereas the bill rate is normally the loaded rate the buyer pays the seller. Make sure you know the difference.

TIP

I suggest you use the "80/20 rule," discussed in Chapter 8, to focus on the areas that are going to cost the most, especially labor. Also, don't shortchange yourself on the cost of managing the project contract(s) and procurements, which can be independent of project costs. These activities take time, especially if they are unfamiliar, not clear, or are misinterpreted.

Whenever possible you will want to be involved in the contract and procurement process from the beginning of your project. If you are working in a centralized procurement organization, you will need to work closely with that department or group to initiate the proper requests, using the proper forms and procedures. If you attempt to work outside the process, the consequences can be disastrous—for example, not getting the best price from sellers, missing key information in the SOW, or even losing your job. (That's correct! If you don't utilize the right people or processes for procurement, it is often considered a "bypass" and can cost you your job.)

Project Procurement Management Processes

Project Procurement Management includes the processes to purchase or acquire the products, services, or results needed from *outside* the project team. Here's an overview of the four project procurement processes:

- **12.1: Plan procurements (Planning process group)**   Documenting procurement decisions on how you will manage procurements and setting the seller selection criteria on the project

- **12.2: Conduct procurements (Executing process group)** Involves initiating the bidder selection process, obtaining seller responses, choosing a seller, and awarding the contract

- **12.3: Administer procurements (Monitoring and Controlling process group)** Involves maintaining the procurement relationship with the vendor selected as well as monitoring contract performance and managing the changes and corrections needed to ensure compliance

- **12.4: Close procurements (Closing process group)** The process of completing each project procurement transaction and the contract services at the end of the project

NOTE

The Project Procurement Management knowledge area was reduced from six processes down to four in the fourth edition of the *PMBOK*, thus streamlining the processes and making them much easier to understand.

1. Plan Procurements Process

The procurement planning process is all about understanding what needs to be obtained in the way of products, services, or results on the project, and then documenting the purchasing decisions and the approach you plan to take to identify the resources needed, such as marketing, advertising, vendors, subcontractors, and so on.

TIP

It is important to remember the seller is often referred to as a vendor, supplier, subcontractor, provider, or even customer. Also, note the procurement planning process has the highest number of inputs (11) of all the processes in the *PMBOK*, with project schedule being one of the biggest influencing factors during the procurement process (see the detailed list of inputs for this process in the "Inputs" section that follows).

When planning procurements on a project, you have many things to consider, starting with the scope (and scope baseline), requirements document, schedule, budget, and contract type. This process should be closely tied to the cost and time available to deliver the project.

Plan Procurements Inputs, Tools and Techniques, and Outputs

The inputs, tools and techniques, and outputs for the Plan Procurements process are as follows.

Inputs   Because procurement is an important aspect of obtaining resources outside the project team, the list of inputs for this process is long:

- **Scope baseline**   Includes the scope statement, WBS, and WBS dictionary.

- **Requirements documentation**   Includes contractual and legal implications around health, safety, security, performance, environmental considerations, insurance, and so on.

- **Teaming agreements**   The team charter. Are there existing or new legal contracts that need to be honored or established to facilitate the project?

- **Risk register**   Includes risk-related information, such as identified risks, owners, and response strategy as it pertains to contracts and procurement.

- **Risk-related contract decisions**   Is insurance needed or bonding of providers?

- **Activity resource requirements**   Number of people and type of skills needed.

- **Project schedule**   Constraints, timelines, specific deliverables, and target dates.

- **Activity cost estimates**   From procurement activity, bid process, and cost of deliverables.

- **Cost performance baseline**   Sets the approved starting point for tracking/reporting.

- **Enterprise environment factors**   Type of structure, market conditions, supplier performance, relationship and credibility, and terms and conditions of the contract.

- **Organizational process assets**   Formal procurement policies, management systems used, and contract type (it is important to know who bears the burden of risk).

Tools and Techniques   The following tools and techniques are used in the Plan Procurements process:

- **Make-or-buy decision**   A technique used to determine if specific work can be performed with the skills and resources available on the project team or if this needs to be acquired outside the team. Again, the schedule will often influence this decision.

- **Expert judgment**   In the case of procurement planning, the experts sought out may be financial analysts, business analysts, contract or procurement specialists, and so on.

- **Contract types**   There are three primary types of contracts (fixed-priced, cost-reimbursable, and time and materials). These are covered in more detail later in this chapter.

NOTE
Each contract type carries varying degrees of risk between the buyer and seller.

Outputs   The outputs of the Plan Procurements process are as follows:

- **Procurement management plan**   Includes the types of contract to be used, risk issues, and evaluation criteria for vendor selection.

- **Procurement statement of work (SOW)**   Based on the project scope, this is a narrative description of the procurement work to be performed on the project.

- **Make-or-buy decision**   Conclusions and decisions made to perform the work internal to the project team or external to the team. Note that this is a result of the make-or-buy analysis performed as a tool/technique and is also an input to the next process (Conduct Procurements).

- **Procurement documents**   The documents used to solicit proposals from potential sellers, vendors, or suppliers.

- **Source selection criteria**   The key skills, deliverables, cost, and so on that will be considered as part of the vendor selection process.

- **Change requests**   Items that surface during procurement planning that require changes to the selection process or to the criteria when choosing a vendor.

Contract Types

Hundreds of contracts and agreements are available to you as a project manager, so to keep this discussion simple we cover only the ones mentioned in the *PMBOK*.

Another important factor when choosing the contract type to use on your project is who will bear the burden of risk between the buyer and seller. Each contract type carries advantages and disadvantages, depending on which side of the table you are on.

The three primary types of contracts recognized by PMI are detailed next.

Fixed-price Contracts   Fixed-price contracts involve setting a fixed (or lump sum) price for delivery of a product or service. This price is fixed at the time the contract is awarded. There may also be incentives incorporated into the contract—no down payment, delayed payments, factory rebates—but the price is usually the price. Of course, we try hard to negotiate the price down, but whatever price the seller and buyer agree upon becomes the fixed-price contract.

Here are the three types of fixed-price contracts mentioned in the *PMBOK:*

- **Firm fixed price (FFP)**   This is the most common and is favored by most buyers because the price is set and the risk goes mostly to the seller. If the cost of services or materials goes up, the seller bears the burden of risk in this type of contract.

NOTE

A purchase order (PO) is the simplest form of a fixed-price contract. This type of contract is considered to be *unilateral* (signed by the buyer) as opposed to *bilateral* (signed by both parties).

- **Fixed price incentive fee (FPIF)** Gives the buyer and seller some flexibility in that it allows for variations in performance, with financial incentives tied to any agreed-upon results. For example, if the house is completed in time to move in before school starts, the seller gets an incentive fee based on a pre-negotiated amount. Here's an example:

  Contract = $100,000 + $5,000 for each month the project is completed ahead of schedule. (Two months early = $10,000 + $100,000 = $110,000 total contract value)

- **Fixed price with economic price adjustment (FP-EPA)** Used when the seller's performance period spans a considerable number of years, allowing for changes in labor and material costs. It is a fixed-price contract, but with a special provision allowing for predefined annual or final adjustments to the total price of the contract. Here's an example:

  Two-year contract = $100,000 ($50,000/year) + $5,000-per-year cost of living adjustment (COLA) starting year two for the added cost of labor. (Year 1 = $50,000, year 2 = $55,000. Total contract value = $105,000.)

Cost-Reimbursable Contracts This contract category is advantageous to the seller and is commonly referred to as a "cost plus" (CP) contract. It involves payments (cost reimbursements) for all legitimate actual costs incurred for the work performed and includes some type of incentive (or added profit) if the seller exceeds predefined objectives (such as schedule, cost, or performance targets). Cost-reimbursable contracts tend to pass the risk to the buyer. They also allow flexibility in the contract if the scope is not clear or if there's a high number of expected changes. This contract type is commonly used with research and development (R&D) projects.

Here are three of the more common cost-reimbursable contracts:

- **Cost plus fixed fee (CPFF)** The seller is reimbursed for all allowable costs for performing the agreed-to work of the contract plus a fixed fee usually identified as a percentage. Here's an example:

  Actual cost (for example, labor and materials) = $100,000 + $5,000 (5%) fixed fee = $105,000.

- **Cost plus incentive fee (CPIF)**   The seller is reimbursed for allowable costs for performing the contract work and receives a predetermined incentive fee based on achieving certain performance objectives, such as completing the project on time (similar to FPIF). Here's an example:

  Actual cost = $100,000 + $10,000 incentive at completion = $110,000 total contract value.

- **Cost plus award fee (CPAF)**   The seller is reimbursed for all legitimate costs, but the majority of the fee is earned based on the satisfaction criteria preapproved by the seller and the buyer (for example, the software application performs to requirements). Here's an example:

  Actual cost = $90,000 + $20,000 award fee (if preapproved deliverables are met) = total contract value (if approved) = $110,000.

NOTE

Cost-reimbursable contracts often include direct and indirect costs (see Chapter 7 for details on cost management). A contract of this type is beneficial when the scope of the project is not clearly or easily defined, or there are a high number of changes expected.

Time and Materials Contract   Time and materials (T&M) contracts (sometimes called unit price contracts) are considered to be a "hybrid" type of contractual arrangement in that they have certain aspects of both fixed-fee and cost-reimbursable contracts. They are often viewed as "risk neutral," meaning the burden of risk is shared by both parties.

Sometimes the T&M contract is left open-ended to allow flexibility in the terms and conditions (T&Cs) of contract delivery. T&M contracts can resemble fixed-price contracts when specific parameters are set in the contract's T&Cs. Here's an example:

Time = 1,000 labor hours * the approved hourly rate ($50 per hour) = $50,000 + costs of materials (actual = $58,255) = total contract value of $108,255.

Things to Consider in Contract Selection

A number of factors need to be considered when it comes to the type of contract you (or your organization) selects for your project.

TIP

As a PM, you may not always be directly involved with, or be the decision-maker in, the selection of which contract type will be used on your project (especially if you operate in a centralized procurement organization). However, for the purposes of the PMP exam, you need to be able to put yourself in the procurement manager's shoes and answer questions on the exam as if you are making these decisions as the PM from the buyer's perspective.

Here are some things you need to consider as part of the contract selection process:

- Contract type (sometimes predetermined by your company or organization).

- Relationship with the seller/vendor/supplier.

- Vendor's reputation and past performance. For example, do they deliver on time, with skilled responsible people? Do they invoice in a timely manner? Are the invoices accurate? Do they stand behind their work? Do they comply to industry standards?

- Vendor's willingness to adjust schedule, skills, cost, and so on to meet project needs.

- Competition. (How does the seller compare to their competition?)

- Degree of risk on both parties (ideal is shared risk).

- Contract terms and conditions. (Are they rigid or flexible?)

- Other specific considerations unique to your project.

Advantages/Disadvantages by Contract Type

Table 12-2 provides a comparison of the contract types in the three primary categories and the advantages and disadvantages of each.

TIP

There will be a few questions on the PMP exam regarding contract types, so I recommend you become familiar with the types, who bears the burden of risk between them, and the advantages/disadvantages of each contract type.

Keep in mind that contracts can be complex, even if the project is not. This can be exacerbated when you are managing multiple projects or subcontracts at the same time. Each project life cycle can end at different times. With this in mind, it is important to keep a keen eye on the way one project may affect another when it comes to procurements. You may require certain skills, equipment, or other resources across many projects, and keeping everything organized by project may be a challenge. This is where strong organizational skills are essential (for example, don't fall into a trap by signing a one-year lease for equipment on a six-month project).

Risk-Related Contract Decisions

Contract decisions should be based on the related risk. The main purpose of a contract is to protect you and the other party. From a PMI perspective, contacts are arranged according to the level of risk to the project manager (buyer). The sliding scale in Figure 12-1 shows how risk shifts between the buyer and seller. You should be able to recognize who bears the burden of risk for each of the seven contract types typically used and recognized in the world of project management.

Fixed-price (Lump Sum) Contracts	
Advantages	**Disadvantages**
Very common and easy to understand. Buyer knows the total price at the start of the project.	Can be more expensive than cost-reimbursable contract to help cover added risk to the seller.
Buyer has less risk and less work to manage (or audit) the invoices. FP contracts work well when the scope is clearly defined.	Seller may underprice the bid and overprice add-on services, features, or upgrades for higher profit.
Seller is responsible to control the costs.	Quality of work may suffer or the seller may cut corners if costs run higher than estimated. Also, there's little flexibility for change.

Cost-Reimbursable (CP) Contracts	
Advantages	**Disadvantages**
Typically less work to write the contract/SOW. CP contracts work well when additional or critical skills are needed to augment your staff.	Buyer has higher involvement to audit seller invoices closely. Additional procurement and administrative uplift (burden).
Seller has less contract risk.	Seller is not motivated to control costs.
Generally lower cost than FP contracts because of cost reimbursement instead of having to add in for unknown contingency.	Total price is unknown.

Time and Materials (T&M) Contracts	
Advantages	**Disadvantages**
Easy to create/manage, T&M contracts are effective when work needs to begin right away.	Profit margins are built in to the hours billed.
Add flexible workforce (supplementing staff).	Seller has no incentive to control costs.
Usually for very specific products or services over a shorter, more manageable period of time.	Usually only appropriate for smaller projects.

Table 12-2 Advantages/Disadvantages of the Contract Types

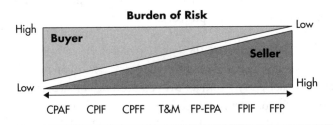

Figure 12-1 Contract risk scale

Procurement Management Plan

To be successful in managing procurements, you should always have a plan. The procurement management plan should describe how the procurement processes will be managed. It should define the key characteristics of the project (such as concerns or issues that need to be considered during the process) and the policies used to select suppliers—for example, single source, preferred (preapproved) vendors, performance measurements, billing requirements (such as electronic, net 30-day, payment by auto-deposit, and so on).

Key components of the procurement plan may include the following:

- The type of contract to be used, terms and conditions, and who the signers will be
- Assumptions and constraints
- The risk plan and contingencies
- The bidder selection process and who will manage it
- The schedule, with date and time requirements or estimates
- The billing and reconciliation process
- The escalation or exception process (to handle grievances or disputes)
- Contract termination language (for example, 30-day written notice, nonperformance penalties, and early termination clause)
- The communications plan (for example, frequency of meetings, format of documentation, where the documentation is kept, who takes minutes of the meetings, and level of participation from suppliers in the project processes)
- Performance measurements and evaluation criteria
- The overall schedule, documented deliverables, and major milestones

NOTE
The procurement management plan can be very detailed or high level. It can be formal or informal, depending on the needs of the project and the relationship (history) between the buyer/seller, as well as the level of confidence the seller will deliver as agreed to in the contract.

Make-or-Buy Analysis

The make-or-buy analysis helps the PM decide whether it is cost efficient to produce the products/services inside the project team or buy them outside the team from a supplier or vendor. There are times when it is more efficient to farm out (outsource) the work or lease equipment than to do the work internal to the team or purchase the equipment.

Many factors need to be considered, such as frequency of use, overall cost of the alternative, proprietary property, schedule, resource availability, and so on.

Procurement Documents

As an output to the Plan Procurements process, you develop documents that will be used to solicit proposals from sellers/suppliers. These documents represent a detailed view of the work to be performed, products, or results expected as part of the vendor performance.

The term "proposal" is used generally to describe any one of the following documents to solicit proposals (bids) from prospective sellers or suppliers:

- **Request for proposal (RFP)** Sometimes called a "request for tender." An RFP calls for a price from the seller and usually a detailed proposal of how the seller will perform the work, handle billing, receive payments, and so on.

- **Request for information (RFI)** Requests detailed description of how the seller can and will perform the work.

- **Request for bid (RFB) or invitation for bid (IFB)** Requests a price for the work to be performed (typically, the bid received has a time limit; for example, 30 or 60 days).

- **Request for quote (RFQ)** Requests a price quote per item-hour or per unit of work.

NOTE

As the *buyer,* you (the PM) structure the request or invitation to meet your specific project needs. The documents should have sufficient details to address the specific products, services, or results you need to accomplish from the procurement.

Here are the steps to follow when the final decision is made on the type of documents you plan to use for soliciting proposals:

1. Identify the potential sellers. This is normally accomplished either by current or past relationship with sellers (some companies have a preferred vendor/seller list) or by referrals from others. You can also simply use a phone directory or an Internet search.

2. When you have a list of sellers, you need to assess their ability to provide the needed products, services, or results in the time frame they are needed.

3. Send out the invitation to bid to prospective sellers.

NOTE

The invitation should be clear on the requirements, return date, and bidders conference information (described in the next section). This could include location, time, format, time allocated to each seller to present, and question-and-answer period.

Source (Seller) Selection Criteria

This process begins with distributing requests for products or services using the documents created in the preceding section. The documents describe the work to be performed and the initiation of the source selection process.

Assessment of potential sellers may include the following:

- **Overall life cycle cost**   What is the total cost of ownership in the work to be performed (purchase cost plus operating cost—for example, office equipment, office space, and disposal fees)? Are there licenses or royalties that will need to be paid for their services?

- **Capability to meet the needs of the contract**   Staffing technical skills, management or specialty skills (such as CAPM or PMP), and track record on past projects. Also, is training required and/or available if needed?

- **Risk rating**   Level of risk to the seller, past performance, and mitigation strategy.

- **Management approach**   Will the seller provide supervision, HR management (including payroll), and standard processes, methods, and procedures for the services to be performed?

- **Technical approach**   Does the seller have proven methods, measured results, and positive trends in quality performance? Do their services meet the procurement document requirements?

- **Warranty requirements**   Does the seller warrant the finished product and for what time period? Are there property rights (licenses) for products or services the seller provides?

- **Financial status**   Are they financially sound to take on your project? Do they invoice in a timely manner and pay their bills on time? Can they handle wire transfers between banks?

- **References**   Are they willing and able to provide good references from previous clients?

The information and sample selection scoring (weighting) criteria in Table 12-3 represents a bid for call center (help desk) services.

NOTE
Keep in mind the scoring criteria and weight numbering are subjective and must be meaningful and applicable to your specific project.

The best approach is to start with identifying which criteria is required ("must have") as opposed to criteria that you would like to have or your "want" list from the seller.

Category	Weight
I. Functional Characteristics *(This section evaluates the system and technologies.)*	**40**
A. Redundancy/reliability/life cycle of technology proposed	10
B. Flexibility for interconnection with peripheral systems installed at other locations (non-call center)	1
C. System management tools and report capabilities	5
D. System expandability (scalability) ease of adds, deletes, moves, and changes	1
E. Integration of voice, data, video, and Internet	7
F. Flexibility for network and VRU (voice response unit) interface	7
G. User operational characteristics	1
H. Flexibility for multisite virtual network	8
II. Vendor Qualifications *(This section evaluates the vendor's capabilities to get the job done.)*	**25**
A. Strategy for long-range product development	5
B. Training and backup support	2
C. Installation capabilities	3
D. Maintenance capabilities	7
E. Installed base of comparable systems	6
F. Call center management strategy expertise	2
III. System Cost/Revenue Opportunities *(This section evaluates the costs over the useful life of the system or services, and any revenue opportunity enhancements available.)*	**35**
A. Discounted cash flow over system life cycle	5
B. Capability to minimize network costs	5
C. Capability to minimize staffing costs	15
D. Capability to maximize revenue production	10
Total:	**100**

Table 12-3 Sample Scoring Criteria

The must-have criteria might include a set of key performance indicators (KPIs) or service level agreements (SLAs) that are tracked, measured, and reported on a regular basis. If the KPI or SLA is missed, penalties may be assessed on the seller (in this case, the call center service provider). Remember that special or critical support requirements may result in higher risk to the seller and possibly higher cost to the buyer. Here's a sample set of must-have criteria for a call center:

- Ninety percent of all calls to the center will be answered within 30 seconds.

- Once the call is answered, no more than 45 seconds of "hold time."

- Seventy-five percent of caller problems will be resolved at the Level 1 call center without transferring the caller to a Level 2 support group. Note: Being able to resolve the caller's problems on the first call is sometimes known as the "first-time fix rate" or "first call resolution" (FCR).

Each "want" criterion must be given a relative weight to display its importance compared to all the other "want" items. The total of all "want" criteria should be 100 points, or 100 percent of the decision (in our example). For technology acquisitions, it is common to divide the "want" criteria into three major categories:

- Functional characteristics (such as the system and technology to be used)

- Vendor qualifications and capabilities to meet the requirements of the contract

- System cost and revenue opportunity (see the sample criteria in Table 12-3)

2. Conduct Procurements Process

The Conduct Procurements process involves obtaining seller responses and comparing the responses to the scoring (or weight) table. At this time, you have a clear set of selection criteria, procurement documents (such as RFP or RFQ), and a distribution list of the sellers you feel would be able to provide the goods or services you want to acquire.

The request is sent to the sellers, and you begin collecting the responses.

Bidders Conference

In some cases you may conduct a bidders conference (sometimes called a contractors conference, vendors conference, or pre-bid conference). This is usually held at the (requesting) customer's site or a central location for more complex or larger contracts.

The bidders conference is a way to get the request presented in an organized fashion to multiple vendor/suppliers by getting them together at the same time in the same place (co-located). This is a great opportunity to present the goods or services needed and the criteria that will be used in the selection process to ensure all participants hear the same information in an unbiased manner. It is customary to allow a question-and-answer (Q&A) session during the conference in case the suppliers want clarification on any specifics of the project. Normally, the minutes and Q&As are posted online or distributed to all prospective bidders in a timely manner.

Choosing among competitive bids can be a challenging process. It often involves having a committee representing a variety of disciplines and agendas. A fair and impartial analysis that results in a consensus decision is the goal, but competing priorities and hidden biases or agendas often slow down the process. This is where the work in the previous processes pays off—for example, you have an approved procurement plan and associated documents (including scoring criteria).

Source Selection: Selecting a Seller and Awarding a Contract

Once the bids are received from the sellers, your committee begins reviewing and analyzing the bids for compliance with your must-have criteria. Here are some insights into the selection process from the article "Using Selection Criteria in Vendor Bid Analysis" by Maggie Klenke:

"Any ['must have'] failures will eliminate that vendor. Once [the review] is completed, the remaining vendors will be scored against each other on the 'want' criteria. For example, if [process and systems] redundancy is the criteria and it has a weight of 10 points..., then the committee considers all vendors and selects the one that is judged to be the best of all bidders. That bidder is given a score of 10. All other vendors are judged against the best vendor and given a relative score. It is OK to have tied scores and even zero scores. Once all have been scored, then the score is multiplied times the weight that was given to [those] criteria. So the winning vendor in redundancy would receive a weighted score of 10×10 or 100 points. Another vendor given a score of 6 would receive 6×10 or 60 points. This process is repeated for each criteria item until all have been scored. The weighted scores are added to obtain the final score for each vendor. The one with the most points is the winner and generally represents the best-balanced choice for the organization."[1]

Ask the Expert

Q: Do you have an example of a seller selection that can serve as a learning experience?

A: Yes, in response to an RFP from a seller to a bid for 24/7 (three 8-hour shifts per day) call center support, the seller stated they would provide support in two 12-hour shifts per day. When the seller was asked why they proposed different shift coverage, they said that it would be more efficient and save money to provide two-shift 12-hour coverage instead of three 8-hour shifts. When the truth came out, the company didn't have enough trained staff to perform coverage for three shifts. Needless to say, they were not awarded the contract.

Conduct Procurements Inputs, Tools and Techniques, and Outputs

The inputs, tools and techniques, and outputs for the Conduct Procurements process are as follows.

Inputs   There are many inputs to be considered in the Conduct Procurements process and the inputs in most cases are the outputs from the previous (Plan Procurements) process.

- Project management plan
- Procurement documents
- Source selection criteria
- Qualified seller list
- Seller proposals
- Other project documents
- Make-or-buy decisions
- Teaming agreements
- Organizational process assets

Tools and Techniques   When it comes time to work the Conduct Procurements process, there are a number of tools and techniques available. Each has its purpose and may be predetermined by your PMO, procurement department, or organization. The PM should be involved in this process even if it is being handled or managed by a centralized procurement department or group. A few of the tools and techniques available are

- Bidders conference, contractor conference, or vendor conference
- Proposal evaluation techniques using selection criteria based on procurement policies
- Independent cost estimates
- Expert judgment
- Advertising, Internet search
- Procurement negotiations

Outputs   The outputs of the Conduct Procurements process are

- Selected sellers and procurement contract award (contract or agreement)
- Resource calendars (work schedule, work periods, and so on)

- Change requests
- Project management plan updates
- Procurement document updates

NOTE

You should remember that the outputs from a given process typically become the inputs to the next process. Watch for the links—this will help when studying for PMI exams.

3. Administer Procurements Process

The Administer Procurements process involves managing procurement relationships and monitoring contract performance to ensure the work (or product) is meeting quality requirements. The legal nature of the contractual relationship makes it extremely important for the project team to be fully aware of the implications of their actions when administering procurement. This is what is often referred to in the business world as a "bet your job" situation.

Most companies have established procurement policies and follow strict business conduct guidelines pertaining to how contracts should be managed.

TIP

The best way to "do good and avoid evil" is to stay current on all your business conduct guidelines. Ensure you follow all regulatory requirements and your company's code of ethics. The PMI professional and social responsibilities/ethics are available on the www.pmi.org website. I highly recommend you print it out two to three weeks prior to taking the exam to get very familiar with this section and the two key categories ("Mandatory" and "Aspirational").

Managing the Relationship

The key to success when it comes to procurement is the relationship between the buyer and the seller. As the PM (assumed buyer), it is extremely important that you manage this relationship. The best way to manage the relationship during the administration of procurements is with a formal document of agreement (DOA) or statement of work (SOW) to establish the ground rules and roles and responsibilities between the buyer and seller.

Statement of Work (SOW)

Most project managers use SOWs or a similar type of document. For performance-based contracts, the SOW is often referred to as the "performance work statement" (PWS). An SOW is a narrative description of the services (or products/results) to be delivered on the project. Other titles include work order, request for service, service request, service order, and document of understanding (DOU). It doesn't matter what you call it in your world; you need to be familiar with the SOW from PMI's perspective, especially if you plan to take and pass the PMI exam.

The SOW should be developed from the approved scope baseline and defines the specific work that will be performed from outside the project team. It can be viewed as a legally binding document and should sufficiently describe the work, quality deliverables, features, functions, metrics, due dates, specifications, estimated hours, duration, and so on. It should also include details of the location where work will be performed, hours of service, billing requirements, and key contacts (see the upcoming sample list of SOW contents). Some great SOW templates are available on the Internet. One example can be found at the CVR/IT Consulting LLC website (http://cvr-it.com/PM_Templates/TemplateDetails8.html).

Sample List of Topics in a Statement of Work

Here are some key components you might see in a statement of work:

- Introduction to the project (business need or justification).

- Problem statement or background (what the project will fix or address).

- Scope statement/baseline.

- Seller and buyer requirements, deliverables, and milestones.

- Schedule duration (period of performance, target completion date, and so on).

- Change management plan, system, process/procedures.

- Specific type of services and deliverables.

- Rate structure (by skill type, expected hours, constraints, and costs).

- Hours of support or coverage.

- Communications plan and expectations for meetings and status reporting.

- Special needs, training, mentoring, and so on.

- Payment schedule and type (for example, invoices must be paid within 30 days of receipt).

- Nondisclosures (for example, handling of confidential or proprietary information).

- Physical and logical security (for example, user IDs, access codes, and passwords).

- Travel and discretionary expense reimbursement guidelines.

- Approval signatures.

Administer Procurements Inputs, Tools and Techniques, and Outputs

The inputs, tools and techniques, and outputs for this process are as follows.

Inputs   The Administer Procurements process has a number of inputs to consider, with key focus on the contract and other specific performance and procurement agreements. The inputs are as follows:

- Procurement documents
- Project management plan
- The contract
- Performance reports
- Approved change requests
- Work performance information

Tools and Techniques   The tools and techniques for the Administer Procurements process focus on results reporting, tight change control, and accountability in the process. The tools and techniques for this process are

- Contract change control
- Procurement performance reviews
- Inspections and audits
- Performance reporting
- Payment system
- Claims administration
- Records management system

Outputs   As with all outputs, keep in mind the ripple effect (progressive elaboration). When administering the procurement process, you need to keep all procurement and project documents up to date. The outputs of this process include

- Procurement documentation
- Organizational process assets updates
- Change requests
- Project management plan updates

It is important to note that many organizations treat contract and procurement administration separately from operational or functional support. Although a PM may be involved with the administration of contracts and procurement, they may have supervisory/management support to administer this process.

Contract Change Control

As mentioned previously, change control is essential, especially when you are managing procurements and contracts. When it comes to legal documents and liabilities, this is not a topic you want to take lightly. Changes to a project can have a direct effect on the contract, such as a modification to the scope of work, or deliverables. Also, there may be a change in overall cost (price increases for products, materials, or services). It is important to ensure that all contract changes are reviewed, documented, and approved by both parties prior to implementation. I highly recommend you seek support from your contracts and procurement experts when drafting/managing contacts and procurements.

TIP

You should be aware of the doctrine of privity of contract, which refers to the contractual relationship between the buyer and seller. You may see a question on the PMP or CAPM exam around this term. Simply stated, if Seller A enters into a contract to build a house for Buyer B, and Buyer B contacts Seller C (electrician) to install additional features in the house (such as wiring for a home theater system), and the house burns down because of faulty wiring by Seller C, Seller A will not be liable for the damages.

4. Close Procurements Process

The Close Procurements process involves completing each procurement activity and verifying that all work and deliverables were performed according to the terms and conditions of the contract. The closure of procurements may be for the entire project or one or more phases.

The Close Procurements process also includes administrative activities such as finalizing any open claims, updating records, and archiving all pertinent documents for future use.

The best place to start when it comes to closing procurements is the contract terms and conditions to make sure all contractual obligations have been fulfilled. Once you are sure you and the team have successfully completed all deliverables of the contract/procurements, you need to obtain formal acceptance from the sponsor (or sponsors) of the project. In some cases, a formal audit may be performed prior to final payment.

A couple of things to think about when closing out the procurements are to ensure you obtain formal acceptance of all deliverables on the contract, verifying that the work is satisfactory, complete, and warranted as appropriate and that all invoices are paid. And to make sure you have complete administrative closure. Administrative closure simply refers to those activities associated with claims processing, tracking changes to completion, record retention management, payments, and so on.

Close Procurements Inputs, Tools and Techniques, and Outputs

The inputs, tools and techniques, and outputs for this process are few but extremely important to ensure that all aspects of the contract procurement are brought to a satisfactory close.

Inputs There are only two inputs to the Close Procurements process:

- Project management plan
- Procurement documents

Tools and Techniques A few tools and techniques for the Close Procurements process focus on ensuring proper control, handling any unsettled procurements, and making sure your records are complete and accurate on your project. The tools and techniques are

- **Procurement audits** Structured review of the procurement process.
- **Negotiated settlements** If settlement of contract deliverable cannot be achieved through direct negotiation, some form of alternative dispute resolution (ADR) may need to be explored.
- **Records management system** Consists of a specific set of process-related control functions and tools that are part of the overall project management information system.

Outputs The last thing you need when managing procurements on your project is loose ends. You must ensure all procurements are closed properly. This includes

- **Closed procurement** Formal written notice from the buyer to the seller showing satisfactory acceptance of the project deliverables.
- **Organizational process asset updates** Includes procurement document updates, deliverables acceptance, and lessons learned documentation reflecting the final status of the procurement.

Try This Fixing Issues Before Turning Out the Lights

You are the PM on a large project and are closing the procurements by conducting a lessons learned meeting. The customer makes a comment that some of the work was not completed properly and they will not sign a formal acceptance statement for satisfactory project completion until the work is complete. Take a few moments to decide what you would do first and what you would do second. Then consult the following answer.

Answer:

1. Interview the customer to understand what work they feel was not completed.

(As it turns out in this case, the work the customer is referring to was not in the original scope baseline, and the work was begun by the project team later in the life cycle.)

2. Interview the team to collect status and estimated completion. Find out why the work was started even though it was not in scope. Then work with the customer to document the work as follow-on activities given that it is not in the scope baseline. Explain that you will be happy to complete the work as a follow-on phase to the project once it is approved; however, you need to officially close the original project.

Contract Termination   Sherrie Bennett states the following in her article "Contract Termination" at Lawyers.com:

> "There are many ways to terminate the obligations of a contract. Most often, parties conclude their contract obligations by performing them. However, sometimes problems arise and parties cannot or will not complete their obligations under the contract. Therefore, contracts may be terminated by reasons of *rescission, breach, or impossibility of performance.*"[2]

Here are definitions of these three reasons for termination:

- **Breach of contract** (also called default)   Either one or both parties have failed to perform an obligation as agreed to and expected under the contract. A breach may occur when one party

  - Refuses to perform the deliverables of the contract.

  - Does something that will prohibit the contract from being delivered.

  - Prevents the other party from performing their obligations.

There two types of breaches: material and immaterial.

- **Material breach of contract**   This goes to the heart of the contract. The injured party can seek damages such as monetary payment to cover losses resulting from the breach of contract. For example, a rock star who shows up at a concert but doesn't bring his guitar has materially breached the contract to perform if he cannot play.

- **Immaterial breach of contract**   This is more trivial and does not kill the contract. For example, let's say you have a service contract to maintain the air conditioning system at the events center. The system is to be checked weekly on Fridays to ensure the temperature in the arena is a constant 60 degrees (±2 degrees). Contrary to the contract, the service person misses a Friday inspection and comes in on Saturday instead. This act is a technical breach of the contract, but it is immaterial, unless for some reason the inspections needed to be done on Fridays as opposed to any other day.

- **Impossibility of performance**   The contract can be terminated if an unforeseen event prevents the performance of the contract. For example, you contract with a famous singer to perform a concert and the performer gets laryngitis and is unable to sing. The contract is terminated by impossibility of performance. As always, there may be exceptions.

- **Rescission**   This may terminate the obligations of a contract in a variety of circumstances. One party may have the legal right to rescind the contract, or the parties together agree to terminate the contract. For example, event ticket sales are extremely low and the event center has another client to fill the spot (date), so both parties agree to a rescission of the contract.

Additional Contract and Procurement Terms

Here are some additional terms you should be familiar with (especially for the PMP exam).

Force Majeure   According to Wikipedia, *"force majeure* (French for "superior force") is a common clause in contracts which essentially frees both parties from liability or obligation when an extraordinary event or circumstance beyond the control of the parties, such as a war, strike, riot, crime, or ... an 'act of God' (for example, flooding, earthquake, volcano) prevents one or both parties from fulfilling their obligations under the contract. However, *force majeure* is not intended to excuse negligence or other malfeasance of a party, [if the] non-performance is caused by the usual and natural consequences of external forces (for example, predicted rain stops an outdoor event), or where the intervening circumstances are specifically contemplated."[3]

Letter of Intent or Letter of Agreement   Letter of intent (LOI) and letter of agreement (LOA) are terms that refer to the buyer's express interest in the seller. Even though these letters from the buyer are not normally considered to be contracts, they may be used during the engagement or proposal phase of negotiations to commit to a closer (best and final) review of the seller's proposal. There may be financial compensation written into the LOI or LOA that allows for a period of due diligence for the seller to verify the size and complexity of the project prior to entering into the final contract. LOIs and LOAs are often used when there are many unknowns associated with the project, such as new technology, unique conditions, uncertainty in the overall size or complexity of the project, and so on.

Due Diligence   *Due diligence* is a term used for the performance of an investigation of a business or person. A common example of due diligence in various industries is the process through which a potential buyer evaluates a target company's assets to ensure they accurately stated inventory, revenues, and so on, prior to the acquisition (the goal is full disclosure of the buyer's status and no surprises to the seller after the contract is signed).

Single and Sole Source   You should be familiar with these terms of noncompetitive procurements:

- **Single source**   A single source contract is made directly with a preferred seller, often without going through the full procurement process. This is normally used when you have a prior long-term relationship with the seller. It is based on trust and confidence.

- **Sole source**   With a sole source contract, there is only one seller due to special conditions, patents, or special skills that may exist with that seller.

NOTE
Single and sole source contracts carry higher risk of nonperformance due to putting all your eggs in one basket.

Performing Contract Closure
Contract closure involves making sure all the unfinished work (loose ends) are tied up and formally completed. Many steps are involved with procurement closure. These steps include product verification, administrative closure, financial closure (payments are made/received), final reports, lessons learned, and updating all project documentation.

TIP
You will likely see situational questions on the PMI exams asking whether the project is closed. Also, you may see questions asking the difference between contract closure and administrative closure. The difference is contract closure should occur first and then administrative closure.

All contract documents, such as the procurement plan, scope statement, WBS, and so on, need to be reviewed to ensure satisfactory completion. Reviewing all the project documentation (not just the contract) will assist with contract and procurement closure. Documents and areas of consideration include the following:

- Scope baseline

- Approved schedule, deliverables, and milestones

- Budget reports and other financial documents (such as invoices, payments)

- Inspections and audit results (as appropriate)

- Substantial completion. (This is defined by The American Institute of Architects, AIA, as "the stage in the progress of the Work where the Work or designated portion is sufficiently complete in accordance with the Contract Documents.")

- Final completion (formal acceptance)

- Inventory closeout

- Release of liens/claims (formal)

Once the deliverables have been accepted by the customer and the contract has been closed, it's time to collect all the contract, procurement, and project information (conduct a lessons learned meeting) and finalize the project control book for record retention. Remember, lessons learned should have been collected throughout the project, making the final lessons learned meeting even more effective. Make sure more than one person knows where the contract files/documents are stored and that you have more than one key. This sounds simple enough, but entire warehouses are full of old project documents needed for

Ask the Expert

Q: **Can you provide an example of project documents needed on an old project?**

A: Yes, a young PM called me a couple of years ago and asked if I had the scope statement, SOW, or WBS for a project I had worked on "some time ago." I finally found the documents in my archives. They were from over seven years ago, and the customer's recollection of the deliverables of the project was much grander than what was captured in these project documents. Needless to say, these documents saved the day and allowed the new PM to get and give a clear picture of the original project. This enabled the new PM to manage the customer expectations more effectively as they initiated Phase II of the project.

audit or customer review but the project manager has since retired or moved on to another company. When the client comes back for Phase II or III of the project, unless you have key documents you will have to start all over; otherwise, you could fail an audit if the documents cannot be produced when needed.

Summary

Here are the things you need to remember about contract and procurement management:

- Know the different types of contracts and who bears the burden of risk between the buyer and seller for each.

- Know the four procurement management processes (and be familiar with inputs, tools and techniques, and outputs of each).

- For the PMI exam, think of the PM as the buyer in the buyer/seller relationship.

- Be familiar with the elements of a legally binding contract.

- Understand the SOW and contract/agreement details on your project.

- Understand the evaluation criteria. Make it as objective as possible.

- Know the importance of good negotiation skills and the need to maintain a good buyer/seller relationship.

- Ensure contract performance reporting/documentation is complete and accurate.

- Know the importance of obtaining formal acceptance and effectively closing procurements.

NOTE
Additional information on project closure is provided in Chapter 13.

References

1. Klenke, Maggie. "Using Selection Criteria in Vendor Bid Analysis," The Call Center School, http://www.swpp.org/newsletter/fall08/managing.html.

2. Bennett, Sherrie. "Contract Termination, Lawyers.com, http://consumer-law.lawyers.com/Contract-Termination.html.

3. Wikipedia, http://en.wikipedia.org/wiki/Force_majeure.

Chapter 13

Closing the Project: Are We There Yet?

Key Skills & Concepts

- Importance of properly closing the project

- Formal acceptance (getting the signoff in writing)

- The two closing processes

- Reverse engineering

- Lessons learned

- Exit criteria and common closure activities

- Conducting lessons learned/closure meeting

- Rewards and recognition

- Finding team members/assets a home

- Final project closure report

- Plan for record retention

- Celebrate!

- Reminder of the A.I.M. strategy

- Next steps—where to go from here (steps to apply for a PMI exam)

You are approaching the end of your project (and this book). Closing the project is probably the least planned and potentially the most difficult part of managing a project. So how do you ensure you bring your project to a successful close? The answer is by using good sound project management discipline. You want to manage the project closure phase of the project life cycle just like any other phase—by using the five process groups, as appropriate. You should remember them by now; they are Initiating, Planning, Executing, Monitoring and Controlling, and Closing. You might think you can focus only on the Closing process group and that is not the case. As mentioned before, all process groups work interactively.

Importance of Project Closure

Closing the project or phase is as important as starting a new project. As the PM, you need to manage project closure as a project in itself. That's right, you need to initiate project closure, verify the scope and deliverables of project closure, make sure you have authorization to close out the project (potentially a separate project charter with focus on the closing phase), plan for it, and ensure proper staffing, adequate time/schedule, sufficient budget, and so on, to meet the approved closure dates and deliverables.

Formal Acceptance

One way to ensure proper project closure is to make it official by getting the final acceptance (sign-off) in writing. We talked about risk management in Chapter 11 and how you must plan for and manage risk throughout the project life cycle. This is especially important during project closure. The project is not officially complete until the paperwork is done and signed by the approving sponsor(s).

Most project managers have a fear of surprises. Surprises are great for birthdays, but not when closing a project. One of the greatest surprises on any project is when you go to the project sponsor (customer) to obtain formal acceptance of project completion and you discover they don't want the project to end. Either they really like the work performed and thus feel confident about adding more features or, on the other side of the coin, they feel they didn't get all they expected and want you to deliver more.

If you have planned well and properly documented the project scope and deliverables (what I call "lining up your ducks") by defining the acceptance criteria, communicating the plan and measurement objectives, and obtaining formal acceptance from the sponsor(s), then you should experience few or no surprises at the end of the project.

TIP

At the end of the project, the success or failure of a project depends entirely on measured results and perception. For example, a project may be on time and on budget, but may not meet the customer's expectations. PMI feels issues/conflicts should be resolved in favor of the customer. Therefore, you need to manage customer expectations effectively early and often *especially* when closing the project.

Three Takeaway Points

A really good way to manage customer expectations, the project as a whole, and project closure is to remember the three key "takeaway points" from Chapter 2. In my opinion, they are essential to helping you close down your projects. Hopefully, by now you remember them. If not, now is a good time to ask the expert for a refresher.

Ask the Expert

Q: What are the three takeaway points needed for success on any project or phase?

A: At this point, you should be able to recite these from memory. If you can't, learn them now:

- **Stay focused on the end goals and objectives** You should be able to answer the following question confidently: Did you do what you said you would do on the project? For example, did you meet all project deliverables, effectively manage constraints, meet the approved budget and schedule, perform in a quality manner, and meet customer expectations?

- **Use the tools available** Did you effectively manage the resources and did you effectively use tools such as standard processes, templates, checklists, this book, your organization's assets, and the *PMBOK?*

- **Work as a team** Did you manage the team effectively? Did you help grow the team and the individual team members through mentoring, partnering with the team, and other team building activities?

Closing Processes

There are only two processes in the Closing process group of the *PMBOK:*

- **Close project or phase** The process of finalizing all activities across all the project management groups to formally complete the project or phase (Chapter 4.6)

- **Close procurements** The process of completing each of the procurements on the project (Chapter 12.4)

Reverse Engineering

Reverse engineering (sometimes called "right-to-left planning") is a great way to close a project. You normally have a set (or fixed) target date for closure. So start by backing into the target date and allow enough time to properly shut down the project. The amount of time needed to close a project depends entirely on the size, type, and complexity of the project. In general, allow at least 60 to 90 days due to the written notices you need to send to suppliers to cancel services, to write lease (or license) termination letters for hardware and software, and to give people sufficient notice to plan for their next assignment.

It doesn't matter if you are closing a long-term project that you have been working on for some time or if you are brought in on a fairly new short-term project that someone else has been managing, the approach should be the same. Manage the closing phase as a project (charter to close).

The Past Is a Crystal Ball Into the Future

Wouldn't it be great if you knew how to reach success on your project before you even began? You can, and you don't even need a crystal ball to see into the future. The past has provided a lot of great historical information about why projects fail. We should be able to simply learn from past mistakes and move on to greater project success.

You may remember that in Chapter 2 we talked about why projects fail, and these reasons apply even when closing a project. To refresh your memory, here's a short summary:

- Lack of project management discipline (risk management, communications, change, time, cost and scope management, and so on). When closing a project, we tend to get in a hurry and think we just need to get to the "end of the game" and the project will be complete. However, you still need to exercise good PM practices for successful closure.

- Lack of user (key stakeholder) involvement. (Don't leave out the customer or users.)

- Lack of project sponsor commitment. (Sponsors tend to lose interest at the end of the project; remind them of what needs to be done and the need for their support.)

- Projects ending for the wrong reasons (assuming the problems *are* solved, or due to lack of sponsorship).

- Lack of properly trained or skilled people to work the project.

- Lack of cultural skills and ability to manage in multicultural environment.

Exit Criteria

The exit criteria for a given project tends to be unique no matter how many times a similar project has been conducted. Even if the project has been done before, there are always certain factors that require a slightly different approach to the closing process for each project.

Exit criteria must align to the agreed-to measures for the project and may include quality, quantity, conformance to specific requirements, key deliverables such as products, services, and results.

Project Closure Activities

Here are some of the more common project closure activities:

- Provide final written reports (financial status, earned value reports, milestones, changes, successes, open issues, the location of updated documentation, and so on).

- Conduct contract closeout and overall administrative closure.

- Get formal acceptance (extremely important) of all deliverables.

- Conduct a lessons learned session to capture what worked and what didn't work (include the customer).

- Update documentation for record retention. (Check with your asset manager or business controls coordinator for state and local, federal government [IRS, SEC], and company-specific requirements.)

- Conduct team and individual evaluations. Provide feedback to the employees and their managers.

- Provide rewards and recognition to the team and individuals for their contributions.

- Celebrate!

Sample Project Closure (from the BEC Case Study)

To carry on with our events center case study, see Table 13-1 for a real-world example of project closure. After each event/project, this checklist is used to determine the status of the facility, equipment, and preparedness for the next event. All identified follow-up activities will be initiated as appropriate.

Conduct Lessons Learned/Closure Meeting

History is our best teacher. It shows us how to do things better if we take the time to learn from our mistakes. If we don't apply the knowledge learned, we truly miss out on some valuable lessons that can be costly to our future projects. Too often we just dive in to the water before we realize we don't have on a life preserver. The words of Clarence Darrow are appropriate here: "History repeats itself. That's one of the things wrong with history."

To help assess the results of your project, schedule a project team meeting and include the customer. Plan for at least two hours (more if the project is large or complex). Also, set the stage and expectations by sending an agenda ahead of time and be sure to capture the minutes of this meeting. The lessons learned/closure meeting works best if you provide questionnaires or surveys ahead of time so people can think about their

Resource/Owner	Activity Description	Complete? Yes/No	Comments/Follow-Up
Building operations	Walk through a visual inspection for damages.		Schedule repairs if necessary.
Preventative maintenance	Check all building equipment and systems to ensure good working order.		Schedule maintenance as needed.
Sponsorships	Create a detailed report outlining fulfilled elements of the event sponsorships.		Create action plans as needed.
Marketing	Reconcile all advertising audit reports with each media partner (radio and television spot times and newspaper tear sheets).		Ensure event advertisement is cancelled to match event completion and billing, as appropriate.
Sales	Analyze box office sales and determine return on investment (ROI) in relation to each media buy.		Use results for future marketing trend analysis and strategy.
Manager on duty	Create a report detailing building cleanliness, attendance, staff performance, issues/concerns related to the event, successes of the event, accidents/injuries, patron behavior, police reports, and recommendations for future events.		Communicate status results. Create action plans as needed.
Finance manager	Process all payments, expenses, and financial settlements, and report financial status with event promoter/manager.		Handle reconciliations and payments disputes. Ensure that retention of financial reports meets all company external agency requirements.

Table 13-1 Sample Project Closure

answers prior to attending the meeting. Here are some key questions that need to be asked and answered:

- How did we do overall on the project? (Were the results achieved and anticipated?)
- Did we meet our documented objectives? (Did we deliver what we said we would?)
- Are the products or services at the approved quality levels?

- Did we manage the customer and team expectations properly?

- Did we effectively manage change by enforcing the control process?

- What caused the most problems, and how can we keep them from coming back on our next project?

- Was the budget managed properly, or did we have to beg for more funding halfway through the project life cycle?

- Did we make the best use of our resources? (Did we use the right skills at the right time in the right place?)

- Did we use the lessons learned from previous similar projects and did we capture lessons learned from the current project effectively?

Some great lessons learned templates are available on the Internet. You can see a partial example in Figure 13-1.[1]

Documenting Results and Action Items

The project is not over until the paperwork is done. Documenting the results of the lessons learned and project closure meetings needs to be concise with specifics of key findings, a clear short summary of events, feedback from the team, milestones, deliverables, and any/all follow-up action items, warranty period contacts, and so on. Here are the steps to take:

1. Completely and accurately document the project results. (This should match the scope baseline and milestones as well as address all approved changes.)

2. Document accomplishments and team member recognition.

3. Capture minutes of all meetings, especially lessons learned and closure meetings, including input from all stakeholders (customer, team, yourself as the PM, sponsors).

4. Plan for process improvement (remember Deming's "Plan-Do-Check-Act" cycle).[2]

Most project managers like checklists or surveys to tell them how they did in managing the project. Table 13-2 is a sample post-project survey (from *Identifying and Managing Project Risk, Second Edition,* by Tom Kendrick) that includes questions about project definition, planning, defect and issues management, decision making, teamwork, leadership, and managing dependencies.[3]

1. Project Lessons-Learned Check List

No.	Lessons Learned	Yes	No	N/A	Impact Low 1	2	3	High 4	5

Yes = The project team agrees with the statement.

No = The project team does not agree with the statement.

N/A = This statement does not apply to the project.

Impact = The extent to which this factor had an impact on your project.

Add a >comment to any question where supporting detail would be helpful

Project Planning

No.	Lessons Learned	Yes	No	N/A	1	2	3	4	5
1.	Business objectives were specific, measurable, attainable, results-focused, and time-limited. >								
2.	Product concept was appropriate to business objectives. >								
3.	Project plan and schedule were well documented, with appropriate structure and detail. >								
4.	Project schedule encompassed all aspects of the project. >								
5.	Tasks were defined adequately. >								
6.	Stakeholders (e.g., sponsor, customer) had appropriate input into the project planning process. >								
7.	Requirements were gathered to sufficient detail. >								
8.	Requirements were documented clearly. >								
9.	Specifications were clear and well documented. >								
10.	Test plan was adequate, understandable, and well documented. >								
11.	External dependencies were identified and agreements were signed. >								

Figure 13-1   Sample lessons learned template

Please evaluate each of the following statements using the scale: 1-Strongly disagree, 2-Disagree, 3-No opinion, 4-Agree, 5-Strongly agree						**Comments**
1	2	3	4	5	Project developed and used a project and risk plan.	
1	2	3	4	5	Problems were dealt with quickly and escalated properly when necessary.	
1	2	3	4	5	Schedule/budget problems were dealt with effectively.	
1	2	3	4	5	Resource problems were dealt with effectively.	
1	2	3	4	5	Specifications were modified only through approved change control/management.	
1	2	3	4	5	Project reviews were done at appropriate times.	
1	2	3	4	5	Communications were thorough, timely, and complete.	
1	2	3	4	5	Documentation was consistent and available when needed.	
1	2	3	4	5	Project status was reported honestly throughout the project.	
1	2	3	4	5	Reporting project difficulties resulted in solutions.	
1	2	3	4	5	Standard processes were used properly.	
1	2	3	4	5	The project had appropriate sponsorship and support.	

Table 13-2 Sample Project Closure Survey

Rewards and Recognition

Most of us thrive on rewards and recognition. We like to know that we are appreciated and recognized for the extra effort we put forth on project activities (the long hours, hard work, and sacrifices we make to do well). Therefore, as a project manager you need to make sure team members' efforts and good deeds are rewarded, even if it's only a pat on the back and a nice note or letter to the team member and their boss. Monetary rewards are great as well. Remember, your team is the number-one asset on your project, and team members need to feel needed and appreciated.

Finding Homes for the Team and Assets

Breaking up the team is always the hard part. This is called the "adjourning" phase in the Bruce Tuckman model. When it comes time to close a project, emotions are mixed. Some PMs feel sad that the project is coming to an end, the project team is moving on to the next project, and the fear of the unknown (the next project and starting all over again) tends to creep in. Some PMs are happy to see their hard work coming to successful closure and new project opportunities appearing just around the corner, where they can apply all the lessons learned and their new experience to the next big project.

This is no time to shortchange the team. It is extremely important to work with each team member to find them a good project home to move to. If you look out for the team members, they will look out for you. We work in a small world, so don't be surprised when you go into a new project and find people you previously worked with are now your customer or boss (this has happened to me several times).

TIP

Another measure of success for you as the project manager is when people are willing to work with you on the next project. I view this as the biggest compliment one can receive. The team (or at least key members of the team) is confident enough in your PM skills and ability to work with you again on future projects.

When it comes to finding a home for the assets, you need to be thorough and get transfer acceptance in writing. Find a home for all the equipment and then properly transfer the equipment. Cancel all appropriate software licenses or hardware leases, as needed. The last thing you want to happen is to have a supplier call you three to six months after the project is closed down looking for payment of an invoice. This has happened to many experienced PMs, and dealing with this situation is not fun especially when the project budget is closed.

Final Project Report

The primary purpose of the final report is to acknowledge the accomplishments of the project and to communicate to everyone involved that the project is officially complete. A final project report should also thank all stakeholders and contributors as well as address who to contact if questions arise or if records are required after the project is closed.

Regardless of the size of the project, here are some fundamental steps that, if used, will help you ensure successful closure on your projects:

1. Use proven project management disciplines. This includes using organizational assets by documenting and managing scope baseline, change, risk, scope, time, and cost diligently.

2. Review and report status frequently and honestly (I recommend weekly).

3. Ensure clear two-way communications (use active listening).

4. Work with the stakeholders to ensure they are focused on the closure activities.

5. Be an advocate for your project team (catch them doing something right!).

6. Verify the overall health of the project by asking yourself and the team the following questions:

- Were deliverables produced on time, within the approved scope, and within the approved budget?

- Did the project satisfy the business requirements of the stakeholders? (For example, was the problem solved or business result accomplished?)

- Has the project met the business value goals? (Such goals might include cost savings, increased market share, and streamlined processes needed to improve quality.)

- Most importantly, do the business owners (sponsors) believe the project was successful? Did you deliver a quality product and meet stakeholder expectations?

- Last but not least, document, document, document and communicate project results.

Plan for Record Retention

As part of formal acceptance you should ensure that all final reports have been completed, reconciled, and approved. Make sure you have documented and planned for how to store the project documents. This includes record retention, e.g., where to store the project documents, for how long, who will have access to the documents, who the backup person is in case the primary contact is not readily available? Make sure these bases are covered in writing and are fully communicated to all the key stakeholders, especially when dealing with particular industries, PMs should be aware of their document retention policies or requirements.

Celebrate!

Now it is time to celebrate. No matter how the atmosphere has been during the closing days of your project, bring it to a positive conclusion. Celebrate the success of the team, the individuals on the team, and the key support managers. A dinner or luncheon works best, but this might not be possible if the team is geographically dispersed or if some team members have already moved on to other projects. Still, you should strive to rally the team together to acknowledge their good work, even if the project was not a complete success.

Moving on to the next assignment/project is much easier for people when they have a chance to bring their last project to a friendly conclusion. For global or distributed teams, you might want to arrange a similar event for each location at roughly the same time and then conference in the different subgroups for a final thank-you and sendoff.

Next Steps: Where to Go from Here

The best way to reach success is to always have a plan and a strategy. I recommend the A.I.M. strategy (discussed in Chapter 2). I feel strongly about this strategy for life in general and project management. Here it is again, as a reminder:

1. *Analyze* the situation. (Develop the plan as a team and obtain formal acceptance for the project plan.)

2. *Implement* the approved plan. (Use available tools and resources.)

3. *Manage* the whole project, and nothing but the project.

Here are the steps you should follow if you are planning to take a PMI exam:

1. Apply for the exam online at www.pmi.org.

2. Study using the key resources (books, study groups, sample exams) available to you.

3. Consider creating index (flash) cards with questions on one side and answers on the back. Study them until you know all the answers, and then reverse the process by looking at the answers and being able to describe the questions.

4. Stay focused (make a project plan and stick to it).

5. Don't be too hard on yourself (allow for some downtime).

6. Don't cram for the exam the night before you take the test.

7. Celebrate your achievement upon successfully completing the exam.

Many great project managers are successful without being certified. You, too, can be a successful PM by following these simple rules (the three P's):

1. *Plan* well (preparation is the key).

2. *Perform* your role with clear direction and clear communications.

3. *Practice* (you need to keep developing your skills, apply lessons learned for continuous improvement, and stay current with latest processes, tools, concepts, and methods).

Ask the Expert

Q: How do I get the most out of my project management effort and experience?

A: I would like to offer these words (from an unknown author): "The best way to get where you want to go is to act like you are already there." This means you have a much greater chance of being successful if you perform with integrity, conviction, and commitment. Act like a leader. To be successful, you must demonstrate your abilities, take charge, and then take action to move your projects forward with determination and direction.

Project Objectives for this Book

Here are the objectives I set for the "project" of writing this book:

- Provide useful information that the reader can apply to their projects immediately.

- Provide the reader with proven checklists to help guide them in managing their projects to a higher degree of success.

- Offer tips to help the reader better understand what they need to do to apply for and prepare for the PMI exam.

I consider this book a success if I have accomplished one or more of these goals. However, the only way I will know is through feedback from you, the reader. Feel free to contact me through my website (www.eagle-business.com) to offer your feedback and suggestions and to let me know if I met my project goals.

Go Confidently in the Direction of Your Dreams

I would like to leave you with a quote from Henry David Thoreau: "Go confidently in the direction of your dreams! Live the life you've imagined. As you simplify your life, the laws of the universe will be simpler."

To follow your dreams and get where you want to be you must have a clear strategy. The one that has worked for me over the years is **"Line up your ducks and feed them well."** This is a motto that I live by and it has worked extremely well for me in life and in the dynamic world of project management. I hope it works as well for you.

References

1. CVR/IT Consulting LLC, http://www.cvr-it.com/PM_Templates/.

2. Wikipedia, http://en.wikipedia.org/wiki/PDCA.

3. Kendrick, Tom. *Identifying and Managing Project Risk: Essential Tools for Failure-Proofing Your Project, Second Edition* (AMACOM, New York City), 2009, pages 296–298.

Index

D

E

F

U

V